# The House at Work

*Edited by Joseph Cooper and*
*G. Calvin Mackenzie*

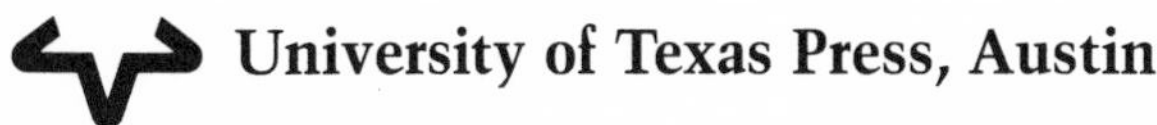

University of Texas Press, Austin

The editors wish to acknowledge with gratitude the financial support received during the preparation of this volume from Rice University and from the Social Science Grants Committee of Colby College.


Printed in the United States of America

First Edition, 1981



Library of Congress Cataloging in Publication Data
Main entry under title:
The House at work.
(The Dan Danciger publication series)
Includes bibliographies and index.
1. United States. Congress. House. I. Cooper, Joseph, 1933–
II. Mackenzie, G. Calvin.
JK1319.H68 328.73'072 81-2987
ISBN 0-292-73017-9 AACR2

**To Congressman David R. Obey**
for his courage, integrity, and dedication
to the House as an institution.

# Contents

# Introduction

# Coping in a Complex Age: Challenge, Response, and Reform in the House of Representatives

*G. Calvin Mackenzie*

The second half of the twentieth century has not been kind to the United States House of Representatives. Decades of rapid social change, economic diversification, and international terror have had a profound effect upon the character of the House and the expectations the American people place on its members. The contemporary representative in Congress is now beset with an incessant flow of constituent demands for personal services, with a spiralling responsibility for making legislative decisions, and with growing obligations to oversee an expanding sprawl of federal agencies and programs. The modern House is a full-time enterprise; its members are full-time public servants.

It hasn't always been that way. In the early years the House was rarely burdened by the weight of its own agenda. The government, as James Sterling Young (1966, 28, 31) reminds us, was

> a small institution, small almost beyond modern imagination. . . . Almost all of the things which republican governments do which affect the everyday lives and fortunes of their citizens, and therefore engage their interest, were . . . not done by the national government. The administration of justice, the maintenance of law and order, the arbitration of disputes, the chartering and supervision of business enterprise, road building and the maintenance of transportation systems, the schooling of the young, the care of the indigent, even residual control over the bulk of the military forces—these functions fell principally within the province of state and local governments to the extent that any governmental bodies performed them.

In those years, its legislative business rarely kept the House in session for more than a few months each year. Members had little contact with their constituents while in Washington. And, with the exception of an occasional special investigation or confirmation controversy, oversight was confined almost entirely to the appropriations process.

Nor were things much different in the early decades of this century. Listen, for example, to the description of the House by a young man who came to clerk in his father's congressional office in 1917 (Dies 1954, 31).

> Congress sat for six months the first session and three months the second session. A representative got about 15 letters a week. Only at rare intervals would a constituent come to see him. He had no pressure groups to contend with. Because Congress enacted only a few bills each session, legislation got the deliberative attention it deserved. Every member had plenty of time to study bills in committee before they came to the floor. Debate was important in the consideration of every bill. A member did not take the floor until he had carefully got together as many facts as were available. When he spoke, he knew his subject. A good debater had no trouble getting a large audience in the chamber. Most of the member's time was spent on legislation. There was little else for him to do.

Things have changed in the House. In the past three decades the changes have been rapid and substantial. No matter what measure one chooses to apply, the evidence shows consistently that the House has gotten busier and busier. Table 1 demonstrates this.

These measures only begin to capture the extent to which the legislative environment has been altered by the increasing pace of congressional activity. They do not reveal, for instance, the extent to which constituents have come to call on their representatives with individual problems. There are no reliable data on the growth in constituent casework but, as John Johannes indicates later in this book, the unanimous consensus of the old hands on Capitol Hill is that these demands have increased steadily over the past few decades. These data also fail to demonstrate any increase in the number of contacts between special interest groups and members of Congress. Yet again, those who have long experience on the Hill are quick to point out that the number of such contacts has grown enormously in recent years. One needn't belabor this point further. The fact is starkly clear: the contemporary Congress is an extraordinarily busy institution.

**Table 1.** ***Average Measures of Legislative Activity in the U.S. House of Representatives by Decade, 1947–1976***

| | *Averages per Congress* | | |
|---|---|---|---|
| *Measures of Legislative Activity* | *1947–1956* | *1957–1966* | *1967–1976* |
| Days in session | 269 | 303 | 321 |
| Hours in session | 1,172 | 1,242 | 1,583 |
| Number of bills introduced | 10,244 | 15,383 | 19,582 |
| Number of resolutions introduced | 1,011 | 1,451 | 2,163 |
| Number of committee meetings | 3,210[a] | 3,635 | 5,486 |
| Number of quorum calls | 166 | 278 | 369 |
| Number of Yea and Nay votes | 182 | 248 | 564 |

SOURCE: Commission 1977, 1 (*Work of the Commission*):99.
[a]Figures available for 84th Congress only.

## THE SOURCES OF CHANGE

What accounts for these changes in the workload and responsibilities of the Congress?

### Population Growth

The most obvious answer is that the country has grown. Between 1910 and 1975, the American population increased by 229%. In that same period, however, the size of the House of Representatives changed not at all.[1] There were 435 members in 1910 and there are 435 members today. In 1910 the average population of a House district was 212,429; in 1975, it was 486,855. Hence the first reason for the increase in congressional activity is simply that the House is serving a lot more people than it used to.

### The Changing Role of the Federal Government

The period from 1933 to the present has been marked by persistent redefinitions of the role of the federal government in American society and of the role of America in the world. The effect of these redefinitions has been unveeringly expansionist. In virtually every area of public activity, the federal government has become the dominant actor on the American stage. Little that we do is unaffected by government policy. Few of our social or economic objectives can be accomplished without government help or acquiescence. Naturally, of course, this has expanded the range and frequency of our interaction with the federal government and increased our reliance on the members of Congress who are our principal liaison with it.

The 1960s and 1970s saw the enactment of a number of federal programs designed to transfer funds to individuals through various forms of entitlement or to public and private agencies at the state and local levels through grants-in-aid. By 1980, hundreds of billions of dollars were being distributed annually in this fashion. Those are high stakes and, not surprisingly, demands for readjustment of distribution formulas and correction of distribution errors have become a common and ever more burdensome part of the congressional workload.

The growth in the jurisdiction of the federal government has thus enlarged the workload of the House in two ways: first, by increasing the scope of House legislative concerns; second, by stimulating a substantial demand from members' constituents for ombudsman services. The effect is the same in both cases: more work.

## Expansion in the Number and Sophistication of Special Interest Groups

Few trends have been as marked in the last few decades of congressional history as the increased involvement of special interest groups in the legislative process. Interest groups have been with us throughout this century, but the contemporary period has seen an explosion in their numbers, the development by them of new and compelling tactics of influence, and substantial increases in their ability to raise funds and to spend them to their political advantage.

Perhaps the most significant of the recent changes in the role played by interest groups in Washington has been the appearance and rapid attainment of influence by two types of groups. One of these is the so-called "public interest groups" whose principal objective has been to counter the traditional influence of producer groups and other special interests in the policy decisions that most affect them. Their success in doing this has varied from one issue to the next, but overall the public interest groups have quickly become a factor of considerable magnitude in the legislative process (Berry 1977).

Equally significant is the appearance of what have come to be known as "single issue groups." Unlike the large, coalitional, multilithic interest groups of the past, the single issue groups concern themselves solely and often passionately with a single legislative concern. Demanding and uncompromising in their relations with the Congress, they have become the kamikazes of American politics. They concern themselves only with the battle at hand. They save nothing for tomorrow.

Each of these changes in the nature of special interest groups and their role in the legislative process has had the effect of increasing the burden on both the House of Representatives and its members. Virtually every issue now has at least two sides that are well represented in the halls of the House office buildings, in the lobbies of the Capitol, and in most congressional districts. Journalist Meg Greenfield (1978) wrote, "I can't remember a time in Washington when interest group issues and politics so dominated events. And the units of protest and concern seem to be subdividing into even smaller and more specialized groupings."

Members receive more mail on legislative issues, they see and hear more lobbyists, and they constantly find their decision-making calculations more difficult. This complicates their own decision processes and, in so doing, it compounds the problems faced by the full House in making collective legislative decisions. Whatever the representative advantages in the recent explosion in the number and skills of special interest groups—and there are many—this is a development that has added immeasurably to the complexity and arduousness of legislative decision making.

### Advances in Communications and Transportation Technology

In a great many ways, the Congress is closer to the people than it has ever been. Members used to go to Washington, stay the session, and go home. Now, with jet travel, most members go home once or twice a month. Many of those whose districts are east of the Mississippi River go home every weekend. Wide area telephone service (WATS) now makes it a simple matter for members and their staffs to deal with constituents directly over the phone. WATS lines, and the official allowances available to pay for them, have allowed members to open offices in their districts where staff can handle constituent casework as quickly and as effectively as if they were in Washington.

Television, the preeminent instrument of modern communications, has had a significant though largely indirect impact on the congressional workload. Most members, for instance, have recognized the opportunities that television provides as a vehicle for communicating with their constituents and, in some cases, for communicating with broader segments of the American public. They take advantage of this in a number of ways: by making and distributing their own videotapes, by submitting to interviews with television news reporters, by staging media "events" in Washington and in their districts, and by appearing on regularly scheduled television programs like *Meet the Press* and *The MacNeil-Lehrer Report*. Doing these things, and especially preparing for them, takes time, both the time of the member and the time of his or her staff. Television, for all of its benefits as an instrument of communication, has added a new dimension to the public lives of many members of Congress and—unavoidably—a new demand on their time as well.

Television has had other impacts on the House workload. It strongly influences Congress's agenda. It has an unmatched capacity for forcing new issues into the public consciousness and into the sphere of active concern for public institutions. In recent times we have seen this with focused issues like the Santa Barbara oil spill, the saccharin ban, and kepone contamination, and also with larger issues like civil rights and Vietnam and energy shortages. By contributing to public awareness and public concern, television encourages, in some cases even forces, Congress to respond immediately. Hearings are quickly scheduled, new legislation is introduced, members have to develop new positions, and so on. The uncontrolled nature of this agenda-setting complicates the efforts of House leaders to plan legislative schedules, it crowds committee calendars with unanticipated business, and it adds yet another set of dislocations to the already frenetic lives of most members.

Television has also had a profound influence on the recent attention the House has paid to its code of ethics. On the whole, television journalism does not do an especially good job of covering the activities of the Congress. It is not an easy institution to cover. It is large and complex, much of its important activity is not visible or comprehensible to the untrained eye, and it lacks a focal point. Hence regular news broadcasts rarely capture anything more than an occasional dimension of congressional decision making.

Television journalism, however, has been rather good at identifying and magnifying the warts that sometimes mar one or the other of the bodies of Congress: extensive overseas travel by members ("junkets" in journalistic parlance), violations by members of ethical mores or regulations, and legislative politics in some of its rawer forms. This, of course, is one of the duties of responsible journalists, to rake muck where there is muck to be raked. But the performance of this duty, particularly its aggressive and highly visible performance by television reporters, has added yet another burden to legislative life. It has forced legislators to exercise extreme care in their campaigns, in the management of their offices, and in their interactions with special interests; that is, to avoid even the slightest appearance of impropriety. These are not new concerns, to be sure, but the widespread publicity, particularly the televised publicity, of the difficulties of people like Adam Clayton Powell, Wilbur Mills, and Wayne Hays has made virtually all members more cautious than ever before. It has forced them to keep more detailed records, to file more frequent and elaborate reports, and to focus more attention on administrative details. It has further detracted from the time they can spend on the business of legislation.

**The Complexity of Modern Issues**

We noted earlier that the contemporary Congress has had to deal with a much broader range of issues than did its predecessors. But there is a difference in the nature as well as the quantity of these issues. The age of scientific discovery, the onset of interdependence among nations, and the ever more apparent scarcity of essential resources have placed issues of unprecedented scope and complexity before Congress. Every generation of Americans has faced its share of significant challenges, but none has ever faced a range of problems as complicated and compelling as those that loom over the present.

Joe Martin, whose service in the House began in 1925 and lasted more than 40 years, pointed emphatically in his autobiography (1960, 49) to the changing character of the issues that came before Congress in his lifetime.

> The great difference between life in Congress a generation ago and life there now was the absence then of the immense pressures that came with the Depression, World War II, Korea, and the cold war. Foreign affairs were an inconsequential problem in Congress in the 1920s. For one week the House Foreign Affairs Committee debated to the exclusion of all other matters the question of authorizing a $20,000 appropriation for an international poultry show in Tulsa. This item, which we finally approved, was the most important issue that came before the committee in the whole session.
>
> From one end of a session to another Congress would

> scarcely have three or four issues of consequence beside appropriation bills. And the issues were fundamentally simpler than those that surge in upon us today in such a torrent that the individual member cannot analyze all of them adequately before he is compelled to vote.

More complex issues mean more information to gather, more interests to consult, more time in legislative preparation, and more uncertainty in choosing courses of action. Issue complexity adds to the workload of individual House members and subtracts from their satisfaction with their accomplishments; and it adds to the workload of the House as a whole and subtracts from public satisfaction with its accomplishments.

For these reasons principally, but for others as well, the contemporary Congress no longer resembles the part-time, avocational, deliberative body that developed in the nineteenth century and carried over through the first third of the twentieth. It has become instead a large, bustling enterprise, trying—not always successfully—to keep pace with a changing polity and a demanding clientele. The impact of those changes and demands, and the House's responses to them, are the topic of this book.

## THE HOUSE RESPONDS

The history of the House of Representatives is an interesting amalgam of change and stability. In some essential characteristics, the contemporary House is similar to its predecessors of a generation or even a century ago. Its members still have to juggle legislative and representative roles, they still have to balance local and national interests. The acts of bargaining and compromise are as much the foundation of legislative decision making as they have always been. And the skills of political leadership remain relatively unaltered despite substantial variations in the institutional support for their exercise.

In broad perspective however, and despite these filaments of consistency, institutional challenge and reform loom as the most prominent characteristics in the development and growth of the House of Representatives. There has rarely been a time when proposals for change in its rules, procedures, and organization have been absent from the House agenda. History reveals a typical pattern of development in the House. After a spate of change, a period of stability sets in. Then, slowly, new challenges and demands upon the

House begin to mount. Reform pressures, often accelerated by an influx of new members, accumulate and gradually come to a head. When they do, change begins to take place, often in large and concentrated doses. This occurred in the aftermath of the Civil War, in 1911, in 1921, and in 1946. In the 1970s it has happened again. The responses to the self-examination of the last decade have taken several forms and in this book we will explore those that affect the internal operations of the House and the manner in which its members perform their jobs.

## Redefinition of Members' Jobs and Responsibilities

It would be a logical expectation, given the growing technical complexity of public policy, that contemporary members of the House would devote ever larger chunks of time and resources to their legislative responsibilities. We should expect that, like Alice, they would find it necessary to run harder just to keep up. That, however, is not the case. Representative, rather than legislative, functions have been the growth sector in the official activities of this generation of House members. In defining their jobs—that is, in setting priorities among the array of tasks and opportunities that confront them—members in recent years have been pouring ever larger amounts of effort and energy and staff resources into their relationships with their constituents.

To understand this development, we must begin by recognizing that public policy has become more complex in two ways, not just one. It is technically more complex, as we have noted. But it is also politically more complex. Issues are broader in scope and harder to compartmentalize. Government policy tends now to have multiple, and often conflicting, impacts on the peculiar heterogeneity of interests that compose the political environment. Consensus is more elusive and policy objectives are harder to attain. Members of Congress continue to introduce proposals for what they regard as sound and effective programs. But then they encounter one frustration after another as those proposals wend their way through the political torture chamber of the legislative process. Even when they succeed in bringing their legislative seedlings to fruit, the external rewards rarely seem to justify the effort. Some citizens will warmly welcome a new program and praise its sponsor; but others will vigorously oppose it for its substance, its cost, or the precedents it sets.

To this complex and frustrating political environment, members have been responding by gradually shifting their focus from the legislative to the representative arena. In the latter, at least, the rewards are easier to define and achieve. Devotion to the needs and demands of constituents has two quite clear attractions for members of Congress. First, unlike legislative efforts, constituent service engenders little stress or opposition. It is, to put the matter simply, a whole lot easier than legislating. Its second attraction is the more important one, however, and that is that its rewards are palpable and direct. And, by all odds, its principal reward is reelection.

Nothing has so shaped the structure of priorities, the job definitions, of modern representatives as the recognition that their participation in the legislative policy-making process has little direct correlation with their ability to stay in the Congress. There is little to suggest that creative legislators are more likely to be reelected than are those incumbents who participate only occasionally or passively in the legislative process. But there is a growing body of evidence suggesting that members who pay dedicated attention to constituent service and who avoid the taint or appearance of ethical impropriety can expect to be reelected for as long as they choose to run.

To a large extent, the way members of Congress define their jobs and set priorities on their time and resources is a function of the personalized incentive systems under which they operate. Reelection looms large as an incentive for nearly all members. It is the single, essential prerequisite to everything else they hope to accomplish in their congressional careers. Their recognition of the high correlation between constituent-oriented activities and reelection, on the one hand, and the low correlation between legislative policy making and reelection, on the other, has quickly become one of the governing factors in the way most members of the House now define their jobs.

The nature of this development and its very important implications, both for the internal operations of the House and for its public esteem, are explored in the first three articles in this volume. Glenn R. Parker notes the growing dichotomy between the popularity of House incumbents in their districts and the unpopularity of the Congress as an institution. Using survey data, he explores the sources of Congress's institutional unpopularity and the likely persistence of that phenomenon.

Thomas E. Cavanagh examines the relationship between the reelection goals of members of Congress and their performance of other legislative and oversight functions. Working with a rationalist model of congressional behavior, he conceptualizes two different "arenas" of congressional activity: the electoral and the institutional. The former is dominated by the demands the public makes on individual representatives, the latter by members' perceptions of the responsibilities of the House. The objectives that prevail in these two arenas are often in conflict with each other and the resolution of these conflicts has a direct bearing on the way members allocate their own time and resources. Cavanagh explores this process of resolution and its impact on the role the Congress can and does play in the development of public policy.

In contrast, though more narrowly focused, John R. Johannes's chapter casts some doubt on both the burdens and the benefits of the "electoral connection." The growth in constituent casework has contributed mightily to the expanding workload of the offices of House members. Johannes focuses on this specific aspect of member office operations. From interviews and survey data, he has drawn a portrait that details the scope of the casework burden, the division of labor effected within member offices to cope with that burden, the kinds of people who normally become caseworkers, and the degree of satisfaction they are able to achieve in trying to resolve constituent problems. Johannes's analysis is especially noteworthy for its sensitivity to the relationship between casework and the broader functions that members perform: legislation, representation, and oversight.

A final factor of growing importance for the job of the representative is the heightened concern of the past decade with the question of congressional ethics. Several instances of individual misconduct in Congress and the Watergate scandal in the presidency have focused unrelenting public and press attention on the manner in which public officials acquire, spend, and account for public funds. Many members believe that public perceptions of the House of Representatives are directly affected by these ethical concerns,[2] and this has inspired the House to take a good hard look at the use and abuse of public funds by its own members. Allan J. Katz's article explores some of these concerns, focusing particularly on the major effort undertaken by the House in 1977 to revise its code of ethics. Katz looks closely at the politics of ethical reform, at the substantive concerns of those who participated most directly in this effort, and at the nature of their interaction. In his positions as General Counsel of the U.S. House Commission on Administrative Review and as Counsel of the House Select Committee on Ethics, Katz had abundant opportunities to observe these activities at first hand.

## Development of Resources

As its workload has grown, the House has sought to keep pace by enlarging the resources available to its members. This has helped. But it has also created a new set of problems revolving around the need to effectively manage and deploy this growing array of resources. Resolving these problems has not been easy; indeed many of them remain unresolved. The reason for that has a great deal to do with the nature of the House, in fact with the nature of all democratic legislatures as institutions. The essence of good management is the adaptation of means to ends, first to clarify objectives and then to develop and utilize resources in the efficient pursuit of those objectives.

In a legislature, that is extraordinarily difficult. There is rarely consensus on institutional objectives in anything other than the most general sense. Institutional objectives are defined politically, through an elaborate and traditional bargaining process. They are ad hoc and impermanent, changing with the public mood and with the natural alterations in the membership of the House wrought by frequent elections. In a business corporation, profit maximization provides a constant institutional objective to which resource development and management choices can be related. But in the House, no such constant or measurable objective exists. Hence every debate over resource and management questions is potentially tortuous because there is no consensual standard to use in determining what is appropriate and what is adequate.

Its character as a legislative body poses a further impediment to the effective development and utilization of resources in the House. The House is a nonhierarchical organization. In making decisions about internal procedural and structural questions, it operates very much like a confederation of autonomous units, each of which places a high value on its own independence. Members and committees and other operating units are reluctant to surrender any significant measure of control over their workplaces or their workforces. In most cases, then, development and management of resources is not a centralized function in the House.

Yet another compelling factor in House decisions on internal operations is the perceived relationship between the deployment and control of resources, on the one hand, and political influence, on the other. Organizational patterns in the House are generally the product of a series of decisions, often narrow or minor decisions, made at different points in its history. They derive from no single blueprint and they adhere to no apparent set of consistent organizational principles. To a management specialist, unfamiliar with the ways of legislatures, the organization of the House might well appear illogical, inconsistent, even irrational. And indeed there may well be instances where that is clearly the case. Existing patterns of organization and operation cannot be changed, however, without confronting and challenging a set of existing political realities and thus incurring the determined resistance of their beneficiaries.

The absence of consensual institutional objectives, the relative autonomy of individual units, and the political significance attached to the control of resources and direction of administrative activities have persistently set the parameters of recent efforts to manage more effectively the workload of the House. Part 2 of this book looks at several of these management issues and provides assessments of the successes and inadequacies of recent House attempts to deal with them.

Perhaps the most important of the resources available to the House and its members is time. The growth in demands on the contemporary House has meant that there are simply fewer and fewer hours available to devote to any one issue or function. The problem of time management is explored by Thomas J. O'Donnell. O'Donnell examines the nature of the demands on the time of contemporary members. He notes the implications of these compelling demands on the ability of members and of the House as an institution to make thoughtful, informed, and deliberate decisions. He then outlines the new scheduling procedures adopted by the House in 1977 and assesses the early evidence of their effects.

Despite these efforts by the House to manage its time better, it has become strikingly clear in recent years that the 435 members of the House will never have enough time to cope alone with the rapid growth in their workload. This has forced the House to pay more and more attention to the development of another important resource: House staff. The past two decades have witnessed an increase in both the size and quality of House staff that is nothing short of phenomenal. The Legislative Reorganization Act of 1946 recognized formally for the first time that House committees needed professional staff support and authorized each full committee to hire two professional staff members. At that time, members were permitted to hire no more than five people and to spend no more than $9,500 per year in aggregate salaries for their personal staffs. In the period since then the size of House staffs, both clerical and professional, has grown steadily. Table 2 indicates the pace of this staff expansion.

Like any development of this magnitude, the growth in House staff has generated its own set of problems. In general, these are problems attendant to personnel management in any institution, issues such as recruitment, training, compensation, fringe benefits, and so forth. In the House, however, these are especially perplexing issues because of the decentralization of personnel management re-

**Table 2. *Committee and Personal Staff Employees, U.S. House of Representatives, Selected Years***

| *Year* | *Committee* | *Personal* |
|---|---|---|
| 1930 | 112 | 870 |
| 1935 | 122 | 870 |
| 1947 | 193 | 1,440 |
| 1957 | 375 | 2,441 |
| 1967 | 589 | 4,055 |
| 1972 | 783 | 5,280 |
| 1976 | 1,548 | 6,939 |
| 1978 | 1,844 | 8,432 |

SOURCE: Adapted from *Congressional Staffs*, by Harrison W. Fox, Jr., and Susan Webb Hammond (New York: Free Press, 1977), p. 171; and from H. Rep. 96-866, pp. 535–541, U.S. Congress, House. 96th Cong., 2d sess.

sponsibilities. Individual units have independent responsibility for hiring, for firing, and for the determination of most other personnel practices. Hence there is not one personnel management system in the House, but hundreds. David W. Brady's chapter examines the way personnel issues are handled in these offices and he explores the implications of this for the effective utilization and equitable treatment of personnel in the House as a whole and in its individual offices.

The growth in the personnel and material resources available to House members, committees, and leadership offices has created a new and inevitable set of burdens on those offices. That is the need to find an effective and efficient way to employ those resources. This is a management problem and, like most of the issues surveyed in this volume, it is a problem that all offices share, but which they tend to cope with individually. Susan Webb Hammond writes about the nature and scope of these office management problems. She concentrates on the frustrations the individual House units encounter in trying to cope with these problems and she identifies the most common and most successful of the arrangements that House offices now employ.

Another area in which the House has been attempting to manage its work better is in the provision of more abundant and more efficient administrative support for its operating units. With the growth in workload and the concomitant growth in personnel and other resources to handle that workload, extensive new demands have been placed on the House administrative system. There are more people to be housed and fed, broader and more sophisticated equipment needs, more money to be handled, more mail to be processed, and so forth. This has required continuing adjustments that would have been difficult for any administrative system. They have been especially difficult for the House because its administrative structure, like so many other aspects of its operations, is without a single central focal point. It has not one leader, but several. Responsibility concentrates, not at one point, but at a half dozen or more. Rooted in a set of traditional, often politicized relationships, it is a clumsy system. And despite the conscientious efforts of its managers, the House administrative system has not always succeeded in providing the kind of comprehensive, efficient support required by an institution as complex and demanding as the modern House of Representatives.

Jarold A. Kieffer has had a long and distinguished career in the management of private and public institutions, and in his analysis of the House administrative system he makes a special effort to examine it in the perspective of more traditional kinds of administrative structures. He sketches an outline of the administrative system, concentrating on the distribution of responsibility and authority for the performance of administrative tasks and carefully identifying the special problems of administering a legislature. He then goes on to indicate those functional areas in which administrative support systems have failed fully to keep pace with internal demands for administrative services. In the same way that looking around in a private home can reveal a great deal about the people who live there, Kieffer's look at the internal administration of the House is pregnant with suggestive implications about the nature of that body as a working institution.

## Coping with Information Needs

The growing complexity of American political life has produced several different kinds of demands on the House and its members. Members have been required to reconsider, and in some cases to redefine, the character of their own jobs. The House, both as a whole and as a compendium of individual operating units, has been forced to develop, reorient, and more effectively manage its personnel and material resources. But the House has also had to come to grips with a new set of substantive demands, demands for policy proposals or for responses to policy proposals, that require it to be better informed about a broader range of topics than at any time in its history. In attempting to meet this substantive set of demands, the House has come to recognize that for much of its history it has operated without a truly productive or genuinely independent apparatus for generating essential information on national and international policy issues.

Sandy Maisel's chapter sets these concerns in perspective. Maisel begins by looking at the dimensions of member and committee information requirements, at the kinds and quantities of information they need to satisfactorily carry out their responsibilities. He also identifies the primary sources, both official and informal, from which they draw this information. His primary contribution, however, is his rich and well-documented analysis of actual habits of information reliance and utilization. Drawing on interviews and surveys of House members and their staffs, he is able to map the normal patterns of information flow. His findings have also allowed him to identify some of the inadequacies in the House information support system and the problems that members and committees continue to encounter as a result.

The House's information needs demand not only reliable sources but also an effective capacity for organizing and communicating existing information. To satisfy this latter need the House has become an increasingly heavy user of computers and other information processing technology. In the early 1970s it established an organization called House Information Systems to oversee and manage the application of computer technology to House operations. In his chapter, Jeffrey A. Goldberg describes this development, shedding light on its successes and its problems. Since many applications of computer technology are just beginning to take shape, Goldberg looks thoughtfully at the probable impact of these on the operation of individual offices and of the House as a whole.

Some of the most visible and most significant of the improvements in House information support have come from the expansion in the number and the capabilities of the legislative research units appended to the Congress: the Congressional Research Service of the Library of Congress, the General Accounting Office, the Office of Technology Assessment, and the Congressional Budget Office. James A. Thurber's article traces the development of these research units and examines a number of salient characteristics of their composition and operations. He gives considerable attention to concerns about the effectiveness of the units, both individually and as the collective components of the House's information support system.

## THE OBJECTIVES OF THIS BOOK

At the heart of this book is a simple but important notion: that examining the way institutions perform fundamental tasks reveals a great deal about their character and their possibilities. In organizing the book, we have attempted to answer two primary questions: How do members get their work done? and, How does the House get its work done? In looking at the House at work, the authors of the individual papers collected here employ both micro- and macro-level analysis. Some of those papers focus on individual members of Congress, on how they define their responsibilities, how they organize their time, how they manage their offices and their staffs, and how they cope with the fundamental problem of decision making. Other chapters will look at a different dimension of the House: at the traditions and responsibilities that constrain the way it operates, at the scope of its institutional burdens, and at the structures and processes that compose its internal organization. In each case, our objective has been to describe existing arrangements for handling the workload, to analyze their operations, and to assess their impact and effectiveness.

This volume falls outside the more traditional approaches to the study of the Congress. Our focus is not on political processes, on elections, on roll call voting, or on legislative reform *qua* reform. Nor do we attempt to penetrate the mysteries of any single committee or leadership office. Our intention, quite simply, is to view the House as a whole, to examine it as an organization operating in a complex environment and forced to cope with multiple needs. Our focus, therefore, is on the fundamental operations and relationships that are the flesh and blood of a dynamic institution. We think there is much to be learned about the House by examining the manner in which it operates *as an organization*: the way it defines objectives, the way it integrates its parts to each other and to the whole, and the way it manages its day-to-day responsibilities.

This is fundamentally a book about institutional development and institutional adaptation to change. But it is also a book about a peculiar kind of institution, a legislature. One of our principal concerns, one that is treated directly in Joseph Cooper's conclusion and in the prologue to each Part, has been to identify the distinctive organizational characteristics of legislatures and the distinctive ways in which they respond to environmental changes. Almost all models of institutional change and development are derived from the experience of hierarchical organizations. But legislatures are almost invariably nonhierarchical, and in their complexity, their diffusion, and their lack of consensual objectives they pose unique problems for both the theorists and the practitioners of legislative change and development. It is our hope that this volume addresses those problems and helps in some way to suggest a framework for resolving them.

In undertaking this project, we have been doubly blessed. Our first blessing is the unprecedented scope and quality of the information on which these papers draw. Many of them make extensive use of data and materials gathered by the U.S. House Commission on Administrative Review (the Obey Commission) in 1976 and 1977. That commission's analysis of the internal operations of the House was the broadest ever undertaken. Among the sources of information it developed were a national survey of public attitudes toward the Congress, more than 300 lengthy interviews with members of the House and almost 200 interviews with personal and committee staff employees, a detailed and systematic study of the way members allocate their time, and a formal census of the 11,000 employees of the House. We found this to be a rich lode of information, full of new insights about the operations and capabilities of the House of Representatives, and worthy of the further probing that occurs in the papers collected here.

Our second blessing in organizing this volume has been the unique qualifications of the contributing authors. Most are academic political scientists; most have also held positions of considerable responsibility within the House of Representatives. They are not strangers to the institution that is the subject of this book, nor to the tradition of congressional scholarship that this volume is intended to extend and expand. In almost every case, the papers collected in this book are written by people whose intellectual interest in the issues about which they write is buttressed by some significant practical experience in dealing with those issues.

Our ultimate hope is that this book says something about congressional behavior and congressional performance. For the House of Representatives, the past decade has been the best of times and the worst of times. These have been good years for the House because of their intense introspection. They have revealed the willingness and the ability of the House to examine its own operations and procedures, to subject them to harsh assessments, and to change those things that have failed to measure up. Few decades in congressional history have been filled with as much self-questioning or with as many creative attempts to find new solutions to both old and new problems.

But these have been hard years for the House as well. Turnover has been high, traditional sources of stability and continuity have declined or disappeared, significant legislative accomplishments have been elusive, and poll after poll has indicated distressingly low levels of public satisfaction with congressional performance. Is it possible that a decade of introspection and reform has left the House a weaker, rather than a stronger, institution? Have the demands of an ever more heterogeneous population and the confounding complexity of modern issues overloaded the capacity of the House—indeed of any democratic legislature—to respond effectively?

Our concern with these questions was a major factor in our decision to proceed with this volume. We do not pretend that we have answered them. We hope, however, that by exploring the fundamental operations of the House, we have provided information and judgments that will advance the ongoing effort to determine a feasible and appropriate role for the Congress in a modern policy-making system. Our interest in this volume and the issues it explores stems from our shared belief that the manner in which the House defines, organizes, and manages its work reveals a great deal about the determinants of congressional behavior and about the quality of congressional performance.

## NOTES

1. Briefly, after the admission of Hawaii and Alaska to the Union in 1959, the House expanded to 437 members to accommodate a single representative from each of the new states. In the reapportionment following the 1960 census, the size of the House reverted to 435.
2. When a sample of House members was asked by the Commission on Administrative Review to indicate the "most serious problems the House has in terms of how the public regards it," 11% cited the "cultural stereotype of the Congressman as crooked, lazy, self-serving, corrupt, incompetent"; 16% indicated that "abuses by a few members damage the image of the institution as a whole"; 32% blamed the "personal ethics of Congressmen, morals scandals, scandals in general"; 9% said "conflicts of interest"; 15% pointed to "financial ethics problems"; and 9% suggested "junkets, excessive foreign travel." (Multiple responses to this question were permitted.) See Commission 1977, 2(*Survey Materials*): 892–894.

## REFERENCES

Berry, Jeffrey M. 1977. *Lobbying for the People*. Princeton: Princeton University Press.

Commission on Administrative Review, U.S. Congress, House. 1977. *Final Report*. 2 vols. 95th Cong., 1st sess. H. Doc. 95-272.
Dies, Martin. 1954. "Truth About Congressmen." *Saturday Evening Post*, October 30, 1954.
Greenfield, Meg. 1978. "Thinking Small." *Washington Post*, April 19, 1978.
Martin, Joe. 1960. *My First Fifty Years in Politics*. New York: McGraw Hill.
Young, James Sterling. 1966. *The Washington Community, 1800–1828*. New York: Harcourt, Brace, and World.

# Part I. Defining the Job

## *The Context of Job Performance*

Chester Barnard long ago aptly defined organizations as coordinated systems of effort. As such, one of their primary concerns must be to prescribe and regulate the conduct or behavior of their participants in ways that are conducive to the preservation of the organization and the attainment of its purposes. This, in turn, involves the specification and control of a variety of forms of conduct or behavior: conduct or behavior that is directly and immediately involved in producing the outputs of the organization; conduct or behavior that defines or orients interpersonal interaction within the organization; and conduct or behavior that defines or orients modes of exchange or transaction between members of the organization and external sources of demand and support.

As in other organizations, analysis of the job of the member of Congress thus requires attention to several dimensions of activity, not a single dimension. Institutional prescription and regulation of member conduct or behavior, to be sure, involves work or task activity (e.g., bill introduction procedures or limitations on the use of staff or expense resources). But it also involves prescription and regulation of interpersonal interaction (e.g., bans on insulting language or discriminatory treatment of staff), and prescription and regulation of modes of environmental transaction (e.g., disclosure requirements or limits on campaign financing). Indeed, in recent decades prescription and regulation along each of these dimensions have grown in response to a variety of pressures and circumstances—expansion in the role of the federal government, increases in staff and expense resources, changes in public attitudes on openness, chronic public dissatisfaction with congressional performance, soaring campaign costs, and emergence of service in Congress as a career. Nonetheless, the House remains a very distinctive organization with severely limited capability to determine or control the manner in which members perform their jobs. As a result, these pressures and circumstances have posed a number of serious problems for the House as an institution.

## SOURCES OF CONSTRAINT

All organizations are constrained in their ability to prescribe the jobs of their participants and to regulate conduct or behavior so that it accords with or satisfies job prescriptions. In part, this is due to the nature of their operating environments, including values, forms of linkage, and exchange positions relative to input needs and output demands. In part, it is due to the character of their work, including the nature of the raw materials they seek to process, the complexity and range of their products, and the state of technological knowledge with respect to their work or productive processes. In part, however, it is also due to the dilemmas all organizations confront by virtue of the fact that what they seek to order are segments of the activities of whole human personalities. Prescription may be necessary to maintain a system of coordinated effort. However, it inevitably involves limitations on judgment and initiative as well as the impairment of job satisfactions. Regulation or control through the allocation of organizational rewards and penalties may also be essential to keep performance in line with prescription. However, to establish systems of power or control over organizational rewards and penalties is inevitably to breed envy and resentment over both the system of power per se and its concrete impacts or results.

These general or pervasive sources of constraint function with highly restrictive effects in the case of the House. The House is a democratic legislature, operating in a separation of powers and bicameral framework of government. Its members are chosen through plurality elections in separate and distinct constituencies, have a fiduciary relationship to their constituencies, and are accountable to their constituencies on a regular basis as a condition of continuance in office. The House thus must accord each member formally equal status, must operate in a collegial manner basing authoritative action on deliberation and voting, and must take care not to bias or interfere with the ability of a member to represent his constituents. Concomitantly, the work of the organization is highly abstract, value laden, and dependent on the aggregation of voting coalitions. Its substance is accordingly not highly subject either to analysis or determination on the basis of criteria or techniques derived from some discipline or field of knowledge. The job rather remains far more of an art than a science. Finally, the basic character of its operating environment and work, combined with the pressures of the modern workload and the current difficulties of assembling majorities behind important policies, make the cost-benefit or inducement-contributions balance of service in the House quite fragile.

## IMPACTS ON JOB PRESCRIPTION

The consequences for the prescription of job behavior are varied, but on the whole quite negative. Through both the explicit language and the underlying assumptions of the rules and statutes that govern its operations, the House vests its members with the tasks of representation, legislation, oversight, and constituent service. Moreover, certain procedural aspects of these tasks or activities can be and are specified in great detail. However, the House can do little to specify the substance or content of these tasks or to prescribe how conflicts within them or among them should be resolved. Such determinations must be left primarily to the members themselves as individual representatives of their constituents, except in periods when party is strong enough to order and direct such choices. Since the present era is not one of great party strength, the modern House must depend far more than most organizations simply on informal work norms to specify the kinds of task behavior that serve the institution's interests (e.g., specialization, hard work, apprenticeship). The situation with respect to interpersonal interaction is quite similar. Here too the equal status of members and their ties and responsibilities as representatives of their constituencies impede institutional prescription of conduct or behavior. Here too, to the degree that party is not strong enough to provide a substitute basis for specification, the House is highly dependent on sets of informal norms to control conflict and coordinate interpersonal relationships so that they serve institutional needs (e.g., "to get along, go along," "take half a loaf," "disagree without being disagreeable").

Conversely, the House's ability to prescribe conduct or behavior involved in modes of exchange or transaction with its environment exceeds that of most organizations. Its status as a key public institution and the need to preserve confidence in the integrity of the fiduciary relationship that exists between members and constituents expands the leeway for specification. In addition, because the House is publicly financed, greater leeway also exists with respect to a tangential aspect of task activity or behavior—use of organizational resources for private or personal purposes. Nonetheless, once again the basic character of the type of fiduciary relationship that exists, that is, political representation, creates substantive and political limits or barriers to prescription of no mean significance. Forms of improper conduct or behavior past outright bribery or simple thievery are difficult to define without impinging on the representative ties and responsibilities of the members per se. The House thus tends to prescribe the conditions or context of behavior rather than its substance, such as limits on campaign contributions or requirements to disclose sources of income. Even so, results may be very ambiguous, such as the ban on use of staff for "political" purposes. Moreover, the objects of action must be matters of broad consensus if prescription is to contribute to public confidence; severe costs may be imposed on the retention and recruitment of able members; and action is always contingent on the willingness of a majority of members to define their jobs in ways that impair their personal privacy and financial or career interests.

## IMPACT ON JOB REGULATION

The consequences for regulating or controlling the manner in which members actually perform their jobs are also quite negative. The ties and responsibilities of members to their constituencies, the collegial character of House decision making, the non-amenability of political decision making to technological regulation or routinization, and the low boiling point of House members relative to differential distributions of power or inducements all serve to limit organizational power. On the one hand, they impair the ability of the House to generate a fund of rewards and penalties that can be subject to discretionary control. Thus, the House has far less ability than most organizations to distribute pay, benefits, and resources to members in a differential manner as well as far less control over the selection and retention of members per se. On the other hand, they impair the ability of the House to establish systems of power that will distribute the discretionary rewards and penalties that can be generated in ways that lead or induce members to serve institutional needs rather than personal career interests. Once again party strength is an important variable. It both adds to the fund of discretionary rewards and penalties that exist and provides incentives and mechanisms for their application that strengthen institutional capacity for policy outputs. However, in the absence of substantial party strength, not only is the fund of inducements reduced, but applications of those that do exist are marked by substantial degrees of caution or reserve. Thus, in the modern House members are rarely subject to sanctions or penalties because of their job performance, party leaders seek and tend to rely on neutral or general principles in distributing rewards, and considerable leeway is extended to members to use institutional resources for personal, career advantage.

As a result, the degree of articulation between the allocation of rewards and penalties and the inducement of task or interactive behavior that serves institutional effectiveness is quite lax in the modern House as compared with many organizations. Members who adhere to informal norms and/or display substantive or political competence are rewarded with power and prestige. But so too are relatively undistinguished members, when favored by political circumstances, tenure, or accident, and mavericks, when they possess media or legislative skills. Nor can the House rely, as many organizations can, on environmental pressure or discipline to supplement deficiencies in its institutionalized capacity to allocate inducements. In many organizational contexts environmental dissatisfaction with performance has harsh and immediate consequences for individual well-being and career prospects. In the House, however, the tie between members and constituents and the collegial character of decision making allow members to separate themselves from environmental dissatisfaction with institutional performance. Moreover, given limited ability to regulate the use of organizational resources, expansions in these resources expand this capacity rather than simply contributing to task performance. In short, then, the House in motivating job behavior that serves its performance needs must depend far more on diffuse feelings of institutional loyalty and personal desires for policy outputs and/or internal power than most organizations. These, to be sure, are often quite effective, but their impact is necessarily highly variable and fragile when not reinforced or supported by substantial institutionalized capacity to reward or punish and environmental sanctions for performance failures.

Institutional capacity to control or regulate prescribed conduct relative to environmental transactions or use of institutional resources is also highly restricted. Special forms of inducements and mechanisms have to be relied upon because those used in the regular work or productive processes are immersed in politics and hence subject to suspicion regarding their impartiality. Even so, members are extremely reluctant to act as policemen and judges over one another. Not only is this at odds with their equal status as representatives and the maintenance of feelings of comity and camaraderie that are essential to the operation of a collegial institution; in addition, the specter of abuse for purposes of partisan advantage is always present. The few internal control mechanisms that are created, such as the Ethics or Standards Committee, are thus operated with great caution. Rather, the House prefers to rely on electoral discipline or legal sanctions. But these have serious disadvantages as well. The enactment of civil or criminal penalties provides a highly inflexible means of regulating forms of conduct that are subtle and complex. The creation of special regulatory or enforcement agents, such as the Federal Election Commission, can compensate for this defect. But the House is understandably quite reluctant to place great power over the daily life and future careers of members in the hands of outsiders, many of whom might well not be experienced politicians. As for reliance on elections, the ability of members to establish personal relations with their constituencies that override general or institutional considerations has had an impact on broad forms of behavior or conduct as well as task behavior. Members are often now impervious to defeat even when they have engaged in the most egregious forms of personal conduct.

## PROBLEMS AND ISSUES

As stated earlier, it is the interaction of the House's distinctive limitations in prescribing and regulating the conduct of its members with the pressures and circumstances to which it is now subject that underlies the problems and issues it confronts in securing job performance adequate to its needs. These problems and issues may be summarized briefly as follows both to conclude this analysis and to place the articles in this section in perspective.

First, the House's ability to perform its law-making and oversight responsibilities under the Constitution effectively is currently very much in question and thus so too is its longrun ability to maintain its role or position in the broader political system. Yet the House has limited capacity to prescribe or regulate the behavior or conduct of its members. Nor can it rely on environmental dissatisfaction with its collective performance as an instrument of inducing task performance that serves its needs since members now more than ever can separate electoral judgments of their performance from electoral judgments of the institution's performance. Moreover, ironically enough, perhaps the most decisive action the House can take to enhance task performance, that is, expansion in staff and expense resources, can well have counterproductive effects. The degree to which they do is of course debatable; but the general problems of a wide gulf between institutional needs and individual career interests and the mixed benefits of additions to the resource base remains quite serious and difficult to resolve.

Second, maintenance of trust in the integrity of the fiduciary relationship between members and constituents requires more effort and poses more problems than ever before. Yet, as long as dissatisfaction with output performance remains high, it appears that action in this realm can only limit discontent, not enhance support. Moreover, both the nature of the action that should be taken and the House's willingness to take it are highly uncertain and tenuous. In the former regard the precise implications of general ethical notions or concepts as well as the degree to which it is fair or expedient to constrain all members because of the possible misbehavior of some present difficult and highly controversial issues. In the latter regard the House is a very human organization and as such its members are just as prone to self-righteousness and self-protective behavior as members of other types of organizations in this society. And yet it remains true that the House cannot ignore acts of its members that betray or prejudice their fiduciary relationship to their constituents. A final, but devastating, irony of the House's current situation is that whereas the public will often not hold members accountable for either institutional performance failures or their personal behavior, it holds the institution closely accountable for both.

# 1. Can Congress Ever Be a Popular Institution?

*Glenn R. Parker*

## INTRODUCTION

One of the most distinctive features of Congress is its lack of widespread public esteem. The public appears to disregard the unusual accessibility and responsiveness of Congress in forming their evaluations of congressional performance. Institutionalized features of Congress that insure citizen access enhance the popularity of the representative, but not of Congress. For instance, the traditional letter to the representative provides citizens with a direct opportunity for demanding services, voicing complaints, or seeking solutions to problems. Further, constituents can be fairly certain that letters to their representatives will probably carry more influence and inspire more action than similar letters to the president. Yet, such ombudsman functions of Congress are ignored in evaluating overall congressional performance, or are attributed to the efforts of individual representatives. Representatives, not Congress, receive (and take) credit for protecting citizen interests. Perhaps we expect more from the collective wisdom of 535 members of Congress than from our own representative.

The extent to which Congress is unpopular is evident in the fact that Congress has received more negative than positive evaluations in over 80% of the survey measurements of congressional popularity[1] between 1939 and 1977; during this period, congressional unpopularity has a mean of 52%. Clearly, Congress is more unpopular than popular. In fact, popular Congresses can be viewed as aberrations created by unusual circumstances. For example, the relative lack of public dissatisfaction with the 83rd Congress (1953) is probably influenced by the fact that a truce in the Korean War was initiated while the opinion survey was under way; this coincidence may have served to increase favorable evaluations of Congress (fig. 1.1). As for the other most popular Congress, the 89th, one of its most

Figure 1.1. *Congressional Unpopularity: 1939–1977*

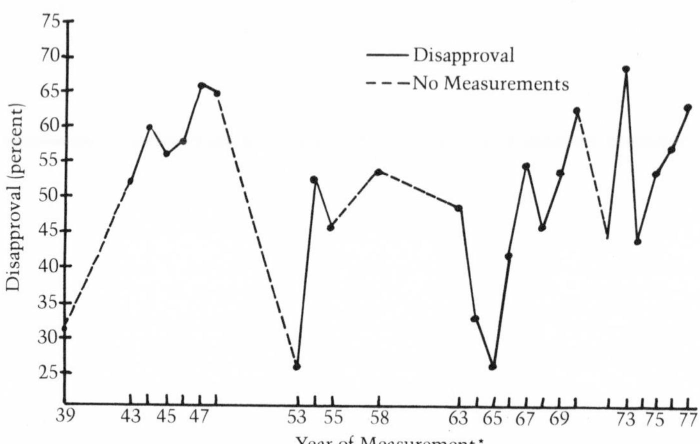


*Since there have been multiple measurements of congressional unpopularity during some years, only the *latest* measurement of congressional disapproval during a specific year is charted.
*Source*: American Institute of Public Opinion.

distinctive characteristics is the unusual degree to which it supported President Johnson's legislative initiatives: approximately 70% of the over 450 presidential measures submitted to Congress were approved during the first session of that Congress.

Unfortunately, congressional unpopularity is often treated by the mass media and political observers as a malady in desperate need of remedy. Americans are expected to be appalled by the inability of this major representational institution to generate greater public support. On the other hand, the consistently high levels of congressional unpopularity suggest that we should be more accustomed to frequent and sizable amounts of dissatisfaction with Congress. That is, it could be argued that we should expect congressional performance to receive low marks.

This is not to suggest that we ignore drops in congressional popularity. On the contrary, severe declines in popularity may critically impair the ability of Congress to execute its functions and responsibilities "in the public's name." This relationship between popularity and prescribed influence is evident in the Survey Research Center's 1974 and 1976 Election Studies: those dissatisfied with congressional performance frequently indicate that Congress should exercise less influence within the political system (r = .26 and .28, respectively).[2] Since congressional popularity and institutional influence are theoretically and empirically linked, questions of institutional effectiveness and capability are apt to arise during periods of declining popularity. As a consequence, public skepticism over the amount of influence Congress should exercise is likely to mount. Thus, Congress may find it increasingly difficult to defend its constitutional prerogatives and legislative actions in clashes with a popular president. Our point is, however, that low levels of popularity may be endemic to Congress and beyond its immediate control. In short, attacks on Congress for its lack of public prestige serve no useful purpose: Congress, like Prometheus, is inevitably bound to suffer indignities.

Further, comparisons between the popularity of Congress and that of its members are misleading. Individually, members of Congress are far more popular than the institution in which they serve. This discrepancy is not so difficult to understand if the criteria used to evaluate Congress and its members differ significantly. In short, it may be difficult for Congress to attain the same degree of popularity as individual members because of the nature of the institution and the standards that are applied in evaluating congressional performance.

The purpose of this chapter is first to discuss the sources of Congress's low level of popularity, and then to examine the sources of evaluations of individual members. In the process, we hope to clarify the reasons for the relatively low regard for Congress and the greater public esteem of the individual representative. We can attribute Congress's lack of public esteem to: (1) the nature of Congress and the tasks it is expected to perform; (2) the affective attachments between an individual and the political system; and (3) the impact of institutional and political conditions which structure perceptions of congressional performance.

## MAJOR SOURCES OF EVALUATIONS OF CONGRESS

### The Nature of Congress and Its Work

The very nature of the legislative process may not only dampen citizen interest in Congress, but also generate negative impressions of congressional performance. We observe, for example, that congressional style and pace is one of the most frequently cited criteria for evaluations of Congress (table 1.1). Not surprisingly, these evaluations are largely negative: in both the 1968 and 1977 Louis Harris opinion surveys, negative evaluations based on the congressional environment contained frequent references to the slow, inefficient, and unproductive nature of Congress. The negative impact that the complexity of the legislative process can have on citizen evaluations of congressional performance is not lost on House members: 18% cite the lack of public understanding of the complexity of the House as seriously diminishing the popularity of Congress (Commission on Administrative Review 1977, 892).

The substance of congressional work—public policies and laws—also contributes to public discontent with Congress. The significance of policy actions (or inactions) in congressional evaluations is evident in the frequency with which policy considerations enter such assessments: over half of the responses in 1968 and almost one-third of the responses in 1977 made some mention of political issues or policies as bases for evaluating Congress. The range and volume of policies and problems for which Congress is held accountable by the mass media and the public create numerous opportunities for generating dissatisfaction with Congress. Since no policy action is likely to completely satisfy everyone, most congressional outcomes produce some discontent. Conversely, avoidance of such decisions provides no salvation. The lack of congressional action on significant societal problems only serves to reinforce impressions of congressional ineffectiveness.

Although political issues can generate favorable evaluations of Congress, the result is more likely to be a mixed or negative evaluation as in 1968 and 1977. Foreign and defense policies generated negative congressional evaluations in 1968 but these issues were mentioned infrequently in 1977. The decline in the saliency of foreign and defense issues in 1977 is probably a result of the lack of American involvement in a foreign conflict, such as Vietnam, and the increased importance of domestic issues. Domestic issues are far more salient than foreign policy concerns in congressional evaluations; hence, such issues exercise a stronger impact on congressional popularity. The impact of domestic issues on congressional popularity was decisively negative in 1977, but the actions (or inactions) of Congress may not be totally responsible for this increased negative association. The domestic issues which presently confront Congress (energy, inflation, unemployment, pollution, welfare) are extremely controversial. These issues are by their very nature divisive, and any congressional action in these areas seems likely to produce significant dissatisfaction with Congress. Thus, current policy issues seem more likely to create negative, or at best mixed, evalua-

**Table 1.1.** ***Bases of Evaluations of Congress***

| Reason cited as basis for evaluation | 1968[a] (1,370 Responses) | | | | 1977[b] (1,813 Responses) | | | |
|---|---|---|---|---|---|---|---|---|
| | % citing this reason | (N) | Favorable evaluation of Congress | Unfavorable evaluation of Congress | % citing this reason | (N) | Favorable evaluation of Congress | Unfavorable evaluation of Congress |
| Issues | **51.8%** | | | | **30.8%** | | | |
| Domestic | 46.3 | (634) | 54% | 46% | 30.1 | (545) | 7% | 93% |
| Foreign-Defense | 5.5 | (75) | 35 | 65 | .7 | (13) | 100 | — |
| Legislative-Executive Relations | **6.5** | | | | **19.6** | | | |
| Presidential support | 3.1 | (43) | 72 | 28 | | | — | — |
| Presidential opposition | 3.4 | (46) | 56 | 44 | 19.6 | (355) | 25 | 75 |
| Congressional Environment | **16.0** | | | | **37.1** | | | |
| Congressional style and pace | 10.2 | (140) | 38 | 62 | 23.1 | (418) | 30 | 70 |
| Congressional ethics | 2.4 | (33) | — | 100 | 4.9 | (89) | — | 100 |
| Congressional self-seeking | 3.4 | (47) | — | 100 | 9.1 | (165) | — | 100 |
| Treatment of Interest Groups | **4.2** | (58) | 66 | 34 | **1.4** | (25) | 50 | 50 |
| Other | **6.4** | (88) | 27 | 73 | **8.4** | (152) | 33 | 67 |
| Respondent Repeats Closed-end Question | **12.0** | (165) | | | | | | |
| Don't Know/Not Ascertained | **3.0** | (41) | | | **2.8** | (51) | | |

[a] "How would you rate the job Congress did this past year in 1968—excellent, pretty good, only fair, or poor? Why do you feel this way? Any other reasons?" *Source*: Louis Harris and Associates, Study #1900 contracted by Roger Davidson.
[b] "Overall, how would you rate the job Congress as a whole—that is, the House of Representatives—has done during the past 2 or 3 years—would you say the Congress has done an excellent job, a pretty good job, only a fair job, or a poor job? Why do you feel this way? Any other reasons?" *Source*: Louis Harris and Associates, contracted by Commission on Administrative Review 1977.

tions of congressional performance. In short, both the nature and substance of the legislative process contribute to low levels of congressional popularity.

**Individual Affective Attachments to the Political System**

The degree to which citizens harbor positive feelings (affect) toward the political system structures their perceptions of the performance of those institutions within that system. Like most political institutions, Congress suffers from citizen alienation from government. When the political system is an object of contempt, no institution in the system is apt to be spared from this discontent. Dissatisfaction with government is likely to spill over and influence evaluations of the institutional structures which comprise the government. This relationship is evident in the sizable correlations between evaluations of congressional performance and affective attachments[3] to the political system in 1974 and 1976 ($r = .64$ and .54, respectively). These relationships illustrate that congressional popularity is dependent to some degree upon the affective ties between citizens and their government.

This is not to say that these affective attachments between citizens and the political system are not influenced by the actions of one or more governmental institutions. Certainly unfulfilled expectations of institutional performance can sour citizen attitudes toward the larger political system. Nevertheless, other forces that are totally beyond the influence of government also damage these affective attachments to government. For example, political orientations originating in personal or societal conditions, such as feelings of political impotency, anomie, misanthropy, and estrangement, enhance alienation, even though these attitudes may have little connection to the performance of the political system or its component institutions. Thus, dissatisfaction with Congress may be rooted in political orientations for which Congress is only slightly responsible.

There are two alternative explanations for this relationship between affect and evaluations of Congress. It might be argued that this relationship conceals the influence of political cynicism—an orientation closely related to affect. As a general political orientation, cynicism (or trust)[4] can structure evaluations of governmental institutions and foster intense antipathies toward individual governmental structures like Congress. This relationship between political cynicism and evaluations of Congress is evident in the survey data derived from the Survey Research Center's 1974 and 1976 Election Studies: the greater an individual's level of political cynicism,[5] the more negative the evaluation of Congress (r = −.37 and −.30, respectively).

A related aspect of political cynicism that might also account for the relationship between affect and congressional popularity is external efficacy—the extent to which the political system is perceived as being susceptible to citizen influence and control.[6] Perceived institutional insensitivity to citizen opinion can lead to negative evaluations of institutional performance. If citizens feel incapable of exercising a measure of influence over political leaders and institutions, they are unlikely to develop favorable perceptions of institutional performance. Under these conditions, the intrinsic representational nature of Congress is apt to be forgotten or viewed as serving only the interests of "big business" or other elitist segments of society. The pluralistic nature of Congress and the political process may further fuel impressions that groups, not citizens, influence the legislative process.

We can evaluate the accuracy of these alternative explanations for the relationship between affect and congressional popularity by entering these variables into a multiple regression analysis where respondent evaluations of Congress serve as the dependent variable. Multiple regression analysis enables us to separate the independent effects of affect, trust, and external efficacy on congressional popularity. The relative influence of each of these variables is related to the size of the standardized regression coefficients ("betas") in table 1.2; the greater the magnitude of the standardized regression coefficient, the more influential the variable.

As the regression results in table 1.2 illustrate, each of these variables—political trust, affect, and external efficacy—significantly influence evaluations of Congress. The affective relationships between the individual and the political system, however, appear to be far more important in explaining congressional popularity than the other variables. In fact, more than 25% of the variation in individual evaluations of Congress can be explained by the affective ties between the individual and the political system. In sum, the relationship between affect and the popularity of Congress is certainly not spurious; affective attachments to the political system appear to be critical in individual assessments of congressional performance. Influences which weaken these affective attachments are apt to distort perceptions of congressional performance, and therefore increase congressional unpopularity. Once again the amount of influence Congress can exert over these affective attachments, and hence congressional evaluations, is tenuous.

**Table 1.2. *The Impact of System Affect on Evaluations of Congress***

| | *1974* | | *1976* | |
|---|---|---|---|---|
| | *Regression Coefficients*[a] | | | |
| | *Unstandardized (b)* | *Standardized (Beta)* | *Unstandardized (b)* | *Standardized (Beta)* |
| *Variables* | | | | |
| Political trust | −.057 | −.053 | −.053 | −.053 |
| External efficacy | −.048 | −.050 | −.110 | −.108 |
| System affect | .239 | .596 | .194 | .487 |
| *Regression Characteristics* | | | | |
| Intercept | 1.57 | | 1.77 | |
| Standard error of estimate | 1.30 | | 1.24 | |
| Multiple correlation coefficient | .64 | | .55 | |
| Coefficient of multiple determination | .41 | | .31 | |
| Number of cases | 1691 | | 1529 | |

SOURCE: Survey Research Center's 1974 and 1976 Election Studies, University of Michigan.
[a]All are statistically significant at .01 level.

## The Political Context

International crises and economic malaise are two political forces which influence the public standing of political institutions; international crises are one of the few contextual forces that enhance the popularity of political institutions. A commonly observed feature of presidential popularity is the tendency for intense crises to "rally" support behind the chief executive (Mueller 1970, 25–28). A distinction is made between international and domestic crises because domestic crises are as likely to exacerbate conflict as they are to diminish tensions. International crises not only enhance the public esteem of the president, however; they may also have a generalized effect on the political system by generating positive attitudes toward government in general. As a result, international crises tend to increase both congressional and presidential approval. The conduct of a national opinion survey within weeks of an international event such as the Cuban missile crisis, the Bay of Pigs invasion, or the attack on, and recapture of, the *Mayaguez* could "inflate" congressional popularity by about 16 percentage points.[7] As the international crisis slips from the public's consciousness, the "rallying" influence of the crisis subsides and congressional popularity declines.

In contrast to the influence of international crises, economic malaise diminishes the popularity of Congress and the president (Mueller 1970, 28; Parker 1977, 101–106). Congressional unpopularity is increased by declines in economic conditions; improved economic conditions, however, can be expected to enhance the public standing of Congress perhaps because congressional actions may appear more judicious in times of economic boom than during times of economic decline. Between 1939 and 1977 a one percent increase in the unemployment rate increased dissatisfaction with Congress by about three percent.

Since wars are widely perceived as reducing the popularity of presidents, they might also be expected to dampen the popularity of Congress. Inasmuch as wars can only be waged with congressional approval, or at least acquiescence, Congress, as well as the president, could be held culpable for the existence of wars. Despite the logic of this argument, the influence of wars on congressional popularity is suspect. The president's position as commander-in-chief, his preeminence in the area of international affairs, and the historic participation of presidents in the conduct of wars may overshadow Congress's constitutionally prescribed power to declare war. This may account for the insignificant relationship between the existence of wars and trends in congressional popularity (Parker 1977, 104–105).

### Institutional Context

The prevailing institutional context also influences the level of popular dissatisfaction with Congress. The institutional context is structured by the nature of legislative-executive relations. When Congress and the president are at odds, the resulting conflicts have usually been accompanied by declines in congressional popularity (Davidson, Kovenock, and O'Leary 1968, 59–60). For example, the intense hostilities between President Ford and the 94th Congress were cited by a number of respondents as the reason for their negative evaluations of Congress (table 1.1). Active-positive presidents seem to be particularly susceptible to such conflict. This type of president is characterized as one who expends an inordinate amount of energy in the performance of responsibilities, and appears to enjoy such effort (Barber 1972). These presidents possess a political style conducive to conflict: "They seek out—even create—opportunities for action, rather than waiting for the action to come to them" (Barber 1972, 210). The impact of active-positive presidents on congressional popularity is extremely significant: such presidents (Roosevelt, Truman, Kennedy, Ford) contributed about 11 percentage points to congressional unpopularity between 1939 and 1977.

There are at least two explanations for the impact of the presidency on congressional evaluations. It might be argued that congressional resistance to the president's legislative program accounts for the impact of an active-positive president on congressional popularity. Active-positive presidents have had a difficult time securing congressional approval of their legislative programs. The assumption implicit in this argument is that the public expects Congress to cooperate with the president's legislative requests; therefore persistent congressional opposition to the legislative initiatives of presidents—and especially active-positive presidents—diminishes the popularity of Congress.

An equally plausible argument is that the public evaluation of the president, rather than his style of governing, is responsible for shifts in congressional popularity. That is, the declines in congressional popularity associated with acrimonious legislative-executive relations are a consequence of unpopular presidents fighting controversial legislative battles. The more unpopular the president, the less willing Congress may be to follow the president's leadership (Edwards 1976, 112–113). Unpopular presidents are more susceptible to congressional attack, indifference, and/or obstinacy than popular presidents (Neustadt 1960). Thus, the absence of harmonious relations between Congress and an unpopular president may account for the declines in congressional popularity associated with active-positive presidents.

Despite their plausibility, neither presidential popularity nor the character of legislative majorities exercise a significant influence on congressional popularity—only the presence of active-positive presidents heightens dissatisfaction with Congress (Parker 1977, 105). Thus, the political and societal conditions which exist at the time of measurements of congressional popularity may sharply influence the direction of evaluations of congressional performance.

## MAJOR SOURCES OF EVALUATIONS OF THE REPRESENTATIVE

The criteria for evaluating members of Congress are neither as varied nor as negatively toned as evaluations of Congress. One of the major differences between evaluations of Congress and evaluations of individual members of Congress is that political issues and policy matters rarely impinge upon the citizens' evaluations of their own representative, but they are very important in assessments of Congress. Evaluations of members of Congress tend to focus on the incumbent's personal characteristics and/or service to the district. This can be expected to have some impact on the tone of evaluations of individual representatives, since evaluations of Congress that are based on political and policy issues tend to be negative.

## PERSONAL ATTRIBUTES

The personal attributes of House incumbents are important concerns to their constituents: personal characteristics were mentioned in more than one-third of the responses to the query eliciting the criteria utilized in evaluating the representative. Table 1.3 confirms our suspicion that the personal attributes of incumbents tend to cast them in a favorable light. By and large, House members occupy the highest educational and occupational levels of society; in fact, most House members rank higher in the social hierarchy than the vast majority of their constituents. But citizens do not perceive their representatives in social, demographic, or occupational terms; rather, the personal attributes that are salient to constituents pertain to socially prescribed ethics, norms, and mores. For instance, the honesty, conscientiousness, fairness, and hard work of their representative are the personal characteristics which attract the attention of constituents. These criteria generally insure the representative of a relatively high level of popularity.

Applying these socially prescribed standards to the performance of incumbents may, however, create problems for constituents since most lack even a rudimentary awareness of their own representative. As a result, citizens form only vague impressions of the performance of their representative—"he's done a good job; he works hard; he's well-informed." Only salient violations of these standards are apt to detract from the positive images of incumbents. Even in these instances, constituent reaction to such exposés is generally benign. Constituents have displayed a penchant for effectively rationalizing the ethical transgressions of their own representative. This may help to explain why constituents have returned to office—by significant electoral margins—House incumbents who have been charged with ethical and legal violations (e.g., Adam Clayton Powell, Charles Diggs, Daniel Flood). In sum, personal attributes appear to generate positive evaluations of congressional incumbents and insure a high level of popularity for the individual representative.

**Table 1.3.** ***Bases of Evaluations of the Representative***

| | *1968*[a] *(N = 1,203)* | | | | | | *1977*[b] *(N = 985)* | | | | | |
|---|---|---|---|---|---|---|---|---|---|---|---|---|
| | *Mentioned by* | | *Positive* | | *Negative* | | *Mentioned by* | | *Positive* | | *Negative* | |
| *Salient Concerns* | N | % | N | % | N | % | N | % | N | % | N | % |
| *Policy* | | **12.4** | | | | | | **3.6** | | | | |
| Vague reference | 105 | 8.7 | 72 | 69 | 33 | 31 | 18 | 1.8 | — | — | 18 | 100 |
| Specific reference | 44 | 3.7 | 21 | 48 | 23 | 52 | 18 | 1.8 | — | — | 18 | 100 |
| *Constituent Service* | | **51.7** | | | | | | **47.2** | | | | |
| District attention | 345 | 28.7 | 260 | 75 | 85 | 25 | 164 | 16.6 | 164 | 100 | — | — |
| Constituent assistance | 29 | 2.4 | 29 | 100 | — | — | 155 | 15.7 | 155 | 100 | — | — |
| District conditions | 34 | 2.8 | 31 | 91 | 3 | 9 | 46 | 4.7 | 46 | 100 | — | — |
| Informs constituents | 214 | 17.8 | 38 | 18 | 176 | 82 | 100 | 10.2 | 82 | 82 | 18 | 18 |
| *Personal Attributes* | | **29.4** | | | | | | **44.4** | | | | |
| Personal characteristics | 212 | 17.6 | 176 | 83 | 36 | 17 | 82 | 8.3 | 82 | 100 | — | — |
| Reputation | 127 | 10.6 | 121 | 95 | 6 | 5 | 356 | 36.1 | 238 | 67 | 118 | 33 |
| Personal acquaintance | 14 | 1.2 | 14 | 100 | — | — | 0 | — | — | — | — | — |
| *Treatment of Groups* | 79 | **6.6** | 46 | 58 | 33 | 42 | 46 | **4.7** | 46 | 100 | — | — |

[a]"How would you rate the service your Representative gives in looking after this district in Washington—excellent, pretty good, only fair, or poor? Why do you feel that way? Any other reasons?" *Source*: Louis Harris and Associates, Study #1900 contracted by Roger Davidson.

[b]"Overall, how would you rate the job the Congressman who has been representing this area during the past two or three years has done—would you say your Congressman has done an excellent job, a pretty good job, a fair job, or a poor job? Why do you feel this way? Any other reasons?" *Source*: Louis Harris and Associates, contracted by Commission on Administrative Review.

**Constituency Service**

One of the most notable features of recent Congresses is the amount of time members spend on constituency-related matters. Meeting with constituents, answering district mail, pursuing constituent complaints, and mending political fences within the district are constituent activities that consume vast amounts of the time and energies of representatives. Despite the belief of most House members that constituent work interferes with the performance of other legislative responsibilities (Commission on Administrative Review 1977, 875), there is evidence that district attentiveness has increased over the years (Fenno 1978, 206–210; Parker 1980). An examination of the criteria utilized in evaluations of members of Congress suggests some reasons for this emphasis.

As table 1.3 demonstrates, district service is frequently cited in citizen evaluations of their representative: approximately one-half of the responses mention some aspect of constituency service as a criterion for evaluating their representative. It would be a mistake, however, to assume that the public has lost regard for the strictly legislative responsibilities of House members. Table 1.4 illustrates a strong popular consensus that House members should devote time to the study of proposed legislation (71%), conduct legislative oversight of executive agencies (64%), develop legislation within committees (62%), and engage in floor debate and voting (76%). Why, then, do citizens focus attention on constituency-related activities as bases for evaluating their representatives?

The combination of a poorly informed electorate and the emphasis of House incumbents on constituency service may help to explain the saliency of district service in popular evaluations of members of Congress. There is a general lack of citizen knowledge about their representative, as evidenced by the fact that rarely can more than half of the electorate identify their representative (table 1.5). Public awareness of their representative's policy positions is even less extensive (Stokes and Miller 1962). Perhaps it behooves incumbents to keep it that way: the less constituents know about the Washington-based activity of their representative, the less he or she may have to explain or justify during visits to the district. Of course, incumbents have an incentive to advertise their effectiveness in legislative matters, and even to boast of their legislative accomplishments. Incumbents are always quick to point out, however, that their legislative skills and effectiveness are being used to further district interests. In a sense, attending to constituent affairs is often characterized by incumbents as an all-consuming task, and for some it truly is that dominant. As a consequence, other aspects of legisla-

**Table 1.4.** ***Citizen Views of the Importance of Constituency and Legislative Activities***[a]

| *Activity* | N | *Very Important (%)* | *Fairly Important (%)* | *Only Slightly Important (%)* | *Not Important (%)* | *Not Sure (%)* |
|---|---|---|---|---|---|---|
| Meeting personally with constituents when they come to Washington | 1,529 | 48 | 32 | 14 | 3 | 3 |
| Getting back to district to stay in touch with constituents | 1,528 | 68 | 25 | 4 | | 3 |
| Helping people in district who have personal problems with the government | 1,531 | 62 | 28 | 7 | 1 | 2 |
| Staying in touch with local government officials in district | 1,530 | 63 | 29 | 6 | | 3 |
| Debating and voting on legislation on the floor of the House | 1,528 | 76 | 17 | 2 | | 4 |
| Keeping track of the way government agencies are administering laws passed by Congress | 1,529 | 64 | 24 | 6 | 1 | 4 |

| | | | | | | |
|---|---|---|---|---|---|---|
| Taking the time to explain to citizens what their government is doing to solve important problems and why | 1,530 | 67 | 26 | 4 | 1 | 2 |
| Studying and doing basic research on proposed legislation | 1,531 | 71 | 21 | 3 | | 4 |
| Sending newsletters about the activities of Congress to people in district | 1,530 | 49 | 34 | 12 | 3 | 3 |
| Taking time to gain first-hand knowledge of foreign affairs | 1,527 | 50 | 30 | 11 | 4 | 6 |
| Working in committees to develop legislation | 1,530 | 62 | 29 | 4 | 1 | 5 |
| Making sure district gets its fair share of government money and projects | 1,530 | 77 | 17 | 3 | 1 | 2 |

SOURCE: Commission on Administrative Review 1977, 828–829.

[a]Question: "Now, I'd like you to tell me how important you feel your Congressman ought to treat each of these activities."

**Table 1.5. *Citizen Awareness of Their Representative***

| *Date of Survey* | *% of Sample Correctly Identifying Their Representative*[a] |
|---|---|
| March 1942 | 51 |
| March 1943 | 53 |
| January 1946 | 54 |
| June 1946 | 48 |
| August 1947 | 42 |
| June 1957 | 35 |
| November 1958 | 52[b] |
| September 1973 | 46[c] |
| January 1977 | 50[d] |

[a]Unless otherwise identified, all the data are from the American Institute of Public Opinion.
[b]Data from Survey Research Center's (University of Michigan) 1958 Election Study.
[c]U.S. Congress, Senate, Subcommittee on Intergovernmental Relations, *A Survey of Public Attitudes*, part 1 (December 1973), p. 249.
[d]Commission on Administrative Review 1977, 814.

tive performance, such as roll-call voting, never come to the consciousness of constituents, except when that behavior becomes a campaign issue; hence, district activity becomes a basic criterion in constituent evaluations of the performance of their representative.

Citizen concern with district service also may be generated by the emphasis that House members place on constituent attention. For instance, those individuals who base their evaluations on district service criteria perceive that their representative places greater emphasis on district-related activities such as securing federal funds for the district ($r = .19$), spending time in the district ($r = .22$), helping constituents with government-related problems ($r = .23$), and informing constituents about congressional activity ($r = .18$).[8] Yet, these respondents attribute no greater significance to these activities than those who cite other criteria in their evaluations. This suggests that Americans focus their evaluations of their representative on constituency service because of the emphasis that House members place on such activity, rather than as a result of the importance that constituents assign to these services.

**Will Congressmen Ever Be Unpopular?**

Since constituency service tends to be positively evaluated (table 1.3), the emphasis that House members place on it is apt to have a positive effect on the member's popularity within the district. The increased emphasis on district service by House members is likely to strengthen their levels of district popularity. We can expect that as long as constituency service continues to be positively evaluated, members will continue to be popular. It also seems unlikely that members will decrease their emphasis on constituency service as long as it is salient to and positively evaluated by their constituents—especially when such service provides other benefits. For example, constituency service may color constituents' perceptions of the relative effectiveness of incumbents. While 60% of those respondents with a district service orientation evaluate their representative as "better than most," only 22% of those citing non-district related criteria in their evaluations reach the same conclusion. Clearly, some of the positive affect attached to district service is due to the fact that most constituency assistance is well-performed (Cavanagh 1978). If popularity and performance translate into votes, constituency service is the basis of the exchange.

There are other equally compelling reasons for emphasizing constituency service. House members themselves see the performance of district service as exceedingly more effective than the performance of other legislative roles (Cavanagh 1978). This may be one area where members feel that they can exercise a significant impact on society. Perhaps most importantly, constituent service may supply incumbents with an electoral advantage. The persistent erosion of electorally marginal congressional districts has been attributed to the successful performance of constituency service by House incumbents. The growth of the federal government and federal programs has made district service a valuable commodity, and it is assumed that incumbents possess enough experience in Washington to deal with the vast federal bureaucracy. "Thus, so long as the incumbent can elude a personal morality rap, and refrain from casting outlandish votes, he is naturally preferred over a newcomer" (Fiorina 1977, 180).

Since the perquisites of office enable House members to effectively "advertise" and "claim credit" for such district service (Mayhew 1974), another side benefit of constituency service may be that it improves recognition of individual members. For instance, those mentioning constituent service in their evaluation of individual representatives are twice as likely as respondents citing other criteria to correctly identify the incumbent representative's name (r = .33) and political party (r = .33).

Moreover, those concerned with constituent service may be easier to mobilize during elections, since they take a more active interest in legislative politics. For example, they are more likely than those without a district orientation to have voted in the 1974 congressional elections (r = .20); to have attended a meeting with their representative (r = .21); or to have read or heard something about the incumbent in the mass media (r = .22). This strata of the population may be an invaluable electoral resource for the representative because voter turnout is normally quite low in congressional elections. Thus, the electoral benefits of district service can be extremely important to a member's congressional career.

In short, numerous incentives exist for House members to emphasize constituency service in the operation of their legislative offices. House incumbents may emphasize constituency service because of the saliency of such activity to the constituents. Further, such activity generates favorable perceptions of congressional incumbents.

## CONCLUSIONS: WILL CONGRESS EVER BE POPULAR?

The preceding analysis demonstrates that the relatively low esteem of Congress is partially a function of the standards and criteria that individuals use in evaluating Congress: certain criteria are associated with positive evaluations, while other criteria are identified with negative evaluations. The criteria that *dominate* evaluations of Congress are largely negative in valence and are apt to generate negative impressions of institutional performance. The most salient criterion in evaluations of the representative is congressional district service. This attention is handsomely rewarded in terms of popularity, recognition, and perhaps even electoral security. Clearly, the tasks assigned to Congress by the public and those ascribed to the individual representative are different and generate divergent evaluations. For Congress as an institution, citizens ascribe the task of resolving national ills; this responsibility is far more hazardous than the tasks expected of the individual representative. In sum, the standards utilized in evaluating Congress and its individual members contribute to the differentials in their popularity (Parker and Davidson 1979).

It is clear from the preceding sections that congressional evaluations are predicated on several criteria: (1) the nature of the legislative process, (2) the political issues which form the substance of Congress's tasks, and (3) the affective ties between citizens and the political system. Evaluations based on the first two criteria are likely to be negative in nature. In addition, congressional popularity is influenced by contextual factors such as international crises, economic malaise, and the existence of an active-positive president. It should be equally clear that Congress has very little latitude in changing any of the above mentioned criteria.

It should also be evident from the preceding discussion that Congress is likely to continue to be an unpopular institution. The issues which presently concern Congress are extremely divisive, and any congressional action is apt to produce discontent with congressional performance. The mass media, which could help Congress rid itself of some negative characterizations by better informing the public about congressional actions and procedures, instead tend to strengthen the existing negative impressions. Despite the public's desire for more information about Congress,[9] media coverage of congressional politics remains limited. This is understandable because Congress is a difficult institution to cover; daily congressional activities include numerous committee hearings, meetings, and conferences, in addition to floor actions. The multitude of activities occurring in Congress at one time taxes the resources of the mass media and precludes in-depth coverage of congressional activities. Television coverage is a good example of the difficulty inherent in covering Congress: the number of newsworthy events requiring immediate and extensive television coverage and the amount of programming time devoted to national news result in scanty or nonexistent coverage of daily congressional actions. Furthermore, the public often lacks the basic understanding of the legislative process that would lead to an appreciation of the significance of legislative actions. As a result, congressional coverage is usually compressed into a few minutes, and only information that is easily grasped by the television viewer is apt to be presented.

These factors may also explain why so little media attention is devoted to congressional politics in comparison to the attention received by presidents (Cornwell 1959). Presidential news is far easier for the media to cover and report. The president is a single individual, and policy making in the White House can be described almost totally in terms of presidential messages, actions, or press releases. In addition, daily White House briefings reduce the information acquisition costs associated with reporting the news. Is it surprising, therefore, that the mass media, like the mass public, follows the presidency more than Congress (Parker 1976, 417–420)?

Even when Congress receives media attention, however, the coverage may generate further dissatisfaction with congressional performance. For example, although legislative politics were unusually salient during 1974 as a result of the impeachment proceedings, newspaper coverage of Congress was relatively critical: 42% of the articles about Congress were critical of the institution (Miller, Goldenberg, and Erbring 1979). Moreover, the topics that tend to attract the greatest media attention are usually sensational in nature, such as ethical transgressions and explicit displays of self-interest (e.g., raising salaries); these topics normally place Congress in an unfavorable light (table 1.1). Perhaps this explains why so many House members (36%) cite "unfair" media treatment as the cause of Congress's low public esteem (Commission on Administrative Review 1977, 892). For these reasons, it is doubtful that Congress can alter its generally unpopular image to any substantial degree. The public, therefore, should expect to live with an unpopular institution.

The persistent unpopularity of Congress would be an acute problem indeed, if dissatisfaction with congressional performance accumulated with time. Fortunately for Congress, there is little reason to suspect that discontent will aggregate with time as more and more people become disillusioned with congressional action. Although presidential unpopularity increases with time (Mueller 1970; Stimson 1976), the contrasts between the nature of Congress and the presidency may limit congressional dissatisfaction from accumulating with the same force as presidential dissatisfaction. In the case of the president, dissatisfaction accumulates with the passage of time as citizen expectations of presidential performance go unrealized (Stimson 1976, 9–10). In the absence of citizen expectations, however, dissatisfaction may accumulate more slowly. Unlike presidents, Congress has no programmatic platform that citizens could use as a basis for the development of performance expectations. For instance, there is no significant relationship between congressional evaluations and the salience of expectations regarding congressional performance.[10] As a consequence, discontent with Congress is unlikely to coalesce at a significant rate (Parker 1977, 103).

Can we expect the American public to accept the unpopularity of Congress when its own members are unlikely to be sympathetic to Congress's plight as an unpopular institution? One of the salient characteristics of congressional campaigns is the extent to which incumbents campaign against Congress (Fenno 1975, 280–281). While it is difficult to understand the motivation underlying such attacks, "running against Congress" may be a rational way for incumbents to separate their actions from those of the institution in which they serve. Perhaps they worry that their own popularity will suffer if they appear supportive of the institution; or they may fear that their own popularity will be damaged by popular dissatisfaction with Congress. Whatever the reason, there seems little need for congressional incumbents to campaign against Congress: House members are evaluated on the basis of a different set of criteria, and these standards place incumbents in a favorable light among their constituents. Further, attacks on Congress by House members probably reinforce negative impressions of congressional performance. Some House members even suggest that the solution to Congress's low public esteem lies in convincing congressional incumbents not to attack the institution during district visits (Commission on Administrative Review 1977, 894). In conclusion, Congress is unlikely to become a popular institution while its members can be expected to continue their existing high levels of popularity.

## NOTES

The primary sources of the data utilized in this analysis are the public, member, and staff surveys conducted for the Commission on Administrative Review, and the election studies conducted by the Center for Political Studies of the Institute for Social Research, the University of Michigan. Data from the election studies were made available through the Inter-University Consortium for Political and Social Research.

1. The basic form of the question is: "In general, do you think the present Congress in Washington has done a good job or a poor job?" In this chapter, congressional popularity refers to the positive evaluations of Congress while congressional unpopularity refers to the negative responses.
2. The questionnaire item is: "How much influence and power should Congress—that is, the U.S. Senate and the House of Representatives—have?"
3. The measure of affective attachments is a respondent's summary evaluation of the performance of the federal government, the presidency, and the Supreme Court; these performance ratings are highly correlated. The respondent's evaluations of each of these structures are summed to provide a single measure of the individual's affect toward government. The data are from the Survey Research Center's 1974 and 1976 Election Studies.
4. For an excellent analysis of political trust in government, see Miller (1974).
5. Cynical responses to the following items are summed to provide a measure of citizen distrust of government:
    a. How much of the time do you think you can trust the government in Washington to do what is right—just about always, most of the time, or only some of the time?

b. Would you say the government is pretty much run by a few big interests looking out for themselves or that it is run for the benefit of all the people?
c. Do you think that people in the government waste a lot of the money we pay in taxes, waste some of it, or don't waste very much of it?
d. Do you feel that almost all of the people running the government are smart people who usually know what they are doing, or do you think that quite a few of them don't seem to know what they are doing?
e. Do you think that quite a few people running the government are a little crooked, not very many are, or do you think hardly any of them are crooked at all?

For a more extensive discussion of the nature and properties of the index of political trust, see Miller (1974).

6. External efficacy is a Guttman scale based upon the following items:
   a. I don't think public officials care much what people like me think.
   b. Generally speaking, those we elect to Congress in Washington lose touch with the people pretty quickly.
   c. Parties are only interested in people's votes but not in their opinions.
   d. People like me don't have any say about what the government does.

   The external efficacy scale is based upon the number of statements agreed to by the respondent. The scale has a reproducibility of .88 and a scalability above .6 in both the 1974 and 1976 Election Studies of the Survey Research Center. These statistical characteristics of the external efficacy scale support our contention of the scalability of the items and their use as a unidimensional measure.
7. The impact of crises and economic malaise is based upon a time-series analysis of congressional popularity between 1939 and 1977. The regression statistics are as follows:

| | | *Regression Coefficients* | |
|---|---|---|---|
| | *r* | *Standardized (Beta)* | *Unstandardized[a] (b)* |
| *Independent Variables[c]* | | | |
| Crises ("rally around the flag") | .26 | .51 | 6.65[b] (1.45) |
| Economic decline ("economic slump") | .44 | .62 | 2.84 (.51) |
| Active-positive presidential character | 44 | 50 | 11.22 (2.36) |

| *Regression Characteristics* | |
|---|---|
| Intercept | 50.93 |
| Standard error of estimate | 7.14 |
| Multiple correlation coefficient (R) | .79 |
| Coefficient of multiple determination ($R^2$) | .63 |
| Number of cases | 38 |

SOURCE: Measurements of congressional unpopularity, 1939–1977. For an explanation of the construction of the variables, see Parker (1977).

[a] The standard errors for the respective partial regression coefficients are shown in parentheses. To be regarded as statistically significant, a regression coefficient should be, conventionally, at least twice the observed standard error.

[b] This is the regression coefficient for a *natural* logarithmic transformation of the variable; the regression slope for a common logarithmic transformation of this variable is 15.31.

[c] The identifying terms which Mueller (1970) assigns these variables are given in parentheses.

8. Unless otherwise noted, the correlations described in this and the following sections are based upon data from the 1977 opinion survey conducted by Louis Harris and Associates for the Commission on Administrative Review. The measure of the concern of respondents with constituency service is based upon the criteria utilized in evaluations of the representative. Respondents who mentioned some aspect of district service in their evaluations are assumed to be more concerned with constituency service than those who failed to mention such criteria in their assessments. This dichotomous variable is then correlated with other items on the 1977 survey. We should point out that these perceptions of constituency service may not necessarily be grounded in reality—more than two of every three respondents citing service criteria in their evaluations *cannot* recall any services that their representative has provided the district.
9. Sixty percent of the electorate would like to receive more information from the newspapers and television about the activities of and legislation being considered by Congress (Commission on Administrative Review 1977, 853).
10. The questionnaire items reflecting expectations are based upon the Louis Harris 1977 opinion survey conducted for the Obey Commission. The expectations refer to the role of Congress in:
    a. Expressing what the people who elected them want in voting on legislation.
    b. Studying and voting on proposed legislation.
    c. Initiating new policies and establishing long-range goals for the country.
    d. Acting to curb executive branch abuses when a president gets out of line.
    e. Providing people in their districts with a direct line to the federal government.
    f. Holding investigative hearings to reveal wrongdoing both in and out of government.

g. Making sure that laws passed by Congress are being properly and effectively administered.
h. Informing the public about the important issues facing the country.

The salience of individual expectations is derived from a summated score based upon the importance which the respondent attributes to each of the expectation items. An analysis of the relationship between an individual item (expectation) and evaluation of congressional performance also failed to produce any significant associations.

## REFERENCES


Barber, James David. 1972. *Presidential Character*. Englewood Cliffs, N.J.: Prentice-Hall.

Cavanagh, Thomas E. 1978. "The Two Arenas of Congress: Electoral and Institutional Incentives for Performance." Paper presented at the 1978 annual meeting of the American Political Science Association, New York.

Commission on Administrative Review, U.S. Congress, House. 1977. *Final Report*. Vol. 2 of 2, *Survey Materials*. 95th Cong., 1st Sess. H. Doc. 95-272.

Cornwell, Elmer E. 1959. "Presidential News: The Expanding Public Image." *Journalism Quarterly* 36: 275–283.

Davidson, Roger H.; Kovenock, David M.; and O'Leary, Michael K. 1968. *Congress in Crisis: Politics and Congressional Reform*. Belmont, Calif.: Wadsworth.

Edwards, George C., III. 1976. "Presidential Influence in the House: Presidential Prestige as a Source of Presidential Power." *American Political Science Review* 70(March):101–113.

Fenno, Richard F., Jr. 1975. "If, as Ralph Nader Says, Congress Is 'The Broken Branch,' How Come We Love Our Congressmen So Much?" In *Congress in Change: Evolution and Reform*, ed. Norman J. Ornstein, pp. 277–287. New York: Praeger.

———. 1978. *Home Style: House Members in Their Districts*. Boston: Little, Brown.

Fiorina, Morris P. 1977. *Congress: Keystone of the Washington Establishment*. New Haven: Yale University Press.

Mayhew, David R. 1974. *Congress: The Electoral Connection*. New Haven: Yale University Press.

Miller, Arthur H. 1974. "Political Issues and Trust in Government: 1964–1970." *American Political Science Review* 68(September):951–972.

———; Goldenberg, Edie N.; and Erbring, Lutz. 1979. "Type-Set Politics: Impact of Newspapers on Public Confidence." *American Political Science Review* 73(March):67–84.

Mueller, John E. 1970. "Presidential Popularity from Truman to Johnson." *American Political Science Review* 64(March):18–34.

———. 1973. *War, Presidents and Public Opinion.* New York: Wiley.
Neustadt, Richard E. 1960. *Presidential Power.* New York: Wiley.
Parker, Glenn R. 1976. "A Note on the Impact and Saliency of Congress." *American Politics Quarterly* 4(October):413–421.
———. 1977. "Some Themes in Congressional Unpopularity." *American Journal of Political Science* 21(February):93–104.
———. 1980. "Sources of Change in Congressional District Attentiveness." *American Journal of Political Science* 24(February):115–124.
———, and Davidson, Roger H. 1979. "Why Do Americans Love Their Congressmen More Than Their Congress?" *Legislative Studies Quarterly* 4(February):53–61.
Stimson, James A. 1976. "Public Support for American Presidents: A Cyclical Model." *Public Opinion Quarterly* 40(Spring):1–21.
Stokes, Donald E., and Miller, Warren E. 1962. "Party Government and the Saliency of Congress." *Public Opinion Quarterly* 26(Winter):531–546.

# 2. The Two Arenas of Congress

*Thomas E. Cavanagh*

To describe a typical week in the life of a member of Congress is to invite incredulity. The making of public policy can be given only piecemeal attention, sandwiched in among a host of competing concerns. The representative must endure a daily blizzard of phone calls, staff interruptions, and constituent visits. Committee sessions degenerate into public relations charades or stand idle for want of a quorum. Afternoons are broken up by repeated strolls from the office to the floor. And many weekends are devoted to exhausting rounds of handshaking and speechmaking back home in the district.

The incoherence of the House member's schedule reflects a fundamental tension in the congressional process. In this chapter, we shall explore that tension as it is actually experienced by members of the House of Representatives. Our authority is the perceptions of the members themselves, as articulated in interviews conducted by the Commission on Administrative Review in 1977. Quotations in this chapter are from these interviews. All respondents were guaranteed anonymity.

We shall find that the central dilemma of congressional existence is an incessant alternation between two competing modes of political activity. The members must not only deal with their colleagues; they must answer to the voters as well. We shall discover, in short, that there are two arenas of congressional performance: the institutional arena in Washington, and the electoral arena in the member's home district.[1]

The electoral arena encompasses those interactions with constituents which make it possible for a member to serve in Congress. As a candidate, the incumbent's goal is to identify potential voters and mobilize their support on election day. This is done through the merchandising of an image of "responsiveness" to constituent concerns. Like any aspiring entrepreneur, the representative must devise a marketing strategy to locate a clientele of "customers" whose political desires the candidate can satisfy.[2]

In the institutional arena, the member seeks to attain and wield influence in the making of decisions on public policy. Influence—which is to say, power—is acquired through accumulating expertise and bargaining skillfully in committee and subcommittee. In Congress, institutional influence is the true measure of success. It is valued not only in its own right, but as the instrument needed to accomplish the member's legislative goals.[3]

This delineation of incentives highlights two critical but frequently neglected aspects of the congressional process. First, competing successfully in the electoral arena is a necessary but not sufficient condition for success in the institutional arena. And second, it is the hope of success in the institutional arena which is the ultimate motivation for seeking election in the first place.

With these member goals in mind, we shall examine the nature of congressional responsibilities and public demands as seen by the 153 members of the House interviewed by the Commission on Administrative Review. These perceptions will be juxtaposed with the preferences expressed by a cross section of the public in a contemporaneous survey conducted by Louis Harris and Associates. By comparing and contrasting the perceptions of the governing and the governed, we may better comprehend the clashing incentives for congressional performance, and their implications for the American policy process.

## THE INSTITUTIONAL FUNCTIONS OF THE HOUSE

We shall begin by noting the functions which members prescribe for the House. The Commission's sample of members was asked in January 1977, "What roles *should* the House play in the federal government—what do you believe *ought* to be its one or two most important functions?" This is not quite the same as asking what the members as individuals ought to be doing; rather, it serves the purpose of determining which institutional functions are valued most highly. The results, summarized in table 2.1 and expanded upon in the analysis below, illustrate the primacy of policy determination and implementation in the members' views of the responsibilities of the House.

**Table 2.1.** ***Members' Views on Roles House Should Play***

| Role | % of Respondents |
|---|---|
| Legislative | 82 |
| Oversight | 41 |
| Ombudsman | 27 |
| Representative | 18 |
| Constitutional | 12 |
| Educational | 3 |
| Political | 3 |
| All others | 1 |
| No answer, don't know, not sure | 1 |

NOTE: Total weighted N = 146. Multiple responses were possible.

## The Legislative Role

Not surprisingly, the centrality of the House's institutional role as a legislature was overwhelming. It was volunteered by 82% of the members, and 72% cited it first. The focus here was on initiating policy and programs in response to the major problems facing the nation and its people. One member declared that the role of the House is "to try to draw up a legal framework for wise policy decisions and directions for the entire country. To try to create a framework for an environment in which the American people can develop their best potential." Another summarized the thoughts of many in saying:

> One of the chief roles is to identify problems needing legislative action, and to initiate legislation and procedures in Congress which develop a solution. This is different from waiting for the Administration to say what it wants and doesn't want, and it's different from a "don't rock the boat" attitude. The House as a branch of government should be most sensitive to "people problems" in their initial stages.

A number of structural problems were thought to impede the legislative capacity of the House. Overlapping committee jurisdictions, poor scheduling of committee and floor business, and institutional inertia were each blamed by 20% or more of those citing legislative shortcomings as contributing to the problem. A lack of cohesion was a prime cause of inertia in the eyes of some. "I go for the honeycomb theory," one representative volunteered. "There are too many guys here doing their own thing. There's not enough pooling of efforts."

Legislative overload was also decried, as in the complaint that "Congress operates on a crisis-to-crisis basis. . . . The legislative body scurries around to find instant solutions. There's no luxury of thought. It's difficult to take time to sit down and establish priorities. There's always such an atmosphere of emergency." Or as another member cautioned, "We have legislated into so many areas that no set of human beings could have the capacity to be really well informed on even most of the matters that we deal with."

Moreover, the personal incentives for genuinely addressing a potential problem have ironic limitations:

> A person who, by virtue of his foresight, is able to do something today that avoids a problem five years from now successfully, is a man without credit. Because if he's successful in doing it, then the problem never arises! Suppose he says, "Do you realize that by my action in 1976 I kept you from this disaster?" No one believes him! So you're pushed to respond to immediate problems which the public and the press see as immediate. There are very few rewards for solving future problems.

### The Oversight Role

If solving present and future problems is the province of legislation, then investigating the efficacy of these solutions is at the core of oversight, which involves monitoring programs to insure proper implementation. It is revealing that while 82% of the members prescribed a legislative role for the House, only 41% suggested that the House should review the effectiveness of its enactments through oversight. In explaining the need for oversight, one representative commented, "The regulatory agencies don't administer the laws the way we like them. The agencies waste a lot of the taxpayers' money. If we could streamline the agencies and regulate their activity, their actions would represent our will and thus be closer to the will of the people." Another felt that "the House ought to operate in a more meaningful manner in the oversight area. It ought to draw on its roots as 'the grand inquest of the nation,' and conduct more meaningful, more penetrating investigations into government operations."

Complaints on the lack of follow-through in the oversight process were legion. The administration of programs was generally thought to be overlooked rather than overviewed. The major reason, cited by 34%, was that the oversight role is so diffused that no one has a responsibility to perform it effectively. As one member viewed the process, "We're not geared up properly for oversight. We don't have anyone with the responsibility to perform oversight. The information we develop in hearings and investigations gets put into books and isn't used by anyone. It becomes worthless."

Among 18% of the respondents, oversight was thought to be neglected because of the lack of any incentive to perform it. "Oversight doesn't have the political sex appeal of new legislation," one representative commented; according to another, "It's easier and we get more publicity in enacting a new program than in studying an old one and trying to make it work." In a similar vein, the incentives afforded by the press were considered dysfunctional to effective oversight. One member complained that "the press only covers sexy oversight hearings," while another noted:

> There is a tendency on the part of committee and subcommittee chairmen to try to make a name on oversight—to dramatize, rather than do the boring, methodical oversight that is needed, but neglected. Rather than taking on organizations that need controlling, we look for newsworthy minor scandals. We are not getting at the big job, but concentrating on what tends to be trivial.

The coziness of committees and agencies in the familiar "Iron Triangle" relationship was also a source of frustration: "What happens is one little subcommittee has the only responsibility for a particular area and they become a protector rather than an overseer."

> It really depends on the committee. The House is nothing more than committees, in looking at oversight. . . . There's a built-in inertia. The system has grown up. The people who grew up in it were taught, "Don't rock the boat," and they believed it. Now they own most of the oars and the sails to the boat, and they prefer to sail with the wind rather than go with steam power. People should ask, "Why should we do that, rather than try this?" But that mentality just doesn't exist.

> . . . In many instances, there is a very happy marriage, wrongfully I believe, between the executive and the legislative branch.

Of course, even those with the initiative to challenge the agencies can find themselves at a loss:

> You can't match the staff and the resources of the executive branch. The bureaucrats tie up hearings with charts and facts. It's hard for a member with limited staff, limited information, and limited access to computers to counter the executive's defense. You can't rebut their arguments. So, since you would achieve nothing, you would just end up by making enemies in the agencies. So you don't even bother.

**The Ombudsman Role**

Helping constituents deal with the federal bureaucracy was volunteered by 27% as a proper role for the House. Perhaps the general line of thinking was captured best by the respondent who stated that the ombudsman role was performed by the members "as individuals, not as the House." To the extent that it was thought to have an institutional role as an ombudsman, the House was seen as a middleman between the citizen and the government. One member called it "a watchdog for individual rights," helping constituents "when their rights are abused by the government." The importance of the role appeared to be increasing over time. "The longer I'm around," said one member, "the more impressed I am with the ombudsman role. You're dealing with constituents who don't know where to turn for help with the federal government." And another veteran remarked, "The federal government today is involved directly in the lives of all my constituents. Life is much more complicated—the requests come to us."

**The Representative Role**

For 18% of the respondents, the House was a conduit to allow the people to participate in the government. This, at least, was what the representatives appeared to mean by the word "representation." As one member said, "The first job of the House is to represent. I believe the House is the people's forum—a place where people have input. It goes back to what Hamilton meant when he said, 'Here, sir, the people govern.'" The two-year term was volunteered by some 5% as an asset to this process of representing "the views of the people in Congress. We are elected every two years, so we are close to the pulse of the people." Asked to define the role of the House, another responded:

> To be a bridge between the government and the people. . . . To stay close to the public as a whole, and be responsive to the cross currents of American thought. We should be a representative of them and their problems in relation to the government. Thus, we should try to reflect popular attitudes in trying to bridge the gap. We should try to reduce the "us and them" syndrome that afflicts the governed and the governing.

The House was also seen as a collection of ambassadors and advocates for various points of view within the population: "The House is a melting place of regional interests. The House reduces all interests to a general consensus. Farmers' interests, business interests, environmental interests—all are represented and absorbed by the House."

**The Constitutional Role**

Some 12% of the respondents construed the House's role in an explicitly constitutional framework, emphasizing its place in the overall system of checks and balances more or less independently of any specific substantive task or function. One stressed the "role the Constitution enumerates: the House must keep a close eye on the activities of both the executive and judicial branches." And another discussed this role at length:

> We're dealing with a couple of generations of representatives who came of age after the time of FDR, when the executive was painted bigger than life. There was an emphasis on executive direction, and a decline in the stature of Congress as a coequal branch, an acceptance of less than equality. The only direct representatives of the people are the House, and now, since the amendment of 1912, the Senate. We should accept the responsibility of this role in a more demanding fashion than we have. We should not be spoonfed, or accept a denial of information. Of the three supposedly coequal branches, the more equal is clearly the Congress, not the executive. There is a desire to placate and please the executive rather than fulfill an obligation to the people who sent us here.

Other institutional roles were occasionally cited, such as the educational role of making people aware of issues and government activities (3%), and the political role of getting reelected and serving as a party or political leader (3%). Overall, as we have seen, the vast bulk of the responses concerned the policy-oriented roles of legislation (82%) and oversight (41%). Thus, it seems clear that the prescribed activities in the institutional arena of the House are dominated by the adoption and review of federal programs.

## THE DEMANDS OF THE PUBLIC

The incentives in the electoral arena are structured by the preferences of the public. At the same time that the House members were being asked their views on the functions of the House, a national survey of the public was being conducted by Louis Harris and Associates. When asked, "What kinds of jobs, duties, or functions do you expect a good congressman to perform?" the preferences of the public were at once less pronounced and more district-oriented than the members' prescriptions for the House as a whole. Note that the public was asked to give its expectations for individual members, as opposed to the entire House, making the question more relevant to the electoral situation.

The various aspects of legislative activity were cited by a total of 58% of the public respondents. The education and communication role, mentioned by 41%, involves the establishment of a regular two-way flow of information between the representative and his constituents. Almost as many respondents (37%) volunteered constituency service as a desired member activity. This was defined in terms of meeting local needs, aiding constituents, and working to solve local problems. Representation, mentioned by 35%, refers to expressing the desires of the district. Personal character, in terms of honesty and resistance to political pressure, was cited by 13%, and general competence in the job by 3%. The oversight role was of so little salience to the general public that it barely merited a coding category, receiving mention by only 1%.

The member and public coding schemes are not completely comparable, because of the different questions asked and the different responses received. Nevertheless, contrasting the two sets of results is at least indicative of the differences between member prescriptions for the House and the public's expectations of individual members. The two policy-related roles are mentioned more frequently as institutional functions: legislation is cited by 82% of the members as opposed to 58% of the public, while oversight is all but invisible to the public despite its mention by 41% of the members.

Activities involving some form of direct linkage with the public, on the other hand, are more frequently expressed as public demands upon individual members. Education and communication is volunteered by 41% of the public but only 3% of the members; and lesser gaps exist for constituency service (37% of the public vs. 27% of the members citing the ombudsman role) and representation (35% of the public vs. 18% of the members). All in all, the incentives for performance in the electoral arena are clearly distinct from the prescriptions for performance in the institutional arena of the House.

## THE FUNCTIONS EXPECTED OF REPRESENTATIVES

There remains the question of which set of expectations is more salient to House members in their everyday activity—those of the public, or the institutional functions cited by their colleagues. The members were asked by the commission to list "the major *kinds* of jobs, duties, or functions that you feel you are expected to perform as an individual member of Congress." The question does not specify any single set of expectations, but rather asks the member for his perceptions of the entire gamut of expectations from any and all sources. These perceptions are presented in table 2.2, and the results make clear that the importance of the electoral imperative renders the public's demands far more weighty than the members' own prescriptions for the functions of the House.

### The Legislative Role

Once again, this role predominates, being perceived as an expectation by a near-universal 87% of the members. Whereas the institutional responsibilities for legislation tended to be defined in terms of collective problem solving, the expectations of individuals were centered more on the accumulation of policy information. "My first responsibility," declared one representative, "is to develop committee expertise. I'm expected to learn all there is to be known on an issue, to stay with it on a day-to-day basis. I want to be an expert, sought out by other members and able to help them."

**Table 2.2.** ***Members' Views on Functions Expected of Members***

| *Role* | *% of Respondents* |
|---|---|
| Legislative | 87 |
| Constituency service | 79 |
| Education and communication | 43 |
| Representative | 26 |
| Political | 11 |
| Oversight | 9 |
| Institutional | 7 |
| Office management | 6 |
| "To be everything" | 6 |
| All others | 4 |

NOTE: Total weighted N = 146. Multiple responses were possible.

### The Constituency Service Role

However, almost as important in the overall field of expectations was constituency service, volunteered by 79%. The ombudsman role alone was cited by half of the sample, while 9% discussed public works and 6% aiding local officials in their dealings with the federal government. It is a responsibility felt keenly by the individual member. Some of the flavor of these responses can be gleaned from the following comments:

> Constituent work: that's something I feel very strongly about. The American people, with the growth of the bureaucracy, feel nobody cares. The only conduit a taxpayer has with the government is a congressional office.
>
> To get programs for the district, pork stuff, to make sure (member's part of state) doesn't get short shrift. Not that we should get more—just to make sure (member's part of state) doesn't get dealt out.
>
> People turn to their congressman or senator for help when the rest of the system fails. They don't vote for the Small Business Administrator, or the Farmer's Home Director, or the EDA As-

> sistant Secretary. They probably never see them. They don't vote for the Social Security Administrator. They do vote for their congressman and senator. They see them, know them, touch them, talk to them, write to them.

In these responses, one also begins to sense how these differing expectations are weighed and assessed in the political calculus which every member must continually make. In a word, constituency service is seen as vital to electoral success. "A near idiot who has competent casework can stay in Congress as long as he wants, while a genius who flubs it can be bounced very quickly." "You do whatever you can that is good for the district. Nobody's going to criticize you in an election campaign for not devoting enough time to the broad issues. Or if they do criticize you, you need not worry about its impact."

**The Education and Communication Role**

Slighted as an institutional function, this role was perceived as an individual expectation by 43% of the members. "The role of the educator," according to one member, is "first to learn, to assess the feelings of the district on particular issues, and to educate other members as to the aims of your constituency. To take the views of Washington back to the district. It's a two-way function." Other comments highlighted the interactive facets of the role:

> Staying in contact with the people in my district. Answering the mail. That's my first priority, because it may well be their only contact with the office. You let them know you represent them. I have hearings, personal appearances, and seminars in my district. I go to the important charitable functions. A politician doesn't have a personal life, but that is the sacrifice you make. We must encourage participation in the government. I send out a questionnaire every three months.
>
> I think a congressman has a duty to educate the public. You present both sides of an issue to your district and you try to persuade them to the way that you think is correct. I invite public participation in my decision-making process. I think I can teach my people why certain programs, such as the federal minimum wage, are right and important. Sometimes they convince me.

**The Representative Role**

An expectation for 26% of the members, this role was perhaps most aptly summarized by the respondent who attempts "to express the desires of my district, either by speech or by vote." Another declared that if his district has problems, "they're *my* problems, if they involve the federal government. I have a collateral responsibility to the country as a whole, which my constituents are part of, but that's almost secondary. I'm supposed to be a spokesman for our constituency and our constituency's point of view." Yet another member's "constituents expect me to be a symbol of their connection with the federal government. They want to have pride in me. They want to be able to vent their frustrations through me."

Additional expectations abounded: the political obligations of reelection and party leadership (volunteered by 11%), oversight (cited by a mere 9%), fulfilling general institutional responsibilities as a member of the House (7%), and supervising office staff (6%). And 6% said wistfully that they are expected "to be everything!" "You are expected to perform everything from the role of entertainer on occasion to being a personal adviser to your constituents. You're a jack of all trades. If you take it all seriously, it's impossible to do it. You're supposed to be a miracle-maker, to do the impossible."

Reviewing the set of expectations perceived by individual members of the House, we find that legislation and constituency service are almost universal expectations, while education and communication, as well as representation, are perceived by significant numbers. Oversight, meanwhile, is left far behind. In sum, the demands of the institutional arena do not appear to be focused on the individual member unless they are reinforced by demands emanating from the electoral arena. One can conclude that the incentives for performance in the electoral arena are the predominant force in determining the expectations perceived by individual members.

## THE CLASH OF INCENTIVES

This distinction between the two arenas is confirmed when one asks members about their most precious resource of all: "What are the *differences* between how you *actually* have to spend your time and what you would *ideally* like to do as a member of Congress?" By far the most frequent complaint, offered by 50% of the members, was that constituent demands interfere with legislative and other congressional activity. The tradeoffs engendered were a source of frustration for a large number of members:

> There's a role conflict. The incredible demands of constituent service interfere with constructive legislation.
>
> The problem-solving part of the job I would like to see abated somewhat. I spend every Saturday in the mobile office, listening to people complain. . . . I would like to shift time from that to the legislative side. I spend too much time on things like finding a high school band a place to stay. . . . That actually consumed half a day—that's nuts!
>
> I have an ombudsman-like role. I came down to Washington with great ideas, but I don't have the time to deal with them.
>
> When I came here, I was interested in being a national legislator. I didn't see my role as getting a dam for the home district, or some sewer project, or being an ombudsman for people needing a Social Security check. I don't denigrate these tasks, but they shouldn't be the prime tasks. . . . One reason we are not able to formulate better national policy is because we have become the ombudsman and the last hope of individuals who are despairing of dealing with the federal bureaucracy.

Perhaps the key effect of this role conflict is to take time away from the less visible aspects of the legislative process, and particularly the careful analysis of alternative policy options:

> Ideally, I would like to spend my time studying and reading, so I might always vote intelligently and have the time to contribute to solutions to major problems. I find myself constantly pulled in all directions by the demands of constituents and quorum calls and committee meetings and so on that just reduce my efficiency.
>
> I actually spend my time handling anything from trivia to matters of great moment to the people in my district. . . . I would like to be exclusively a legislator, but custom has made that impossible. I would like to have time for reflection, so for every vote I could come in well-armed and contribute to the discussion.
>
> I would prefer some other system, so we don't have to spend so much time on casework. I would feel more fulfilled if some-

> body else were doing it. I would prefer a more philosophical pursuit and deeper discussions. What are the *assumptions* behind our legislation? We never get around to assumptions and premises around here.

The motivations underlying this state of affairs are abundantly clear to any practicing politician:

> The service function . . . includes Social Security, veterans' problems, immigration, casework, community projects, business problems, labor difficulties—they're all things you must do if you realistically want to be reelected.
>
> My role as a representative of the people to the bureaucracy is not a constitutional function, but it's a function that has grown out of tradition and a desire to get political gain. Here's where you do yourself the most good politically.
>
> I would rather go to committee meetings. . . . I have to meet with Boy Scouts and have my picture taken. It's a waste of time, but it's important to the people back home.
>
> Legislation takes a back seat. It can be neglected without any immediate adverse impact on a congressman. He can miss a committee hearing, not be on the floor, neglect material necessary for an informed decision, and who's ever gonna know? But he cannot avoid, except at the risk of the peril of constituent hostility, responding to constituent requests. So constituent requests take a priority over legislation. You have a turning upside down of what the priorities ought to be.
>
> That's a flight from reality, that question. . . . I'd love to leave all considerations of Inaugural tickets and constituent problems and whether we get such and such a contract and all such considerations to my able, alert staff, while I serve the future interests of the country by producing a sparkling new . . . law. It's very unlikely to happen that way.

In short, when asked to spontaneously prescribe a set of institutional functions for the House, the views of House members diverge markedly from the expectations placed upon individual members by the public. And in reconciling these differences in their expenditure of personal time, the members' preferences for policy making give way to the demands of the voters. The representative has a kind of split personality, heeding one set of incentives emanating from Washington and another from the district. This political schizophrenia is so common that it has generated any number of summary aphorisms. A sample:

> At home, I'm a social worker, I do casework. Here, I improve legislation, and create new laws.
>
> You are a servant-leader. As a servant, you are an ombudsman. As a leader, you are a legislator.
>
> There are two sets of expectations. They come from (1) constituents, and (2) the institution, or colleagues. The people back home—they expect me to be an ombudsman, help them with Social Security problems, legislate in their interests, be responsive to letters, and keep them informed. By our colleagues, we're expected to participate in committee work, be on the floor to vote and participate, and project a good public image.
>
> The best politician is a combination of introvert—someone who is a good study, who can be a good student—and an extrovert—someone who can make love to his constituents.

Thus, the two arenas of Congress are not merely a construct; they are a vivid reality to many members of the House.

## THE EFFECTIVENESS OF PERFORMANCE

The clash of incentives between the two arenas has important implications for the effectiveness of the House in performing its functions. Table 2.3 presents the results when members were asked to evaluate the House's performance of the institutional functions volunteered earlier in the interview. The most effective job is done on the ombudsman role, where performance is rated positively by 77% and negatively by only 22% of the members. Representation is given a positive rating by about three-fifths of the members, and legislation is given a middling rating, about half positive and half negative. Oversight, however, is rated positively by only 22%, and negatively by 77%. The general pattern is clear: casework and other functions desired by the public are performed most effectively; while oversight, for which there is no electoral demand, is performed indifferently, if at all. In looking at the performance of Congress as a whole, the electoral imperative appears to predominate.

**Table 2.3.** ***Member Ratings of Effectiveness of House Performance of Volunteered Roles House Should Play***

| *Roles House Should Play* | *Very Effective* % | *Fairly Effective* % | *Only Somewhat Effective* % | *Not Very Effective* % | *Weighted Cases*[a] (N) |
|---|---|---|---|---|---|
| Ombudsman role | 42 | 35 | 10 | 12 | 35 |
| Representative role | 13 | 48 | 35 | 4 | 24 |
| Legislative role | 12 | 39 | 35 | 14 | 130 |
| Oversight role | 4 | 18 | 33 | 44 | 60 |

[a]The number of cases varies because the question on effectiveness of performance was asked only of those members who had previously volunteered a given role.

The members' air of self-congratulation on their handling of casework deserves a closer look, for it is perhaps the most direct contact that members have with their constituents. The survey by Louis Harris and Associates revealed that 15% of Americans lived in households that had at one time requested congressional assistance. Of these, 63% were "very satisfied" with the help received, and an astonishing 66% *volunteered* that the representative's office "did their best" or "could not have done more" to help!

The political dividends appear to be sizable. Among households containing casework alumni, 71% gave their representative a favorable job rating, as opposed to 62% among households never touched by congressional assistance. Incumbents received an even higher 78% favorable rating from respondents who were "very satisfied" with the disposition of the household's case. Overall, casework may well be one of the most politically profitable activities in which a member can engage.[4]

### Priorities in Time Expenditure

The effectiveness of congressional performance is a direct consequence of the members' allocation of their limited resources of time and staff. The commission asked members to estimate how much time they spend on a variety of activities, as well as how important each of these activities should be. The differences between how members would like to spend their time and how they actually spend their time are striking. An instructive example: getting back to the district is considered "very important" by 74% of the members, and accorded "a great deal of time" by 67%, a fairly good fit.

However, while studying and doing basic research is rated "very important" by an equally impressive 73% of the members, it is given a great deal of time by only 25%. The gap is almost as great for oversight (56% vs. 16%), floor work (64% vs. 30%), and mobilization on legislation (55% vs. 22%). On the whole, one finds only a modest divergence between ideal and actual time priorities on constituency-oriented activities: casework (58% vs. 35%) and grantsmanship (44% vs. 24%) are typical of this trend. Yet one also finds, as we have seen, seriously suboptimal time expenditures on legislative and other policy-related activities. Once again, it appears, the electoral imperative wins out.[5]

As one might expect, members enjoy more freedom from electoral considerations as they attain seniority. Table 2.4 demonstrates that floor work, mobilization, and oversight are given considerably more attention by senior members than by their junior colleagues, significantly lessening the gap between their actual and ideal priorities for time expenditure. Some of the difference is undoubtedly due to the increase in electoral safety which accrues with seniority. As one member commented, "We're not expected to be planners or developers, so it isn't done except when you have the luxury of a safe seat." Or as another lamented, "Ideally I would like to have a political cushion so I could concentrate on substance rather than appearances—so I could be a legislator for causes I believe in, rather than contriving things to attract attention, which I must do because my seat is uncertain."

## Staff Allocation

The importance of the electoral arena is even more dramatically seen in staff allocation patterns. In June 1977, the Commission on Administrative Review asked administrative assistants in member offices to list the number of people performing a given function in their office. The results indicate that staff time is overwhelmingly devoted to satisfying the demand for constituency service. The average House office contains 4.2 caseworkers, 3.1 clericals, 2.2 office supervisors, 2.2 legislative researchers, 1.4 legislative correspondents, 1.3 communications specialists (i.e., press secretaries and field representatives), 1.2 personal secretaries, and 0.2 people under other headings.

Just as enlightening is the division of staff resources between the Washington and district offices. Of the 15.7 people employed in the average House office, 9.5 are situated on Capitol Hill and 6.2 are working in the field. Not surprisingly, virtually all of the district-

**Table 2.4.** ***Members' Actual vs. Ideal Priorities for Selected Activities, Controlling for Tenure***

| | *2 Terms* | | *3 to 5 Terms* | | *6 or More Terms* | |
|---|---|---|---|---|---|---|
| *Member Activities* | *Should Be Very Impor-tant* % | *Spend Great Deal of Time* % | *Should Be Very Impor-tant* % | *Spend Great Deal of Time* % | *Should Be Very Impor-tant* % | *Spend Great Deal of Time* % |
| Studying and doing basic research on proposed legislation | 78 | 24 | 72 | 18 | 76 | 32 |
| Debating and voting on legislation on the floor of the House | 60 | 27 | 75 | 22 | 61 | 40 |
| Working in committee or subcommittee on oversight activities | 62 | 11 | 54 | 4 | 57 | 30 |
| Working informally with other members to build support for legislation about which you are personally concerned | 62 | 15 | 56 | 24 | 51 | 25 |
| Weighted N | 38 | | 50 | | 58 | |

based personnel are involved in some aspect of constituency service: 3.0 perform casework, 1.2 are clerical staff, 0.9 manage the office, and 0.6 specialize in communications. Thus, the importance attached to satisfying the public's demand for constituency service is a critical factor in a member's allocation of scarce staff resources; this allocation has important consequences for the institutional performance of the House.

## SUMMARY AND CONCLUSION

The competing incentives for performance in the two arenas of Congress are an explicit reality for members of the House. They feel that the institution as a whole should be primarily concerned with the policy adoption and implementation functions of legislation and oversight. However, the public is relatively less concerned with legislation and altogether ignorant of oversight. Electoral demands are centered around such district-oriented activities as constituency service, representation, and the two-way process of education and communication linking representatives with their constituents.

These conflicting electoral and institutional perspectives are clearly perceived by the members. They are generally conscious of playing a dual role—emphasizing legislation while in Washington and constituency service in their more direct contacts with constituents. The clash of incentives is generally resolved in favor of the demands of the electorate, both in terms of the member's personal time and the allocation of personal staff.

This fragmentation of roles is so striking that one wonders whether there are any incentives for a *coordination* of congressional functions. The "ideal-type" legislator who monitors constituent complaints in the hope of improving legislation may be a rare species indeed. The individual constituent who brings a case to the individual member of the House is interested in an individual remedy. There are no immediately apparent benefits to the member in undertaking the more gargantuan task of patching up an entire delivery system. Given the perceived political benefits of casework, the incentives may appear to run in precisely the other direction—that is, in the perpetuation of a bureaucracy that creates opportunities for member intervention in constituents' daily lives.

A more comprehensive approach to policy making requires careful study, the sifting of alternatives, and the mobilization of support on the floor and in the public for a solution. It is necessary and vitally important work for the proper functioning of the policy process. It is also tedious, conflictual, and largely hidden from public view. The audience for the conscientious legislator is limited to one's conscience, one's colleagues, and a handful of lobbyists and subject-matter specialists—for even the press and political scientists are unlikely to notice. Not a large public, that. The image of "responsiveness" is almost certainly more lucrative merchandise for the congressional entrepreneur.

It is an ingenious and disturbing system. While satisfying the most keenly felt desires of both the candidates and the public, it does nothing to safeguard the long-term national interest in coherent policy formulation and implementation. As is all too clear from the public's negative evaluations of Congress, the public senses the problem, but not its source.[6]

It is easy to dismiss constituency service activities as too trivial or demeaning for the Congress to engage in. But to the extent that they satisfy the legitimate needs and desires of constituents, they serve the purpose of quite literally bringing the government closer to the people. It is the tradeoffs they engender that are a source of strain for congressional performance. Member inattention to pending bills today means poor legislation, and poor implementation, tomorrow. The chronic lack of effective oversight only compounds the problem. And increased casework is the result, which in turn aggravates the existing misallocation of member time and staff.

If we are to halt this spiral of dysfunction, we might do well to heed the member who advised:

> All of these goddamn political science courses are interested in the legislative function and the sinister influence of lobbies. They should be seeing how these things are working out in the district where the money comes out of the spigot. Political science is preoccupied with Congress in place here in Washington. That's just the tip of the iceberg. You've got to rub your nose in it.

To understand Congress as its members experience it, we must recognize that what the electorate demands and what the institution requires are often quite distinct. It is this tension that we see reflected in the shortcomings of congressional performance. In an era when the need for coherent national policy making is keenly felt, professional politicians may not be the only ones whose futures depend on the clash of incentives between the two arenas of Congress.

## NOTES

I would like to thank Joseph Cooper, Robert Dahl, Roger Davidson, Michael Denney, Victor Fischer, Calvin Mackenzie, Steven Rosenstone, and especially David Mayhew for commenting upon earlier versions of this paper.

1. For a more complete description of the electoral and institutional arena models, detailing their derivation from other theories in the literature, see Cavanagh (1979). A structural-functional model of the "two Congresses," with internal and external inputs and outputs, has been presented in Davidson and Oleszek (1980). A game theory model of congressional roll call voting, which poses a similar contrast between electoral demands and member goals, can be found in Fiorina (1974, chap. 2). And Fenno (1978, 33) has touched on the conception of two arenas in his recent research on "home style": "The job of a congressman requires that some things be done in Washington and others be done in the district. At the least, legislation is passed in one place and elections occur in the other. . . . And this built-in strain between the need to attend to Washington business and the need to attend to district business affects the work of each individual and the work product of the institution. The strain is both omnipresent and severe. Members give up the job because of it. Congressional reforms are advocated to alleviate it."
2. This is essentially the Downsian electoral marketplace as modified by Mayhew's substitution of individual candidates for parties. Cf. Mayhew (1974) and Downs (1957).
3. This treatment draws heavily from Fenno (1965).
4. Fiorina (1977) is the most prominent advocate of the view that the growth of casework explains much of the electoral advantage currently enjoyed by congressional incumbents. For more data on casework, see Cavanagh (1979).
5. Twelve items concerning priorities for member time expenditure were asked of both members and the public in the studies conducted by the Commission on Administrative Review. In general, there was a substantial correspondence between member and public priorities, although grantsmanship and staying in touch with local officials were more highly prized by constituents than by members. A more striking finding was the complete lack of correspondence between the member and public perceptions of how members of the House actually spend their time. The mass public appears to have a civics-book conception of congressional activity as being primarily legislative. The public's lack of awareness of the extent of district-oriented activity may contribute to the intensity of demand for such activity perceived by members.
6. For a detailed analysis of public attitudes toward Congress, see Glenn R. Parker's article, "Can Congress Ever Be a Popular Institution?" (chap. 1).

## REFERENCES

Cavanagh, Thomas E. 1979. "The Rational Allocation of Congressional Resources: Member Time and Staff Use in the House." In *Public Policy and Public Choice,* ed. Douglas W. Rae and Theodore J. Eismeier, pp. 209–247. Beverly Hills: Sage Publications.

Davidson, Roger H., and Oleszek, Walter J. 1980. *The Two Congresses.* Washington: Congressional Quarterly Inc.

Downs, Anthony. 1957. *An Economic Theory of Democracy.* New York: Harper & Row.

Fenno, Richard F., Jr. 1965. "The Internal Distribution of Influence: The House." In *The Congress and America's Future,* ed. David B. Truman, pp. 52–76. Englewood Cliffs, N.J.: Prentice-Hall.

———. 1978. *Home Style: House Members in Their Districts.* Boston: Little, Brown.

Fiorina, Morris P. 1974. *Representatives, Roll Calls, and Constituencies.* Lexington, Mass.: D. C. Heath.

———. 1977. *Congress: Keystone of the Washington Establishment.* New Haven: Yale University Press.

Mayhew, David R. 1974. *Congress: The Electoral Connection.* New Haven: Yale University Press.

# 3. Casework in the House

*John R. Johannes*

One of the least understood aspects of congressional life is casework: helping constituents in their dealings with the federal bureaucracy. Not a day passes in a representative's office without letters, calls, and visits from constituents seeking assistance. Whether it is a government check that is late in arriving, a tax dispute with the IRS, a delay in processing a passport application, ambiguous language in some agency's regulations, or a federal housing grant application by a community in the member's district, constituents seek out their representative for help.[1] Often called the "errand boy" function of Congress, this means of redressing grievances and improving access—a veritable "re-presenting" of citizens to executive branch administrators—constitutes a booming growth industry on the Hill. And along with the growth comes staff expansion, specialization, and sophistication—and some interesting consequences and controversies.

Until recently, little was known about constituency service. But two new studies have provided sufficient data to take a serious look at how the House handles cases for individuals and projects for local governments. The first is the work of the House Commission on Administrative Review (the Obey Commission); the second is an intensive examination of casework I conducted.[2]

## CASES AND CASELOADS

What are these cases like, and just how many of them do congressional offices process? By far the most common types of cases deal with social security and Veterans Administration benefits: late checks, reductions in benefits, or eligibility disputes. Military cases (exemptions from the draft during the Vietnam war, discharges, and transfers), Labor Department matters (Workmen's Compensation and black lung program benefits), and immigration problems come next in frequency. (These five categories constituted nearly three-quarters of all the cases mentioned in surveys of members and their aides.) The vast majority of cases and projects are routine and common, but some are complex and even bizarre: a Soviet seaman who jumped ship and sought asylum in the United States, for example, or a constituent whose new invention was spurned by the Air Force in favor of a more costly but apparently lower quality substitute manufactured by a corporate giant. Some cases are "tear-jerkers": parents and children separated by the vicissitudes of immigration laws; elderly men and women eating dogfood because they had not properly applied for social security or other government benefits; and husbands in the military trying to get to the bedsides of their dying wives. Every caseworker can relate story after story of this type. Other cases, of course, are less momentous: the college student writing her representative in hope of changing dormitory roommates or the father demanding that the representative do something about a low grade his son received in a political science course at a state university.

The types of cases vary from district to district and time to time. During the 1960s, for example, military cases dominated the mail; when the war ended, veterans' cases proliferated. Members from coastal and border regions are flooded with immigration problems; those from mining areas receive disproportionate numbers of black lung claims; members from the sunbelt hear from retirees complaining about social security red tape; and Maryland and Virginia representatives seem to have a near monopoly on civil service cases.

Caseloads, too, vary. The 131 representatives who responded to the Obey Commission's survey indicated that the number of "requests for help in dealing with the personal problems" their constituents had with the federal government averaged nearly 12,000 annually, ranging from a low of 20 to a high of 95,000. (Problems of definition, naturally, enter into such estimates.) The author's survey asked members and staffs for their normal case and project loads (defined to include not only problems with the federal government but also those with state and local governments and private institutions that ended up in congressional offices). Responses indicated a mean weekly caseload of 112 for 177 offices of current and recent members, with a low of 10 and a high of 465.[3] About four-fifths of these cases came from individuals, another seven or eight percent from state and local governments, and the remainder from businesses and other groups. Although comparable caseload data do not exist for previous years, two-thirds of the members and staffers agreed that caseloads have been rising in recent years. Only one out of 190 respondents thought that they had decreased. Among the most important reasons for the growth of casework is the tendency of members, especially those elected in this decade, to employ devices such as mobile offices, newsletters, town meetings, and random phone calls to constituents in a determined effort to solicit cases and requests for services. Other factors include heightened public expectations, burgeoning and more complex government programs, and bureaucratic snafus.

## CASEWORK STAFFS

Members of Congress, themselves, spend little time on case and project work (see below). Rather, they have increased steadily the sizes of their casework staffs and moved them to offices in their home districts. Between 60 and 70 percent of all casework is done "back home." The most frequently heard reason for shifting casework operations to the district is that there is too much work with insufficient office space in Washington. In addition, caseworkers can be closer to the constituents and closer to the federal bureaucracy's regional and area offices (where records are kept, decisions that caused the problems made, and initial appeals examined). Other members want to concentrate Washington staffs on legislative duties.

How large are casework staffs? The Obey Commission's interviews with members found that they had an average of 1.2 aides "involved in the substantive disposition of casework" in Washington and another 3 in home offices. The author's data suggest that these figures probably underestimate the size of case and projects staffs by as much as a third.

Staff organization differs by office, perhaps more so in district offices than on the Hill. In Washington and in some home offices, most representatives designate one or more aides as "caseworkers" (with or without that exact title). Many others choose not to have caseworkers per se, preferring to have legislative assistants (LAs), administrative assistants (AAs), personal secretaries, press assistants, and others to carry out the casework burden—in part to make better legislative use of information discovered while handling constituent problems. The remainder employ both casework specialists and others to handle cases, usually reserving to the LAs, AAs, and personal secretaries the "tough" and nonroutine cases. In district offices, especially when there are only one or two staffers, each tends to be a "jack of all trades." But larger district offices resemble those in Washington in terms of staff specialization.

Where there is more than one designated caseworker, the work is divided either by type of case (typically one staffer handles military and veterans problems, while another does social security, immigration, and so on), alphabetically, or on a first-come-first-served basis. Among professional caseworkers there is considerable dispute as to which system is better: specialist or generalist. The former enhances expertise and familiarity with agency liaison personnel (specialists who work with congressional aides to resolve cases and, generally, to smooth interbranch relations). The latter makes it easier to cover for a caseworker who is absent, and it allows for continuity when a staffer leaves his or her job. For dealing with federal projects, staffing patterns are somewhat different. Unlike the Senate, few House offices can afford a specialist for federal grants applications and other projects. Thus projects are done by a variety of staff members.

Two other points deserve mention. First, caseworkers work alone, with very little direct supervision by members, AAs, or office managers. Two-thirds of responding staffers in Washington and over four-fifths in district offices reported high degrees of operating independence, compared to about 10 percent who said they were closely supervised. While such staff autonomy could mean that little importance is attached to their activity, or at least points out that most casework is routine, it has significance. In combination with other characteristics of casework operations (complexity, well-boundedness, adaptability, and stability), it emphasizes the growing professionalization and institutionalization of this particular congressional function. Such institutionalization tends to enhance the influence of case and projects specialists and may lead to a set of norms and behavioral patterns which insulate caseworkers from some of the political pressures associated with "doing favors" for constituents.

A second characteristic worth noting is that each congressional office works alone. Over half of all responding staffers indicated that, in working on cases and projects, they never or rarely worked with other offices. Conversely, 4% said they often pooled either case data or efforts with others. The two situations leading to interoffice cooperation include: (1) state- or area-wide federal projects, on which several offices (often including the senators from the state) get together to help push applications; and (2) instances—about 15% of all cases—in which constituents contact several members of a state delegation simultaneously. The consequences of this lack of coordination are two: caseworkers lost the opportunity to compare operating styles and systems, and it becomes harder to utilize casework for purposes of integrated oversight of the executive bureaucracy.

Perhaps the most striking characteristic of caseworkers, on Capitol Hill, is that almost all (90%) are women. In district offices, where staff specialization is much less pronounced, about half of those doing case and project work are men. Why so many women caseworkers in Washington? The answer may have something to do with the supply of and demand for jobs and workers at the low to medium salary range in which caseworkers fall (Commission 1977*a*, 85–100; Johannes 1978*b*, 10–12). Or it could be related to what virtually everyone in Congress thinks are the traits that make good caseworkers. Easily the most frequently mentioned characteristic was empathy with and sensitivity to people's problems. Knowledge of agency structure and personnel (having good contacts in the executive branch), patience, and perseverance are also valued. Other aides talk about dedication, hard work, the ability to listen and to communicate, speed, and an ability to "read between the lines." Whether women possess these traits in greater measure than do men is unclear. Preliminary analysis suggests, at least, that women caseworkers are no more successful than men.

Other caseworker traits can be summarized quickly. Caseworkers in general are well educated, with most having finished college. Overwhelmingly, they share the party identifications of their employers. Three-quarters feel that they know both their bosses and their districts "very well." Over half of the Washington-based caseworkers have had previous Capitol Hill experience, whereas caseworkers in home offices are considerably less experienced at casework and projects. A sizable minority of aides remain as caseworkers for years, even decades, although they may work for several members during that time. It is among these staffers that a distinct casework career has developed on the Hill. Meanwhile, a majority of caseworkers in Washington (unlike aides in district offices) are under 30 years old and tend to leave their positions at a relatively high rate—largely because (1) they view casework as an entry-level job and a stepping stone in the congressional staff hierarchy, and (2) the pressure, tension, emotional drain, and often boredom of casework prove unpopular.

These age and experience differences appear to have consequences. Younger, better educated, and less experienced case and project workers tend to see Congress's legislative and oversight functions as more important than serving constituents. Older, less educated but more experienced aides tend to see representation and casework as more crucial than do the other group. Such differences probably will remain in the future. However, if younger aides who value the policy aspects of legislative life remain as caseworkers, there may, over time, be greater pressure to use case experiences as sources of legislative and oversight activity.

## CASEWORK PROCEDURES

Most cases come to staffers when constituents write their representatives. Phone calls to and walk-ins at district offices are common. Members personally pick up cases when visiting their districts. In Washington, a small number of members read all incoming mail, screening certain cases for special handling. A few others take constituent phone calls, giving the aggrieved citizens a preliminary hearing before turning them over to the caseworkers.

The procedures for doing casework are simple. A constituent's inquiry is quickly acknowledged by a letter (sometimes preceded by a phone call if further information is needed). Unless a few words of explanation or advice are sufficient, the caseworker opens a file on the case. Either by phone, letter, or buckslip (a preprinted referral form), and occasionally by a personal visit, the aide contacts the relevant liaison person in the federal agency having jurisdiction over the case. (The military services and the Civil Service Commission locate their liaison staffs in offices on Capitol Hill. Some veteran aides and some who simply disdain liaison staffs take their cases directly to the operating or program levels of agencies, thus bypassing several layers of bureaucracy. Others, especially those in members' home offices, make most of their contacts with administrators in regional or area offices of departments and agencies. Frequently, such offices are located in the same cities, and even in the same federal buildings, as the congressional offices.) Once the constituent's problem is communicated to the executive, it becomes merely a matter of time until a decision is made and a reply drafted, cleared through several levels of the agency, and sent to the representative. To alert them when administrators fail to reply within a given time, most caseworkers employ some sort of "tickler system." Interestingly, despite the growing use of computers on the Hill, fewer than 10% of House offices use computers to track casework. Most of those who do report considerable satisfaction.

When the agency's reply is received, it is forwarded or paraphrased to the constituent over the representative's signature, which often is penned by the AA. (In a few offices the caseworkers use their own names in dealing with constituents in order to establish familiarity and confidence, even at the risk of destroying the illusion that the representative personally is involved.) If the agency's response is judged by the caseworker to be inadequate, it is returned—usually to a higher-ranking administrator—with a request that it be investigated further. If nothing results from this appeal and the case still is judged meritorious, or if the agency has been less than fully cooperative, the member may be asked to place a call personally to a high-ranking official, perhaps the department secretary or agency head. Nearly nine of ten caseworkers interviewed for this study reported taking cases to the secretarial or even presidential level at one or more times in their careers.

Procedures for federal projects differ according to the type and significance of the project. Strictly routine endorsements of grant applications or pro forma arrangement of meetings between applicants and agencies are handled almost automatically. Major projects necessitate considerable research efforts, several meetings, and close work between congressional staff, executive administrators, and often uninformed local government officials. Some congressional offices see their role as informal "grants coordinators" for their districts, particularly in rural areas whose many small towns and villages cannot afford to hire professional grants writers. In short, the more important the project, the greater attention it receives.

Overall, the caseworker-agency relationship is amazingly fluid and satisfactory. Asked to assess the quality of cooperation from agencies on casework, 24 of 28 representatives, 18 of 25 administrative assistants, 32 of 45 caseworkers in Washington, and 90 of 109 aides in district offices rated cooperation as always or usually good. The Labor Department and, to a lesser extent, the Immigration and Naturalization Service received most of the negative evaluations. Both the commission's interviews and those of the author turned up some unhappiness with the bureaucracy's ability to process cases and provide information relevant to cases and projects quickly, but such complaints were in the minority. Not only are most agency officials anxious to help citizens who have valid complaints, but they perceive it to be in their self-interest to be as cooperative as possible with the Hill.

## CASEWORK: AN ASSESSMENT

In assessing the constituent service function, scholars—and members of the House—are divided. Defenders see it as a necessary and laudatory function with numerous beneficial consequences. Critics (Clapp 1963, 56–57, 61, 90–91; Gellhorn 1966, 72, 125–129) view it negatively, concluding that casework is ineffective, disorients members of Congress, interferes with more important congressional duties, is unfair and unjust, and has damaging side effects in terms of protecting incumbents from electoral challenges.

Does casework have an impact? That depends, in part, on how one measures success, and from whose perspective it is viewed. Staffers in this study were asked to estimate the proportion of cases which resulted in "decisions favorable to the constituents." The mean response from 198 aides was a surprising 39.5%; the median was 35.2%. In addition, 13 former members of the House estimated success rates at nearly 50%. These figures include only bureaucratic actions that were reversed or altered. If one added instances in which constituents received either speedier answers or clear explanations of why benefits were denied, the "favorable" figure would double. It is true that many of these successful results come in routine cases which the constituents themselves could have pushed to their conclusions. But many constituents are incapable of doing so, and others simply become so frustrated with bureaucratic red tape that they quickly turn to their representatives.

Critics also complain that, relative to other functions, casework is too time-consuming and distracts representatives from their primary tasks. Some scholars (Mayhew 1974; Cavanagh 1978) have argued that constituent demands and expectations for casework, "pork barrel" projects, grants and loans to local governments, correspondence, visits to the district, meetings with local government officials, and similar "constituent" activities constitute an "electoral arena" that is distinct from and disruptive of the more important "institutional arena" (legislative and oversight duties) of congressional life.

A definitive judgment about the validity of such charges rests on too many variables and requires better data than are now available. Although it certainly is true that members allocate a good deal of time and resources to their constituencies (Fenno 1978), and that the public expects individual members to do so, it does not follow that casework per se is the culprit. In several respects it can and must be distinguished from other constituent services and reelection activities such as "advertising," "credit-claiming," and "position-taking" (Mayhew 1974, 49–64). To argue that casework interferes with more serious tasks is to argue that: (1) inherently, casework is relatively unimportant; (2) members spend a lot of time on it; (3) the time spent on and resources devoted to casework are taken away from other duties; and/or (4) those other duties actually suffer because of casework (or, alternatively, that casework contributes nothing to the accomplishment of those duties).

Is casework unimportant? When the Obey Commission asked members to name the two most important roles the House should play, the most frequent response (cited first by 72% of the members and second by 19%) was the legislative role. Oversight was named by 10% on the first response and 32% on the second; representation by 11% and 8%; and the ombudsman (casework) role by 2% and 25%. That is, fully 27% of the members surveyed felt that casework was one of the two most important jobs of the House of Representatives (Commission 1977*b*, 865–867). Note that the commission's interviewers were instructed to accept only two responses from members. How many members would have listed constituency service or casework as their third choice if they had been able to? Moreover, when asked how importantly members should treat certain activities, 58% said that they should treat "helping people in [their] district[s] who have personal problems with the government" as very important. Only 14% said it should be "not" or "only slightly" important (Commission 1977*b*, 880). Caseworkers in my study were virtually unanimous in assessing casework as important, while administrative assistants were slightly less so. Of course, one does not know *why* members and staffs think casework is important. Mayhew and Cavanagh would argue the "electoral connection." But many members and their staffs participating in this study stressed other motives (see below), which, while not incompatible with the electoral hypothesis, are legitimate and distinctive in their own right.

Do members spend inordinate amounts of time and resources on casework? Saloma (1969, 184) found that members of the House in the early 1960s spent about one-quarter of their time "running errands." Of the Obey Commission's respondents, 35% reported spending a "great deal" of time helping constituents who have problems with the government—a figure surpassed on only three other activities—32% said they spent at least "some" time doing so. (Another 32% reported spending "only a little" or "hardly any" time on casework.) Such data are impressive, but they may be misleading. Saloma's figures seem to include all sorts of constituency-related activities; moreover, they were gathered fifteen years ago. The commission's results neither include definitions of "a great deal" or "some," nor do they distinguish between time spent in Washington and time spent back home in the districts talking with and taking cases from constituents. Furthermore, one should be skeptical of hasty judgments arising out of these particular data. The commission asked members how much time they spent on each of seventeen different activities (nine of which are clearly institutional tasks, while the others are either electoral or could fit into either category). At least half of the respondents reported spending a "great deal of time" or "some" time on no fewer than thirteen of those activities. Overall, when the four response categories are collapsed to two (a "great deal" and "some" time versus "only a little" and "hardly any"), casework itself ranks ninth out of nineteen functions in terms of members' time. Ahead of it are five purely institutional activities and three representational—or electoral—ones.[4] In short, whether or not constituency service activities waste members' time depends on how one defines those activities. It is hard, using commission data, to argue that casework itself does so.

Perhaps a more accurate picture can be had from the staffs, rather than from the members (who obviously regard themselves as incredibly busy). Aides in 135 House offices reported that the members for whom they worked spent an average of fewer than six hours weekly (with a median figure of only three) on cases and federal projects when they were in Washington. And in half the offices, the staff estimates were two hours or less per week. Lending support to these figures is an interesting datum from the commission's work (1977*a*, 18). In its study of how members spend their time, the commission found that on average, when members were in Washington, they were in their offices for only three hours and nineteen minutes per day. Even assuming, generously, that half that time is spent on casework, the average representative could not possibly spend more than eight hours per week helping constituents. Back home in the district, naturally, the picture is different: representatives often are besieged with constituent requests for help. And many members, especially new ones, go out of their way to drum up even more cases by holding office hours, visiting different areas in their districts with mobile vans, and so on. But it is their staffs that do the actual work.

Members' personal involvement in casework usually is triggered by two causes. Either staffers have done all they could with the bureaucracy and require extra clout that only members can provide; or the cases are of special significance: emergencies, hardships, cases with policy implications, or federal projects. Additionally, members are more likely to become personally involved in cases when they are the ones who first made contact with constituents about them and when the constituents requesting help are friends or local VIPs back in the district.

Though members do not spend much Washington time on casework, they do utilize their staff resources. Cavanagh (chap. 2) has argued that constituent demands of all types—not just casework—force members to orient their own staffs away from legislative and oversight tasks and to seek out other staffs. Hence the proliferation of independent subcommittees, each with its own staff. The question is: in the absence of constituency service duties, especially casework, would office staffs be devoted in greater measure to "more important" tasks such as legislation or oversight? It is hard to say. Indeed, it is likely that, since staff growth has come largely in response to increased constituent demands for attention and services, without those demands there would not be nearly as many aides available for any function, including legislation and oversight. The issue is moot.

Finally, does casework interfere with more important jobs? Commission data are confusing. On the one hand, asked what are "the obstacles which stand in the way of the House in doing a better job" of performing its roles (as mentioned by members in a previous question), only 7% said casework interfered with the first mentioned role (predominantly legislation) while 8% cited the two-year congressional term as the major problem (Commission 1977*b*, 870–873). Adding all district-related demands together, only 19% of the members found constituent-related duties to be obstacles. When the same question was put to members concerning the obstacles to what they took to be the second most important role of the House, 17% cited district demands, almost all of which were casework. Interestingly, when asked for recommendations to help Congress overcome the obstacles to accomplishing its most important tasks, only a small percentage responded in terms of larger staffs or other casework or constituency-related matters. The bulk of recommendations dealt with improving scheduling, better information, changes in committee structure, and revisions of floor rules.

The commission (1977*b*, 881–885) also asked members about the biggest obstacles that each encountered in trying to do his or her job the way he or she wanted to do it. Only 6% complained about casework burdens directly; but 80% cited lack of time, caused mainly by institutional (legislative, oversight)—*not* electoral—problems.

On the other hand, members were asked to identify the major differences between how they actually have to spend their time and the way they ideally would like to. A total of 50% responded in terms of constituent demands: 39% said that time demands for constituent services detract from the legislative function, and 2% said they detract from oversight. Reelection pressures and time spent in the districts for ceremonial duties constituted most of the remainder of the 50%. Scheduling problems were cited by 36%, and structure by 9%; 16% said there were no differences.

Thus a clear judgment on whether casework in particular and constituent or electoral pressures in general disrupt institutional work is not easy to reach. Obviously, any time away from legislative or oversight work is by definition a distraction. But if listening to and helping aggrieved constituents is seen as part of the representative function of Congress, and if such activities help restore the public's faith in Congress, surely time spent on such activity is a useful contribution to the legitimacy that underpins the legislative function. And electoral pressures that force members to return to their districts may be precisely what the founding fathers had in mind when they sought incentives to keep members attentive to constituents' views.

There is another side to this coin. When the commission (1977*b*, 957–980) asked members where they and their staffs turn to get information needed to handle their committee duties and to deal with matters they must vote on or be knowledgeable about, about one in five responded in terms of district input, including feedback from constituents. Could such electoral or representational factors actually help members and staffs in their jobs of legislating and watching over the bureaucracy? Asked in my questionnaires how effective and valuable case and project work is for providing ideas and incentives for legislation, 21 of 28 members, 13 of 23 AAs, 36 of 51 caseworkers on the Hill, and 117 of 149 aides in district offices responded "very" or "somewhat" effective. In each category, only a small number answered "rarely" effective and valuable. Almost identical responses were obtained when respondents were asked about oversight.[5]

Casework's utility for such tasks arises in three ways. First, cases sometimes lead directly to formal oversight (hearings, audits, staff investigations) and to the introduction of remedial legislation. Close to two-thirds of House staffers indicated that their offices at least attempted to generalize about problems uncovered in casework in order to discover underlying causes and solutions—though almost none do this systematically—and virtually every Washington office contacted in this study was able to supply several examples of legislation that resulted from casework. It appears that the program areas in which this most often occurs are those dealing with eligibility for various benefits, where constituents can pinpoint problems easily, and where remedies are not hard to enact.

Second, the very act of intervening to correct a problem for a constituent is a form of instant oversight that alleviates the effects of bureaucratic error, delay, or abuse. Third, constituency service, to varying degrees, serves as a potentially valuable source of administrative feedback to agency officials interested in spotting and correcting weaknesses in their programs and operations. Interviews in departments and agencies confirm that such activity in fact takes place. Thus, without exaggerating, and taking into consideration the optimism and bias of casework staffs, it nonetheless seems safe to say that there are distinct benefits, in terms of oversight and legislation, to doing casework.[6]

Another primary criticism of the casework function is that it is unfair and unjust. When confronted with this argument, caseworkers and AAs were incredulous. "Unfair? How could anyone say that—everyone is free to write their representative." Nearly 90% of members and staffers surveyed disagreed or strongly disagreed that casework gives some people an unfair advantage over others. True, some citizens have the good fortune of living in districts represented by senior members of the House, committee chairs, and party leaders. But caseworkers for such members reported no significantly higher—and in some instances lower—success rates. Indeed, only one of four aides cited the identity or committee assignments of their bosses as relevant factors in casework success. (Over half felt the key factor is the inherent merit of the cases, while the remainder cited the skills and tenacity of the caseworker.) In competing for federal grants and projects, some advantage probably does accrue to strategically placed members. But the evidence, such as it is, is mixed and thus inconclusive.

Casework could be unfair in other ways. Do some constituents (VIPs, friends, relatives, or local political leaders) receive better or faster service from congressional offices? Over 60% of the 153 staffers responding to this question said no, compared to about 20% answering in the affirmative. Quite a few indicated either "I wouldn't know such people if I saw them" or "nearly everyone who writes claims to be a cousin or an old friend of the representative." Asked what reasons account for exerting special efforts on certain cases (why one case might be pushed harder or to a higher level than another), 11% answered in terms of friends of VIPs, while 50% referred to "the nature of the case." Indeed, some suggested that their evenhanded professional approach to casework served to inhibit favoritism by their employers.

Lastly, unfairness could result from some members' requests receiving preferential treatment from the executive because they were of the same party as the president. Respondents split about evenly on this question, suggesting that such favoritism does exist. Of course, if administrations continue to alternate between Democrats and Republicans, such political preferences would "average out" over the long run.

A related criticism is that justice is subverted, or at least tampered with, because administrators tend to violate rules, make exceptions, or spend disproportionate amounts of time on some cases in order to please members, irrespective of the merit of the cases. A recent study of twenty-two agencies by Technical Assistance Research Programs (1976, 12-3) found that agencies often pay more attention to citizens' complaints, however trivial, channeled through congressional offices than to serious problems brought directly to the attention of administrators.

To examine the question of meritless inquiries, this study asked members and staffs to estimate what proportion of cases they receive lacked substantive merit. The mean response was just under 20%, with the median about five points lower. Respondents also indicated that roughly one in five constituents failed to tell the whole truth when contacting congressional offices for help, but, as many staffers said: "People tell you their side of the story. They're not usually lying as such. Actually, when we dig out all the facts, we sometimes come up with a better case than they thought they had."

Critics argue that casework disrupts the operations of federal departments and agencies. Needless to say, representatives and their staffs disagreed, although some believed this to be true. Interestingly, 14 of 25 agency liaison staffers in Washington also disagreed. As one put it: "Sure, I suppose the people downstairs and down the hall are distracted from their jobs when a 'congressional' comes in. But they should be if there is a good reason for the complaint." A liaison specialist in a regional office called such disruption the "cost of doing business—like overhead." The charge of hurting agency efficiency would be more serious if it could be shown that a large proportion of constituents take their problems to Congress without having exhausted normal channels of redress within the executive branch. Apparently such is the case. Estimates from staffers of the number of citizens who fail to exhaust normal administrative channels approached 50%. But even here, there are extenuating circumstances. Said one caseworker: "Many of these people just don't know where to go. If they don't come to us, they wouldn't get any help because they'd give up without trying."

A final major complaint relates to political impact. Not a few observers (Fiorina 1977; Mayhew 1974) have expressed the fear that successful casework is undermining competition in congressional elections, leading to a situation in which service replaces legislative performance as the criterion for reelection. The reason, according to Fiorina (1977, 45) is that "pork barreling and casework . . . are almost pure profit." According to Fiorina, Congress enacts programs and creates bureaucracies to administer them, knowing full well that those bureaucracies—because of red tape, inadequate funding, or whatever—will make mistakes, will delay delivery of benefits, and will at times insult and abuse constituents. People, naturally, turn to their friendly representative for help, which is gratefully remembered at election time. The case is built on circumstantial evidence, but it is potent. Furthermore, recent data make it even more plausible.

The Obey Commission (1977*b*, 831) asked a nation-wide sample of voters whether they had ever contacted their representatives for assistance on problems they had with the government. Of those who had, 61% said they were "very satisfied" with the results; another 7% indicated they were "mostly" satisfied. And those who were satisfied seemed to give their representatives higher performance ratings (see chap. 2). Such potential electoral benefits are not lost on members and their staffs. When 226 aides and 26 former representatives were asked if they believed that people who received casework help would vote for the members supplying that assistance, only nine (including two members) disagreed. Well over 80% answered affirmatively. Over 90% thought that casework was "very" or at least "somewhat" valuable and effective in strengthening an incumbent's electoral base.

Two questions arise. First, do members engage in casework solely or primarily for electoral purposes? Second, do—or how do—members exploit constituency services for votes?

When the members and staffs in this study were asked whether the primary reason most members do casework was reelection, more responded negatively than affirmatively. Most insisted that, to quote one staffer, "you just can't separate the election benefits from the other reasons." Those reasons include a dedication to representation (of which constituency service is an integral part); a sense of the humanitarian importance of making government work for "the little guy"; a satisfaction in helping people; the challenge of tackling problems and taking on the bureaucracy ("we hate the bureaucrats," said one AA, whose boss corroborated that sentiment moments later); and legislative and oversight uses. To be sure, members realize that *not* doing casework will jeopardize their political careers and that votes can be influenced by favors done. But that is not quite the same as saying they handle cases and projects specifically in order to win reelection. In short, while electoral motives undoubtedly place high, or even highest, on the list of reasons for (and rewards of) casework, they exist amidst—and often intertwined with—others. Members not only believe that helping constituents is good politics, but most—and nearly all their aides—believe it to be a way of insuring that the average citizen gets a fair chance with the bureaucracy.

The electoral benefits that do accrue to constituency service do not derive from using casework records to solicit campaign funds or to recruit campaign workers, since only a small minority of offices do so. Rather, they apparently are produced by a combination of subtle and not-so-subtle "advertising" and "credit-claiming" (Mayhew 1974, 49–60). Substantial pluralities of respondents indicated that casework recipients' names were added to mailing lists; successes, at least in aggregate terms ("I helped 2500 constituents last year") are included in newsletters; and occasional cases are described in detail in campaign literature or speeches. Almost all agreed that the best dividend from casework came from word-of-mouth publicity.

Still, the electoral effects of casework have not been proven. No one knows for sure whether and to what extent voters cast their ballots simply to reward good casework or pork barreling. Some aides are skeptical. Many casework recipients are not even registered voters (half, according to one caseworker). Most constituents expect members of Congress to provide assistance when asked, regardless of who is asking. Nearly one-third of those who requested help were not satisfied. And only a third of all cases end in concretely favorable results. Finally, if either quantity or quality of casework produced greater electoral margins, the effect should be apparent in an examination of the relationship between 1977–78 caseload and success rates, on the one hand, and the electoral margins in the 1976 or 1978 election, on the other. No such relationships emerged.

## CONCLUSION

Casework on Capitol Hill and in district offices has become a semi-professionalized and semi-institutionalized function which some fear may threaten not only more important roles of Congress but electoral competition as well. For some congressional districts, such fears may be real, but available evidence must be stretched to argue that the problem is yet as serious as critics claim. Moreover there is no denying that this function does provide citizens with a relatively efficient and effective means of redressing grievances, and that some useful legislative and oversight spillovers—not to mention better representation and, perhaps, some measure of reduction in public cynicism—occur.

The problem is not the system as it now works. The problem is that caseloads are likely to continue to expand, thanks in large measure to members and staffs who stimulate constituents to request their services. Such expansion inevitably leads to pressure for still larger staffs, both in Congress and in the executive. And although casework is rather independent of other office activities, and although such autonomy has its benefits, sooner or later an undesirable layering of staff and isolation of the members may occur. Complaint-handling, paradoxically, could become a barrier not so much to legislation and oversight but to the very representation that underpins the legitimacy of the House.

Some commentators have suggested that Congress abandon or at least alter the way it goes about case and projects work, perhaps by creating a Scandinavian-type ombudsman. Others, including several members of the House and the Senate, have introduced legislation to establish in Congress a centralized office for handling the routines of casework: a place where the "legwork" could be done so as to achieve economies of scale and to utilize casework data for oversight better. Neither idea is popular with members and staffs in the House, attracting support from only ten percent of those surveyed. Not only would the "personal touch" be lost but, according to many, so would the motivation for effective service, once the political elements were removed.

What is needed, and what is being done to some extent, is more and better training for caseworkers (who currently undergo little formal training other than visits to various executive agencies to be briefed); more computerization of records (strongly resisted by some offices, but clearly the wave of the future); more interoffice coordination; and a greater inclination to use casework for purposes of oversight and legislation. For, in a real sense, there is no better way to learn how well or how poorly laws are working than to examine the numbers and types of complaints from citizens.

## NOTES

The author wishes to thank the Marquette University Committee on Research for a Summer Faculty Fellowship and Research Grant and the American Philosophical Society for a Johnson Fund Grant.

1. This discussion deals only with *casework* (intervention with federal

agencies on behalf of constituents who, as individuals, groups, or businesses, have difficulties in dealing with the bureaucracy) and *federal projects* (helping state and local governments secure grants, loans, and construction projects from Washington). Members of Congress engage in all sorts of other constituency relationships and service: arranging White House tours, corresponding politely about legislative issues, providing information and government documents, and helping with service academy appointments. Such non-casework and non-projects activities are excluded from this paper.

2. The House Commission included questions on casework in its surveys of 153 representatives, their staffs, and the general public. The author independently has compiled data—based on 57 personal interviews, 23 telephone interviews, and over 200 mail questionnaires—for 176 current and 23 former members of the House. Additional data were collected from 28 federal agencies and bureaus. When data presented are not specifically identified with the Commission, the reader should assume they are from the author's surveys.
3. Using medians rather than means (to eliminate the effects of extreme values) produces a commission (1977*b*, 890) estimate of about 135 cases per week and my own estimate of 100. Since the commission's figure was obtained from members, who generally do little casework and probably are not as aware of the flow of cases as are their staffs, and since definitions of casework vary, the lower figure (obtained from caseworkers) may be closer to the truth.
4. Whether such "representational" activities as returning to one's district to keep in touch with constituents and with local government officials, or taking time to explain to constituents what government is doing should be considered "institutional" or "electoral" arena duties is unclear. To the extent that they are electoral, they necessarily detract from time that could be spent in committee or on the floor of the House. But are they merely electoral?
5. Interviews with agency liaison officials in Washington tended to support this judgment. Ten of the twenty officers interviewed felt that casework was very or somewhat valuable for oversight or for legislation.
6. A more complete argument can be found in Johannes 1978*a*.

## REFERENCES

Clapp, Charles L. 1963. *The Congressman: His Work As He Sees It*. Garden City, N.J.: Doubleday, Anchor Books.

Commission on Administrative Review, U.S. Congress, House. 1977*a*. *Administrative Reorganization and Legislative Management*. Communication from the chair. 2 vols. 95th Cong., 1st sess. H. Doc. 95-232.

———. 1977*b*. *Final Report*. 2 vols. 95th Cong., 1st sess. H. Doc. 95-272.

Fenno, Richard F., Jr. 1978. *Home Style: House Members in Their Districts*. Boston: Little, Brown.

Fiorina, Morris P. 1977. *Congress: Keystone of the Washington Establishment*. New Haven: Yale University Press.

Gellhorn, Walter. 1966. *When Americans Complain: Governmental Grievance Procedures*. Cambridge: Harvard University Press.

Johannes, John R. 1978*a*. "Casework As a Technique of Oversight of the Executive." Paper presented at the 1978 annual meeting of the American Political Science Association, New York.

———. 1978*b*. "Congressional Caseworkers: Attitudes, Orientations, and Operations." Paper presented at the 1978 annual meeting of the Midwest Political Science Association, Chicago.

Mayhew, David R. 1974. *Congress: The Electoral Connection*. New Haven: Yale University Press.

Saloma, John S. 1969. *Congress and the New Politics*. Boston: Little, Brown.

Technical Assistance Research Programs, Inc. 1976. "Feasibility Study to Improve Handling of Consumer Complaints: Evaluation Report." Second portion of the Federal Central Office Phase of Contract Number HEW-OS-74-292. December 1976.

# 4. The Politics of Congressional Ethics

*Allan J. Katz*

All institutions have a difficult time confronting the problems of the ethical behavior of their members. Delineating proper conduct is a difficult task. The Congress of the United States has had to face this question more directly than perhaps any other body. As an institution its basic character has changed dramatically from its origins in the late eighteenth century when it was primarily a place for people of means to spend a few years of their lives. Today that job is a career, and certainly by any measure one of the more demanding ones.

The process of devising suitable standards of conduct for the House of Representatives has evolved dramatically during the past ten years in response to the increased scope of the federal government and changing public attitudes toward "openness." Other institutions have undergone significant changes during that period of time as well, but the House of Representatives faces a unique dilemma in establishing an appropriate code of ethics. Most other institutions exercise some measure of control over membership selection, but the House does not. Its problem is to create a suitable set of ethical standards for a membership that is elected by 435 individual constituencies.

The role of party politics in the operation of the House constitutes another factor of great importance. While the decline of party over the past twenty-five years has been evident in the Congress, there is no question that partisan advantage is an integral part of the daily workings of the House. Yet the impact of party allegiance is complex, not simple. When the issue of disciplining members has come before the House, great effort has been made to avoid the appearance of partisanship. While that has made the process slow and laborious, it has created certain built-in safeguards without which the ability of the institution to govern itself could be undermined.

It is also important to remember that because all the members of the House are subject not only to the whims of the voters every two years but also to the criticisms of the press, there is a camaraderie out of adversity which most members feel especially on questions of ethical standards. They feel that in many cases they are perceived by the public as guilty until proven innocent. This breeds an inherent defensiveness not only toward anyone attacking them individually but also against those who attack other members of the institution.

These underlying factors must be kept clearly in mind in attempting to understand exactly how the House of Representatives was able to pass a comprehensive Code of Ethics in March 1977 (H. Res. 287). While some have pointed to certain flaws that exist in that code, it was widely heralded by the press as one of the toughest and most comprehensive codes of ethics in existence anywhere. Analysis of its passage thus casts light on an important dimension of the job of the member and on the processes of change as well.

## BACKGROUND EVENTS

Exactly how the House of Representatives was able to pass a Code of Ethics that received such unprecedented approval is a story of political necessity as well as institutional recognition of a need to meet a problem in public credibility that threatened to undermine its effectiveness.

Ironically enough, it was made possible by two occurrences that made life most unpleasant for many members of the House. The first was the undoing of Wayne Hays which forced members to take individual responsibility for changes in the allowance system. The second was the need to deflect anticipated criticism of a congressional pay raise, the first, other than one minor cost of living adjustment, since 1969. This, coupled with other events, brought about changes the effects of which are still being felt today.

During the second session of the 94th Congress (1976), several events took place which had a significant impact on subsequent ethics legislation. The first was the disclosure that Robert L. F. Sikes, Chairman of the House Appropriations Subcommittee on Military Construction, had a conflict of interest which he had not reported as specified under the disclosure requirements of the House. Common Cause, a self-styled public interest group, led the move to have Sikes brought before the Standards of Official Conduct Committee. This effort led to the reprimand of Sikes by the House and, ultimately, to the loss of his subcommittee chairmanship at the start of the 95th Congress (1977). It also added to the support that Common Cause had attempted to build for expanding the disclosure requirements for members of the House.[1]

Two other significant events occurred in 1976 which created the appropriate atmosphere for a thorough revision of the Code of Conduct for the House of Representatives. The first was a story that appeared in the *Wall Street Journal* (March 23, 1976) written by Jerry Landauer, dubbed the "Phantom Driver" story. In it Landauer revealed how a number of members of Congress had claimed to have driven to their districts when, in fact, they had actually flown there. The reason for the false claims was that, through a recently passed regulation by Representative Wayne Hays's Committee on House Administration, members were entitled to receive twenty cents per mile if they drove, as opposed to fifteen cents per mile reimbursement for other means of transportation. Consequently, members would receive a greater amount in travel reimbursement than the actual cost of a plane ticket. Landauer's story underscored the lack of accountability of the Committee on House Administration, which since 1971 had had the ability to change regulations on allowances through a committee order without calling for a full vote of the House. This led to a flurry of press stories and concern by the leadership of the House. Most of the members listed in the story wound up reimbursing the House of Representatives for the differences in mileage claimed.

Shortly after the Landauer story appeared, the *Washington Post*, beginning May 23, broke the story that Wayne Hays was involved in an affair with Liz Ray, an employee of the House Administration Committee. Ms. Ray told *Washington Post* reporters that she couldn't take dictation, or type, or even answer the telephone. The revelation that a mistress of a powerful chairman was kept on a committee payroll strictly for sexual favors caused a thunderstorm of criticism descending upon the House and particularly upon Wayne Hays. Hays admitted having an affair with Ms. Ray but denied that was the only reason she was on the payroll. Nonetheless, the criticism grew, and for the first time Hays was in serious trouble with his colleagues in the House.

It is significant to note that Hays had long been viewed as one of the most powerful members of the House by virtue of the chairmanship of the Committee on House Administration. Because the committee, under his leadership, could increase members' allowances without the members themselves voting on them, he became a lightning rod for criticism of congressional excesses regarding expense allowances. As long as Hays remained the main source of the criticism and the members themselves were free from any personal responsibility, Hays's power was secure. Once he became the source of that criticism and could no longer fend off the burst of publicity surrounding those allowances and how they were obtained, members who had supported Hays in retaining his chairmanship at the beginning of this Congress abandoned him with incredible swiftness. Even his erstwhile ally, Phil Burton, was strangely silent during this time.[2]

Meanwhile, the leadership, which had never been comfortable with Hays, saw this as an opportunity to get rid of that problem once and for all. More importantly, the leadership understood the necessity of taking steps to assure the public that the credibility of the House could be restored.

On June 4, the Speaker appointed a three-man task force from the Democratic Steering Policy Committee to look into the accounts system of the House and to make recommendations to the caucus on improving the "propriety and appearance of propriety" of the accounts system of the House of Representatives. The task force was chaired by Congressman David R. Obey of Wisconsin; the other two members were Congressmen Lloyd Meeds of Washington and Norman E. D'Amours of New Hampshire.

The task force met for the first time on Monday, June 7, 1976, and, at that time believing it was under a deadline of September 1, began to pull together all the information available on how the accounts system was set up in the House.

As the task force began to compile information, the pressure grew on Hays to resign, which he ultimately did. The deadline moved up for the task force. They were asked to have a report to the caucus prior to adjournment in early July for the Democratic National Convention.

In the process of looking through the accounts system of the House, the task force became aware that there were several problems that needed immediate attention. The first was the source of Hays's power. The ability to change and increase members' accounts by the House Administration Committee without a vote of the House had to be changed. The task force thus recommended that the committee no longer have the power to change accounts without a vote of the House.

The next obvious problem was that of the phantom drivers. Therefore, the task force recommended that the mileage reimbursement be reduced to fifteen cents per mile. Other complaints that had surfaced in the press regarded certain allowances that could be "cashed out." Members could take the cash in lieu of the allowance and declare it as income while disbursing it for office expenses as they saw fit. This amounted in some cases to over $10,000 and the task force recommended ending this option for members.

In a letter circulated to members, the task force asked what features of the allowance system they would most like to see changed. The primary complaint by members was the inflexibility of the old allowance system as well as the areas of potential abuse and embarrassment listed above.

The old allowance system was set up into fourteen different categories. Members could spend their allowances only for those categories. Therefore, if a member needed more money for traveling to his district more frequently, this could only be paid out of his own pocket. Thus, the task force recommended a consolidated account whereby all members would be free to use the accumulated allowance for whichever uses best fit their needs in representing their constituents.

As an added safeguard to this consolidation feature, the task force recommended that all expenditures and allowances be reported on a quarterly basis and on a member-by-member basis. The idea was that members could spend the money as they saw fit for official purposes, but if it was reported fully and completely to their constituents, they could be held accountable.

As the task force accumulated its information and tried to look at the overall account system, the administrative structures of the House and its lack of organization became very clear. Consequently, as the final recommendation of the task force, a page was lifted from the recommendations of the Committee on Committees of the 93rd Congress. The task force resurrected the proposal for the establishment of a Commission on Administrative Review to review the entire administrative structure of the House and to make recommendations to the House regarding changes in this system, including the allowance system and other fiscal matters as well. An additional recommendation of the task force was that the Democratic members of the Committee on House Administration be appointed by the Speaker. This was felt to be an important element because it would give the leadership some control over a sensitive area that affected the credibility of the House.

The recommendations were discussed at length with the leadership and finally presented to the Democratic Steering and Policy Committee. Objections arose immediately over the proposal for appointment by the Speaker. The objections came from the members of the California delegation, most of whom had served in the California legislature under the very powerful Speaker, Jesse Unruh. Objections to the overall package were raised by some members of the committee, but the Steering and Policy Committee voted to accept the recommendations of the task force. A method of implementing these changes as soon as possible was then set in motion.

The basic strategy was to have the House Administration Committee take up the matters and pass them by committee order as they still had the power to do. Once they had done this as their final act with the power to make changes in allowances, a resolution would be put before the House which would strip them of that power. A very risky tightrope was being walked, but it was the only practical approach to solving the problems in the existing time frame.

In order to get the House Administration Committee to move quickly and in order to get the Rules Committee to vote out the so-called "stripper resolution" as well as the resolution creating the Commission on Administrative Review, a resolution from the Steering and Policy Committee went before the caucus on June 23. The intention was to have the caucus vote to instruct the Democratic members of both committees to proceed according to the recommendations and implement the leadership's strategy.

The opposition to the Speaker appointing Members of the House Administration Committee began to harden and Majority Leader Thomas P. O'Neill, who was going to be the Speaker in the new Congress, stood up in the caucus and moved to strike from the report that particular recommendation. Even then there was significant opposition to what the task force recommended and the caucus, which had been planned to begin at 9:00 A.M. and conclude by noon, concluded in disarray with no action taken and a subsequent caucus scheduled for 6:00 P.M. that evening.

Throughout the day there was extensive maneuvering with the leadership doing all they could to bring a majority of the Democrats in line to support the task force report. At the same time there was intense activity on the other side aimed at gutting the recommendations. That evening the caucus, after a very stormy session, voted to adopt the task force report. On June 28 the House Administration Committee adopted those portions of the task force report on which it could act and on July 1 the House passed the stripper resolution (H. Res. 1372) and the resolution which created the Commission on Administrative Review (H. Res. 1368).[3]

It is interesting to note that the diverse forces at work on the task force recommendations were involved primarily because of the fight over the majority leadership which was to take place at the beginning of the 95th Congress. Countless maneuverings could only be explained in terms of setting the groundwork for a later fight.

Many members liked the notion of a consolidated account but felt that these changes were being made too quickly. Consequently, the major thrust in the caucus to gut the task force recommendation failed by only twenty votes.[4] That part of the task force recommendation which received the smallest amount of attention was the creation of the Commission on Administrative Review. That commission was to be the vehicle which would bring about the most sweeping changes in the Code of Conduct for the House of Representatives during the next year.

## THE WORK OF THE COMMISSION

On July 21, 1976, the Speaker of the House announced the appointment of fifteen members of the Commission on Administrative Review. It included eight members of the House and seven members of the general public. The chairman was Congressman David R. Obey of Wisconsin and the ranking Republican was Bill Frenzel of Minnesota.

Immediately the commission began the task of selecting a staff, and the first organizational meeting was held on September 12, 1976. During that meeting some of the acrimony that would pervade the deliberations of the commission became apparent. The minority members were trying to get the commission to act on recently publicized abuses, especially with an election less than two months away. However, the chairman was under a charge from the Democratic leadership to concentrate on the problems of scheduling and to report recommendations to the House that could be implemented by the beginning of the 95th Congress. Consequently, the initial thrust was aimed not at ethics but rather at a more procedural issue, much to the dismay of the Republican members.[5]

Shortly after this meeting, however, a number of events led the commission to the subject of ethics legislation. The first was the activity of the Commission on Executive, Judicial, and Legislative Pay (the Pay Commission), and the second was the Democratic Caucus in December 1976.

The Pay Commission recommended that congressional pay be substantially increased along with that of the judicial and executive branches. The raise totaled $12,900, from $44,600 to $57,500. However, they recommended that the pay raise needed to be accompanied by a commitment to limiting outside earned income. The premise for this recommendation was that members of Congress should be well paid for being full-time legislators and, consequently, should avoid potential conflicts of interest with other occupational earnings. Chairman Obey testified before the Pay Commission in favor of the proposal, and it became clear that the Pay Commission would in all likelihood recommend to the president that congressional pay increases be included in the budget to be presented to the Congress in January 1977 (Commission 1977*a*, 311–406).

There was tremendous concern on the part of many members of Congress that politically the pay raise would be an issue that many of their colleagues would be unwilling to face and that a newly elected Democratic president would be afraid to endorse. Consequently, a number of them traveled to Atlanta during the campaign to meet with Democratic candidate Jimmy Carter and were successful in convincing him to withhold any statement on the proposed pay raise until after the election.

The primary issue dominating the Democratic Caucus was that of the election of a new majority leader. Richard Bolling, Phil Burton, Jim Wright, and John McFall were all seeking that post. McFall's entanglement with what was soon to be dubbed "Koreagate" made his chances of moving up from majority whip position to that of majority leader remote at best. Ultimately, Jim Wright defeated Phil Burton by one vote.

As the caucus turned its attention to procedural matters, a number of members of the House began to propose changes in the Code of Conduct. The impetus for such proposals came not only from the impending pay raise, but also from the Hays scandal the previous spring and the recent newspaper revelations that Korean agents had dispensed millions of dollars in cash and gifts to members of Congress in an attempt to create a favorable legislative climate for South Korea (Congressional Quarterly 1980, 36–47; H. Rept. 95-1741).

Specifically, new rules on financial disclosure, gifts, travel, and unofficial office accounts, as well as the pay raise and outside income, were discussed. The leadership wanted these matters handled in a different fashion than in an open caucus with little forethought given to the ideas. The vast majority of these issues were thus referred to the Commission on Administrative Review or, as it became known, the Obey Commission. As one senior staff member of the leadership later commented, "If the Obey Commission hadn't existed, we would have had to invent it." Consequently, at the conclusion of the Democratic Caucus, the Obey Commission found itself facing a number of ethics issues that were not on its original agenda.

Once the commission was faced with the responsibility of dealing with ethics legislation, it became apparent that this legislation would be closely related to action by the Congress on the pay raise. The deadline for action on the pay raise was February and the clamor to defeat it, by various members as well as certain segments of the public and press, was increasing.

The commission took those issues which had been referred to them by the caucus as well as those issues which related to the pay raise and attempted to develop a realistic approach and basis for ethics legislation.[6]

**Financial Disclosure**

While there had been a financial disclosure rule in the House for almost ten years, it was essentially ineffective in terms of revealing potential conflicts of interest. Similarly, while a number of disclosure bills had passed the United States Senate with great fanfare and by impressive majorities in prior years, it was always with the implicit assurance that there was no chance that this legislation would ever come before the House.

Common Cause had been advocating and lobbying for financial disclosure legislation for several years. While they had been successful in the Senate, they continued to be unsuccessful in the House. Therefore, the commission offered a good vehicle to accomplish what they and others had wanted to do but had been unsuccessful in accomplishing.

The commission took the previous year's most prominent disclosure bill and began to analyze it. The criterion used to evaluate the effectiveness and efficacy of the bill was whether it disclosed those areas of financial interest that represented potential conflicts of interest. While early advocates of financial disclosure talked in terms of net worth statements or income tax returns, it became clear that both of those had significant disadvantages.

Net worth statements often attribute values that are illusory. Income tax returns represented to the commission too great an invasion of privacy. Whether or not there were medical bills in a family or how much or how little one contributed to charity, all readily accessible on these returns, were deemed to have no real value except to satisfy the curiosity of the public. Neither accomplished the goal of financial disclosure, that being an intelligent method of disseminating information that was relevant to the performance of a legislator and of giving his constituents an opportunity to measure any potential conflict of interest believed to have existed at the time legislative action was taken.

There was a general consensus among commission members, the press, and members of the House that improved disclosure rules were necessary and important. Consequently, the commission was dealing primarily with the details of accomplishing a meaningful disclosure rather than having to convince people that the whole notion was necessary. Its aim was to balance the need for disclosure rules that would identify potential conflicts of interest with the need to avoid unnecessary invasions of the privacy of members. In essence, what it recommended was disclosure of the sources and exact amounts of income and gifts in excess of $100 plus the disclosure of debts in excess of $2,500 and holdings and transactions in excess of $1,000 in terms of broad categories of value (e.g., under $5,000, $5,000–$15,000, etc.). The difficult issue of spouse disclosure was resolved by requiring it in cases where funds or assets were "constructively controlled" by the member.

**Unofficial Office Accounts**

Probably the most memorable public exposure of unofficial office accounts came during the 1952 presidential election when Richard M. Nixon, then a candidate for vice-president, in his famous "Checkers speech," admitted that businessmen had set up an account for him. The public forgave Nixon his indiscretion, but the practice has continued and flourished in recent years.

In many instances the unofficial office accounts—or as the press liked to refer to them, "slush funds"—existed because of the inadequacy of official accounts. Members of Congress merely requested contributions to these accounts which would be used for expenses as diverse as buying stamps and stationery for the office or entertaining visiting constituents. The sources of these contributions were disclosed only at the members' discretion, but after the revelations surrounding Tongsun Park and Congressman John McFall, the press and public began to focus clearly on these accounts and their potential for abuse.

The commission examined the issues surrounding the need for these accounts and concluded from its own survey that approximately 40 percent of the members of the House maintained them for a variety of purposes. Some members used them to pay for student interns from their districts to spend a few weeks in Washington. Others used them for entertainment, while still others used them for supplementing service to constituents back in the district. The main reason given for these accounts was the lack of adequate official allowances by the House. A significant number of members who did not have these accounts pointed out that they used their campaign funds for similar expenditures. The commission concluded that the vast majority of the members of the House of Representatives were using some form of outside funding to supplement their official expenditures. Ultimately, the commission recommended the abolition of these accounts along with an increase in official allowances of $5,000. This recommendation led to the most acrimonious debate to take place during the commission's deliberations.

The Republican minority were vehement in their opposition to increasing official allowances. While they approved of eliminating the unofficial office accounts, they also believed the present allowances were sufficient.

It is important to understand that there were political incentives to bolster the opinions of both sides of this argument. The Democrats enjoyed a two-to-one margin in membership. Increasing allowances, thus allowing younger and more vulnerable members of the House to increase constituent services, would be one way of helping the Democratic incumbents remain in office. Republicans, on the other hand, holding only one-third of the seats of the House, wanted to do nothing to enhance the longevity of the more vulnerable Democrats.

In one vehement public session of the commission, Representative Bill Frenzel, the ranking minority member, denouncing the linkage between the increase in official allowances and the abolition of unofficial office accounts, said that he was "tired of the rest of us being raised to the level of the pigs." This brought an acerbic response from the chairman, David Obey, and a shouting match erupted between several members of the commission (Commission 1977*a*, 255–259; Commission 1977*b*, 25, 29; Congressional Quarterly 1980, 49–50). It also reinforced the mutual distrust between the chairman and the ranking minority member that was never really dissipated throughout the life of the commission.

**Gifts**

The existing House rule on gifts was that no member or staff person could receive a gift of "substantial value" from anyone with a "direct interest in legislation before the House." The problem with enforcing that rule was twofold. First, defining "substantial value" and, second, determining who had a "direct or indirect interest in legislation before the House."

Under the old definition by the Committee on Standards of Official Conduct, substantial value meant that it had to be of substantial value to both the donor and the donee. Under that definition, a gift of $50,000 to a staff member from Nelson Rockefeller might not have qualified as having "substantial value." The existing definition was thus clearly unworkable.

"Direct or indirect interest in legislation" was even more difficult to define. Technically every American has an interest in tax legislation. Drawing any distinction is quite difficult and was clearly a question beyond the scope of what the commission planned to address. Consequently, the commission proposed the following: "Substantial value" was changed to $100, and anyone with a "direct interest" included, but was not limited to, people who had to register as lobbyists under any future statute. The belief at that time was that a new Lobbying Reform Act would pass during the 95th Congress and take care of this difficult definitional problem.

The commission went on to exempt gifts from relatives and to deal with certain threshold minimums regarding gifts. There was general agreement that there was no point in members and staff people keeping track of every single item including a cup of coffee or a hamburger that was purchased by someone with an interest in legislation. A threshold of $35 was established. Thus, only gifts over $35 counted toward the $100 limit. The limit was cumulative in one year. While this created some concern on the part of a few, the commission members all agreed that these were reasonable and necessary modifications of the $100 limitation.

**Use of the Frank**

A wide variety of outside groups have long maintained that there is abuse by members of Congress of the franking privilege set forward in the Constitution. The various uses of the frank have become more sophisticated as the methods of reaching constituents have improved.

At the time the commission was considering a series of proposals on ethics, the chairman was approached by Congressman Morris Udall, head of the Franking Commission of the Post Office and Civil Service Committee. After extended discussion, the chairman brought to the staff of the commission a series of recommendations for them to examine to see whether or not workable solutions to the problems that existed could be found.

There were two major problem areas. The first was the extensive use of the frank. Some members were sending out literally millions of pieces of mail to their constituents at virtually no cost to them. The other problem was that virtually anything could be sent under the frank, with little regard to content or the source of the printed material. Ultimately, the recommendations were settled along political lines.

The Republicans were very interested in limiting the number

of postal patron mailings (newsletters) that were sent out by the younger, more vulnerable Democratic members of the House. They wanted this limitation because they felt that mass mailings of such material made constituents more likely to reelect someone who had become quite familiar to them. The Democrats, on the other hand, liked the advantage of sending out these large numbers of newsletters. What they were concerned about, however, was that the Republican National Committee, which traditionally has far more money for its candidates than the Democrats, was bankrolling the printing of newsletters for incumbent Republican members of Congress. This meant that with the investment of $3,000 by the committee for printing, Republican members could get their newsletters into the homes of 200,000 of their constituents with the government picking up the tab for the postage. Even though the material was not political in nature, it was clearly good politics for them, just as it was for the younger Democratic members. Furthermore, this use of political funds to finance newsletters ran contrary to the basic thrust of the argument for eliminating unofficial office accounts, that argument being that official expenditures ought to be paid for out of official funds and no official funds should be associated with things which were not official expenditures.

Consequently, the commission produced a series of recommendations on the frank which accommodated the partisan interests of both Democrats and Republicans. These proposals limited the number of newsletters that could be sent in a given year; limited the time period within which a newsletter could be sent prior to an election; prohibited the mass mailing of any material under the frank that was not printed with official funds; and provided that all such material would be mailed third class. All of their restrictions promised a potential savings to the House of Representatives and the taxpayers in the neighborhood of $9 million.

### Foreign Travel

The Democratic majority on the commission was unwilling to deal with the complexities of the problem of foreign travel given the time constraints that existed. They adopted an idea that had been floating around for several years which received quick Republican concurrence. No member of the House would be permitted to travel on public funds after he had been defeated or after the end of the session if he had announced his retirement. This effectively put an end to lame duck travel once and for all.

## Outside Earned Income

This issue came to be the flashpoint of the entire ethics debate. There was probably no other issue that members personally became as well versed on during the 95th Congress and probably no other issue that sparked the kind of gut-wrenching concern and true antagonism between certain members of the House.

Based on the deliberations of the Pay Commission and upon the beliefs of the chair of the Obey Commission as well as the chair of the Task Force on Financial Ethics, Congressman Lee Hamilton of Indiana, a move started within the commission to impose a limitation on outside earned income for members of the House. This move was resisted strongly by the minority members of the commission.

The argument of the majority was fairly simple. Members of the House were full-time legislators. Thus, the public had a right to expect them to make that their full-time occupation. Consequently, rendering personal services for income in other professions was, on its face, suspect. The potential for influence peddling, especially with activities involving law firms, was obvious.[7] The opponents of the limitation pointed to the fact that the commission had not touched investment income. Their argument, therefore, was that if you were lucky enough to have been born wealthy, you could continue to clip your coupons, while if you had been unfortunate enough to have to work for a living, your ability to do this was going to be precluded. They also argued that to limit outside income would be to make members overly dependent on congressional careers.[8] As a compromise, the commission recommended the imposition of a ceiling on outside earned income equalling 15 percent of a member's congressional salary.

There were long and stormy debates among members and the staff of the commission over what this 15 percent really applied to. The question of ownership of a small business and whether reimbursement from that business represented income for personal services or a return on an investment was closely scrutinized. Drafts and redrafts by the commission staff tried to squarely address the problem. A large number of members of Congress sought out the chairman or other members on a one-to-one basis to explain their personal financial situations, and the staff was consulted to determine whether they would indeed come under the limitation. As one member of the commission later put it, the amount of disclosure of personal finance that went on during that period was probably greater than at any previous time in the history of the House of Representatives.

**Select Committee on Ethics**

One final recommendation that came from the commission was the creation of a Select Committee on Ethics. This was done primarily to create a vehicle to issue rules and regulations and put into permanent law any changes that were necessary based on these proposed rule changes.

A select committee was recommended for a number of reasons. First and foremost, the Speaker of the House had announced that such a committee would be created and members needed an authoritative entity to resolve ambiguities in their personal situations. Also, the Committee on Standards of Official Conduct had such low credibility that to entrust to them any such activity would have been viewed as making a sham of the entire effort.

## PASSING THE ETHICS BILL

The commission faced a number of procedural and legislative obstacles as well as severe time constraints in its attempt to bring ethics recommendations to the House and have them acted upon and implemented. First, the leadership felt that it was essential that an ethics package come before the House in early March since the $12,900 pay raise was slated to go into effect in mid-February. This necessitated having the package completed by the end of January so that the necessary committee votes could be completed during the month of February. Secondly, the Senate was preparing to take similar steps. The Senate did not face the public relations problem the House did, not having been immersed in the Wayne Hays or Koreagate scandals. Consequently, the House leadership wanted to be the initiator of the activities.

The major stumbling block was to devise a method of implementing the proposed changes without having to go through both the House and Senate and ultimately involving the president as well. The commission staff devised a method to avoid dealing with the Senate or president on this matter.

The rules of the House are set by the House. All of the commission's recommendations could thus be passed as rules of the House. As such, they would, of course, be binding only for the remainder of the Congress in which they were passed. But since the rules are readopted at the beginning of each Congress, the feeling was that once they were in the rules they certainly would never be withdrawn. Furthermore, this approach allowed most of the proposed rule changes to be considered by the Rules Committee as the committee of original jurisdiction, instead of going through the Standards of Official Conduct Committee. It was a fairly unusual procedure, but it seemed to be the only way to accomplish what was needed given the time pressures that existed.

The other major hurdle was the need to ensure the cooperation of the committees of jurisdiction involved in the proposed rule changes. The commission was fortunate that there had been a number of rule changes in the House of Representatives, both as a result of the Bolling Committee effort and as a result of some fairly slick maneuvering by the leadership staff in the organizing caucus for the 95th Congress. Thus, the Speaker had gained the power to make split committee referrals of legislation with a time specified for reporting by the committees. What that meant for the ethics resolution was that various parts of it could be and were assigned to the appropriate committees of jurisdiction, along with a deadline to meet in reporting out its portion. This guaranteed that the ethics package would reach the floor when the leadership wanted. This rule, in effect, gave the Speaker of the House the ability to discharge a bill. Normally in order to discharge a bill the signatures of a majority of the members of the House were needed.

The commission was concerned about the ability of the three committees involved to function smoothly. The Standards of Official Conduct Committee could not be avoided on the issue of gifts. The committee met and promptly dropped the $35 exemption that had been included by the commission. The committee chair, John Flynt, expressed dismay at the time pressures they were under and ultimately adjourned the committee, having passed the gifts portion of the ethics legislation with the committee amendment eliminating the exemption for any small gifts. The House Administration Committee received the part of the bill that dealt with the elimination of lame duck travel and the substitution of $5,000 in official allowance for unofficial office accounts. The Committee's first vote approved the elimination of lame duck travel, but deleted the proposed $5,000 increase in allowance. This led to a furious lunch-time lobbying session with the Speaker of the House working very hard with the committee chair to reverse the decision. Leon Panetta, who had voted to eliminate the $5,000, was convinced by the leadership to request a reconvening of the committee two hours after the initial vote. This was done amid an outcry by those who opposed this proposal. This time the additional funds passed.

The vast majority of the package went before the Rules Committee as the committee of original jurisdiction and all the other pieces of the package went to them for an appropriate rule. The major areas of discussion centered on the outside income limitation.

Since this is the one committee where all Democratic members are appointed by the Speaker, the Speaker should under normal circumstances have great control, especially on an issue that he felt strongly about. However, a number of the members of the Rules Committee had their own sources of outside income. It was clear that several of them were vehemently opposed to the outside income limitation and they were all very frank in their discussions both privately and publicly on the issue.

The Speaker of the House, after the House Rules Committee had held two days of hearings on the issue, met for breakfast with the Democratic members. A wide variety of different versions of that breakfast circulated around the Hill. They ranged from the committee members reproaching the Speaker to the Speaker screaming and yelling and threatening members of the committee. One story surfaced that the Speaker sidled up to one of the members after that breakfast and said, "I know I can count on your support on this important piece of legislation because I would sure hate to see all my good friends on the District of Columbia Committee next year."

Whatever the true story of that breakfast and whatever the content of the numerous phone calls back and forth, the committee voted to report the ethics resolution to the floor of the House with a rule, requested by the leadership, which greatly restricted amendments. The final vote was a straight party line vote.

The bill was taken up by the House on March 2.[9] The floor manager of the rule was Congressman Richard Bolling, who was the ranking Democrat on the Rules Committee. He, probably more than any other member, possessed a sense of timing that was crucial in the debate. As the minority members and those who opposed the outside income limitation urged the defeat of the rule, Congressman Bolling sat back and watched what was happening. He obviously felt that partisan juices needed some stirring because he closed the debate by taking the rostrum, turning his back to the Republican side of the chamber, and addressing his fellow Democrats in the following manner: "We know why they want this rule defeated." And then as the Republicans began to jeer, Bolling held his hand out to them and still addressing his fellow Democrats said, "Let them jeer, they reveal themselves." Bolling gave a rousing partisan speech, demanding that the Democrats do what the Democratic Congress needed to do to preserve the public's faith in the Democrats of the House. After he sat down the roll was called and the rule was adopted by a large margin, almost totally along partisan lines.

The debate which then ensued was one of great intensity and breadth. There were long monologues on the need for disclosure. Abuses of the frank and travel allowances were detailed; the failure of the commission to deal with certain other abuses was pointed out. Through all this time the Republicans argued that the outside income limitation was a terrible injustice and would indeed change the very nature of the House of Representatives.

Meanwhile, the members of the majority party sought to respond to each and every charge leveled at them by both Republicans and disenchanted Democrats who opposed the outside income limitation. It is significant to note that there was virtually no Democratic opposition to the package except by those who believed that the income limitation was unjust. The House easily moved through the disclosure provision and the first real debate began on the amendment to eliminate that section of the resolution which prohibited unofficial accounts and created an additional $5,000 in official allowances for members. The amendment offered by Congressman Frenzel was a reargument of the donnybrook that had erupted in the commission. Congressman Frenzel said that he had supported the abolition of unofficial office accounts and indeed had a resolution to achieve just that. He said he planned to introduce it immediately upon the passage of the amendment that he proposed.

The increase in allowances and the abolition of unofficial office accounts were put together deliberately, not by accident. The leadership of the commission and the House felt that standing alone the increase in allowances would certainly be defeated. Consequently, if the increase in allowances was to be salvaged at all, it was imperative that it be tied closely to the abolition of unofficial office accounts. Abolition of these accounts was an issue which was viewed as akin to motherhood and, consequently, the hope was that by tying the $5,000 increase to it, members would have the political courage to vote for it.

The vote on Congressman Frenzel's amendment turned out to be the closest vote of the day. The amendment was rejected, however, and subsequent amendments caused virtually no change in the commission's proposals.

When Morgan Murphy of Illinois offered his amendment to eliminate the limitation on outside earned income, it was already late in the evening. Still the debate raged on. A significant number of Democrats opposed the limitation. Otis Pike of New York and Claude Pepper of Florida gave perhaps the most eloquent denunciations of the impact the income limitation would have on the lives of members, their dependence on reelection, and their desire to remain in Congress. Finally, near the end of the debate, with the leadership and staff of the commission growing nervous about the possible outcome, the Speaker of the House went into the well to speak. One of the junior Democratic members sitting in the back row, noticing Tip O'Neill moving toward the rostrum—it is highly unusual for the Speaker to participate in the debate on an amendment—leaned over to his seatmate and whispered, "Uh oh, school's out."

Tip O'Neill stood before the House and in quiet tones eloquently and sternly pointed out to them that the outside income limitation was the "heart and soul" of the package, that much of what had been going on had gone on for the wrong reasons, and that this issue had to be faced. His speech was probably one of the most incisive ever given before the House of Representatives. It cut through the mood like a knife and, at the conclusion of his remarks, there was little doubt in anyone's mind what the final outcome would be.

When a vote finally came on the amendment, the first vote, a nonrecorded division, showed that the amendment was failing, but not overwhelmingly. Then a roll call vote was requested and the number of members that were willing to publicly register their vote against the income limitation reduced drastically. Upon the completion of that vote, the House moved quickly to pass the package by a large majority.

## CONCLUSION

In retrospect it is important to understand just how significant and how difficult it was for the House to undergo this process and pass the Code of Ethics.

Substantively, the basic issues involved were and remain fraught with uncertainties and conflicting considerations. What is the best balance to be drawn between the need to ensure conduct that will maintain the credibility of Congress and the need to make the job feasible and attractive? To what degree should the freedom and flexibility of all members be restricted to ward off the possibility of abuses of power or privilege by a few members? More specifically, how much financial disclosure is necessary and how can it be instituted and enforced without creating undue and unfair burdens for members? Should outside earned income be strictly limited to ward off serious potential conflicts of interests or will such limits ultimately have highly negative effects in making members overly dependent on congressional careers and in keeping persons of substantial worth or ability out of the Congress? How can gifts be handled so as to protect the integrity of the institution without unduly punishing members simply because they are members or making the task of record keeping burdensome? What resources do members need in terms of office expenses, travel, and the frank to do their jobs and how can highly political or personal uses be identified and controlled?

Politically, only the combination of a set of rather special events made passage of the code possible. First, great pressure for change was created by the Hays affair and Koreagate and by the passage of the pay raise. Indeed, the successful inclusion of a 15 percent income limitation can only be understood in the context of the roughly $13,000 salary increase that preceded it by only a few weeks. This pressure was mediated and maintained by the press and electronic media, which gave ethics reform wide coverage and strong support. In addition, the commitment of the leadership to reform was unusually strong. The issue was of great importance to Speaker O'Neill both substantively, because of his concern for the reputation of the Congress and politically, because he had played a key role in the passage of the pay raise. Thus, he deliberately chose to make ethics reform the first major test of his Speakership and he was unrelenting in his support.

Nonetheless, the victory was not gained without cost. The commission compromised on a few issues, left implementation questions vague in some areas, and avoided tackling hard questions in still other areas. Equally important, the ability of the leadership to work its will in the House on subsequent program proposals suffered. Certainly, resentments stirred by the passage of the Ethics Code played an important role in the defeat of the commission's administrative reform package six months later. But the impact extended beyond reform issues. Many members strongly resented the imposition of an outside income limitation, but politically they were unable to vote against it. Later, however, this was reflected in opposition to the leadership in a variety of ways. Furthermore, it was necessary to literally push aside certain powerful members of the House in bringing about ethics reform. These members were not without their resources and the bruised feelings that resulted subsequently manifested themselves in numerous ways which undercut the ability of leadership to push a variety of programs through the House. The control the leadership exhibited in passing the Code of Ethics thus has rarely been displayed on subsequent issues that have come before the House.

Both the substantive and political facets of this case study accordingly underscore the difficulties the Congress has in coming to grips with ethical issues. Nonetheless, the significance of the passage of the Code of Ethics should not be underestimated. It is true that conflict over the code continues, particularly with reference to the limitations on outside earned income (Congressional Quarterly 1980, 54–56, 84–88). In the House attempts have been made to suspend this provision and to limit its stringency in implementation. Moreover, the Senate, in fact, did defer the implementation of its rule until 1983. Still, the fundamental underpinnings of the code remain intact with regard to financial disclosure, unofficial office accounts, and gifts in both bodies and outside earned income in the House.[10] Indeed, the disclosure provisions, which at the time received so little attention in the floor debate, today provide the grist for annual newspaper stories of the income and assets of various members of Congress.

It is also true that the passage of the code has not prevented serious scandals (e.g., Abscam) or improved public perceptions of the Congress. In the former regard, however, adequate legal penalties against bribery have long been in force and it is fair to say that recent revelations have been a surprise to most members of Congress as well as the public. The critical problem is enforcement and here as elsewhere this issue raises problems that are exceedingly difficult to resolve. In the latter regard, no Code of Ethics Congress may implement is likely to improve public perceptions of the institution greatly. Approval or positive perception is primarily determined by policy performance. This was well understood by O'Neill, Bolling, Obey, and Hamilton at the time of the passage of the Ethics Code. Consequently, the passage of the code is a tribute to those who pushed it through the House. They believed that fundamentally the institution needed a revised Code of Ethics. They well recognized that the political benefits would be limited and temporary and in many ways their behavior can be seen as an act of political courage. In essence, the code gave members nothing politically, but rather subjected them to greater potential criticism by the media and opponents as well as greater limits on their freedom to conduct their personal affairs.

The passage of the Ethics Code was a necessary exercise for the House. Additional reform may be needed and may in the future be implemented. However, the House's actions in early 1977 represented a significant step by an institution that did what it had to do, not only because of the political conditions that existed at the time, but more importantly, to maintain its integrity and preserve its long-term ability to govern.

## NOTES

1. On the Sikes affair see Congressional Quarterly 1980, 22 and H. Rept. 94-1364.
2. See *Congressional Quarterly Weekly Reports,* June and July 1976.
3. For details on the task force recommendations see Congressional Quarterly 1980, 92. For floor debate see *Congressional Record,* 94th Cong., 2d sess., 1976, 21788–21825.
4. Even so, the proposal for a consolidated account system had to be modified to secure caucus approval and it was not until 1979 that a fully consolidated allowance system was instituted. See Congressional Quarterly 1980, 92, 95.
5. The first report of the Obey Commission dealt with scheduling changes. It was issued in late November 1976 and approved by the Democratic Caucus in early December 1976. Those reforms which required changes in rules were made in January 1977 at the start of the 95th Congress. See H. Doc. 95-23 (Commission 1977*c*).
6. The commission's ethics recommendations and supporting arguments can be found in its report, H. Doc. 95-73 (Commission 1977*b*). See also Commission 1977*a*, 219–279 for the record of its discussions and voting on these recommendations. In addition, see Congressional Quarterly 1979, 153–163.
7. For recent figures on outside earned income see Congressional Quarterly 1980, 75–88.
8. For a fuller account of Republican views see Commission 1977*a*, 235–248 and Commission 1977*b*, 25–29.
9. The debate can be found in *Congressional Record,* 95th Cong., 1st sess., 1977, H1566–H1633 (daily ed.).
10. Disclosure requirements in both bodies have been modified as a result of the 1978 Ethics in Government Act, P.L. 95-521. See Congressional Quarterly 1980, 56, 77, 80.

## REFERENCES

Commission on Administrative Review, U.S. Congress, House. 1977*a*. *Financial Ethics: Hearings and Meetings.* 95th Cong., 1st sess.

———. 1977*b*. *Ethics Report.* 95th Cong., 1st sess. H. Doc. 95-73.

———. 1977*c*. *Scheduling the Work of the House.* Communication from the chair. 95th Cong., 1st sess. H. Doc. 95-23.

Congressional Quarterly. 1980. *Congressional Ethics.* Washington: Congressional Quarterly Inc.

———. 1979. *Inside Congress.* Washington: Congressional Quarterly Inc.

# Part II. Managing the Work

## *The Context of Work Management*

Defining the jobs of individual participants constitutes an important facet of organizational design. However, there is more to organizations than the specific jobs or roles accorded to individuals. These jobs or roles are themselves patterned or interrelated, and they form organizational structures when viewed statically as sets of positions and organizational processes when viewed dynamically in terms of operations. Thus, though it is useful for some purposes to focus on jobs or roles from the perspective of the individual participant, it also must be recognized that these jobs or roles are not defined in isolation. Rather, they are defined in conjunction with one another and must be ordered so as to establish a system of coordinated effort, to establish what Chester Barnard aptly identified as the very basis of an organization.

### BASIC CONCEPTS

The articulation of jobs or roles so that they form or compose organizational structures and processes occurs primarily through the specification of differences in the content of the jobs or roles involved. These differences, in turn, derive from nonuniform distributions of two basic factors—organizational power and functional tasks.

Organizational power may be viewed as the ability to direct the conduct or behavior of other participants. As created or established by the organization, it derives from differential distributions of both authority and influence. That is, it involves and requires both differential distributions of normatively sanctioned rights to direct the conduct or behavior of others and differential distributions of control over the use of organizational rewards and penalties. The degree of hierarchy within the organization thus depends on the degree to which authority is differentially distributed and supported or reinforced by differential distributions of influence.

Similarly, organizations distribute or allocate tasks in differential or nonuniform ways. That is, they establish divisions of labor and the more elaborate and distinctive these divisions the higher the degree of specialization. Moreover, just as organizational authority and influence tend to be distributed in conjunction with one another, organizational power and functional tasks are not distributed at random or in a separate and independent manner. On the contrary, since organizations define structures and processes to satisfy output demands, distributions of tasks provide the context or framework for distributions of power. Distributions of power and tasks are thus interrelated so that the structures and processes established may satisfy both functional or specialization needs and integrative or coordinative needs.

It is true, of course, that the character of organizational structures and processes is also significantly affected by the degree of formalization, that is, by the degree to which the discretion or choices involved in performing specific jobs or roles is restricted or regulated by explicitly stated substantive or procedural rules. Formalization can modify and even serve as a substitute for differential distributions of power and can also substantially affect the nature of the division of labor. Nonetheless, the point remains that the structures and processes of an organization embody and conjoin distributions of power and tasks and take their basic shape and much of their basic character from the manner in which they do so.

Organizational structures and processes, in turn, can be classified in a variety of ways. For the purposes of this portion of the book, which focuses on managing the work, two very primary subsets may be identified and relied upon to frame the analysis. These are the support system and the productive system. The first may be seen as the set of structures and processes that mobilize and allocate both the raw materials required to produce organizational outputs and the goods and services required to transform these raw materials into outputs. The second may be viewed as the set of structures and processes that are directly and immediately engaged in doing the work of the organization, in producing the outputs.

## THE PRODUCTIVE SYSTEM

Productive systems are defined or elaborated with reference to the desired outputs of the organization as identified by their operating environments. In the case of the House these outputs are multiple and complex. They include legislation, representation, oversight, constituent service, and education. Nonetheless, separate structures and processes have not been elaborated for each of these outputs. Rather, power and tasks are distributed primarily with reference to producing legislative outputs, and other outputs are provided for or handled either through the structures and processes so defined or through partial extensions of them.

The productive system thus consists of four basic work units: member offices, committee offices, party offices, and the floor. These units organize discrete aspects or facets of the jobs or roles of members. In addition, member offices, committee offices, and party offices now also have sizable numbers of employees of their own, employees who, despite their formal designations as staff, are directly and integrally involved in doing the work of the units, in line activities or functions.

These four basic units, in turn, act and interact in various ways to perform the work of the House. Legislative outputs involve the staged and highly formalized interaction of all four. Constituent service is provided by member offices acting in a highly autonomous and piecemeal fashion. Oversight is in large part a product of work done by committee units both as part of the lawmaking process and ancillary to it. In contrast, representation and education are inchoate in the work of all units and the operation of all processes.

So defined and organized, the productive system of the House is currently subject to great stress. Two interrelated sources of stress exist. One derives from the same basic constraints previously identified in our discussion of individual job prescription and regulation, that is, democratic and separation of power values, electoral linkages, and the abstract and value-laden character of the work. These constraints are significant at the macro as well as the micro level. They limit capacity for specialization and integration and are largely responsible for the basic character and configuration of the units and processes which have long characterized the House. The other derives from more situational factors, primarily the current states of the workload and party strength.

The combined effects of these constraints and conditions pose a variety of difficult issues and problems for the House. More specialized capacity is needed for effective performance, but efforts to create it face a number of obstacles. The House's environment and work deny it an advantage that many organizations possess. It cannot control the time of its key participants nor compartmentalize their activities. Rather, members must be involved in all types of units and in all processes. As a consequence, finer divisions of labor entail finer divisions of members' time and more time conflicts, conflicts which the members themselves have power to resolve as they see fit. Conversely, efforts at reorganization or consolidation are also limited in their potential. Member offices are necessarily discrete and highly autonomous. Committee offices provide blunt mechanisms for dividing labor but are difficult for political reasons to realign.

Distinctive problems and issues also surround the use of staff as a means of enhancing specialization. The House's environment and work endow members with a legitimacy that staff cannot share. As has been suggested, it is this qualitatively-defined and normatively-based status, rather than the character of tasks performed, that primarily accounts for the designation of all nonmember participants on the work units as staff. Yet, the distinction between members and staff is not without functional significance. Members must be in control, must be the ultimate decision makers. The rub, however, is that the precise implications of this imperative, aside from the actual task of voting, are unclear. The result is to create a quandary for the House with respect to further additions of work unit staff. Workload pressures and the personal and political interests of members encourage such expansions. At the same time, there is both suspicion that staff additions multiply the workload and fear that they render members captives of those they are supposed to direct.

Performance needs include the enhancement of integrative capacity as well as specialized capacity. Throughout the House's history democratic values and electoral linkages have restricted differential distributions of authority and influence and, except in a few periods of unusual party strength, have severely limited its tolerance for hierarchy. The House has responded in large part by extensive formalization of its decision-making procedures. However, while procedural formalization can order and reduce conflict, it has limited ability to contribute positively to majority construction, to stimulate or produce legislative action. As a result, integrative capacity has typically been more fragile or tenuous in the House than specialized capacity.

This is even more true today than in past decades. Division of labor in the House has grown more elaborate and refined, placing greater demands on integrative capacity, as shown by the impact of the growth in the number and role of subcommittees. At the same time the ability of party to justify concentrations of power and to provide a nexus for majority construction appears to have waned, as reflected in the proliferation of ad hoc groups and the character of the contemporary caucus. Yet, opportunities for expanding integrative capacity are bleak. Extensions of formalization are limited in possibility and potential benefit. Steps that increase the power of party leaders raise the spectre of undemocratic practice and must be highly incremental (e.g., greater control over appointments to the Rules Committee or more flexibility in reference). Even then, they must be and have been exercised with caution to avoid provoking a counterreaction. Crisis can, of course, expand the potential for change and has done so recently in the budget process. Nonetheless, in general, the House faces the following dilemma with respect to integrative capacity: the need for expansion is generally perceived and acknowledged, but neither conceptions of authority nor the configuration of interests support extensive remedial action.

## THE SUPPORT SYSTEM

Support systems are not defined or elaborated with reference to the desired outputs of an organization, but rather with reference to the mobilization and allocation of the resources such outputs require or use. Hence, their structures and processes are differentiated in terms of basic and essential services or functions that pertain to the mobilization and allocation of the raw materials, goods, and services required for productive work, and they vary in terms of needs and costs in these regards as well as the character of the productive system involved. Prime examples of such services or functions are budgeting, personnel, information management, and procurement.

In all organizations overlaps exist between the productive system and the support system. In part, they occur because control of the support system constitutes an important aspect of overall direction and management. As a consequence the top echelons of an organization typically sit astride both systems. In part, however, they also occur because to varying degrees effective performance is promoted by vesting support functions in productive system units, such as recruitment of personnel.

In the case of the House the degree of overlap between the productive system and the support system is especially pronounced. The House, to be sure, has established a host of units which are external to and separate from the work units and which provide them with a variety of administrative and legislative support services. The units range from the Finance Office to the Doorkeeper's Office to the Barber Shops to the Congressional Research Service. Nonetheless, in terms of both task or activity and power or autonomy, support services or functions are less clearly and consistently differentiated and elaborated than in the case of many organizations.

First, the support units play no role in mobilizing and allocating the basic raw materials, that is, citizen demands and interests, that the House employs in doing its work. These are and must be mobilized and allocated by the work units themselves.

Second, the work units play substantial roles in mobilizing and allocating the goods and services they require or use. For example, they do much of their own recruiting and control hiring; they have great leeway to define staff salaries, jobs, and personnel policies; they have considerable discretion in the use of expense funds; and they mobilize much of the information they require on their own.

Third, a variety of units and processes in the productive system are highly involved in providing policy direction and operational management in the support system. Through statute and rule the floor limits or controls staff sizes, salary ranges, and basic categories and levels of expense spending on both work units and support units. Through the annual Legislative Branch Appropriations Act it funds staff and expense spending by both work units and support units and limits or controls aspects of such spending that are not fixed or permanently authorized. Operating within the parameters established by statute, rule, and appropriations, a number of regular work units and special member units serve as sources of policy direction and oversight with respect to staff and expense spending on other work units and the staffing and general operation of support units. Foremost among these is the Committee on House Administration, but several other standing committees and special committees and commissions are also involved. Similarly, several components of the productive system also participate to varying degrees in the management of the support units. The floor elects the heads of several key units; the Speaker has the responsibility for a number of others; and House Administration directly manages or operates a complex of support units and services of its own.

The manner in which the House currently articulates task and power relationships between work and support units poses a number of serious problems and issues. On the one hand, the restricted scope of the support units entails severe limitations in a number of key support functions. For example, centrally provided personnel services with respect to staff recruitment, job classification, and training are rudimentary. Similarly, no true budget process exists with respect to the mobilization and allocation of staff and expense resources. Rather, once again the House relies primarily on formalization, on fixed rules and formulas, to restrict and control spending. Such discretionary power as does exist is limited and exercised with a bias toward satisfying members, toward insuring that resources will be adequate, not minimizing costs. On the other hand, the complex maze of task and power relationships that exists among work units and support units fosters and entails confusion and redundancy within the set of support units that have been established. Thus, lines of accountability are often unclear and task responsibilities highly overlapping.

Nonetheless, the degree to which these conditions should be altered is far from clear. The present underdeveloped and undifferentiated character of support services or functions in the House is rooted in its character as a legislative body: in its limited tolerance for hierarchy; in the highly politicized character of its work; in the volatility and uncertainty of its workload and work schedule. As a consequence, though leeway exists for extension and refinement of the services support units provide, the bureaucratic model cannot be rigidly applied without entailing far more costs than benefits.

Similarly, the present confusion in lines of accountability and divisions of tasks that characterize the support units reflects more than the highly ad hoc process by which this set of units has developed. In a legislature decisive power in administration as well as legislation must be vested in the body as a whole. Clear lines of accountability, however, require concentrations of power both in House leaders and support unit officials. Such concentrations, in turn, threaten member control and thus must be limited even at the expense of distributions of power that impede effective direction and clear accountability. In addition, since the support units must serve over four hundred highly diverse members and hundreds of individual work units, overlapping and duplication of services have benefits as well as costs. Once again, all this is not to argue that leeway does not exist for clarifying lines of accountability and rationalizing the division of tasks. The point here too is rather that the House cannot rigidly apply the bureaucratic model, that it must feel its way toward distributions of power and tasks that balance universal organizational needs for effectiveness, efficiency, and accountability with its distinctive needs and limits as a legislature.

# 5. Controlling Legislative Time

*Thomas J. O'Donnell*

## INTRODUCTION

The role of the federal government has dramatically expanded as it attempts to find solutions to the range of complex problems facing our society. In particular, the demands placed upon the legislative branch have grown to staggering proportions. Both the expanded government agenda and the complexity of the issues before our lawmakers have severely challenged the ability of the legislature to perform its functions responsibly and productively. The way the Congress structures and uses its time is of critical importance to the quantity and quality of legislation emanating from the institution.

The effects of an expanded federal government agenda manifest themselves in the increase in legislative workload. The number of committees and subcommittees in the House now exceeds 180. In the 94th Congress (1975–77), House committees and subcommittees held 6,875 meetings in comparison to 3,210 such meetings during the 84th Congress (1955–57). Similarly, the number of hours that the House spends in session has almost doubled from 937 in the 84th Congress to 1,789 in the 94th Congress (Commission 1977*a*, 1:634, 636).

Effective time management is a significant challenge to individual members of the House, to committees and subcommittees, and to the majority party leadership. Their success in meeting that challenge bears directly on the ability of the House to carry out its representative, legislative, and oversight responsibilities.

Data gathered by the House Commission on Administrative Review (the Obey Commission) in 1977 shed considerable light on the complexities of time management in the House. In May and July of that year, the commission asked the appointments secretaries of 100 members of the House to keep a log of how those members spent their time over a period of a week. Their cooperation helped to produce a data base of 493 member days. Much of the information in this chapter is the product of five-day averages (Monday through Friday) derived from these daily logs.[1]

Significant time management challenges confront three sets of actors in the House of Representatives: individual members, committee and subcommittee chairs, and party leaders. Each group faces a unique set of time demands and, in attempting to meet those demands, each operates within some specific and imposing constraints. This chapter will look at these three groups in sequence and examine the nature of their time management problems, the success of their efforts to resolve those problems, and the continuing impact of time utilization ineffectiveness on the operations of the House of Representatives.

## INDIVIDUAL MEMBERS

To say that the demands on a member's time are heavy is an understatement. Representatives must allocate the time in their daily and weekly schedules among a host of activities in Washington and out of town, both in their districts and elsewhere. A good share of a member's time is devoted to activities that take place in Washington; some activities such as floor sessions can only take place in the nation's capital. Yet the job also requires that a member spend a good portion of time outside of Washington, visiting constituents, holding hearings, inspecting federal projects or, on occasion, consulting with foreign governments. One member's comments describe well the congressional environment:

> There are just too many votes, too many issues, too many meetings, too many attention-demanding situations. We're going to committee meetings, subcommittee meetings, caucuses—a caucus of the class with which you were elected here, the rural caucus, the steel caucus, you name it—and we're seeing constituents and returning phone calls and trying to rush back and forth to the district, and then we're supposed to understand what we're voting on when we get to the House floor. It gets madcap from time to time. (Drew 1978, 84)

Members vary a great deal in how they allocate their time. Political situations in the home district, length of service, partisan considerations, committee and leadership positions, or personal interest

**Table 5.1.** ***Allocation of Members' Time (Monday–Friday)***

| *Place* | *Average Daily Time* |
|---|---|
| *On the Floor and in Committee* | **4 hrs. 25 mins.** |
| chamber | |
| committee hearings (includes standing and select committee meetings) | |
| committee business | |
| committee markups | |
| committee other | |
| subcommittee business | |
| subcommittee hearings | |
| subcommittee markups | |
| subcommittee other | |
| conference meetings | |
| *In Office* | **3 hrs. 19 mins.** |
| with constituents | |
| with organized groups | |
| with state, local, and executive branch officials | |
| with personal and committee staff | |
| with other members | |
| answering mail and signing letters | |
| preparing legislation and speeches | |
| reading | |
| on telephone | |
| other (with press, Senators, office management, and other) | |
| *In Other Washington Locations (including Capitol Hill)* | **2 hrs. 2 mins.** |
| with constituents in the Capitol | |
| at events | |
| with the leadership | |
| with other members | |
| with informal groups | |
| at party meetings | |
| with state, local, and executive branch officials | |
| personal time | |
| other | |
| *Outside Washington* | **1 hr. 40 mins.** |
| travel time | |
| time in the district | |
| time spent elsewhere | |

SOURCE: Commission 1977*a*, 1:631.

in some issue or substantive area all may lead them to develop different sets of priorities dictating how time should be spent. If this assumption—that members' priorities differ—is correct, then one should expect to find discernible patterns among subsets of legislators as to how time is spent across a whole range of activities. On the other hand, given the number of responsibilities members share, we should also expect to find a fair amount of time being spent by all members on a variety of common or familiar activities. In addition, one would expect the priorities of some members to remain relatively stable over time with, for example, an emphasis on constituent work, while in other cases priorities shift as influence in the House increases.

The Obey Commission's final report documented the fact that members' days are long, fragmented, and often unpredictable (Commission 1977*a*, 1:633). Following the work of that commission, further analysis has been completed which reveals the existence of various patterns of time use among subgroups of the House.

The way legislators allocate their time can be condensed into four general categories: time on the floor and in committee and subcommittee meetings, time in their offices, time in other locations in Washington including Capitol Hill, and time outside of Washington. Table 5.1 lists the various activities that compose each of these four broad categories and the average time spent on each.

The Obey Commission study reported that, on the average, members worked an eleven-hour day in which 4 hours and 25 minutes were consumed on the floor and in committee and subcommittee meetings, 3 hours and 19 minutes in their offices, 2 hours in other locations in Washington, and, finally, 1 hour and 40 minutes outside Washington (Commission 1977*a*, 1:631).

Further analysis of these data indicates that factors such as party, seniority, and number of committee assignments directly affect the allocation of time by members. The data presented in table 5.2 show that Republicans spent an average of almost 40 minutes more a day on the floor than did Democrats. However, Democrats were found to spend an average of 30 minutes more than Republicans in committee and subcommittee meetings. Furthermore, the amount of time spent by Democrats in subcommittee meetings was almost double that of Republicans. Approximately 43 minutes per day was spent by Democrats in subcommittee meetings in comparison to the 25 minutes spent by Republicans. Democrats evenly divided their time in subcommittee sessions between markups and hearings, while Republicans spent almost twice as much time in subcommittee hearings as in markups.

**Table 5.2. *Allocation of Representatives' Time by Party (Monday–Friday)***

| *Place* | *Democrats (N = 332)* | *Republicans (N = 161)* |
|---|---|---|
| *On Floor and in Committee* | **4:27** | **4:32** |
| Chamber | 2:45 | 3:22 |
| Committee meetings | :49 | :36 |
| Hearings | :11 | :04 |
| Business | :03 | :04 |
| Markups | :32 | :22 |
| Other | :03 | :06 |
| Subcommittee meetings | :43 | :25 |
| Hearings | :19 | :14 |
| Business | :03 | :02 |
| Markups | :18 | :08 |
| Other | :03 | :01 |
| Conference meetings | :10 | :09 |
| *In Office* | **3:22** | **3:09** |
| With constituents | :22 | :15 |
| With organized groups | :12 | :03 |
| With state, local, and executive branch officials | :04 | :05 |
| With personal and committee staff | :56 | :49 |
| With other members | :06 | :04 |
| Answering mail and signing letters | :43 | :49 |
| Preparing legislation and speeches | :10 | :17 |
| Reading | :10 | :13 |
| On telephone | :27 | :21 |
| Other | :12 | :13 |
| *Other Washington Locations* | **2:03** | **1:48** |
| With constituents in Capitol | :09 | :09 |
| At events | :35 | :31 |
| With leadership | :01 | :06 |
| With other members | :08 | :07 |
| With informal groups | :05 | :08 |
| At party meetings | :04 | :07 |
| With state, local, and executive branch officials | :05 | :06 |
| Personal time | :35 | :17 |
| Other | :21 | :17 |
| *Other* | **1:35** | **1:41** |

Although both Democrats and Republicans spent just over three hours daily in the office, how they allocated their time there differs when the nature of activity is examined. Democrats met more frequently in the office with constituents and organized groups than did Republicans. In fact, they spent four times as much time with organized groups. On the average, Republicans spent 1 hour and 40 minutes preparing legislation and speeches, answering mail, reading, and talking on the telephone, while Democrats spent 1 hour and 30 minutes on the same activities. In other locations in the Capitol, Republicans spent almost three times as much time meeting with the leadership and in party meetings than did Democrats.

There appear to be several reasons for the differences one finds in the time allocation patterns of Democrats and Republicans. The task of the minority is to offer counterproposals or alternatives to the majority program and, in the face of failure, to obstruct floor business through procedural motions. Galloway (1961, 157) once noted that the task of the minority party should be "to watch and criticize the majority party, to inspect and review the way in which it is conducting business, to point out its errors, and to expose its misdeeds." The results of the Obey Commission time survey indicate that Republicans spend more time on the floor than Democrats and less time in committees. The Republican party's inability to secure approval of suggested alternatives at the committee and subcommittee level in the face of large Democratic majorities spurs them to devote their energies to the floor. The fact that Republicans spend more time on the floor is illustrated by the propensity of at least a few members of the minority to spend countless hours on the floor watching over the majority. Often these members offer procedural motions to obstruct the will of the majority. One account of members' time strategies noted that these individuals "rely on a vigilance, a flair for the dramatic and an intimate knowledge of the rules to embarrass their opponents, to block or delay House actions they oppose, and to bargain for concessions" (*Congressional Quarterly* 1979, 1342).

Organized groups are eager to have their interests considered by the Congress. Consequently, it is not surprising to find them spending more time with Democrats than Republicans, given the fact that Democrats run the committees and generally have a very large say as to the content of legislation that will be considered during a session.

The findings also indicate that seniority influences time utilization by members. Overall, table 5.3 reveals that as seniority increases members spend less time on the floor and in committee and subcommittee meetings. Freshmen spent an average of an hour

**Table 5.3.** ***Allocation of Representatives' Time by Seniority (Monday–Friday)***

| *Place* | *First Term* (N = 99) | *Second Term* (N = 183) | *3–5 Terms* (N = 123) | *6 or More Terms* (N = 88) |
|---|---|---|---|---|
| *On Floor and in Committee* | **5:03** | **4:50** | **4:13** | **3:28** |
| Chamber | 3:54 | 2:53 | 2:52 | 2:06 |
| Committee meetings | :35 | :57 | :44 | :31 |
| Hearings | :10 | :10 | :06 | :09 |
| Business | :05 | :02 | :04 | :02 |
| Markups | :17 | :41 | :29 | :14 |
| Other | :03 | :04 | :05 | :06 |
| Subcommittee meetings | :26 | :52 | :27 | :35 |
| Hearings | :17 | :21 | :14 | :16 |
| Business | :01 | :05 | :01 | :03 |
| Markups | :08 | :24 | :11 | :08 |
| Other | :00 | :02 | :01 | :08 |
| Conference meetings | :08 | :08 | :10 | :16 |
| *In Office* | **3:25** | **3:21** | **3:28** | **2:43** |
| With constituents | :18 | :20 | :18 | :11 |
| With organized groups | :09 | :07 | :14 | :06 |
| With state, local, and executive branch officials | :03 | :04 | :03 | :07 |
| With personal and committee staff | :59 | :56 | :51 | :49 |
| With other members | :07 | :06 | :05 | :04 |
| Answering mail and signing letters | :50 | :45 | :50 | :31 |
| Preparing legislation and speeches | :15 | :12 | :10 | :14 |
| Reading | :08 | :09 | :17 | :10 |
| On telephone | :25 | :28 | :25 | :21 |
| Other | :11 | :14 | :15 | :10 |
| *Other Washington Locations* | **2:10** | **2:05** | **2:05** | **1:40** |
| With constituents in Capitol | :07 | :08 | :14 | :06 |
| At events | :45 | :36 | :28 | :26 |
| With leadership | :02 | :02 | :06 | :02 |
| With other members | :10 | :05 | :10 | :05 |
| With informal groups | :09 | :05 | :09 | :01 |
| At party meetings | :01 | :08 | :05 | :03 |
| With state, local, and executive branch officials | :04 | :05 | :05 | :05 |
| Personal time | :25 | :37 | :24 | :26 |
| Other | :27 | :19 | :24 | :26 |
| *Other* | **1:06** | **1:28** | **1:15** | **3:28** |

more in the House chamber and in committee and subcommittee sessions than members in their second to fifth terms and almost two hours more than senior representatives. Yet, when specific activities within this broad category are examined, different patterns of time use emerge. The second-termers (the "Watergate Class") spent over 30 more minutes in committee and subcommittee meetings than the other groups. Moreover, this class spent 24 minutes and 21 minutes in subcommittee markups and hearings respectively, while the other tenure groups allocated twice as much time to hearings as to markups. The data also point out the propensity of the more senior members to be selected for conference meetings. Representatives who had served for six terms or more spent an average of 16 minutes in conference meetings as opposed to 10 minutes spent by third- to fifth-termers and 8 minutes by first- and second-termers.

In the office, second-termers spent slightly more time with constituents than did freshmen and third- to fifth-termers, and twice as much time as their most senior colleagues. Overall, the more junior members spent considerably more time answering mail and signing letters than did the senior members as indicated by the 48 minutes spent by members with less than six terms and 31 minutes spent by members with six terms or more.

However, senior members seem to be sought out more often in the office by state and local officials and executive branch personnel, as illustrated by the fact that they spent twice as much time with these officials than did any other group of members. Outside the office and off the floor, however, freshmen spent almost twice as long at events on Capitol Hill and in other Washington locations. Members with two to five terms are occupied more often with the leadership and party meetings than are freshmen and senior legislators.

The Watergate class proves to be a very active group of individuals in handling all aspects of their jobs. One majority leader has noted that they are "younger, better educated and more conscientious than other classes" (Rieselbach 1979, 397). They seem to think they have a mandate from their constituents to improve the quality of legislation that emanates from the House. They were found to spend more time than any other group in meetings, which can be attributed to their direct interest in actual formulation of public policy and also the recent decentralization within the institution. The growth and autonomy of subcommittees allowed them to acquire positions of influence in the House at an early stage of their careers. In Randall Ripley's words, they "do not let the fact of their relatively junior status inhibit them from contributing to the legislative process" (1978, 29). The norm of apprenticeship has been severely eroded, as reflected in the activities and input of this class.

In addition, the results of the time survey tend to support Asher's findings (1973) related to the learning of legislative norms. In interviewing freshman members of the House, Asher found that members thought that spending time on the floor to learn House rules was a worthwhile experience. The results reported above indicate that freshmen spent more time in the chamber than any other group. Apparently, freshmen continue to view time spent on the floor as a useful experience not only in learning procedure but also in aiding their reelection chances through good attendance records during votes.

Senior members who have relatively safe seats are generally the most influential members in the House. During their careers they have built up reputations in certain policy areas and special relationships with outside groups both in the government and the private sector. Thus, it is not surprising to find these members spending more time with state and local officials and executive branch officials.

The leadership also recognizes the talents of established members by selecting them more frequently for conference committees. This is confirmed by the finding that they spend much larger chunks of time hammering out legislation with their Senate counterparts. George Goodwin explains the rationale behind this process: "Invariably the leadership is making accommodation to the committee system—especially on important matters, senior members for the majority and minority are designated" (1970, 245).

Another important factor in time allocation is the number of committee and subcommittee assignments a member holds. Those members with seven or more assignments were found to spend more time in all locations in Washington than colleagues with fewer assignments (see table 5.4).

Members with seven or more assignments spent 30 minutes more on the floor and 15 minutes more in committee and subcommittee meetings than their colleagues with fewer assignments. For both groups, time in full committees was devoted primarily to markups and time in subcommittee meetings was evenly divided between hearings and markups. In contrast, the data reveal that those members with fewer assignments spent more time in conference committee meetings. Representatives with seven or more assignments also spent considerably more time in activities in their offices than members with fewer assignments, as evidenced by their spending almost twice as much time answering mail and signing

**Table 5.4.** ***Allocation of Representatives' Time by Number of Assignments (Monday–Friday)***

| *Place* | *6 or Fewer Assignments (N = 250)* | *7 or More Assignments (N = 243)* |
|---|---|---|
| *On Floor and in Committee* | **4:09** | **4:48** |
| Chamber | 2:44 | 3:10 |
| Committee meetings | :42 | :47 |
| Hearings | :06 | :12 |
| Business | :04 | :02 |
| Markups | :28 | :29 |
| Other | :04 | :04 |
| Subcommittee meetings | :31 | :43 |
| Hearings | :15 | :20 |
| Business | :01 | :04 |
| Markups | :12 | :17 |
| Other | :03 | :02 |
| Conference meetings | :12 | :08 |
| *In Office* | **2:55** | **3:32** |
| With constituents | :09 | :22 |
| With organized groups | :09 | :09 |
| With state, local, and executive branch officials | :05 | :03 |
| With personal and committee staff | :55 | :53 |
| With other members | :03 | :08 |
| Answering mail and signing letters | :33 | :57 |
| Preparing legislation and speeches | :11 | :13 |
| Reading | :10 | :11 |
| On telephone | :27 | :24 |
| Other | :13 | :12 |
| *Other Washington Locations* | **1:57** | **2:00** |
| With constituents in Capitol | :09 | :08 |
| At events | :32 | :36 |
| With leadership | :04 | :02 |
| With other members | :09 | :06 |
| With informal groups | :08 | :04 |
| At party meetings | :03 | :06 |
| With state, local, and executive branch officials | :05 | :05 |
| Personal time | :28 | :31 |
| Other | :19 | :22 |
| *Other* | **2:03** | **1:12** |

**Table 5.5. *Allocation of Representatives' Time Outside Washington (Monday–Sunday)***

| | In the District (in minutes) | Elsewhere (in minutes) |
|---|---|---|
| *Seniority* | | |
| First term (N = 99) | 115 | 7 |
| Second term (N = 183) | 107 | 44 |
| 3 to 5 terms (N = 123) | 80 | 20 |
| 6 or more terms (N = 88) | 60 | 112 |
| *Party* | | |
| Democrats (N = 332) | 108 | 42 |
| Republicans (N = 161) | 62 | 42 |
| *Assignments* | | |
| 6 or fewer (N = 250) | 80 | 66 |
| 7 or more (N = 243) | 108 | 19 |

letters and slightly more time meeting with constituents, interest groups, and others. Since members with fewer assignments tend to be more senior than members with more assignments, these results are not unexpected.[2]

We have thus far not commented on the impact of seniority, party, and assignments on time spent outside Washington, because the results in tables 5.2, 5.3, and 5.4 are anomalous and perplexing. Note, for example, that Republicans spend more time out of Washington than Democrats; that senior members spend more time out of Washington than junior members; that those with six or fewer assignments, who also tend to be more senior, spend more time out of Washington than those with seven or more assignments. However, the data in these tables combine all activities outside of Washington and, as noted earlier, are based only on Monday through Friday entries in office logs. If we subdivide the category and expand the time period to Monday through Sunday, so as to include the weekend, most of the difficulties disappear.

Table 5.5 indicates that freshman members do spend more time in their districts than senior members, though senior members spend more time outside Washington totally. Nor is this surprising.

Robert Peabody (1979, 134) describes well the main challenge confronting freshman members: "In the absence of drastic redistricting, a major election tide, or a personal scandal, the vast majority of

Congressmen are most vulnerable electorally at the beginning of their political careers." Conversely, senior members are generally safer politically, better known, more influential in Washington, and more in demand outside the district.

This table also indicates that, with weekends included when Democrats are free of the burdens of running the House, they spend more time in their districts than do Republicans. Similarly, members with seven or more assignments do, in fact, spend more time in their districts than members with six or fewer. As might be expected since they tend to be more junior, they simply spend far less time elsewhere.

In sum, these data suggest that while all members are chronically pressed for time, the relative strength of particular demands on their time may vary according to their positions in the House. The way a member uses his time will be shaped in part by his party membership, by the length of his tenure in the House, and by the number of committees and subcommittees on which he serves. We note, then, not only that there are differences in the way individual members allocate their time, but that these are patterned differences.

But we should also note that all members operate under significant limitations on their ability to fully control their own time. The data indicate that members' time is widely dispersed among a number of activities, and that their ability to concentrate time on any single activity is severely constrained by the abundance and complexity of the demands that confront them. There is just so much to do and so little time in which to do it.

## COMMITTEES

Committees and subcommittees must schedule concentrated work periods, especially around budget deadlines. The manner in which they coordinate their scheduling varies from committee to committee. The continuum runs from developing a long-range plan for an entire session to the opposite of little or no advance scheduling. The degree of coordination between the full committee and subcommittees varies widely as well. Moreover, the workload and jurisdictional prerogatives of each committee influence the scheduling of committee business. Finally, the high number of assignments per member complicates the ability to plan and conduct committee and subcommittee business in a timely and efficient fashion.

Long- and short-range planning are used by committees in bringing legislation to the floor. Both the Budget Committee and the Science and Technology Committee develop long-range planning for an entire session, whereas the Agriculture and Interior committees allow for little if any planning (Committee on House Administration 1977, 5). The majority of committees fall somewhere between these extremes.

Those few committees which engage in long-range planning coordinate their scheduling more closely with their respective subcommittees than those committees which rarely plan a work schedule in advance. The relationship between full and subcommittees has been further strained by the passage of rule changes which have fostered the independent operation of subcommittees.[3] These changes, along with the proliferation of these units, have further exacerbated the difficulties encountered by committees in planning their work. As long as coordination is lacking, long-range scheduling will continue to be the exception rather than the rule.

Room availability and caucus meetings also limit effective advance scheduling. Under the rules of the House, all committees must schedule hearings one week in advance. However, some committees such as Education and Labor must schedule meetings three weeks in advance due to the shortage of available rooms (Committee on House Administration 1977, 5). Other meetings which are scheduled in advance, particularly at the subcommittee level, are sometimes preempted by caucus or full committee meetings. Although the frequency of cancelled meetings is not high, and most meetings are rescheduled, the legislative timetable of some committees is disrupted by these occurrences. A study by the House Information Systems (Committee on House Administration 1977, 9) during the first session of the 94th Congress indicated, for instance, that Education and Labor cancelled twenty-five to thirty percent of its full committee meetings and the Interior Committee cancelled three out of four meetings. The study reports that the Democratic Caucus was the biggest cause of cancelled meetings cited by committees.

The scheduling of committee business is not only affected by the absence of advance planning on the part of a large number of legislative units, but also by the uneven distribution of work among committees and subcommittees. Table 5.6 indicates that some committees such as Appropriations, Interstate and Foreign Commerce, and Agriculture are very busy, while other committees have little to do.

During the first session of the 95th Congress, for example, 25% of all meetings that took place in the House were conducted by the Appropriations Committee and its subcommittees (Commission 1977*a*, 1:646). One can well understand the problems encountered

**Table 5.6. *Number of Meetings by Committee, 95th Congress, 1st Session (January–May)***

| *Committee* | *Full Committee Meetings* | *Sub-committee Meetings* | *Total* | *Percent of Total* |
|---|---|---|---|---|
| Agriculture | 61 | 91 | 152 | 6.0 |
| Appropriations | 25 | 609 | 634 | 24.9 |
| Armed Services | 39 | 112 | 151 | 5.9 |
| Banking, Finance, and Urban Affairs | 21 | 83 | 104 | 4.1 |
| Budget | 32 | 0 | 32 | 1.3 |
| District of Columbia | 5 | 22 | 27 | 1.1 |
| Education and Labor | 15 | 100 | 115 | 4.5 |
| Government Operations | 6 | 71 | 77 | 3.0 |
| House Administration | 31 | 39 | 70 | 2.7 |
| Interstate and Foreign Commerce | 19 | 163 | 182 | 7.1 |
| Interior and Insular Affairs | 23 | 86 | 109 | 4.3 |
| International Relations | 49 | 102 | 151 | 5.9 |
| Judiciary | 9 | 129 | 138 | 5.4 |
| Merchant Marine | 19 | 62 | 81 | 3.3 |
| Post Office and Civil Service | 8 | 72 | 80 | 3.1 |
| Public Works and Transportation | 9 | 66 | 75 | 2.9 |
| Rules | 37 | NA | 37 | 1.4 |
| Science and Technology | 16 | 121 | 137 | 5.4 |
| Small Business | 4 | 30 | 34 | 1.3 |
| Standards of Official Conduct | 7 | NA | 7 | .3 |
| Veterans | 9 | 20 | 29 | 1.1 |
| Ways and Means | 27 | 52 | 79 | 3.1 |
| Assassinations | 6 | 0 | 6 | .2 |
| Congressional Operations | 0 | 0 | 0 | 0 |
| Energy | 11 | 0 | 11 | .04 |
| Ethics | 5 | 0 | 5 | .02 |
| Narcotics Abuse and Control | 6 | 0 | 6 | .02 |
| Outer Continental Shelf | 9 | 0 | 9 | .04 |
| Aging | 10 | 2 | 12 | .05 |
| Total | 518 | 2,032 | 2,550 | 100 |

SOURCE: Commission 1977*a*, 1:646.

by the chair of the Appropriations Committee and the subcommittee chairs in scheduling meetings. The data above also reveal that most meetings (82%) took place in subcommittees, as the large majority of committees conduct their business at this level. This figure can be partially attributed to the effects of the so-called "subcommittee bill of rights" enacted in 1973. As Morris Fiorina (1977, 4) describes these changes, "subcommittee jurisdictions were fixed, full committee chairmen could no longer establish vague subcommittee jurisdictions in order to maximize their own flexibility in assigning legislation."

A contributing factor to this uneven distribution of work is the jurisdictional overlap in a number of issue areas. Data collected by the Commission on Administrative Review in 1977 for the first session of the 95th Congress revealed that nineteen different committees received energy-related matters and that eighteen committees received health-related matters (Commission 1977*a*, 1:646–647). This practice of overlap precludes the Congress from coordinating its work in various policy areas and from predicting with any certainty when legislation will be ready for consideration on the floor.

The inability of the House to overhaul its committee system since the 1946 Reorganization Act has further worsened the uneven distribution of labor. Each committee is a separate fiefdom competing with others for jurisdictional control over the countless number of bills introduced each session. Some committees have control over large policy areas while others control smaller areas. It is difficult for the House to achieve comprehensive policymaking under the current jurisdictional alignment. Jurisdictions established in 1946 are not as viable today, as the issues have increased both in number and complexity.

Multiple assignments also limit the ability of committees to report legislation to the floor on time. In the first session of the 95th Congress, each member had an average of 6.1 committee and subcommittee assignments; this figure includes over 250 members who had four or more subcommittee assignments (Commission 1977*a*, 1:640–641). It is no wonder that members often had more than one meeting scheduled simultaneously. Some committees, such as Budget and Agriculture, take a member's prior commitments into account when planning meeting times, while others, Judiciary and Interior for example, do not consider members' conflicts in the planning of committee sessions (Committee on House Administration 1977, 8).

Committee scheduling is perhaps the most complicated aspect of legislative operations in the House. The shortage of appropriate rooms, the unevenness in committee workloads, the overlapping of substantive jurisdictions, and the multiplicity of individual assignments make coordination of committee scheduling a Herculean task. In their efforts to effectively plan and manage their time, all committees operate under enormous and persistent handicaps.

## PARTY LEADERS

The House leaders must determine the legislative agenda and then set up a schedule which permits a reasonable length of time for the consideration of legislation. However, a number of factors must be taken into account before the leadership can decide on a firm schedule: fixed elements in the schedule (e.g., constitutional requirements, holidays and recesses, budget deadlines and special calendars), committee and subcommittee timetables, minority party wishes, individual members' schedules, and the time needed to build majorities for the passage of their programs. Consequently, both long- and short-term planning are utilized during each session.

The majority leadership's control over scheduling is not only constrained by law and the House rules, but also by committee and subcommittee leaders, the minority party and—at times—by individual members. The scheduling decisions arrived at by the majority leadership are made primarily after consultation with committee leaders. Both monthly and weekly agendas are hammered out in such sessions. The leadership must often prod committees to report out legislation for floor consideration. Minority wishes are also taken into account in planning a floor schedule. The minority needs time to develop alternatives to the majority program. Finally, individual members' schedules are sometimes taken into consideration before firming up a floor agenda for a particular period. After allowing for the fixed elements in the schedule and these other discretionary factors, the leadership makes choices in managing the time of the House which often result in early session lag, late session rush, and concentration of legislative activity during midweek and before budget deadlines.

Figure 5.1 shows, for instance, that the House spends considerably less time on the floor in the early part of a session than later on. The volume of business conducted on the floor is at its lowest level in January and peaks in June and July and then again in the fall. The House was in session four times more often in June than in January during the second session of the 94th Congress (1976). Similarly, the

Figure 5.1. *Floor Activity, 94th Congress (1975–1977)*

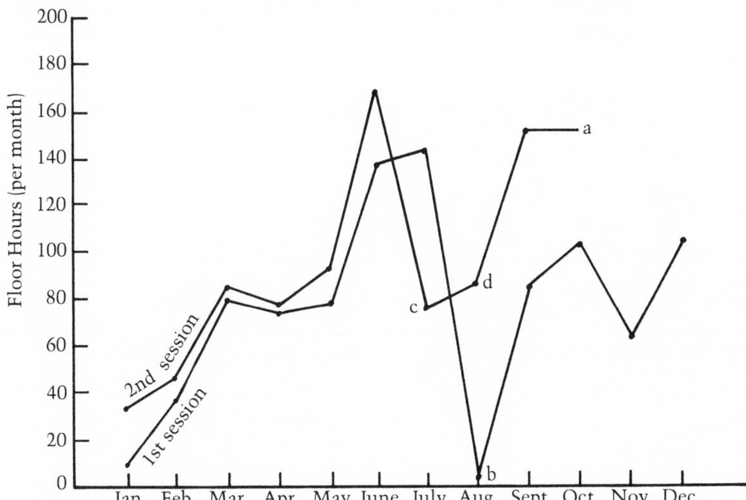


[a]House adjourned October 1, 1976
[b]August recess, 1st session
[c]Democratic party convention
[d]Republican party convention
*Source*: Commission, 1977, 1:19.

number of committee and subcommittee meetings taking place in January is much smaller than in February and March. Over 500 meetings occurred in March of 1976 as opposed to 131 in January of that same year. (See figures 5.2 and 5.3.)

Although the leadership attempts to induce committees to meet earlier in the session, early session lag is still the rule. Members use this time for organizing their offices and servicing district requests. Committees use this opportunity to set legislative priorities and to make plans for handling these priorities. The leadership has made greater use of the suspension calendar to accommodate sponsors of bills, especially during the late part of a session when there is an influx of legislation awaiting floor action. One observer of Congress has noted that "many of these bills would die if they were not moved through the House quickly in this fashion" (Ripley 1978, 215).

Another accommodation which continues to operate is the handling of the bulk of the legislative agenda, both on the floor and in meetings, during midweek. Furthermore, when the House is in

Figure 5.2. *Committee Activity, 94th Congress (1975–1977)*

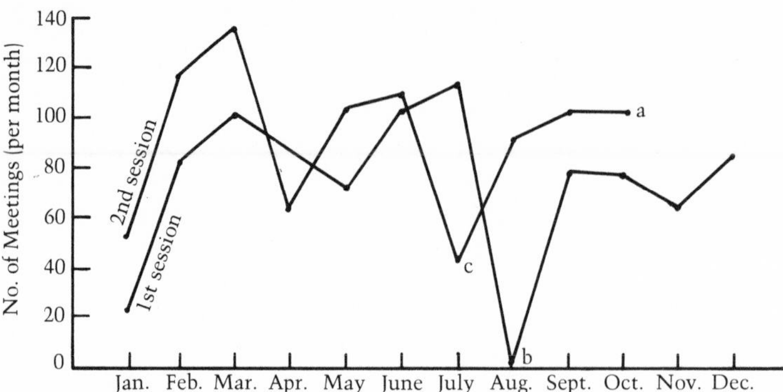


[a]House adjourned October 1, 1976
[b]August recess, 1st session
[c]Democratic party convention
*Source*: Commission, 1977, 1:21.

Figure 5.3. *Subcommittee Activity, 94th Congress (1975–1977)*

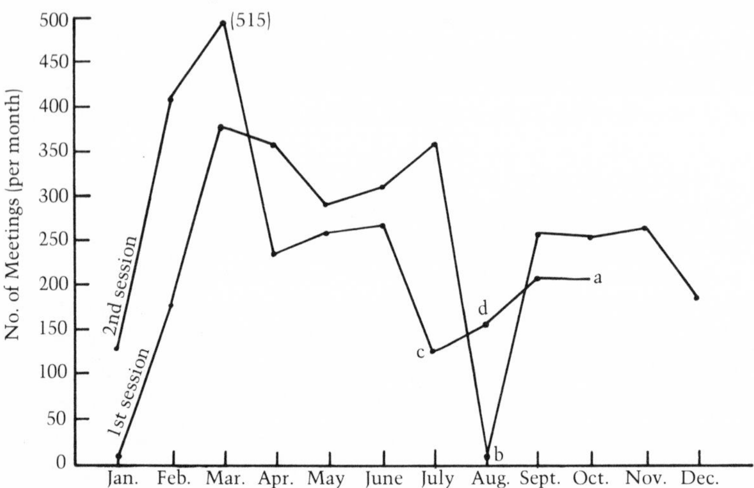


[a]House adjourned October 1, 1976
[b]August recess, 1st session
[c]Democratic party convention
[d]Republican party convention
*Source*: Commission, 1977, 1:22.

session on Mondays, votes are usually taken late in the day so that members returning from their districts will be present to cast their votes.

As a consequence of this crowding, members often have two or more meetings occurring simultaneously. In 1977, the Obey Commission found that on a daily basis 38% of the members had meeting conflicts and that, on the ten busiest days of the first session of the 95th Congress, 91% of the members experience at least one meeting conflict (Commission 1977*a*, 1:642). The Obey report also indicated that 83% of all conflicts occurred Tuesday through Thursday. Interestingly, a good deal of this conflict was among subcommittees of the same full committee.

Scheduling conflicts also occur between the floor and committee and subcommittee meetings. Again, the bulk of legislative work in midweek and the late session rush highlight this problem. The commission found that 85% of all such conflicts occurred Tuesday through Thursday and that, on 54% of the days the House was in session, there were more than ten instances of committee and subcommittee meetings during recorded votes (Commission 1977*a*, 1:644). The need for members to go back and forth to the floor inhibits their ability to deal with any one problem during a particular meeting. The same disruptive effect occurs when witnesses are testifying before a legislative unit. As a glaring example of workday fragmentation, one legislator who occupies an office in the far corner of the Rayburn Building told staff members of the Obey Commission that he consumes about half an hour every time he goes back and forth to the floor.

The suspension calendar has increasingly become a significant legislative tool, as indicated by one staff member's remarks during a late session rush in an election year: "Everybody and his dog are trying to get on the suspension calendar" (Drew 1978, 80). Understandably, the use of the suspension calendar has also come under criticism by some members. Ned Patterson, a retired member from upstate New York, has noted that "this is a symptom of the incredible overload that we deal with every day. There's no way that a member of this body can honestly say that he fully understands what he is voting on" (Drew 1978, 83).

Well-intentioned accommodations can, however, cause havoc in individual committee meetings. For instance, it is very difficult for a committee chair to secure sufficient blocks of time to consider legislative matters if the membership is constantly running back and forth to the floor or other meetings. Indicative of this problem is one chair's remarks that he could finish up his major bill in three days, but it takes one and a half months because it is difficult to get members to attend.[4]

In addition to the above-mentioned accommodations, a number of other proposals have been implemented to deal with aspects of the scheduling problem. The House agreed to Obey Commission recommendations, strongly supported by the leadership, to set forth a fixed schedule of work periods during a session based on budget deadlines which would provide committees with concentrated periods of time, fixed adjournment times, permission for committees and subcommittees to meet while the House is in session, and the clustering of votes on noncontroversial rules.[5] Fixed work periods cemented district times into members' schedules and, in so doing, allowed them more certainty in planning their schedules in Washington and in the district. Also, with fixed adjournment times, members can make it home on Fridays with some certainty. Although these recommendations were well intended and have had some positive results, they were swimming upstream against a tidal wave of legislative business. The persistent growth of the legislative agenda continues to hinder the development of effective solutions to scheduling problems in the House.

Today, the problem of workload is further aggravated by the decentralization of power in the institution. Junior members are wielding considerable power as subcommittee chairs. Their independence from the leadership and from committee chairs allows them great leeway in carrying out their responsibilities. They have a stake in subcommittee government and are likely to fight any proposed changes. The decentralization of the institution severely limits overall coordination in handling legislative business.

Party leaders in the House, particularly the Speaker, do have some resources of authority which they can use to influence individual members and committee chairs to support a more even and efficient scheduling of House business. Ripley (1967, 193) categorizes the principal leadership resources at the Speaker's disposal as the "use of rules, influence of tangible rewards or preference for individual members, influence of psychological rewards or preferment and dominance of the communication process." Some of the more specific powers are: referring bills to committees, negotiating the sizes of committees, appointing select and conference committees, and playing an influential role in the appointment of members to standing committees. However, all of these do not guarantee leadership dominance, because fixed elements in the schedule and individual decisions made by members and committees in response to leadership pleas finally determine when a bill will be considered and brought out of committee.

Leadership attempts to induce committees to begin their work early in the session and to allow for a reasonable period of time to consider legislation on the floor have generally failed. The inability of the leadership to convince committees to get an earlier start, along with the inexorable growth in the legislative agenda, has made a late session rush inevitable. Former Speaker Albert testifying before the Select Committee on Committees (Bolling Committee) noted the problems facing the leadership at the end of the session:

> In every session of Congress the leadership is invariably faced with an overwhelming flood of measures, many of them of major importance, reported by the committee at or near the end of a session. . . . During the entire last session of the 92nd Congress, for example, committees of the House reported a total of 498 bills, but 80 of these including some of the most important were during the last twelve days of the session. (Select Committee on Committees 1973, 5)

Finally, budget timetables, recesses, and holidays also bring about variations in legislative activity during a session. The Obey Commission reported that "an increase in committee work and an extension of floor sessions typically has preceded recesses, summer breaks and budget deadlines, especially during the second session" (Commission 1977*a*, 1:21). The report further added that "a sharp increase in floor activity in June corresponds to the consideration of appropriations bills on the floor and [that] more committees meet before March 15 to report spending requirements to the Budget Committee."

It is thus clear that in scheduling the business of the House, majority party leaders are constrained by a number of factors over which they have little or no control. The necessity for committee deliberation and the political intricacies of majority building allow little room for significant floor activity in the early months of a Congress. Statutory deadlines generate their own flurries of activity. So, too, do district work periods, holidays, and the end of the session. For party leaders, therefore, time management is an art practiced only at the margins of a very tight legislative calendar.

## CONCLUSIONS

Because its supply is short and the demands upon it are enormous, time is one of the most valuable resources of the House of Representatives. In recent years the House has undertaken a number of efforts to utilize that resource more efficiently. But it has met with what one, in all charity, could only call limited success. It continues to be an institution running hard to stay in place, of members constantly frustrated at the distractions that force them to do too many things in too little depth.

Two explanations, above all others, account for this. First, almost every step the House takes to manage its time better turns out to be little more than a holding action in the face of an ever-expanding workload. Like workers whose pay increases fail to keep up with inflation, the House often finds that its marginal improvements in time utilization barely keep up with the annual growth in the demands made upon it.

Second, it is difficult for the House to undertake anything more than marginal steps to improve time management because of the different perspectives in which discrete groups within the House view the time management problem. Individual members want more time to themselves to think and to study, committee and subcommittee chairs want more time for hearings and meetings, party leaders want more time for deliberation and debate on the House floor. These are contradictory positions. Because of its acute scarcity, reallocation of time is a zero-sum proposition. Scheduling accommodations that satisfy the needs of one group often adversely affect another. It is no small task, therefore, to create consensus on the appropriate way to achieve time management efficiencies.

Where then does this leave the House? To what extent can it expect to improve its operating efficiency and effectiveness by manipulating its legislative schedule? The answer—realistically—is probably not very much. The time management problems that result from a decentralized power structure, from a proliferation of subcommittees, and from the inexorable expansion of member responsibilities are simply too imposing to be alleviated solely by scheduling changes.

More radical surgery is necessary. This may involve a reduction in the independence of subcommittees, an enhancement of the authority of party leaders, a realignment of committee jurisdictions, or other measures that will ultimately permit improvements in the central coordination of House operations.

Changes like these will be difficult to achieve, however, because of the redistributive effects they will have on the power and independence of individual members. Until the members of the House become completely frustrated by the longer sessions, the logjam of legislative matters, and their self-perceived inability to do things thoroughly or well, we can expect few changes of the magnitude described here. In their absence, the House will continue to stumble along, rarely enabling itself to make rational coordinated decisions about important national issues.

## NOTES

1. For a fuller discussion of the methodology of the time use survey, see Commission 1977*a*, 1201–1209.
2. Members in the survey with fewer assignments (i.e., less than seven) tended to be more senior. In fact, 61 percent of these members had served for three or more terms.
3. In June of 1973 the House Democratic Caucus approved the "Subcommittee Bill of Rights" which gave subcommittees fixed jurisdictions, referral of all appropriate legislation, and adequate budget and staff resources. (See Ornstein 1975, 105–108 for a fuller discussion.)
4. Interview conducted by the Commission on Administrative Review, 1977.
5. See H. Doc. 95-23 (Commission 1977*b*). The House also adopted the commission's proposal to expand the number of suspension days.

## REFERENCES


Asher, Herbert B. 1973. "The Learning of Legislative Norms." *American Political Science Review* 67:499–513.

Commission on Administrative Review, U.S. Congress, House. 1977*a*. *Final Report*. 2 vols. 95th Cong., 1st sess. H. Doc. 95-272.

———. 1977*b*. *Scheduling the Work of the House*. Communication from the chair. 95th Cong., 1st sess. H. Doc. 95-23.

Committee on House Administration (House Information Systems), U.S. Congress, House. 1977. "Committee Meeting Scheduling Process in the U.S. House of Representatives: An Overview." Unpublished paper.

*Congressional Quarterly*. 1979. "Bauman & Co.: House Guerrilla Fighters." July 7, 1979, 37:1342–1343.

Drew, Elizabeth. 1978. "A Tendency to Legislate." *New Yorker*, June 26, 1978, pp. 80–89.

Fiorina, Morris F. 1977. *Congress: Keystone of the Washington Establishment*. New Haven: Yale University Press.

Galloway, George B. 1961. *History of the House of Representatives*. New York: Thomas Y. Crowell Co.

Goodwin, George, Jr. 1970. *The Little Legislatures*. Amherst: University of Massachusetts Press.

Gross, Bertram M. 1953. *The Legislative Struggle*. New York: McGraw Hill.

Oleszek, Walter. 1978. *Congressional Procedure and the Policy Process*. Washington: Congressional Quarterly Inc.

Ornstein, Norman J. 1975. "Cause and Consequences of Congressional Change: Subcommittee Reforms in the House of Representatives, 1970–1973." In *Congress in Change: Evolution and Reform*, ed. Norman J. Ornstein, pp. 88–114. New York: Praeger.

Peabody, Robert L. 1979. "House Party Leadership." In *The Congressional System: Notes and Readings*, ed. Leroy N. Rieselbach, pp. 118–141. 2nd ed. North Scituate, Mass.: Duxbury Press.

Rieselbach, Leroy N. 1979. "Change in the Congressional System." In *The Congressional System: Notes and Readings*, ed. Leroy N. Rieselbach, pp. 393–410. 2nd ed. North Scituate, Mass.: Duxbury Press.

Ripley, Randall B. 1967. *Party Leaders in the House of Representatives*. Washington: Brookings Institution.

———. 1978. *Congress: Process and Policy*. 2nd ed. New York: W. W. Norton & Co.

Select Committee on Committees, U.S. Congress, House. 1973. "Committee Organization in the House." *Hearings before the Select Committee on Committees*. Vol. 1 of 3. 93rd Cong., 1st sess.

# 6. Personnel Management in the House

*David W. Brady*

## INTRODUCTION

In the past decade the House has attempted to increase its ability to legislate complex problems, oversee the executive branch, serve its constituencies, and increase its power vis-à-vis the president (Dodd and Schott 1979; Rieselbach 1977). The House has therefore increased both the number and importance of staff in member offices and committees and created the Congressional Budget Office, the Office of Technology Assessment, and House Information Systems. In short, not only are staff more numerous than in the past, they are more influential in determining public policies. The validity of this conclusion is attested to by a recent article in *Fortune* magazine (Cameron 1979) on the importance of congressional staff.

This chapter examines personnel policies and practices in the U.S. House of Representatives with special attention devoted to explaining why the House's personnel system is more unorganized and informal than personnel systems in other large organizations. First, there is a general overview of the characteristics of the House's work force in terms of age, sex, education, and salary. Although such data are basic, they have not been available previously in a detailed and systematic fashion. The second and third sections of the chapter examine the basic factors which define the work environments in member offices and committees and then analyze the personnel systems in terms of such factors as recruitment and hiring, training, job descriptions and salary structure, conditions of employment, and tenure. In the final section the impact of the unique political character of the House in determining the character of its personnel system is examined and the limits to beneficial change are discussed.

This analysis utilizes data collected by the Obey Commission staff during 1977. The primary sources are a census of 5,503 House employees in member offices, committees, and administrative units and a sample survey of 154 members, their administrative and legislative assistants, and 42 staff directors of committees and subcommittees.[1] The data on both House personnel and personnel systems thus reflect both as they were in 1977. Some organizational changes have taken place since that time. However, in general, there is little reason to believe that the basic parameters of these samples would be very different if they were taken today. Changes in structure and practice since 1977 will therefore be reported in the footnotes to preserve continuity and eliminate the need for confusing alterations of time.

## GENERAL CHARACTERISTICS OF THE WORK FORCE

The overview of the House work force shows that a majority of the work force, about 57%, is female; 87% of those employed by the House are white, while about 7% are black and fewer than 1% are from any other minority group. In addition, the House's work force is young. Almost 41% are below thirty years of age and another 29% are between thirty and forty years of age. Only 15% of the House's work force is fifty years of age or older.

The work force is extremely well-educated. Almost 61% are college graduates; one-third of the total sample have been to graduate school; about one-fifth of the work force hold graduate degrees.

In general, then, the House's work force is young, well-educated, predominantly white, and more female than male.

With respect to salaries, a majority of the House's employees, about 55%, earn between $10,000 and $20,000, while 7.3% earn over $35,000 per year. The lower end of the salary range includes about 18% of House employees earning less than $10,000 per year. Thus, while in general salaries are relatively high, there are disparities. A number of factors contribute to these disparities, including the type of job performed, where the job is performed, and the fact that part-time employees are reported in the same way as full-time employees. In the separate sections on members' offices and committees, these disparities are analyzed more fully. However, it should be noted here that salary disparity is related to sex and race differences. The data show that women employees and members of minority groups, regardless of educational levels attained or job description, earn less than do their male, white counterparts. This finding must be tempered, however, by the fact that job descriptions do not always accurately describe actual job performance and formal degrees may not correlate with the range of experience or competence a staff job may require.

## STAFF OF MEMBERS' OFFICES

Five factors define the work environment in member offices. First, member offices are in fact highly independent entities. Each of the 439 members, delegates, and commissioners has been elected to the House from a discrete and independent constituency. And since all members are equal and independently chosen, they must be granted great discretion over how they select, organize, and manage their staffs. Thus, so long as members comply with House rules regarding total staff size, total salaries, and nepotism, they are not restricted in whom they hire nor in how they direct their staffs.

Second, members have a great deal of freedom in defining their jobs.[2] Personality, policy, and political considerations all may affect such definitions and may have different effects in different cases. For example, many members very consciously define their roles as voting and representing the specific interests of those who voted them into office. Their policy specialties thus will often reflect the nature of their districts: farm legislation for a rural district; housing renewal and transportation for a big city district. Other members define their constituencies in broader, national terms. They may view the policy areas listed above from a different perspective or they may concentrate on more clearly national interests, such as foreign affairs.

There are other kinds of differences that cause variation in role definition. Some members emphasize their legislative duties, while others stress the service aspects of the job. Some members are most concerned with how their performance is evaluated by their congressional colleagues; others, by those in their districts; still others, by a statewide or national audience. How members weigh these various considerations affects how they define their job. How members define their jobs, in turn, affects the working environment within their offices.[3]

Third, the combination of members' independence and equality, on the one hand, and the differing ways they can define their jobs, on the other, results in a highly diversified working environment when member offices are viewed as a whole. Member offices vary greatly not only in terms of what kinds of work are done but also in terms of how workloads are divided among employees. There is diversity in styles of management, such as the degree of formal or informal organization, as well as in salary schedules, hiring and firing practices, leave policies, and work schedules. Moreover, in the broadest terms, some offices are busier and work under more pressure than others.

Fourth, loyalty to the employing member is a key characteristic of the working environment in member offices. Given the variety of pressures on members, there is a necessity for harmonious working arrangements between representatives and their staffs. Loyalty is expected if not demanded. The guiding principle in each office is to place the member's interest above all else. This doesn't imply saying "yes." It may mean arguing effectively to dissuade him or her. But the point remains that the pressured and politicized character of the work makes loyalty essential.

Finally, the fifth characteristic which describes the working environment in all member offices is the fact that demands on employees are heavy and unpredictable. Members make demands on employees which might seem unreasonable in another setting. These include working long hours in noisy, cramped quarters, working weekends without extra pay, and traveling to district offices. Similarly, unpredictability shapes the environment of member offices. Veteran employees on the Hill realize the difficulty of trying to plan around the legislative process; schedules go awry as fights over amendments run longer than predicted; committee meetings are cancelled for lack of a quorum; emergencies arise in the district, calling for the member's on-the-scene attention; a delegation of visiting farmers, school children or labor union members drops in to see the representative. Such disruptions become an expected part of the "normal" routine.

In sum, the nature of the House as a political institution, the roles members assume as politician–public servants representing widely differing districts, and the demands of an ever more alert public which wants both legislative remedies for complex problems and personal service, result in a complex and variegated working environment. The major points of commonality, despite the differences noted above, are the need for loyalty to the member, the heavy demands made on the employees, and the unpredictable nature of the work day.

With the above as background, this section examines personnel practices for member offices in the House in terms of the following factors: recruitment and hiring, training, job descriptions and salary structure, conditions of employment, and tenure.

**Recruitment and Hiring**

Combinations of the following methods are used to recruit staff: (1) members or their administrative assistants rely on a trusted individual or the "grapevine" of House insiders to suggest staff candidates; (2) members seek advice and suggestions from other members, frequently in the same state delegation; (3) members recruit staff from the home district, either through advisors or from campaign staff; and/or (4) to a lesser extent, members rely on the Office of Placement to supply job applicants.[4]

The first three sources listed above may be considered informal avenues of recruitment, whereas the Office of Placement is a relatively formal vehicle. Because of the political nature of the House the search for staff generally follows informal lines. That is, members need staff who are loyal, particularly at the upper levels within an office, and in order to assure loyalty, the search for staff has focused on finding someone who "fits in." Members who recruit staff via the "grapevine," trusted peers, or their campaign staff and advisors are very likely to get someone who "fits in." In fact, the survey of members showed that slightly over 70% of all member offices hire professional staff through such informal means. Clerical and secretarial hiring in member offices is slightly less informal. Nevertheless, fully 60% of all such employees are hired informally. Another factor related to the predominance of informal recruiting and hiring practices over the more formal practices of the Office of Placement is that often the search for professional staff is geared to finding someone who, in addition to having specific policy and/or political expertise, will "fit in." Other members or House insiders are quite likely to know where such persons can be found, while formal mechanisms for a variety of reasons are far more limited in their ability to identify such persons.

The actual hiring of a member's office staff is generally done by the member and administrative assistants. Members are more active in the hiring of professional staff, with approximately three-fifths of those surveyed claiming a direct role in the hiring of professional staff, and most of the remaining two-fifths claiming indirect control over such hiring. With regard to clerical hiring, one-quarter of the members exerted direct control in hiring with about three-quarters delegating clerical hiring to administrative assistants.

The answer to the question of how staff are recruited to member offices is clear. The pattern is for recruitment to be highly informal and ad hoc in nature. Members rely on informal sources for staff at both professional and clerical levels. The House's formal vehicle for recruiting (the Office of Placement and Office Management) is not used much in recruiting either professional staff or clerical staff. In addition to the informal nature of recruiting, it is also on an ad hoc or need basis. Members' needs vary depending on events and thus so too does the pace and character of staff hiring.

The sources for recruitment vary depending upon the importance of the job. The more important the position, the greater the likelihood that the staff member will have had previous Hill experience.

The initial analysis of where staff is recruited from shows that almost 42% of the member office staff had previous staff experience. The next most important source of staff comes from the private sector with slightly over 25% of staff holding a private sector job previous to their present employment. About 9% of staff were recruited from other branches of government. However, these figures can only be taken as indicative of general trends because sources of recruitment vary by staff position.

In order to determine if variations in recruitment patterns exist at different job levels the following procedure was used. Each respondent on the census of House employees was asked to list his or her last and next-to-last positions. By combining these two questions into a four-point index, ranging from both previous jobs on the Hill to no previous Hill experience, a pattern of where staffers come from is ascertainable. This employment variable was run by job title in member offices and table 6.1 shows the results.

The table indicates that 53% of administrative assistants, 55% of legislative assistants, and 65% of office managers had some previous Hill experience. In addition, 56% of caseworkers had previous Hill experience. In contrast, less than a majority of legislative aides, press secretaries, and clerical staff had previous Hill experience. Though Hill experience is less necessary for effective performance in these jobs, the results still show that the more important the staff position, the greater the likelihood of previous Hill experience. Across all staff positions in member offices, the pattern is for recruitment to be narrowly focused on a pool of individuals who have "been around," and the more important the position the narrower the recruiting base.

A further indication of the narrowness of the recruiting pattern is that among those staff with graduate degrees almost 40% graduated from universities within a 150-mile radius of Washington. Moreover, slightly over one-half of these individuals received graduate degrees at universities located in the District of Columbia.

**Table 6.1.** ***Previous Experience by Present Position in Member Offices***

| | Job Title | | | | | | |
|---|---|---|---|---|---|---|---|
| *Experience*[a] | *Administrative Assistant (%)* | *Office Manager (%)* | *Legislative Assistant (%)* | *Legislative Aide (%)* | *Press Secretary (%)* | *Caseworker (%)* | *Clerical (%)* |
| Last two jobs on Hill | 22 | 35 | 20 | 16 | 10 | 28 | 18 |
| Only most recent on Hill | 27 | 25 | 32 | 25 | 16 | 27 | 21 |
| Only next most recent on Hill | 4 | 5 | 3 | 4 | 1 | 1 | 3 |
| No Hill experience | 47 | 35 | 45 | 55 | 73 | 44 | 58 |
| Total percent | 100 | 100 | 100 | 100 | 100 | 100 | 100 |
| Number | 220 | 77 | 453 | 163 | 146 | 198 | 499 |

[a]Work in district offices is counted as Hill experience.

This analysis leads to the conclusion that the informal, ad hoc recruitment system described above creates a staff whose experience is largely in-House and, consequently, is narrowly defined in terms of both previous employment and geography. Members are not satisfied with this situation, but they have not been able to improve on it. Fully 70% of the members surveyed said that they had problems in recruiting, training, and managing their staffs. Most of these mentioned specific problems with recruiting or with finding qualified people to fill staff vacancies.

Given the identified pattern, recruitment problems are exacerbated for new members. Newly elected members frequently are forced to hire under considerable time pressures without access to good informal sources of recruitment. The rush to judgment in hiring causes staffing problems; often initial decisions must be reassessed quickly. Staff turnover was extremely high for freshmen members of the 93rd and 94th Houses (1973–1977). Thus, recruitment and hiring practices for new members seem to be particularly problematic, and some more formal personnel arrangements would be useful. Further analysis showed that new members used the Office of Placement at about the same rate that more senior members did; therefore, it did not help solve their recruitment problems.

**Training**

There are no continuous, comprehensive programs for training members' staffs. However, in recent years a number of Hill organizations have begun informal training sessions, mostly for new employees and mostly scheduled at the beginning of a new Congress. The development of these training sessions has been piecemeal. The Congressional Research Service, the Democratic Study Group, the Republican Conference, and the House Administration Committee have conducted workshops on various topics. Among the topics covered by these workshops have been legislative research methods, substantive policy questions, and effective office procedures. In addition, occasional seminars run throughout the year by the Congressional Research Service, the Democratic Study Group, the Republican Wednesday Group, the Environmental Study Conference, or outside groups like the Congressional Management Foundation have covered a wide range of topics, often of use to veterans as well as new staff. However, these programs reach relatively few employees.

The training process for staff in member offices is highly informal. On-the-job training is clearly the norm. As one member put it, "I expect my staff to break in new people." Similar comments from other members were frequently offered during interviews. Not surprisingly, the lack of on-going training programs, coupled with the perceived difficulty in recruiting staff, led over one-quarter of the members surveyed to specifically volunteer their support for formal staff training in understanding the legislative process, office management, and equipment operation. In response to questioning, 81% of members thought training programs would be useful for their professional staff, and 67% for their clerical staff. These results demonstrate that members perceive a need for formal training programs to supplement the on-the-job training staff currently receive.[5]

## Job Descriptions and Salary Structure

In both private industry and the federal government, formal job descriptions and salary structures are the norm. The House of Representatives is an exception. Within member offices there is no formal standard for job descriptions or salary structures. Among member offices surveyed, 30% indicated that they used some type of written job descriptions. However, the majority of those surveyed felt that the adoption of standardized job descriptions would slot employees into tightly defined positions, which would make it difficult to use staff effectively in a context where members define their roles differently and have different needs and pressures. For example, depending upon the members' circumstances and personalities, some administrative assistants are the members' alter egos, pinch-hitting on speeches and greeting constituents in their absence; in other offices the administrative assistants direct the legislative program, write speeches, and edit releases. In still others, they serve mainly as office managers.

Despite the independence of each office, there is still some commonality of function. Essentially, most offices strive to perform similar tasks: answering the phone, answering mail, keeping in touch with constituents, and working with legislation. To handle these assignments efficiently, however, most offices employ their own systems of dividing responsibilities and assigning duties. In some offices there is a tight guideline, with legislative assistants and researchers operating apart from clerical staff; in others everyone is required to perform clerical chores and answer the phone; in still others every employee has legislative responsibilities. Emergencies—which often occur daily—mean that all staff pitch in and bail out an assignment area outside their own.

Perhaps the greatest expression of the independence and individuality of member offices lies in salary structure. In some offices the salary schedule is quite high, while in at least one office all salaries are below $15,000. Fewer than 30% of the member offices surveyed reported using a salary structure tied to job descriptions. However, there are some regularities in job titles and salary structures.

As a rule, the Washington office staff earns more than district office staff, often because district salaries are geared to salary rates normal in the home district, almost always less than those paid in Washington. The professional staff positions are paid more than clerical staff. The normal pattern is for administrative assistants to be the most highly paid, with many earning over $30,000 per year. Legislative assistants, office managers, and press secretaries occupy a middle rung with most in the $20,000 bracket; clerical staff are in the lowest pay range. Basically, members pay what they must to hire or keep the employees they want, within the limits set by clerk-hire allowances.[6]

## Conditions of Employment

The term "conditions of employment" can be defined in many ways. In this analysis conditions of employment is taken to mean procedures for evaluating staff performance, sick leave and vacation policy, and grievance procedures.

Employees of member offices recognize that they work in a high-pressure atmosphere, and that their employer, as long as he or she is reelected, has absolute control of the hiring and dismissal of staff. Each member is assured of such control by House rules. The statutory authorization for clerk-hire (2 U.S.C. 92) states, ". . . such person shall be subject to removal at any time by such Member . . . with or without cause." Thus, if an employee is not meeting the standards set by the member, no matter how vague those standards might seem, the employee can expect to be dismissed.

The survey of member offices emphasizes the informal nature of many House offices: for example, only 18% of the members used unwritten formal evaluations and only one office surveyed used written evaluations. The great majority, 81%, indicated that "informal" evaluations were the standard for their offices. The evaluator of staff varied from office to office, with members and administrative assistants normally dividing the responsibility. Two-fifths of the members surveyed reported that they required exit interviews for employees leaving their staff.

Just as evaluation procedures are left to the member's discretion, so too is leave policy. There is no formal House policy on vacation or sick leave. Individual members set vacation and sick leave policy as they see fit. There is, therefore, a wide diversity in policies. Over half of member offices surveyed do not have a formally articulated leave policy while some 43% do have a set policy.

Despite these differences, some patterns emerge. Vacation leave is usually based on earned time, with maximum vacation running from two weeks to one month. Offices establish different kinds of restrictions with respect to when vacation may be taken. For example, some offices do not allow vacations during fall campaigning but allow time off during recesses; others have different policies for professional and clerical staffs.

Sick leave policy is generally liberal, with members carrying staff as long as circumstances permit. Obviously the more senior and/or valuable the employee, the more liberal the sick leave. All of this assumes that highly motivated, loyal staff members will take time off only when illness absolutely prevents their coming to work. In those offices with set policies, the length of absence may be extended for legitimate reasons. The absence of a House provision to cover long-term illness or maternity leave of an employee who wants to return to work places the member and the employee at a disadvantage, particularly if all slots or most of the payroll is committed. Illness may jeopardize an employee's job at a time when he or she greatly needs income.

It is probably true that most offices can survive for short periods without the services of key staff assistants or secretaries. However, fairly long absences can affect the workload of other staff people. Clearly, most members do not lay off a valued employee who is suffering a disabling illness just to hire a temporary replacement. The Committee on House Administration in late 1977 established a "Leave Without Pay Policy" which provides employees with fringe benefits, but no income, during absences resulting from illness. Under the terms of the new policy, the employee on leave without pay is still counted in a member's slot allowance.[7] This policy alleviates some of the problems noted above, but it is not responsive to the income needs of the employee out of work nor to the needs of a member using all eighteen staff slots.

Just as members set policies on evaluation and leave for their offices, so too they decide on what work standards are expected and what actions are appropriate if these standards are not met. This freedom is not totally without limitation. The Congress exempted itself from the provisions of the Civil Rights Act of 1964 and the amendments to it included in the Equal Opportunities Act of 1972, which barred discrimination in hiring, firing, and promotions on the grounds of sex, race, or age, on grounds of the doctrine of separation of powers. However, in approving rules for the 94th Congress (1975), the House passed its own non-discrimination provision (Rule XLIII, clause 9).

No member has yet been charged with violation of this rule, in part at least because it is very difficult for any non-member—in this case an employee who alleges that his or her rights under this rule have been violated by a member—to bring a case before the appropriate body, the Committee on Standards of Official Conduct.

One hundred and six members have joined in an informal arrangement to protect rights and handle grievances. They have established a panel, consisting of three members and three staff persons, to hear grievances and counsel employees or applicants who think they have been discriminated against on grounds of race, sex, marital status, age, or handicap. This committee hears only cases which relate to situations arising in the offices of those members who have joined the committee. Panel members are elected by their peers to serve for one year. In gathering information on the cases brought before them, they attempt to guarantee complete confidentiality and to avoid unnecessary publicity. By the end of 1977 they had handled twelve cases, which they claim to have resolved amicably. No other antidiscrimination cases have been heard within the House and no other in-House procedure exists. However, one employee dismissed by a member who is now retired has brought action through the courts, questioning the restrictive implications of the doctrine of separation of powers and claiming a right to sue members for job bias. That case, *Davis* v. *Passman*, has recently been decided, but the results are inconclusive.[8]

The members of the House are not unaware of problems in the area of conditions of employment. Over 70% of the members surveyed perceived some problems in regard to employees' rights and working conditions. In regard to evaluation, leaves, and grievances, over 75% of the members who perceived some staff problems mentioned these areas as troublesome. Clearly, the members are familiar with problems in conditions of employment and the need for more formal mechanisms to resolve such problems.

## Tenure

The two related factors that come up over and over in regard to personnel policies are the informality and uncertainty of staff life on the Hill. While it is true that there is a corps of Hill regulars, there is also a striking tenure pattern observable on the Hill; namely, for a large number of staff, tenure is short. Almost three-fifths of member office staff have been employed less than two years, and only 5% have been on the Hill more than ten years. However, patterns of tenure vary by job.

Table 6.2 reveals the differences that exist. Specifically, the table

**Table 6.2. *Staff Tenure by Position in Member Offices***

| | *Job Title* | | | | | | |
|---|---|---|---|---|---|---|---|
| *Tenure in present position* | *Adminis-trative Assistant (%)* | *Legislative Assistant (%)* | *Legislative Aide (%)* | *Press Secretary (%)* | *Caseworker (%)* | *Office Manager (%)* | *Clerical (%)* |
| 1 year or less | 38 | 52 | 57 | 49 | 31 | 47 | 41 |
| 1 year to 2 years | 12 | 20 | 27 | 19 | 20 | 13 | 18 |
| 2 years to 5 years | 28 | 24 | 14 | 25 | 31 | 26 | 23 |
| 5 years to 10 years | 10 | 3 | 2 | 7 | 11 | 8 | 11 |
| 10 years or more | 12 | 1 | — | — | 7 | 6 | 7 |
| Total percent | 100 | 100 | 100 | 100 | 100 | 100 | 100 |
| Number | 220 | 453 | 163 | 146 | 198 | 77 | 499 |

shows that administrative assistants have tended to work in their present jobs the longest, with 22% having been in their present positions over five years. Legislative assistants, legislative aides, and press secretaries have held their positions for the shortest times. Nonetheless, this table also supports the general conclusion of high turnover. At least half of those in every job have held their position less than two years.

The survey of members' senior office staffers corroborates these census findings; 58% expect less than one-quarter of present staff to be employed in Congress ten years hence. In addition, when administrative assistants and senior legislative assistants were asked how long they expected to be on the Hill, only 8% and 5% respectively said more than ten years. Fully 40% of legislative assistants and about 25% of administrative assistants said they did not expect to be in Congress longer than the end of the 95th Congress.

The high turnover in member office positions has both costs and benefits for the House. The potential benefits are that, given inbreeding elsewhere in the federal government, high staff turnover may facilitate the House's ability to perform by bringing new approaches and techniques to old problems. The costs of high staff turnover are losses in experience and expertise. However, both effects must be tempered by the realization that some of the turnover is due to old hands changing positions.

## COMMITTEE STAFF

The staffs of the standing committees, as well as those of the select committees, work in environments both different from and similar to member offices. The constituency served is essentially the committee chair, the committee members, and the House membership at large. In many cases there are partisan considerations since there is a division between majority and minority staff.

While member offices deal with constituents' casework, legislative concerns, and some interest groups, committee offices have little contact with casework. Rather, committees are the primary target of interest groups, which train their sights on both members and professional staff in their attempts to influence legislation. Moreover, committee decisions often affect other members' interests, thus focusing the House's attention on their work.

The growing legislative and oversight burdens of the House have spilled over onto the committees, substantially increasing their workloads. The shift away from tightly-run fiefdoms, which considered only legislation of interest to committee chairs, to the more decentralized and open arrangement of responding to the concerns of subcommittee chairs and members has also spurred activity within committees and subcommittees. This growth is reflected in the number of committee and subcommittee meetings scheduled. From the 93rd to the 94th Congress alone (1973–1977), the number of scheduled meetings rose by nearly 17%.

To handle these pressures, committee staff has increased at a rate faster than any other work division within the House. The number of people employed by committees (and subcommittees) has grown from 182 in 1947 to 1,515 in 1977. The additions of staff were accomplished in stages, usually as the result of a specific legislative or House action taken to meet pressing needs.[9]

House rules are more explicit about committee staff than about member office staff. Twenty of the twenty-two standing committees in the House are authorized by law to hire thirty staff members—eighteen professionals and twelve clericals. Statutory staff sizes for the Appropriations and Budget Committees are not specified by law. House rule XI(6) provides for the allocation of one-third of the statutory staff to the minority party (six professionals and four clericals). Both House and caucus rules have provisions regarding the division of staff among subcommittees.

Committee staff positions are not limited to statutory staff; they also include investigative staff. There are no formal limits to the number of investigative staff House committees may hire. Rather, each year the various committees request funds in their annual budgets to hire investigative staff; the Committee on House Administration reviews these requests. In 1977 approximately 900 committee staff members were officially employed as investigative staff.

Salaries for committee staff are determined by the employing committee and funded out of legislative branch appropriations. Unlike the specified clerk-hire allowance, there is no ceiling on the amount committees may request. Top salaries for committee employees are specified by House rule and tied to the Executive Schedule. Two aides in each committee may be paid at the Level IV maximum, while other salaries cannot exceed the maximum of Level V. As shown in table 6.3, committee salaries tend to be considerably higher than those paid to employees in member offices.[10]

The data also show that committee staff have by far the highest salaries. Almost 55% of committee staff are paid more than $20,000 per year, while only 20% of members' Hill staff and 14% of members' district staff are paid that highly. Moreover, nearly 23% of committee staff are paid more than $35,000 per year, while about 5% of

**Table 6.3.** ***Salary Distribution by Employment Location***

| Annual Salary | Member Offices: District (%) | Member Offices: Washington (%) | Committee Offices (%) |
|---|---|---|---|
| $ 0–4,999 | 5.8 | 1.5 | 1.0 |
| 5,000–9,999 | 30.7 | 11.0 | 3.4 |
| 10,000–14,999 | 35.2 | 40.0 | 20.4 |
| 15,000–19,999 | 14.3 | 23.4 | 18.6 |
| 20,000–24,999 | 7.2 | 10.1 | 12.8 |
| 25,000–29,999 | 3.7 | 5.0 | 11.2 |
| 30,000–34,999 | 1.0 | 3.9 | 9.8 |
| 35,000 and over | 1.7 | 4.4 | 22.8 |
| No answer | .4 | .7 | 0.0 |
| Total percent | 100 | 100 | 100 |
| Number | 1,490 | 2,421 | 964 |

the employees in members' Washington offices and 2% in their district offices earn comparable amounts. Thus, given the higher pay and the more predictable nature of the work on committees, it is not surprising that many employees in member offices seek committee positions.

Four factors, in some ways parallel to those described for member offices, define the working environment in committee offices. First, the twenty-two standing committees are independent entities. Each committee under the leadership of the chair is relatively free to structure its staff and develop its annual work calendar as it sees fit. Diversity is found in the number of investigative staff employed by committees, the relationship between the staff director and other employees, and the relationship between committee and subcommittee staffs. However, while few rules limit members in organizing their offices, committees as ongoing divisions of labor created by the whole House have more restrictions. For example, as noted above, one-third of all statutory staff members must be assigned to the minority party. Further, subcommittee chairs and ranking minority members are authorized to hire staff to work under their direction on subcommittee business.

Second, a number of political and policy factors affect the work environment within the various committees. The more critical ones include the degree of partisanship, the substantive content of policies under a committee's jurisdiction, the degree of public concern about committee action or nonaction, the committee's control over matters of concern to the rest of the House, and the degree of interest group involvement.[11] To a large extent these factors are not independent and they are present in different combinations among the various committees. Some committees work closely with affected interests on matters of public concern, whereas other committees shun working with affected interests on such matters. Some committees decide policy questions in a highly partisan manner while others try to seek a bipartisan "committee" solution. In short, because of the various combinations of these factors, committee interests, workloads, styles, and operations vary widely.

Third, the combination of committee independence and the various patterns of political and policy pressures on committees result in a comparatively diversified working environment when committees are viewed in general. Committees vary not only in terms of what kinds of work are done (e.g., investigative, technical, political), but also in terms of how workloads are divided among employees. There is diversity in styles of leadership, salary schedules, hiring and firing practices, leave policies, and work schedules. In addition, some committees are busier and work under more pressure than others.

Fourth, there are some common aspects to working on committees which make the work environment on committees *less uncertain* than in member offices. The substantive policy areas considered by committees remain relatively constant over time. Similarly, the same interest groups and the same executive branch departments and agencies work with committee staffs each year. Thus, staffs are able to develop policy expertise which carries over from one Congress to the next, as well as familiarity with other experts involved in governmental decisions in that policy area. Working conditions are also more predictable in committee offices than in member offices. Although there are peak or slack times in terms of committee activity, and these are reflected in staff working hours, staff members know in advance when these periods are likely to occur.

In general, committees share with member offices independence, role variety, diversity of work, and heavy demands as factors defining the work environment. However, committees as work environments are characterized by more routinized and more certain personnel policies. Committees as continuous nonelected entities offer opportunities for more stable employment than do member offices, and an individual's professional development in areas of committee jurisdiction is usually encouraged. In addition, committee salaries are higher than member office salaries. Thus, from the staff viewpoint, committee positions are considered more desirable.

**Recruitment and Hiring**

The recruitment of committee staff follows the pattern described for member offices. In general, committees use a combination of informal and formal sources to recruit staff. The informal sources are House insiders, the "grapevine," and contacts with individuals and institutions outside the House. These outside sources are generally used to hire subject-matter experts for specific committee investigations. The formal source of recruitment again is the Office of Placement and Office Management.[12] Given the variety of tasks performed by the twenty-two standing committees and their subcommittees, the combinations of these sources vary. However, as was noted for member offices, the general pattern is for recruiting and hiring to be informal and ad hoc in nature.

The commission's survey of top committee staff provides evidence which supports this conclusion. Professional staff recruitment was clearly the most informal, with 87% of the respondents claiming that they did not use the Office of Placement in filling their last professional vacancy. Moreover, even of those who used the Office of Placement, 40% did not hire the person referred by Placement. The most common sources of recruitment for professional staff positions, in order of importance, are other congressional committees, offices, and support units; executive branch agencies; personal contacts; academic and professional sources; the private sector; and finally, the Office of Placement. The informal sources were mentioned almost ten times as often as was the Office of Placement.

The pattern of recruitment for clerical staff is somewhat different. In clerical recruitment the pattern is for formal and informal sources to be about equally important. It is worth noting that even in this area of recruiting, where skills are more easily measurable, approximately half of clerical staff are recruited informally.

The informal nature of recruitment was perhaps best summed up by one respondent who said, "If we had a job open we would find someone we know. . . . It's usually a friend of a friend."

The actual hiring of committee staff varies from committee to committee, depending upon the committee and subcommittee chairs. The committee chair's role varies from acting as staff director—"The Chairman interviews and hires all staff, including clerical help"—to allowing the staff director to do all hiring under a broad mandate. The cumulative results of the survey of committees show that most committee chairs do some hiring personally, but also allow the staff directors to do some of the hiring.

Another important aspect of committee recruitment is the sources from which committee staff come. Again, the pattern parallels the pattern discerned for member offices. Many people come to committee jobs directly from other jobs on the Hill. The base of recruitment varies depending upon the job. Staff positions which require special subject-matter expertise are likely to come from universities and professional organizations, while positions requiring political savvy are likely to come from inside the House.

The initial analysis of staff backgrounds shows that slightly over 40% of committee staff come directly from other jobs on the Hill. The next most important source of staff is the private sector, with 26% holding private sector jobs immediately prior to their present employment. Over 15% of committee staff are recruited from other government jobs, mostly in the federal government.

In order to determine if variations in recruitment patterns exist for different committee jobs, the same procedures described in the member office section were utilized. Again, the measure employed was a four-point index, ranging from both previous jobs on the Hill to no previous Hill experience. This index was compared to job titles to ascertain patterns of recruitment. The results are shown in table 6.4.

The table reveals an interesting pattern. For all positions except staff directors, approximately 40% of committee employees have had some previous experience on the Hill. Many more staff directors, 64%, worked on the Hill in either one or both of their most recent jobs. This result is not surprising, given that the staff director works most closely with the chair and must be both politically savvy and compatible with the chair. In general, the results show that recruiting for committee staff positions is a combination of narrow in-House recruitment and external sources. However, the crucial position of staff director is normally recruited from a narrow base of experienced Hill insiders.

As was the case for member offices, a large portion of committee staffers with graduate degrees received them from District of Columbia schools, which again points to the narrowness of the recruitment base.

In sum, the normal pattern of recruitment for committee staff positions is similar to that discovered in member offices. Namely,

**Table 6.4.** ***Previous Experience by Present Position in Committee Offices***

| *Experience* | *Staff Director (%)* | *General Counsel (%)* | *Legislative Assistant (%)* | *Research Assistant (%)* | *Professional Staff (%)* | *Staff Assistant (%)* | *Clerical (%)* |
|---|---|---|---|---|---|---|---|
| Last two jobs on Hill | 29 | 14 | 17 | 13 | 9 | 14 | 16 |
| Most recent on Hill | 27 | 17 | 26 | 29 | 26 | 26 | 22 |
| Next most recent on Hill | 8 | 7 | 1 | — | 3 | 3 | 3 |
| No Hill experience | 36 | 62 | 56 | 58 | 62 | 57 | 59 |
| Total percent | 100 | 100 | 100 | 100 | 100 | 100 | 100 |
| Number | 48 | 77 | 81 | 52 | 100 | 150 | 135 |

recruitment is informal and in-House. Because committees have a relatively more stable environment, the recruiting tends to be somewhat less informal and in-House, but the general pattern discovered for member offices holds for committees.

## Training

As was the case in member offices, the norm for committee staff has been on-the-job training. However, unlike member offices, committees have funds available to pay for employees' continuing training. Section 304 of the Legislative Reorganization Act of 1970 provides that, with the approval of the Committee on House Administration, contingent funds may be used for committee professional staff to "obtain specialized training." Testimony before the Obey Commission revealed that this provision is seldom used. Among those committees and subcommittees using training funds (24%), no systematic patterns of use could be discerned. No specific training program was mentioned more than twice by the staff directors interviewed; the programs mentioned ranged from data processing and clerical skills training sessions to seminars at the Defense Planning Institute.

Given the informal and sporadic nature of training programs for committee staffs, it is not surprising that the commission survey showed that over 90 percent of the staff director respondents mentioned that training programs would be helpful for staff employees. The most frequently mentioned problem areas where training would be helpful were in understanding House rules and procedures and in acquiring legislative drafting skills. Among others mentioned were office management, policy analysis, account management, and information retrieval from executive agencies. Thus, as was the case for member offices, the need for formal staff training in a number of problem areas is widely recognized.[13]

## Job Descriptions and Salary Structure

Within the broad categories of professional and clerical, and permanent and investigative, each committee may assign specific jobs and set salaries as it sees fit. Most committees do this in an informal way. The only two committees which have formalized both job descriptions and salary structures are Post Office and Civil Service, and District of Columbia. Seven other committees have developed written job descriptions, while Ways and Means and the Budget Committee have developed salary scales. Thus, many different policies are operative within the various committees.

In regard to actual salaries paid, all committees are governed by

House rule XI(6)(c) which provides that committee staff salaries are set by the committee chair. In theory the chair has the power to set all salaries; however, in practice the ranking minority member sets minority staff salaries. Subcommittee chairs and ranking minority members also often set salaries for their staffs. It is worth reemphasizing that committee staff salaries are markedly higher than member office staff salaries.

Despite the lack of formal salary structures, the distribution of salaries among committee employees follows the normal pattern: professionals are paid more than clericals, and staff directors and general counsels more than other professionals. In addition, staff salaries on committees vary not only by job title, but also by sex and race.

**Conditions of Employment**

Following the approach used in the member office section of this chapter, staff evaluations, sick leave and vacation policies, and grievance procedures are included in the definition of conditions of employment.

Committee staff members recognize that they work in a stressful world and that they are subject to termination of employment at the discretion of committee chairs, subcommittee chairs, and ranking minority members. Nevertheless, in comparison to member office staff, committee staff are more protected. They are less subject to electoral pressures and they have often developed policy expertise which carries over from one chair to another. Given this relative stability, one might expect that a number of committees would have developed formal performance evaluations. However, table 6.5 shows that only three committees have developed written performance evaluations—Budget, District of Columbia, and Science and Technology. Only five other committees have a verbal evaluation, while fourteen committees have no "formal" performance evaluations at all. In general, evaluation is controlled by the senior members of the committee and is informal in nature.

Compared to evaluation procedures, sick leave and vacation policy on committees is relatively formal. Although there are no statutory provisions governing leave policies, all but two committees have a stated vacation policy and a number of committees make provisions for extended vacations after a certain period of service. Similarly, sick leave policies for committee offices are more formal than in member offices. Long-term illness does not pose a serious problem for committees because, unlike member offices, their procedures are flexible enough to permit hiring temporary employees. A majority of staff directors surveyed acknowledged that they would carry an employee for an extended time period if necessary.

Grievance policy on committees is highly informal. Nineteen of the twenty-two standing committees have only informal grievance mechanisms. These range from allowing employees to put their complaints in writing to loose verbalization of complaints to fellow staffers.

In general, conditions of employment for committee staff are somewhat more formal than for member office staff. Nevertheless, the overall pattern is marked by variation and informality with relatively few formal mechanisms for resolving problems.

### Tenure

In member offices staff tenure in many job categories was brief. Committee staffs, as has been shown, are somewhat removed from the unpredictability and informality that characterize member office staffs. Thus, it might be hypothesized that staff tenure would be more stable and extended. However, such is not the case.

The data reveal that tenure is brief on committee staffs as well, though not quite so limited as in member offices. More employees in committee offices have held their positions for five years or more. In contrast, as in member offices, there are also many employees who have held their positions for two years or less (at least 50% in all committee job categories). However, to a large extent this finding reflects the increase in the overall size of committee staff recently; thus new employees have been added. Finally, it is interesting to note that staff directors and general counsels do not appear to have held their positions longer than others. This is because there has been a significant turnover in committee and subcommittee chairs recently and the new chairs have wanted to appoint their own staff leaders.

## ASSESSMENT

The analysis of current work situations in member offices and committees clearly points to significant differences between the personnel practices of the U.S. House of Representatives and other large organizations. In comparison to the Shell Oil Company or the Department of the Treasury, for example, House member offices and committee staffs are—

**Table 6.5.** ***Personnel Policies among Committees***

| *Committee* | *Written Policy on Hiring and Recruitment* | *Training* | *Job Classification* | *Job Description* | *Salary Scale* | *Performance Evaluation* | *Grievance* | *Affirmative Action* | *Organizational Charts* |
|---|---|---|---|---|---|---|---|---|---|
| Agriculture | no | no | no | no | no | no | informal | no | no |
| Appropriations | no | no | no | no | no | verbal | informal | no | no |
| Armed Services | no | yes | no | no | no | no | informal | no | no |
| Banking | no | no | no | no | no | no | informal | no | no |
| District of Columbia | yes | no | yes | yes | yes | written | informal | yes | yes |
| Education and Labor | no | no | no | no | no | verbal | informal | yes | no |
| Government Operations | no | no | no | yes | no | no | no | no | no |
| House Administration | no | yes | no | no | no | no | informal | no | no |
| Interior | no | no | yes | no | no | no | no | no | no |
| International Relations | no | no | no | yes | no | verbal | informal | yes | no |

| | | | | | | | | | |
|---|---|---|---|---|---|---|---|---|---|
| Interstate and Foreign Commerce | no | no | yes | yes | no | no | informal | no | no |
| Post Office and Civil Service | no | no | yes | yes | yes | no | informal | no | yes |
| Public Works | no | no | yes | yes | no | no | informal | no | no |
| Rules | no | yes | no | no | no | no | no | no | no |
| Science and Technology | yes | yes | no | yes | no | written | informal | yes | yes |
| Small Business | no | yes | no | no | no | no | informal | yes | no |
| Standards of Official Conduct | no | no | yes | no | no | no | informal | yes | no |
| Veterans' Affairs | no | no | no | no | no | verbal | informal | yes | no |
| Judiciary | no | no | no | no | no | verbal | informal | not written | no |
| Merchant Marine and Fisheries | no | no | no | no | no | no | informal | no | yes |
| Ways and Means | no | no | no | yes | yes | no | informal | no | no |
| Budget | no | yes | no | yes | yes | written | informal | yes | yes |

NOTE: All committees have the same standard package of benefits.

1. recruited and hired much more informally and via the grapevine;
2. trained on the job with no systematic training programs available;
3. not part of a personnel system characterized by formal job descriptions and set salary structures;
4. subject to widely varying conditions of employment in such areas as evaluation, sick leave, vacation policy, and grievance procedures;
5. more likely to have high turnover (or low tenure); and
6. more likely to have loyalty to an individual determine their ability to get and keep a staff position.

In short, whatever the personnel area being considered the House seems to be characterized by unusual personnel policies. Why is this so? The answer lies in the political nature of the House as an institution. In one sense it is silly to compare the House to large corporations or executive bureaucracies. Work situations and personnel practices in the House should be compared, rather, to other political institutions, such as state legislatures or the White House staff. When compared to political institutions, House practices of informal recruiting, on-the-job training, flexible job descriptions, nonbureaucratic salary structures, and informal leave practices seem more the norm than an anomaly. The point is that the House is a political institution and as such there are real constraints on how formal the House's personnel system can become. Representatives are elected from 435 separate constituencies which vary widely in terms of constituent heterogeneity, marginality, and partisan identification, among other factors.[14] Richard Fenno (1978) has shown that members perceive their districts in terms of a number of different constituencies: the geographical constituency, the reelection constituency, the primary constituency, and the personal constituency. Representatives with different constituency perceptions and situations behave differently. For example, representatives who have not built solid reelection and primary constituencies spend more time at home and have less time to spend developing Hill careers. In addition, such representatives are likely to have more of their member office staff located in the district. Thus the variety across and within constituencies leads one to conclude that, in trying to meet constituent needs (and be reelected), member office staffs will be arranged in a myriad of ways to accommodate such needs.

Another source of diversity in the House's personnel system arises from the different goals that members have regarding their

Hill careers. Members have reelection, influence, and good policy as goals. Fenno (1973), Mayhew (1974), and others have shown that these personal goals affect member behavior. It stands to reason that staff placement, job definition, and recruitment and hiring practices will differ, depending upon a member's goal(s). A member whose primary goal is to make good policy will be likely to have more research staff than a member whose primary goal is to be reelected. Thus, the variety of member goals contributes to the irregular nature and helter-skelter appearance of the House's personnel system.

Differences in constituencies and member goals are somewhat sorted out in the committee system as members tend to choose committees where other members share their goals. And, as Fenno (1973), Manley (1970), and others have shown, committees can be understood in terms of the interaction between environmental constraints and member goals. This means that committees will, year in and year out, tend to be dominated by the same norms, deal with the same subject matter, and in general have less diversity than is found in member offices. Thus, the personnel system in committees can be more formal or less chaotic than in member offices.

Variance in constituencies and in member goals are of course ultimately political. Representatives must satisfy constituents and their choice of goals is dependent to a large extent on their ability to be reelected. Thus, as long as members of the House are elected and allowed—within limits—to choose their career goals and policy expertise, the personnel system of the House will be less formal and centralized than the personnel system of Shell Oil, Yale University, or the Department of the Treasury.

With these general points as background, member offices and committees can now be examined as work environments to determine the basis for current personnel practices and to identify the factors that constrain the application of more traditional or familiar personnel practices.

## Member Offices

The relationship between a member and those on his office staff is based on loyalty and trust. The staff member helps the representative in a number of ways, all of which are political. The staff is the representative's eyes and ears, monitoring the flow of events on the Hill and in the district. The staff helps the member make policy judgments which affect his or her constituents and the member's reputation on the Hill. In addition, staff represent the member's views to constituents. In a real way the member's office staff is an extension of the representative's political self. Under these conditions no member can afford office personnel who are unloyal or untrustworthy.

The importance of trust and loyalty in the member/staff relationship leads directly to many of the personnel practices discussed above. For example, the high degree of informality in recruiting is a result of members' needs for loyalty. Given a forced choice between a competent but unloyal AA and an incompetent but loyal AA, a member would always choose the latter. The search for new staff is oriented, among other considerations, to finding someone who will be loyal. Therefore, members and AAs look to those they know personally for recommendations, and trusted insiders know best what traits will lead an employee to work well with a particular member.

Other current personnel practices follow naturally from the need for flexibility. Members need to structure positions and assignments so that their priorities are served and so that they can rely on those they most trust for the tasks they deem most important. Thus, vacation and sick leave policies are informal because members cannot predict district and/or legislative crises. Staff leaves are granted as needed or desired providing that conditions permit. In the same vein, flexibility and loyalty dominate present personnel practices such as on-the-job training, job descriptions, and salary structures. In the aggregate House, personnel practices differ and will continue to do so as long as there are constituency differences and members have different goals. In short, as Fenno (1973, 1978) has so clearly shown, districts differ and member motivations also differ. Members' office personnel policies will therefore vary in relation to district characteristics and individual member choices on goals. The major characteristics of such a system will of course be unstandardized personnel practices—informality.

## Committees

The constraints on committee personnel systems are not as severe as those on member offices. Committees are continuous entities somewhat removed from the electoral pressures faced in member offices. In addition, there are career patterns on committees, based on policy expertise and at least partially independent of any one member. These are differences of degree, however, not of kind, and vary from committee to committee. How they affect personnel practices and how much they constrain more traditional policies therefore varies.

Some examples of these variations are illustrative. The fact that job descriptions and salary structures have been introduced into some committees demonstrates that constraints in committee offices are not so severe as those in member offices. However, the fact that most committees have yet to institute such systems suggests that constraints still operate. There was resistance, for example, when the Post Office and Civil Service Committee instituted its current system. Some members viewed the move as an infringement on their prerogatives. The system is now well accepted, but the real test will come with a change in committee leadership.

Adoption of fixed procedures and policies for employment by several committees indicates that few constraints exist to bar others from doing so. However, individual members, in their capacities as committee or subcommittee chairs, still desire a certain amount of flexibility in how these offices are run. Such members must be assured that any system imposed will not impair their abilities to run these offices as they deem necessary when pressures are high and working conditions tense. Only policies individualized to meet committee needs and written to guarantee this kind of flexibility would be appropriate in committee offices.

## CONCLUSION

For both member offices and committees, personnel policies and practices are constrained by political considerations. However, the existence of constraints does not imply that the status quo must persist or that it represents the best system possible. It does imply that reformers need to seek personnel practices not inherently constrained by the work environment. For example, flexibility in an organization involves disorder, but the House's political character requires a very flexible personnel system to meet changing needs. Personnel policies designed to bring more order to the House's personnel system will necessarily limit flexibility. Change in personnel policy will thus bring improvement only insofar as it conforms to the inherent constraints in the work environment.

## NOTES

1. For details of these surveys see Commission 1977*b*, 1:695–713, 2:769–801, 941–1121, 1210–1215.
2. The classic statement on legislative roles is Wahlke et al. 1962. For applications to Congress see Davidson 1969.
3. These points are explored in detail in a Congressional Research Service mimeo report entitled, "Congressional Office Operations: Aspects of Staff Operation in Washington and the Congressional District" (Novem-

ber 1976). See also the section on members' offices in Commission 1977*a*.

4. The Placement Office was an arm of the Select Committee on Congressional Operations. When this committee went out of existence at the beginning of the 96th Congress (1979), the personnel and management assistance functions performed by the Placement Office were assumed by the Committee on House Administration. In June 1979 this committee established a new unit, the Office of Management Services, to carry on the duties previously performed by the Placement Office. This unit, working under the aegis of the Committee on House Administration, has sought both to expand the reach of congressional recruitment and to work more closely with members so as to tailor their services to individual needs. Nonetheless, though placement services have improved, the basic points made in the text remain valid.
5. Since its establishment in mid-1979 the Office of Management Services has substantially expanded training programs for member office and committee staffs. In the first six months of 1980, for example, over 100 training sessions were held on such topics as casework, office management, computer skills, etc. Staff participants numbered several thousand, and represented the great majority of committees and member offices. Nonetheless, some large and significant portion of the training remains informal and ad hoc, as described in the text.
6. In 1977 the clerk-hire allowance per member was $255,144, with a ceiling of eighteen staff slots and a top salary for one aide of $47,500. In 1979, due to cost of living increases, the total amount had grown to $288,156, but the top salary remained $47,500 (Congressional Quarterly 1980*b*, 90).
7. In July of 1979 the House, acting on a recommendation of the Committee on House Administration, approved a new system of temporary and part-time employment for member office staff. Members, for various specified reasons, including the replacement of a staff member on leave without pay, can hire up to four more temporary or part-time employees without counting them toward the ceiling of eighteen staff slots per office. This change, however, involved no additions to the clerk-hire allowance. See Congressional Quarterly 1980*b*, 90. Thus, while it eases the problem of granting staff leave for maternity, illness, etc., by not counting temporary or part-time replacements against the slot allowance, it does not provide any extra funds for such purposes.
8. The Supreme Court, on June 5, 1979, overturned a Court of Appeals decision which ruled that Davis, a former employee of Passman, had no standing to sue. However, the vote affirming her standing to sue under the due process clause of the Fifth Amendment was 5–4 and neither the Appeals Court nor the Supreme Court directly confronted the issue of legislative immunity under the speech or debate clause of the Constitution. Though the Court appeared to urge prompt resolution of this issue in sending the case back to a lower court, the issue remains unresolved

since Davis and Passman subsequently settled the case privately for an undisclosed sum of money. See Congressional Quarterly 1980*a*, 22A–23A. Though some members now doubt that Congress can act to protect employees from job discrimination, Reps. Schroeder (D-Colo.), Udall (D-Ariz.), and Drinan (D-Mass.) have introduced a resolution (H. Res. 292) to provide a protection and grievance procedure for House employees subject to job discrimination. The resolution in large part formalizes the informal procedures described in the text.

9. See Commission 1977*b*, 1:657–659. The figures in the text are for standing committees only.
10. In 1977 the top salary for Level IV employees was $50,000 and the top salary for Level V employees was $47,500. In 1979 Level IV employees were given a 5.5 percent cost of living increase, further increasing the top salary disparity between member office and committee staff. See note 6 above and Congressional Quarterly 1980*a*, 269–270.
11. For an excellent comparative committee analysis see Fenno 1973. For individual committees see Manley 1970 and Murphy 1974.
12. The Placement Office has been replaced by a new Office of Management Services. See note 4 above. This unit has sought to expand the sources of recruitment for committee staff, e.g., by visiting universities with MPA programs and compiling rosters of candidates. Once again, however, the basic points made in the text remain valid.
13. See note 5 above.
14. See Clausen 1973, Fiorina 1974, and Fenno 1978.

## REFERENCES


Cameron, Juan. 1979. "The Shadow Congress the Public Does Not Know." *Fortune* 99(January):38–44.

Clausen, Aage R. 1973. *How Congressmen Decide*. New York: St. Martins.

Commission on Administrative Review, U.S. Congress, House. 1977*a*. *Background Information on Administrative Units, Members' Offices, and Committees and Leadership Offices*. 95th Cong., 1st sess., H. Doc. 95-178.

———. 1977*b*. *Final Report*. 2 vols. 95th Cong., 1st sess., H. Doc. 95-272.

Congressional Quarterly. 1980*a*. *Congressional Almanac, 1979*. Washington: Congressional Quarterly Inc.

———. 1980*b*. *Congressional Ethics*. Washington: Congressional Quarterly Inc.

Davidson, Roger. 1969. *The Role of the Congressman*. New York: Pegasus.

Dodd, Lawrence C., and Schott, Richard L. 1979. *Congress and the Administrative State*. New York: Wiley.

Fenno, Richard F., Jr. 1973. *Congressmen in Committees*. Boston: Little, Brown.

———. 1978. *Home Style: House Members in Their Districts*. Boston: Little, Brown.

Fiorina, Morris P. 1974. *Representatives, Roll Calls, and Constituencies.* Lexington, Mass.: D. C. Heath.

Mayhew, David R. 1974. *Congress: The Electoral Connection.* New Haven: Yale University Press.

Manley, John F. 1970. *The Politics of Finance.* Boston: Little, Brown.

Murphy, James T. 1974. "Political Parties and Porkbarrel: Party Conflict and Cooperation in House Public Works Decision-Making." *American Political Science Review* 68(March):169–185.

Rieselbach, Leroy N. 1977. *Congressional Reform in the 1970's.* Morristown, N.J.: General Learning Press.

Wahlke, John C.; Eulau, Heinz; Buchanan, William; and Ferguson, Leroy C. 1962. *The Legislative System.* New York: Wiley.

# 7. The Management of Legislative Offices

*Susan Webb Hammond*

Legislative offices in the House of Representatives operate in a decentralized, highly individual, and political environment.[1] There is opportunity for creativity, adaptation, and innovation in managing the workload and in fashioning legislation and policy. At the same time, there are problems of coordination and duplication, and there are concerns based on supports and demands of the political system external to the environment of the House.

## DETERMINING FORCES AND CONSTRAINTS

Although the congressional environment affects different legislative offices somewhat differently, several factors are important in shaping the work environment of every office.

First, the decentralized organization of the legislative subunits of the House reflects the collegial nature of the institution and the linkage between each member and the external environment. The many member, committee, and leadership offices operate as autonomous units with wide latitude and great discretion. House leaders are only first among equals, with few rewards and even fewer sanctions for distribution to colleagues.

Second, the environment in which offices operate is variable. Legislative offices differ in function, in perception of function, and in the various ways their functions are interpreted. The focus for the representative function of the House is the individual member, with his or her ties to the district. The focus for the legislative function is the committee and the subcommittee. Both the legislative and the representative functions are the concern of leadership offices, whose activities include resource distribution and coordination of collegial decision making. Although there is overlap—representation occurs through votes in committee or on the floor as well as through casework handled by the member's office, and legislative decisions are made by individual members with advice from aides on their personal staff—nevertheless, the central focus of each subunit sets the context for its operations.

Perceptions of office function and role, and therefore the character of office activity and workload management, differ and are governed by the type of legislative subunit and, to a degree, by the personality and priorities of the subunit leader—the member, the committee or subcommittee chair or ranking minority member, or the party leader.

Third, the House is a political institution, and the legislative office units are political entities. Members must face election every two years. The concerns and needs of their constituents are of continuing concern. They must respond to their electorates (however that electorate is defined) and, with ease of travel and increasingly sophisticated electorates, their job tends to expand indefinitely. This central facet of the environment—that the House is a political institution—structures the patterns of workload management, including the choice of priorities, resource acquisition and distribution, and staff jobs. Processes for decision making, for resource distribution, and for work management tend to be congenial to a political milieu—equal access, bargaining and negotiation, and partisan organization. Loyalty, trust, and the accountability of aides to the principal employer are key elements. Hierarchical organization of the individual legislative offices has been slow to emerge, and in most offices professionals continue to have direct access to the member. Coordination devices have been developed primarily within each party rather than across party lines. A large number of autonomous subunits under the personal control of a principal employer fulfills the need for both responsiveness and accountability. In order to manage the workload, choices are made and priorities set in the context of a collegial, decentralized, political institution.

Finally, the workload for members, and for the legislative office units they manage, is often overwhelming. The workload has increased significantly in recent years. Members estimate they receive, on the average, 31,600 letters annually. Casework in member offices has doubled since 1968 (Johannes 1978). Although casework loads vary (from 5 or 10 cases a week to as many as 300), the average load is slightly over 10,000 cases per year. There is variation by seniority and region, with senior members (six terms or more) reporting somewhat larger loads (11,000 per year) than junior members (one or two terms), who report slightly over 9,000 cases a year. For committee offices, increasingly complex legislation and renewed concern regarding oversight, more meetings and hearings, and an increased number of subcommittees are elements of a greater workload. For party leadership offices the greater decentralization of decision making, the cross-cutting nature of the issues with which the House must deal, the increased emphasis on efficiency, and monitoring the substance and scheduling of legislation contribute to the workload.

The Obey Commission reported heavy workloads in members' offices in the areas of legislative mail (67% of the offices), casework (59%), and legislative research (44%). Nearly half the committees and subcommittees reported heavy workloads in supervisory (44%) and internal administration (44%) duties, and more than half (51%) said the workload in substantive and legal analysis was heavy.

The work pattern continues to be cyclical and often unpredictable. An external event may contribute to a deluge of constituent mail or an unexpected amendment may require response through additional research, briefings, and new legislative strategy. The Budget and Impoundment Control Act of 1974 is regarded by many staff aides as contributing to a dysfunctional pace of legislative work, with a rush to finish work on authorizing legislation upsetting a deliberate pace for many legislative committees.

These factors, then, establish the framework for legislative office management, shaping the environment in which legislative offices operate and affecting the level and the distribution of resources.

## THE CURRENT SITUATION

### Distribution of Resources

The House has chosen to allocate the same basic resources to similar work units, and to permit maximum flexibility in the way the resources are used by each individual member, committee, and leadership office. As a result of reforms during the 1970s, resources have increased considerably, and are now more widely distributed, but the underlying premise—that each type of legislative office should have comparable resources subject to individual management by each work unit—has not changed.

*Member Offices.* At the start of the 96th Congress, in January 1979, each of the 435 members of the House of Representatives was allotted $288,156 per session for salaries for personal staff aides and an Official Expenses Allowance of approximately $75,000 to cover costs of office operations.

Members may hire up to eighteen full-time aides, and up to four additional aides in any of several categories—part-time, temporary, shared with another member, interns, or on leave without pay. The top salary for any aide was $47,500 per year in January 1979. The clerk-hire allowance is subject to several restrictions, some of them stemming from earlier abuses: staff must work in the member's Washington office or in the district; unused monies may not be carried over from one calendar quarter to the next; and no member may employ a relative, unless that relative was hired prior to December 16, 1968. Members may use $15,000 of their clerk-hire allowance each year for official expenses. Otherwise, the clerk-hire allowance is not transferable. The allowance covers an office in Washington and any office or offices in the representative's district. Each member decides what staff positions to establish and the particular duties of each aide. When federal employees receive a cost-of-living pay raise, the total clerk-hire allowance of each representative increases by that same percentage (in recent years, about 5.5%), although the raise is not automatically given to each employee, as it is in the executive branch.

The Official Expenses Allowance covers costs of office equipment and supplies, travel for members and staff, telephone and telegraph, newsletters, and district office(s) expenses. The allowance is based on the estimated cost of eight categories of expenses. Table 7.1 provides more detailed information on the size and operation of these allowances. Members may also use the frank for official mail.

The number of staff in member offices has increased rapidly in recent years, from 1,440 in 1947 to 4,055 in 1967 and 6,952 in 1979. Staffs now average 16.5 aides. The effect of the larger staffs has been to make available additional resources to more junior representatives, and thus to give them assistance, especially on legislative matters, previously available only to senior members of the House through the control of committee staff. The importance of personal staffs to all congressional functions is underscored by findings from the House Commission on Administrative Review (the Obey Commission): 60% of the House members interviewed report relying on personal staff for legislative work related to their committee assignments; 57% rely on personal staff for other legislative work; 49% report personal staff as a major source of information on issues of governmental and general public concern (Commission on Administrative Review 1977*b*, 1:670).

*Committee Offices.* Committees of the House have more flexibility in obtaining resources although, as with members' offices,

**Table 7.1.** ***Office Allowances for House Members (per session), 96th Congress (1979–1981)***

| *Allowance Type* | *Allowance* |
|---|---|
| Clerk-Hire[a] | $288,156 |
| Official Expenses Allowance[b] | |
| Communication | 5,000 |
| Equipment Lease | 9,000 |
| District Office Rent | 7,000[c] |
| Postage | 211 |
| Office Supplies | 6,500 |
| Travel | [d] |
| Telecommunications (telephone/ telegraph) | [e] |
| Other Official Expenses | 7,000 |
| Equipment Purchase | 5,500[f] |
| Computer | 0[g] |

SOURCE: Committee on Appropriations 1979, 2: 1563–1566.

[a] Members may transfer up to $15,000 from the clerk-hire allowance to the Official Expenses Allowance.

[b] A consolidated allowance with amounts transferable between categories. A member may spend more than the allotment in one category by cutting expenditures in another. Amounts listed serve as a basis for setting the total amount of the allowance: $32,911 plus variable amounts in three categories (travel, telecommunications, and district office rental) due to variations in district distance from Washington, D.C., telephone tolls, and GSA office space cost in the district. Average Official Expenses Allowance is $75,000.

[c] Cost varies: based on cost of renting 2,500 square feet.

[d] Cost varies: based on 32 round trips to the district; minimum: $2,250.

[e] Cost varies.

[f] Plus one automatic typewriter.

[g] In estimating appropriations needs, $12,000–$15,000 per office is budgeted. $15,000 may be transferred from the clerk-hire allowance.

the basic allowances for each committee are similar. Most standing committees may appoint eighteen professional and twelve clerical aides to the permanent staff; the Appropriations and Budget Committees appoint staff under a separate authorization without regard to ceilings on numbers. The distinction between professional and clerical staff is often unclear—on some committees, for example, the staff director is the top clerical aide although the job entails both administrative and substantive duties—and thus the ceiling of thirty permanent employees is the critical limit.

Committees augment their permanent staffs by appointing "inquiries and investigations staffs." Although many of these aides serve on a committee for a number of years (and therefore appear to be permanent), funds for their salaries must be approved annually by the Committee on House Administration and the full House.[2] Most inquiries and investigations staff do not "investigate," but perform various research, legislative, and clerical duties.

Permanent staff increased from 149 in 1947 to 709 in 1978. Investigative staff increased much more rapidly, from 33 in 1947 to 899 in 1978. The House Administration Committee now scrutinizes requests for investigative aides closely, and cuts committee budgets more readily than in the past. Two top aides on each committee's permanent staff may be paid at Level IV of the Executive Schedule ($50,000 in January 1979); all other salaries must not exceed Level V ($47,500 in January 1979).

The procedures for funding standing committee expense spending are also dual in nature. Operating funds for regular legislative functions are provided by the same section of the Legislative Branch Appropriations Act that provides for member expense allowances. Fixed limits or ranges, however, do not exist, though the objects or purposes of such spending are, as in the case of member offices, regulated by House rules and regulations, issued and administered by the Committee on House Administration. In addition, committees can request additional money annually for expenses connected with their investigative work at the same time as and through the same procedures by which they request money for investigative staff. Such funds can be requested and used for purposes that would not otherwise be authorized (e.g., travel, consultants, and leased equipment), as well as to supplement funding for purposes that are generally authorized (e.g., telephone and stationery). Moreover, since, as in the case of staff, there is no hard line between a committee's "legislative" and "investigative" work, such funds in reality support the day-to-day operation of the committee. In the case of special and select committees, all their funding is provided through the use of special investigative resolutions, whereas Budget and Appropriations have their own separate items in the Legislative Branch Appropriations Act for expenses as well as staff.

Variations in staff and expense needs in the case of the great majority of standing committees are thus met through inquiries and investigations resolutions, reported annually by the Committee on House Administration. Standing committees annually submit budget requests to House Administration based on past experience and expected new needs. Their assessment of need is usually accepted, and the funding level is, in effect, set by the requesting committee. Through these procedures committees can obtain fairly generous funding: in 1978 inquiries and investigations funding varied from $275,000 for the District of Columbia Committee to $3.2 million for the Interstate and Foreign Commerce Committee, with eleven committees authorized to spend $1 million or more (Committee on House Administration 1978, 30; Committee on Appropriations 1979, 1604).[3] There is also more flexibility in expenditure than in member offices. Amounts in the funding resolution for consultant contracts and for staff training may not be exceeded, but otherwise there is no limit on the transfer of funds from one category to another. It is possible to transfer funds to or from employee salaries, or to budget for items for which no expenditure is made.

Distribution of staff resources within committees is governed by House, caucus, and committee rules. House rules authorize the chair and ranking minority member of all Appropriations subcommittees and of up to six subcommittees on other standing committees to appoint a staff aide. Democratic Caucus rules direct that *all* subcommittee chairs be permitted to appoint an aide. These requirements have been an important factor in increasing subcommittee autonomy and decentralizing decision making in the House.

House rules also direct that, if the minority requests, one-third of the permanent (statutory) staff (six professional and four clerical) be appointed to a minority staff. Twenty-one standing committees reported employment of 256 minority staff (149 statutory and 107 investigative) in 1976, the second session of the 94th Congress (Commission on Administrative Review 1977*a*, Appendix 2).

Finally, three committees—Appropriations, Rules, and Budget—permit any committee member who cannot otherwise appoint committee staff to hire one aide to assist on committee work. The result is to distribute staff resources more widely and especially to give junior members, who do not serve as chairs or ranking minority members of subcommittees, staff assistance for their committee work.

Some centralization of resource supervision—in contrast to wider resource distribution—continues. Thirteen of the twenty standing committees (65%) surveyed by the Obey Commission reported that the final subcommittee hiring decision remains a prerogative of the full committee leadership. Fox and Hammond (1977) report that 68% of the professional committee and subcommittee aides surveyed considered themselves primarily responsible to the

**Table 7.2. *Appropriations for Leadership and Party Offices***

| *Office* | *FY 1979* | | *FY 1980*[a] | |
|---|---|---|---|---|
| Speaker | $545,300 | | $566,100 | |
| Majority Leader | 384,100 | | 396,500 | |
| Minority Leader | 479,100 | | 491,500 | |
| Majority Whip[b] | 416,800 | | 431,600 | |
| Minority Whip[c] | 321,800 | | 336,600 | |
| Democratic Steering & Policy Committee | 308,900 | $392,500[d] | 323,000 | $408,600[d] |
| Democratic Caucus | 83,600 | | 85,600 | |
| Republican Conference[e] | $542,500 | | $566,900 | |

SOURCE: Committee on Appropriations 1979, 1295–1297, 1519–1526.
[a]Request for FY 1980 presented to Legislative Branch Appropriations Subcommittee, February 1979.
[b]Includes monies for office of Chief Deputy Majority Whip.
[c]Includes monies for office of Chief Deputy Minority Whip.
[d]In addition, in FY 1979 and 1980, six (majority) photographers were paid $158,000 per year from House Doorkeeper's funds; minority photographers were paid by the Republican Conference.
[e]Includes expenses of Republican Research Committee.

committee chair or ranking minority member. As subcommittee aides are usually directed by the subcommittee leaders, the resource is available but loyalties are not always clear.

In summary, core staff resources for committees are distributed fairly equally among committees, with additional staff distributed according to committee request and House approval. Staff distribution within the committees varies considerably. Most committee chairs control much of the recruitment, hiring, and activities of staff, although significant resources are given to subcommittee leaders and, in some instances, to rank and file members. Two changes in recent years—the increase in subcommittees and the requirements regarding subcommittee activity and resources—have had the important effect of distributing resources more widely to subunits of the House or to individual members.

*Leadership Offices.* Resources for leadership offices are also provided in the Legislative Branch Appropriations Act. Appropriations cover staff salaries and office expenses for the Speaker, the majority and minority leaders, and the majority and minority whips. Monies for leadership offices are detailed in table 7.2.

Leadership offices have administrative, legislative, and clerical responsibilities, as well as important informational, political, and coordinating duties. Aides may deal with executive officials on federal projects for the leader's district, or with committee chairs on the substance and timing of legislation.

Resources available to leadership offices are based primarily on need and request, rather than on underlying assumptions about equality between individual office subunits. The Speaker is recognized as having a dual role: the only constitutional officer of the Congress, and the leader of his party in the House. Staff and office duties have fluctuated depending on the wishes of the Speaker in office. An effort has been made to achieve approximate parity in funding the offices of the party leaders and whips ($800,900 to each party in fiscal year [FY] 1979). Functionally, the minority party relies on party organizations for research and analysis more than the majority party, with its control of most committee staff. The Republicans have staffed their party organizations accordingly and have more extensive party research and analysis staff resources. In 1978, staff of the Republican Conference, Research Committee, and Policy Committee totaled twenty-one as opposed to nine Democratic Caucus and Steering and Policy Committee staff. Generally, leadership offices have remained small. Speaker Tip O'Neill (D-Mass.), for example, expanded his deliberately small staff only slightly during the 95th Congress. He considered a small staff more manageable, and he wanted to assess his staffing needs.

Both whip offices rely extensively on organization of colleagues to assist them in their duties, and in recent years, the whip operation of the Democrats has expanded considerably. An organization of twenty-one members now is in place to assist in information and vote-counting activities. Whips may not vote with the party consistently, but they are accurate vote counters and informational assistants whatever their personal ideologies. As the 96th Congress began, the Democratic White House was relying increasingly on the services of the Democratic whip organization in the House (Bonafede 1979).

Leaders also rely on a network of resources built up over time which are not reflected in the funding figures for their offices. In early 1979, the House Democratic leaders—by then in office two years—began to shift staff aides from personal leadership staffs to other positions, thus in typical Hill fashion giving them a network of aides to assist in coordination and management of House business. Ari Weiss, for example, became staff director of the Democratic Steering and Policy Committee, after serving as a legislative assistant to the Speaker.

*Resources External to Individual Offices.* In addition to the resources allotted to the individual legislative offices, various resources are also available from central offices. Services, rather than funding, are distributed. Administrative and management support services are available from central House offices: messengers; housekeeping and repair services; budget, accounting, and disbursing assistance; personnel recruitment and management assistance; Congressional publications, including bills introduced and committee reports; and computer aid. Legislative support agencies, offering information as well as research and analysis services, have been established in conjunction with the Senate: the Congressional Research Service (CRS), the General Accounting Office (GAO), the Congressional Budget Office (CBO), and the Office of Technology Assessment (OTA). Although centrally provided and generally nonpartisan services run counter to the individualized accountability inherent in separate legislative subunits, the contradiction is handled by making services available to each legislative unit separately and on request. In some few instances preferential access is granted to certain legislative offices, as, for example, the provision that CBO works first for the Budget and Appropriations committees. Generally, however, all legislative offices—member, committee, and leadership—have access to assistance from the support groups.

Since 1970, the legislative support agencies have expanded assistance to congressional offices. For member offices the result has been greater and more diverse resources. Offices use the CRS issue briefs for quick reference and briefing and the SCORPIO computer system (see chap. 10) for ready information on bibliographies and bill status. New publications and in-depth analyses are available. The CBO scorekeeping reports, as well as economic and fiscal analyses on particular issues, offer information not easily available to member offices prior to 1975. The major change, however, has been in assistance to committees as a result of the requirements of the Legislative Reorganization Act of 1970 (84 Stat. 1140), and the 1974 Budget and Impoundment Control Act (88 Stat. 297). CBO works with the Budget Committee on economic projections and fiscal policy. GAO has begun working with standing committees to develop program evaluation and oversight procedures. CRS, in addition to identifying programs requiring reauthorization, has detailed staff to several committees (Rules, Obey Commission, Budget, 96th Congress Select Committee on Committees), and has undertaken major studies of current legislative interest for committees on such topics as the legislative veto and the impact of current pension laws. Analytical resources available to the House have been augmented and a

**Table 7.3. *Committee Use of Congressional Support Agencies*[a] *(percent)***

| | *Very Frequently* | *Regularly* | *Just Sometimes* | *Hardly Ever* | *Not at All* |
|---|---|---|---|---|---|
| GAO | 36 | 40 | 19 | 5 | 0 |
| CBO | 19 | 36 | 17 | 21 | 7 |
| OTA | 2 | 5 | 14 | 36 | 43 |
| CRS | 31 | 43 | 26 | 0 | 0 |

SOURCE: Committee Survey, Commission on Administrative Review 1977*b*, 1:696–698.

[a] Committee staff directors were asked, "How often do you or other staffers in your office make use of the support agencies? How often would you say your staff makes use of any of the different services or publications provided by [GAO, CBO, etc.]—very frequently, regularly, just sometimes, hardly ever, or not at all?" N = 42, 22 standing committees and 20 subcommittees.

continuing source of expertise is available without the dysfunctional consequences of expanding committee staff rapidly. Both legislative assistants and committee staff directors report frequent use of congressional support agencies. See table 7.3.

Ad hoc, nonofficial groups, such as the Democratic Study Group and the Republican Steering Committee, also serve as resources. The number of such groups has proliferated in recent years; during the 96th Congress more than thirty existed to serve members' informational, coordinative, and strategy needs.[4] Staff, supplies and equipment are funded by contributions from members' allowances, and the House has recognized the groups by allocating space in House office buildings or annexes.

## Workload Management

Greater resources more widely distributed are changes congenial to the House as a collegial and decentralized institution with an increasingly heavy workload. Within individual legislative offices, added resources have resulted in increasing specialization and the development of intraoffice coordinating mechanisms. Externally, central support services—both administrative and information-analytical—for legislative offices have been augmented; structures and mechanisms for interoffice coordination, such as the ad hoc, nonofficial groups, have been established; and structures to coordinate the work of the House as a whole have become more complex.

*Internal Organization and Management.* In all legislative offices job responsibilities have become more clearly delineated and duties increasingly specialized. Although only 30% of member offices have job descriptions (Commission on Administrative Review 1977*b*, 2:1022), a rough and clearly understood division of labor exists. The administrative assistant remains a generalist (administration, press work, federal projects, some legislative work) in an increasingly specialized office. For other professionals, specialization is along functional lines: at least one aide is usually appointed to handle every major activity—legislation, press work, casework, office administration, federal projects. The major change of the past five years has been the development of substantive specialization. Most offices now have several legislative assistants, an assistant press aide, and several caseworkers (each with a specified area of expertise). In some House offices, professionals may do their own typing and filing as well as their substantive work; in others legislative secretaries handle mail and free legislative assistants for work on research, drafting, and strategy. In a few offices, the workload is divided by subject areas, and professionals handle legislation, press work, and speeches within their particular areas. House member offices often have no clear organizational hierarchy. In contrast to committees, there continues to be an expectation that in an emergency all aides will work on a project such as a mailing, or a returned opinion survey, but most of the time specialization is the governing norm.

On committees, substantive specialization—by subject area and along subcommittee lines—has also grown in the last decade. Aides and some members specialize in certain areas of the committee's jurisdiction. The proliferation of subcommittees and their increasing autonomy and added resources encourage this type of specialization. Some committees deliberately duplicate specialists, with subcommittee staff and a committee aide working on the same issues. Other committees give complete autonomy to subcommittees, with full committee staff working on matters handled only by the full committee or on matters of particular interest to the chair. Several standing committees assign staff to subcommittees on an ad hoc basis. This reduces specialization, but would appear to enhance coordination and centralization.

Leadership offices—although specialized in the sense that they are established to coordinate the work of the House—resemble members' personal offices more than committee offices.[5] In the whip organizations, specialization occurs along area lines; in other leadership offices the specialization is primarily functional. Aides tend to be generalists. They must be attuned to political ramifications of issues and actions, and work with an eye on the political system and environment external to the House, as well as the intricacies of House politics. They are often House political specialists, as well as party or issue experts (Peabody 1976).

Coordination within offices is increasingly important. Personal staffs are divided between district and D.C. offices, and often among several noncontiguous rooms in Washington. Committee staffs are usually widely separated, with subcommittees most frequently housed separately from the committee staff (often in different buildings), and with majority and minority staff separated as well. Various mechanisms are used to facilitate intraoffice coordination. Staff meetings of all professionals, or of all staff, are held on a regular basis to exchange information and ideas on current projects and workload management. Other coordinative devices are regular meetings with the representative and frequent visits by staff directors and administrative assistants to offices in the annexes.

Coordination between Washington and district offices presents particular problems. There is often jurisdictional overlap, especially in federal projects, casework, and press work. One approach has been to delineate the division of workload clearly. Casework is moved to the district, or district offices act as intake offices for cases handled in D.C. Some representatives have computer terminals in their district offices, enabling staff to computerize office files and to use the LEGIS system (see chap. 10) to check the status of pending legislation. Carbons of correspondence are regularly sent from district offices to Washington. In a few instances, a log of daily work performed in the district office is sent to D.C. Some offices keep two sets of casework and federal projects files, if those matters are handled by the district office. Finally, some offices bring district office personnel to D.C. to meet staff and discuss common goals. In virtually all offices, top D.C. aides and the representative return to the district regularly.

*External Administrative and Coordination Support.* The augmented central information and analytical services provided by the legislative support agencies are important resources for individual legislative offices. Two types of central services provided by the House have also been increasingly important in handling legislative office workload: office management assistance and the provision of sophisticated office equipment and advanced technological services, including computers.

In recent years the House has expanded its office management assistance capability; assistance from outside groups, such as the

Congressional Management Foundation or private management consultants, has also increased. Studies have been made for individual legislative offices on mail flow procedures, filing systems, staff organization, office layout, personnel procedures, and workload management. In early 1979, the Office of Management Services was established under the aegis of the Committee on House Administration, as a successor to the Office of Placement and Management run by the Select Committee on Congressional Operations. The office is designed to offer expanded assistance in personnel recruitment and office management to individual legislative offices. Both nonofficial groups and congressional support agencies conduct an increasing number of briefing, training, and orientation sessions for legislative offices on legislative and office procedures and on policy issues.

Although the Congress moves slowly and often in an uncoordinated fashion (it has taken years for the House and Senate to coordinate computerized information used in both), legislative offices have gradually become users of the most recent office technology. Sophisticated office equipment—memory and mag card typewriters, computerized typesetting, microfiche files, CMS mail and file systems—is available to all legislative offices and used by most. In mid-1979, 300 member offices and all of the standing committees reported some use of computers, according to the Office of Management Services. Computer assistance and computer information files are available to legislative offices, and members' district offices have computer terminals linked to the House system. Member offices can contract computer assistance from outside firms for a variety of office needs such as mail, accounts, filing, and newsletters. Committees also use the House computer facility (House Information Systems—HIS) for scheduling, committee calendars, mail and committee accounts, and for research and analysis. Six standing committees and a number of subcommittees reported using computer assistance from outside the House in 1977: five committees used the Chase Econometric Data Bank; Banking and Housing used the Housing and Urban Development Department's computer to calculate block grant formulas; Ways and Means used Department of Health, Education and Welfare computers to figure costs of Medicare proposals. There is also extensive central in-House capability to handle floor votes and office administration matters.

Formal structures and informal arrangements coordinate the work of the individual legislative subunits. Leadership offices are prime actors in the formal coordination structure. In recent years their resources have expanded and their organizations become more complex. They have become increasingly involved in monitoring the flow of legislation as it moves through subcommittee and committee to the floor, and they now follow the content of legislation closely. The power to appoint ad hoc committees to work on specific legislation which falls within the jurisdiction of more than one standing committee has increased the power and coordinative tools of the Speaker.

A number of legislative offices, particularly member offices, participate in informal pooling arrangements. A group of ten Republican representatives in the 95th Congress pooled computer allowances and ran a central computer operation for processing legislative and casework mail. Six offices ran a joint mimeo-mailing operation. Less formally, two or more offices pool salary allowances to hire a staff aide to work on a particular issue, or an ad hoc group or caucus may be staffed by an aide from a member's office.

These nonofficial groups help legislative, and particularly member, offices manage the workload and serve to coordinate the work of the House. By pooling resources—contributing a staff aide to the DSG, for example—members help ensure timely analysis or needed in-depth research. On substantive issues or procedural matters, ad hoc groups or caucuses assist in the development and implementation of strategy—including the coordination of offices in support or opposition. The proliferation of these groups has contributed to coordination problems, but for member offices the arrangement is efficient.

## ISSUES AND PROBLEMS IN MANAGING LEGISLATIVE OFFICES

Although House response to meet the demands of a changing environment and a heavier and more complex workload has been incremental, it has not been entirely random. Gradually, structures and procedures have been developed which have the potential for managing the workload with greater efficiency and increased effectiveness. However, a number of problems and concerns remain. Central issues are the quality and quantity of resources, and the management of resources.

### The Quantity and Quality of Resources

Resources to assist and support representatives in carrying out their duties are today regarded as necessary to efficient and effective performance. However, disagreement continues over the level and distribution of resources.

How much staff is adequate? How much is too much? Different

**Table 7.4. *Workload and Staffing Needs of Member Offices***

| | *Staffing* | | | |
|---|---|---|---|---|
| | *Over-Staffed (%)* | *About Right (%)* | *Under-Staffed (%)* | N |
| Office Supervision | 2 | 90 | 8 | 143 |
| Communications | 2 | 78 | 20 | 142 |
| Legislative Research | 3 | 55 | 44 | 142 |
| Legislative Mail | 1 | 53 | 47 | 143 |
| Casework | 9 | 71 | 20 | 143 |
| Personal or Appointments Secretary | 0 | 98 | 2 | 143 |
| Clerical | 1 | 57 | 43 | 143 |
| Other | 10 | 90 | 0 | 19 |

SOURCE: Commission on Administrative Review 1977*b*, 2:1053–1054, question 22c.

perceptions of member and office roles yield different answers. Nearly half of the administrative assistants interviewed by the Obey Commission felt their offices were understaffed for legislative work. Nearly all felt offices were understaffed in the clerical areas. Of those representatives who identified lack of adequate staffing as a problem in doing their jobs, 25% had served six or more terms in the House; 75% had served five or fewer terms (Commission on Administrative Review 1977*b*, 1:674–676, MQ1a Wave II Survey). For committees with heavy legislative and supervisory workloads, staffing is perceived as adequate in most areas. However, as with personal offices, a sample of committee and subcommittee staff directors interviewed by the Obey Commission felt they could use more staff, primarily for legislative responsibilities. Few report overstaffing. Tables 7.4 and 7.5 explicate this data in more detail.

Some scholars and observers argue that larger staffs work primarily on reelection and constituent service activities (Mayhew 1974; Fiorina 1977). On the other hand, as staffs have increased and become more expert, (1) there are more hearings; (2) oversight activity has increased; and (3) more legislation is introduced (Aberbach 1977; Johannes 1978; Fox and Hammond 1977; Hammond et al. 1977). Legislation is more complex and there are more programs to oversee (Schick 1976; Committee on House Administration 1978). It is difficult to document specifically the results of increased and more expert assistance on data collection and analysis or the effect

**Table 7.5. *Workload and Staffing Needs of Committee and Subcommittee Offices***

| | *Staffing* | | | |
|---|---|---|---|---|
| | *Over-Staffed (%)* | *About Right (%)* | *Under-Staffed (%)* | N |
| Supervisory | — | 98 | 2 | 42 |
| Internal Administration | 3 | 88 | 10 | 40 |
| Communications | — | 84 | 16 | 38 |
| Legal Analysis | — | 80 | 20 | 41 |
| Substantive Analysis | — | 73 | 27 | 40 |
| Secretarial | — | 69 | 31 | 42 |

SOURCE: Commission on Administrative Review 1977*b*, 0:000–000, Committee Staff Survey, question 10c.

of increased casework on oversight and legislation. And as yet there are no systematic data on changes in quality of legislation, oversight, and representation. In the House there is widespread concern about the development of a congressional bureaucracy which is unresponsive, insulates members from their constituents, and requires additional administrative staff and a more hierarchical organization. The Obey Commission recommended, and in 1979 the Select Committee on Committees reexamined the feasibility of, a ceiling on investigative committee staff.

Many members continue to feel that inequities remain in the distribution of staff, and that there is a continuing pattern of differential access to staff resources. Committee members who can appoint or designate one or more aides (committee and subcommittee chairs, ranking minority members, and all members of Appropriations, Budget, and Rules) tend to have smaller personal staffs. In April 1977 these members employed an average of 15.6 aides in contrast to 16.2 in all other member offices. Those same members contribute disproportionately to staffing nonofficial groups—54 of 72 slots (70%) in April 1977—indicating a flexibility in staffing not available to other members. A number of more junior members told the Obey Commission of problems and frustrations relating to staff resources: "Availability of committee staff to members is abominable," and ". . . there ought to be some way of assuring that a member has someone responsible for his committee work available on the committee staff" (Commission on Administrative Review 1977*b*,

1:637). In conjunction with the data on staff as sources of legislative information, such a pattern must be viewed as a significant factor in workload management.

The level of minority staffing of committees and the relationship of minority to majority staff continue to be issues. The Senate provides staff to the minority out of investigative funds, and many Republican representatives would like a similar provision in the House. During the 95th Congress only two standing committees had nonpartisan staffs. On the remaining twenty, minority aides were generally organized to serve all minority members, and the wider distribution of resources has tended to make minority staffing more feasible than in the past. The relationship between majority and minority staff continues to be worked out on an ad hoc basis. On some committees little information is exchanged and the minority is viewed as obstructionist. On other committees the minority plays an important negotiating role. The personalities of committee leaders and top staff and the degree to which majority members need the minority to report and pass legislation are significant factors in determining the pattern of the relationship.

Staff recruitment affects the quality of resources available to legislative offices. Recruitment problems affect management problems whether the issue is lack of competence, a need for training, or divided loyalties based on recruitment practices. Most legislative offices report problems in recruiting clerical help, but little difficulty in recruiting qualified professionals. Still, the picture of recruitment which emerges is one of a narrow network of sources based on resumes in hand and word of mouth. Committee experts are generally sought within the Washington policy subsystem or network (Fox and Hammond 1977). Committee members often refer candidates for committee positions. Several staff directors cited pressure to hire a referral over other (possibly more qualified) candidates as a major recruitment problem. Member office staff may also be drawn from the district, summer interns, or campaign aides—although one member ruefully reported that this ad hoc system does not work:

> But I have found to my chagrin that campaign volunteers don't always make good staff—the kind of person who's good in a campaign is to a certain extent a huckster, a dreamer, in a fever of excitement. To be a good staff person requires a lot more drudgery. There is a lot more glamour in blasting an opponent in the press than in making five telephone calls to make sure a widow in town gets her social security check. But

that's more important. I had a couple of former campaign people who wanted to change the world. They didn't work out.

Many offices emphasized the need for training sessions in office skills, legislative procedures, and congressional information sources. In Obey Commission surveys 74% of the committee and subcommittee staff directors interviewed (31 of 42) identified training programs which would be useful for committee staff. These included parliamentary procedures and mechanics of the legislative process (bill drafting, markup, reports, etc.), legislative policy issues, budgeting and bookkeeping, use of new equipment, filing, and editing. Although twenty committees budget funds for training professional staff, few use them. "We can't let anyone go," "It's just there in case we want to send someone," staff directors say. Slightly more than 80% of the members interviewed supported training programs for their personal office staffs. Since the *Final Report* of the Obey Commission was published, the Office of Management Services of the House Administration Committee has been established with responsibility for staff training programs. Other groups such as the CRS continue training seminars. There is a need for both orientation sessions and programs throughout the year for new staff and for in-service training for others.

The typically short tenure of congressional aides contributes to resource and management problems. Many representatives express concern but also recognize the benefits of the system. One member whose aides regularly leave for better jobs reflected, "I really don't expect staff people to stay [more than two or three years]. I hope to get people who want to be leaders themselves, as opposed to staff people forever. They get training, . . . and then move on to greater responsibility." Another member reported he "fires people systematically to keep from getting too entrenched. . . . I deliberately keep the turnover going." These attitudes may be fairly widespread, particularly in member offices. They exacerbate an environment already keyed to the short-term view—a frenetic pace, negotiable salaries and leave policies, and few clear career patterns. The tradeoffs for a system which brings new ideas through wholesale turnover are that training is more necessary, recruitment takes more time, and employees use the system to gain experience (as it uses them). The House needs to face the dysfunctional consequences of the system.

All these concerns raise questions regarding the proper role and functions of the individual legislative subunits, and of different groups of legislators within the House—senior and junior members or majority and minority party members, for example. Although there is basic agreement that all members and all legislative offices must have access to resources, a change in the level or distribution of resources has both political and policy consequences. Congress cannot, and in fact should not, match the executive in numbers and expertise. On the other hand, enhanced informational and analytical resources can lead to fuller consideration of legislative issues; more constituents may genuinely need assistance; and the increased casework load can assist oversight and policy making.

In the future it is likely that a central concern will be diversification of staff skills and better management of existing resources, although the tensions between those who control resources and those who perceive the need for more or better or differently distributed resources will undoubtedly continue.

**Management of Resources**

Management problems in the House result from the decentralized structure, collegial decision processes, and different backgrounds of members and aides. For the House as an institution there are problems of coordination, duplication, and overlap in the work of the legislative subunits. For individual legislative offices, with larger staffs and augmented resources, there are management and coordination needs that must be met in an institutional environment which permits complete autonomy and makes centralized guidance difficult.[6]

*Office Organization and Coordination.* Office organization patterns and needs underscore the opportunities and constraints of the legislative environment. As one respondent said, "Here [on the Hill], as opposed to the executive branch, each [legislative office] follows its own practices, and, while I know there are drawbacks, there are many advantages over working in a huge bureaucracy with many [standardized] regulations." The lack of hierarchy in the House is often reflected in legislative offices. Interview data from the Obey Commission indicate that offices organized so that aides function as co-equal generalists are often frustrating places to work and produce widespread unhappiness about the working environment. In one office with this arrangement, turnover was far higher (11 in 2½ years) than the House average (6.7 for the same period). An administrative assistant in an office organized for equality noted, "A major problem is dissatisfaction. Everyone is dissatisfied—because everyone is overqualified."

Most representatives and their aides do not have management

training and many do not have management experience. Members and staff have gradually become aware of management deficiencies and needs. There is a perceived need for expansion of existing programs to assist legislative offices in managing personnel and workload. Members interviewed by the Obey Commission repeatedly noted management needs: "A priority problem is management," one administrative assistant noted. A member said, "Some . . . management expert could come in [to my personal office] and help us a lot. I sometimes walk around just to see how people set up desks in the outer office. I suspect there is a reasonably efficient way of setting it up, although I don't know what it is" (Commission on Administrative Review 1977*b*, 1:675). Member offices must distribute and coordinate the workload between Washington and district offices. Committees frequently must coordinate staffs housed in offices which are widely separated and some distance from the chair as well as from members. Appointment of associate committee staff, usually housed in member offices, brings added management problems, at least for the committee staff directors. The autonomy of minority staff varies and may bring difficulties for managerial personnel.

Subcommittees present special management problems. Although the growth in the number of subcommittees and the increase in their autonomy have been among the most dramatic changes since 1970, the relationship of subcommittees to their parent committees remains unsettled. Lines of operational authority often remain blurred, and both subcommittee and committee staff are dissatisfied. Hiring, budgeting, and absence of clear operational autonomy are often cited as problem points. Most subcommittees do not have separate line items in committee budgets, and may therefore be dependent on committees for every expenditure decision. As one aide said, "Subcommittee budgets shouldn't be just a fungible mass within the full committee budget. . . . Sometimes I don't even know the amounts available to the subcommittee."

Final hiring authority may rest with the committee chair or ranking minority members; professionals may operate autonomously but depend on the full committee for support staff; salaries and raises may be set by the full committee, or salary for subcommittee aides may be lower. Final budget decisions are often made at the full committee level, and in virtually all committees financial administration occurs at that level. Subcommittee staff directors frequently complain about scheduling problems vis-à-vis the full committee. They have trouble getting hearing rooms, or focusing full committee time and attention on a major subcommittee priority. It is unlikely that the tension between full committee control and subcommittee autonomy can, or should, be completely eliminated. But the rather surprising picture which emerges from the Obey Commission interviews is of subcommittees which are somewhat less autonomous as a result of the reforms of the 1970s than the literature describes.

*Personnel.* A number of personnel management problems exist. Because salary and leave policies are set by each legislative office there is no uniformity. Committees generally pay higher salaries than personal offices and are able to attract aides from members' offices. There are also salary disparities among committees and among personal offices. Most personal offices (70% of the respondents) do not have established salary schedules and most administrative assistants feel those would not be useful (74% of those without any salary schedule). One standing committee has established salary schedules; of the remaining twenty-one, 70% of the staff directors feel they would not be beneficial. Although most offices do not want salary structure dictated by the House, many would welcome guidelines against which the office operation could be assessed as an improvement on the present ad hoc and random system.

Few offices (41% of committees and subcommittees, and 30% of member offices) have job descriptions, and most managers feel they would not be helpful. In all legislative offices staff can be fired at will; few have established grievance procedures. Slightly more than 40% of the members' offices and 50% of the committee and subcommittee offices report written vacation and sick leave policies. Leave policies, however, are not uniform. Nor is leave transferable between offices, which creates problems when employees move to a different office.

Members, administrative assistants, and staff directors fear uniformity and rigidity from central directives. They emphasize individualism and the individual accountability of each House member. One administrative assistant said: "You simply can't impose a form; [staff] must match what the member's needs are, and he determines his priorities." A member argued, "If a member wants to bounce somebody for the most outrageous reason, he should. It's his choice. They've got to learn I'm on the firing line every two years." The constraints are clear. The problem is to find some acceptable level of structure, including guidelines and standards, which also allow for individual office differences.

*Allowance System.* For member offices, a system of equal allotments, and of individual discretion regarding use, follows from the premises upon which the system is built. Since 1977 the House has moved toward greater flexibility in the management of allowances with the creation of a consolidated Official Expense Allowance for members and the exemption of certain employees from the ceiling of eighteen on personal staff numbers. But in some respects the system remains inflexible and rigid. Half of the members interviewed and half of the administrative assistants report that the rule that not more than 1/12 (since July 1979, 1/10) of the clerk-hire allowance can be spent in any one month is a problem in operating legislative offices. Members and aides would like a simplified voucher system and current allowance expenditures data. One AA said, "You're dealing with 435 fiefdoms, . . . their [House Administration Committee and central administrative offices] problem is in loco parentis, . . . they should let you splurge it all."

As office needs and available technology have changed, incremental changes have been made in member office allowances to meet immediate needs, and the House has moved to correct abuses by various restrictions. The result is a system which meets many specific needs, but is difficult to redesign or change in any comprehensive way.

*Time Management.* Schedule and time management problems are common to all legislative offices. The uneven pace of work sets the parameters. Committees, somewhat more able than member offices to anticipate and control work flow, are beginning to establish hearing and oversight schedules for a session. But generally the unanticipated remains an important factor in management of the workload.

Two findings by the Obey Commission with regard to members' use of time directly affect management of legislative offices: one is the long and fragmented nature of the representative's day, the other is the unpredictable nature of members' schedules. Both personal and committee offices must be organized to work within the constraints of that schedule. Members complain about multiple and conflicting demands on their time—but committees cite difficulties assembling a quorum and legislative assistants complain that they must conduct briefings on legislation as members dash to the elevator for a meeting or a floor vote. Member offices tend to cope by working longer hours when necessary and by scheduling anticipated work demands such as newsletters carefully. Experienced staff have learned that certain patterns can be anticipated—more legislative mail in winter and after holidays, constituent visits during holidays and summer—and organize to meet these patterns. But the workload remains unpredictable and can only be managed by flexibility in staff hours and by jurisdictional overlap in office duties. All offices agree that the scheduling changes in recent years—set hours for convening and a schedule of recesses for a session—have alleviated some of the schedule-management problems.

## CONCLUSION

Institutional and political factors shape the operating environment for legislative offices in the House. The collegial nature of the institution, the representative duties of House members, their strong ties to their constituencies, and the political context in which members and aides work affect the provision and management of legislative office resources.

In this environment, what are the possibilities for meaningful change? Indeed, what constitutes meaningful change? There is little agreement. House members differ regarding the sufficiency, the distribution, and the organization and management of resources. Their views tend to vary with their goals and priorities, and often with party and tenure. Any change is likely to decrease power for some.

The results of the 1970s reforms are a case in point. Change in the seniority system, regarded as much needed by many, has resulted in greater decentralization and more difficulty in coordinating and formulating unified congressional programs. The benefits have been greater participation by more members, earlier use of junior talent, and significant changes in legislation as it moves through the House. Many of the benefits derive from the wider distribution of increased resources. Which resources are increased and how they are distributed significantly affects the roles members play in congressional decision making.

In the future there is likely to be an increasing flexibility in management of accounts and operation of individual legislative offices, and more emphasis on good management practices (with increased House assistance). Some standardization of procedures and centralization of operations will also occur. Indeed a significant number of members and top aides agree that House guidelines would be helpful in several areas such as salary structure and vacation and sick leave policies. In this regard it may be noted that the Committee on House Administration recently began to publish optional leave guidelines for member and committee offices. Some added provisions for coordination among offices also would be desirable: a method to transfer vacation leave from one office to another, for example. Further standardization and centralization of computer technology appears to be both useful and necessary to the efficiency of individual legislative offices and to the House as an institution. Legislative offices can give up some autonomy in order to enhance both efficiency and effectiveness.

But change which impinges on individual office flexibility and individual decision making in the management of offices is less likely, and indeed, may not be in the best interests of either the offices or the House. Members, whether operating personal or committee offices, must perceive that the benefits of the change outweigh the costs and the risks. It is possible that an institutional challenge will bring about rapid change—for example, that enough members will want to achieve coordinated policy formulation to induce them to surrender some individual autonomy and organizational decentralization. But the short-term outlook is for incremental change which simply intensifies the current trends. The changes that occur will be more carefully assessed, will always be opposed by a vocal minority, and will in the long run bring greater efficiency and effectiveness in the institution. This is not necessarily a gloomy scenario.

Change depends on members' goals, ambitions, and perceptions of congressional function, and most basically, on election patterns and their constituents. All offices operate in a political environment. The strengths and the weaknesses of legislative office management stem from the representatives' ties to the constituency—the basis for the existence of the House and the overriding environmental factor.

## NOTES

1. Legislative offices are here defined as offices of individual members, committees (and subcommittees), and party leaders (the Speaker, the majority and minority leaders, and the majority and minority whips). These offices are part of the formal structure of the House and are formally concerned with decisions regarding legislation and policy. Other House offices, such as the Office of the Legislative Counsel, and those of nonofficial informal groups such as the Democratic Study Group or the Republican Steering Committee, also deal with legislative matters, but neither type of office is part of the formal, on-going legislative decision-making structure of the House. In addition, some aspects of the management of these offices, such as resource allocation and distribution, are quite different from member, committee, and party leader office management.
2. House rule 11, paragraphs (5) and (6).
3. The Obey Commission reported that for the first session of the 94th

Congress every House committee overestimated actual expenditures in making their budget requests, in contrast to members, many of whom use nearly all of their clerk-hire and office expense allowances.

4. Although specific groups come and go, the number of groups has increased rapidly in recent years, and many have become institutionalized and semipermanent. Groups form along party, ideological, regional, and class lines: the Democratic Study Group (DSG), United Democrats, New England Congressional Caucus, the 94th Congress Freshman Democrats. They may be based on shared attributes (the Blue Collar Caucus, Women's Caucus), or shared interests (Steel Caucus, Textile Caucus).
5. Each leader has a personal office staff to handle primarily constituent service matters, although the division is not clearcut; often major federal projects are handled by a top assistant in the leadership office, or important district constituents meet in the Capitol with leadership staff aides. Political scientists have rarely focused on the workload of leadership offices (Peabody 1976 is the major exception), although the work of party offices has received some attention (Stewart 1975; Commission on the Operation of the Senate 1977).
6. Congressional offices are crowded. Although space constraints affect office management, discussion is beyond the scope of this paper.

## REFERENCES

Aberbach, Joel D. 1977. "The Development of Oversight in the U.S. Congress: Concepts and Analysis." In *Techniques and Procedures for Analysis and Evaluation*, Commission on the Operation of the Senate, U.S. Congress, Senate. 94th Cong., 2d sess.

Bonafede, Dom. 1979. "Normalizing Relations with Capitol Hill." *National Journal* 11, No. 2 (January 13):54–57.

Commission on Administrative Review, U.S. Congress, House. 1977*a*. *Background Information on Administrative Units, Members' Offices, and Committees and Leadership Offices*. 95th Cong., 1st sess. H. Doc. 95-178.

———. 1977*b*. *Final Report*. 2 vols. 95th Cong., 1st sess. H. Doc. 95-272.

Commission on the Operation of the Senate, U.S. Congress, Senate. 1977. *Techniques and Procedures for Analysis and Evaluation*. 94th Cong., 2d sess.

Committee on Appropriations, Subcommittee on Legislative Branch Appropriations, U.S. Congress, House. 1979. *Hearings on Legislative Branch Appropriations FY 1980*. 96th Cong., 1st sess.

Committee on House Administration, U.S. Congress, House. 1978. "Studies Dealing with Budgetary, Staffing and Administrative Activities of the U.S. House of Representatives." 95th Cong., 2d sess.

Fiorina, Morris P. 1977. *Congress: Keystone of the Washington Establishment*. New Haven: Yale University Press.

Fox, Harrison W., Jr., and Hammond, Susan W. 1977. *Congressional Staffs: The Invisible Force in American Lawmaking*. New York: Free Press.

Hammond, Susan W.; Fox, Harrison W., Jr.; Moraski, Richard; Nicholson, Jeanne B. 1977. "Senate Oversight Activities." In *Techniques and Procedures for Analysis and Evaluation*, Commission on the Operation of the Senate, U.S. Congress, Senate. 94th Cong., 2d sess.

Johannes, John R. 1978. "Congressional Caseworkers: Attitudes, Orientations and Operations." Paper presented at the 1978 annual meeting of the Midwest Political Science Association, Chicago.

Mayhew, David R. 1974. *Congress: The Electoral Connection*. New Haven: Yale University Press.

Peabody, Robert L. 1976. *Leadership in Congress*. Boston: Little, Brown.

Schick, Allan. 1976. "The Supply and Demand for Analysis on Capitol Hill." *Policy Analysis* 2(Spring):215–235.

Stewart, John G. 1975. "Central Policy Organs in Congress." In *Congress Against the President*, ed. Harvey C. Mansfield, Sr. New York: Praeger.

# 8. Providing Administrative Support Services to the House

*Jarold A. Kieffer*

Legislative bodies, like other organizations, have to be structured both to perform their central function and to facilitate the work of the key actors and their helpers. However, in the case of the U.S. House of Representatives, the key actors include: (1) a Speaker chosen by the members to be their presiding officer; (2) over a hundred members, who, through a combination of action by the dominant political party and the workings of the seniority system, are chosen to chair their various policy-recommending and study committees and subcommittees; and (3) three officers—the Clerk, the Doorkeeper, and the Sergeant at Arms—chosen by the members to perform various legislative and administrative support roles on their behalf.

The collegial character of the U.S. House of Representatives—and, for the most part, its sister House, the U.S. Senate—set the organization of the legislative branch markedly apart from that of the federal executive branch.

The president has broad leadership authority and responsibility for the administrative direction of the executive branch. While these sources of authority and responsibility grew slowly, they developed from sweeping constitutional grants to the president to "take care that the laws are faithfully executed" and to make appointments. Then, particularly from the mid-1930s on, law after law granted specific authority to the president in both the policy-making and administrative areas.

In contrast, in the House of Representatives, not even the Speaker of the House has a clear charter from fellow members to direct, make policy for, or oversee the day-to-day administrative affairs of the body. While the Speaker does play an administrative role and does have considerable influence in this area, this is a consequence of the Speaker's party role, rather than any broad constitutional or statutory authority vested in the office.

In the executive branch, the dominant organizational form is a pyramid structure, in which administrative authority is granted to or rests in the president first and then flows from him to the department heads, and so on down the line.

In contrast, the House, in effect, is a committee which, through a collective process, provides itself with services that help it do its work. It commands these services through several bodies made up of its own members (or including U.S. Senators) that are set up to establish or monitor administrative arrangements, and it gives instructions to officers it elects to direct day-to-day operations. It expects the Speaker to keep things moving, listen to complaints, and referee occasional administrative disputes.

The House is different from executive branch organizations in a number of other ways.

The president and his department heads exercise administrative leadership in a context of laws established by the Congress. These executives may have helped shape the thinking of the Congress regarding those laws, but, for the most part, successive presidents and secretaries have taken the statutory administrative support arrangements they found and tried to function under them as best they could.

The president and his associates also must administer their responsibilities with resources and often priorities determined in minute detail by the Congress. Congress has shaped the organizational structures and financial framework through which the executive branch administers, and it has determined the personnel hiring, evaluation, compensation, and termination procedures that must be used. In addition, it often holds the president and his associates closely accountable for actions and results.

In contrast, the House determines: (1) its own program, priorities, and timetable through collective action of the members; (2) its own resource needs and the allocation of those resources to its members and subunits; and (3) its own administrative structure, personnel system, staff compensation, and modes of accountability.

While the Senate and the House could have established a single administrative system to serve their collective needs, they have chosen to do so only in a few areas. Consequently, this chapter focuses on how the House has allocated authority for providing support services for its operations, and how functional processes and responsibilities actually have developed in connection with allocated authority.

In examining these topics or themes it is first necessary to identify the administrative system in the House. For a variety of reasons this is a task for which there is no easy or neat solution. Nonetheless, a useful, working definition can be established by distinguishing those units and related activities that are directly and immediately involved in carrying on the legislative work of the House from those units and related activities that are wholly or largely involved in providing various kinds of support services. The administrative system may thus be seen as the complex of units and related activities or processes that are involved in providing support services to the four primary work locations in the House—member offices, committee offices, party offices, and the floor.

This system has grown quite large and elaborate in the past quarter century. As the volume and complexity of demands on the House have increased and its committee and office staffs have mushroomed, the dimensions of its administrative system have also expanded. Even excluding those legislative branch units that provide services to the federal government generally (e.g., the Government Printing Office, the General Accounting Office, and the Library of Congress), the administrative support system in the House includes more than forty units, has several thousand employees, expends tens of millions annually on its own operations, and plays a variety of important roles in the expenditure of the hundreds of millions that are annually involved in operating the House.[1]

## THE DISTRIBUTION OF MANAGERIAL AUTHORITY

The distribution of policy and operational authority in the administrative system of the House is highly variegated and complex. It reflects the legislative character of the body, the ad hoc development of the units, and their placement in a number of different locations within the House and the legislative branch.

### Central Sources of Policy Direction and Control

The sources of central policy direction and control in the provision of support services are few and their impact varies. They include the House Administration Committee, the Legislative Branch Appropriations Subcommittee, and the Speaker of the House.

*Committee on House Administration.* House rule X gives the Committee on House Administration broad policy-making and review powers over major parts of the House administrative system. This committee, which was created by the Legislative Reorganization Act of 1946, has both legislative jurisdiction and policy control over the uses of the Contingent Fund. This fund is a primary source of money for both staff and operating expenses in the House.[2] It is the source of money for the various allowances, aside from clerk-hire, that defray the operating expenses of member offices. It is with some exceptions the source of money used by standing committees for their regular or "legislative" operating expenses and by internal administrative units for all operating expenses. It is, in addition, a supplementary source of money for staff and expenses (special investigative funds) that standing committees heavily rely upon and that serves as the sole support of special or select committees. All vouchers requiring payment form the fund and all monthly payroll certifications for the House must be approved by the chair of the Committee on House Administration.

Through its authority over the Contingent Fund and through other authorities growing out of law, House rules, and resolutions, the committee exercises the following central policy and control functions:

a. Issues and administers regulations that, within limits set by the House, govern or control spending from the Contingent Fund for operating expenses by member offices, committee offices, and other House units
b. Develops and consolidates budgetary requests with reference to all categories of expenditure in the Contingent Fund for inclusion in the Legislative Branch Appropriations Bill and reviews and approves committee requests for special investigative funds for staff and expenses prior to their submission to the House for final approval
c. Establishes and controls policy and practice under the House Employees Position Classification Act regarding the number, rates of pay, duties, and qualifications of positions in the offices of the Clerk, Doorkeeper, Sergeant at Arms, and Postmaster, and in the House Recording Studio and the Media and Press Galleries
d. Reviews and passes upon all proposed Clerk of the House and House committee contracts for supplying goods and services, including consultant services
e. Establishes policies for and oversees House financial management services, arranges audits for and settles all Contingent Fund accounts, including member travel, and establishes accounting procedures for spending for operating expenses by member offices, committee offices, and other House units

f. Determines the types of furniture and electrical and mechanical office equipment approved for House purchase or lease and establishes the prices involved
g. Establishes policy and controls the collective or institutional development of information and management systems for all House units

*Legislative Branch Appropriations Subcommittee.* Budgets for all House units and activities are included in the Legislative Branch Appropriations Bill and reviewed by the Legislative Branch Appropriations Subcommittee of the House Appropriations Committee. While many items, such as members' salaries and the number of staff personnel assigned to each member are fixed by law or resolution, the subcommittee has authority to recommend changes in the levels of expenditures for a broad range of support categories.

*The Speaker.* The Speaker is given little formal authority for central direction and policy control over the House administrative system. However, as the chief elected officer of the House, he is broadly influential within the dominant party in such matters as the choice of the other officers and the chairs of the Committee on House Administration and its subcommittees. Also, he is regularly consulted and makes policy decisions on issues arising in the operation of House facilities and the allocation of space for House activities.

Finally, the Speaker, by the nature of his overall leadership role in the House, both in the party sense and as the chief elected officer, is the one person naturally held accountable by the opposition party, the media, and the public when a support service breaks down in some area or abuses are uncovered.

**Sources of Specific Policy Direction and Control**

Several units provide policy direction and control over certain specific support units and activities.

*House Office Building Commission.* The House Office Building Commission (composed of the Speaker, who chairs it, and the House majority and minority leaders) provides policy direction to the Architect of the Capitol and his staff relative to all matters involved in the housekeeping, design, construction, renovation, and repair of the physical facilities of the House, with the exception of the garages, the restaurants, and the gym. The commission also sets the policies and settles questions regarding the allocation of space in House facilities to members, officers, committees, and administrative units.

*Committee on House Administration.* The committee establishes use and pricing policies for House parking areas, food services, beauty shop, and barber shops. It provides policy direction for House Information Systems, the unit that provides computer services of various types to members and units on behalf of the House. It also provides policy direction for the Office of Management Services, the unit that now encompasses the old Office of Placement and Office Management and provides recruitment, training, and management consultant services on behalf of the House.

In addition, the committee has legislative jurisdiction and oversight responsibilities with respect to the Library of Congress, the House Library, and the Government Printing Office, and sets policy on printing charges and the printing and distribution of congressional publications, including the *Congressional Record.*

*Select Committees and Boards.* Several specialized House support activities are given policy direction and oversight by units independent of the Committee on House Administration. They include the Select Committee on the House Recording Studios and the Ad Hoc Committee on the Gym. In addition, the Capitol Police Board, composed of the two Sergeants at Arms (of the House and Senate) and the Architect, determines general policy for the Capitol police, and the Capitol Guide Service Board, composed of the same officials, determines general policy for the Guide Service.

**The Nature and Distribution of Operational Authority**

Direct managerial authority over the day-to-day operations of support units and activities is not as clear or as consistent as in the federal executive or large organizations in the private sector. Managerial control thus does not mean the same thing from unit to unit. In some cases, an officer may hold the power of appointment for the chief personnel of a unit, but not approve its budget. In other cases, a unit may report to one officer, but receive day-to-day direction from another officer.

Once again these discrepancies reflect the legislative character of the House and the ad hoc process by which the administrative system has developed. Nonetheless, various elected or appointed officers as well as certain committees have become responsible for the direction, personnel approvals, and budgets of particular support units or sets of units.

The primary officers are the Speaker, Clerk, Doorkeeper, Sergeant at Arms, Postmaster, and Architect of the Capitol. All but the Architect are elected by the House at the beginning of each Congress. The Architect is appointed by the president without a fixed term, but is considered a statutory officer of the Congress. The primary committee once again is the Committee on House Administration, which combines a variety of important policy responsibilities with day-to-day operational control of a number of administrative units.

With these caveats in mind, the following managerial groupings may be identified:

*The Speaker of the House.* The following administrative units and officials are under the formal control of the Speaker:

a. The Parliamentarian
b. The Office of the Legislative Counsel
c. The Office of the Law Revision Counsel
d. The Media Galleries
e. The Democratic Photographers

The Speaker appoints the chief officials of these units, and, to varying degrees, approves the appointment of their other personnel. With the exception of the media galleries, the Speaker also passes upon their payrolls, but does not review or approve their budget estimates. In the case of the employees of the three media galleries, their day-to-day direction and their nominations are controlled by committees of correspondents elected by the media representatives who cover the House and use the respective galleries. The Speaker, however, must approve their appointments, and they are on the Doorkeeper's payroll. The Democratic photographers are carried on the budget of the Doorkeeper, and the Republican photographers are carried on the budget of the Republican Conference.

*The Clerk of the House.* The following administrative units and officials are under the formal control of the Clerk of the House:

a. Enrolling and Digest Office
b. Bill Clerk's Office
c. Journal Clerk's Office
d. Tally Clerk's Office
e. Reading Clerk's Office
f. House Library (Clerk's Document Room)
g. The Reporters of Debates
h. The Reporters to House Committees
i. Finance Office
j. Office Supply Service
k. Office Equipment Service
l. Property Supply and Repair Office

m. Telephone Exchange
n. Records and Registration Office
o. Recording Studio

Salaries of the employees of the above-mentioned offices are funded through a specific line item in the House section of the Legislative Branch Appropriations Act. These estimates are prepared by the Clerk's office and must be approved by the Legislative Branch Appropriations Subcommittee, which controls House funding. While the program and other expenses of these units also must be approved finally by this subcommittee, such expenditures are provided for in the Contingent Fund, and therefore, must first be screened and approved by the Committee on House Administration. Moreover, if funds are needed by the Clerk to automate the processes of any units, House Information Systems must be consulted regarding the format, timing, and costs of the automation plan.

*The Doorkeeper of the House.* The following administrative units and officials are under the formal control of the Doorkeeper:

a. Publications Distribution Service
b. House Document Room
c. Majority and Minority Cloakrooms
d. Custodial Force
e. Doormen
f. Pages
g. Summary of Debate Clerks
h. Barber Shops (for payrolling)
i. Media Galleries (for payrolling)
j. Democratic Photographers (for payrolling)

The Doorkeeper carries the salaries of the employees of these units, with the exception of the Summary of Debate Clerks, on his payroll. The activities of the Summary of Debate Clerks are directed by the Doorkeeper, but they are on a payroll controlled by the Committee on House Administration. While the barbers are payrolled by the Doorkeeper, the Committee on House Administration manages the barbershop operations and sets the charges to patrons. As previously mentioned, while the media gallery employees are payrolled by the Doorkeeper and are nominated and directed by the elected committees of correspondents of the respective galleries, their appointments must be made by the Speaker.

*The Sergeant at Arms of the House.* The following administrative units and officials are under the formal control of the Sergeant at Arms:

a. House Bank
b. House Contingent of Capitol Police
c. Majority Pair Clerk
d. House Contingent of Capitol Guide Service

The rationale for placing the Bank, Majority Pair Clerk, and House Contingent of the Capitol Police under the Sergeant at Arms relates to the personnel and budgetary powers of this office. Salaries for all these employees are carried on the budget of the Sergeant at Arms, who prepares the estimates and also approves personnel actions. In the case of the Capitol Guide Service estimates are prepared by Senate units which also direct day-to-day operations. However, half of the approximately two dozen employees are apportioned to the House and appointed by the Sergeant.

*The Architect of the Capitol.* The following administrative units and officials are under the formal control of the Architect:

a. Superintendent of House Office Buildings (including operation of the gym)
b. Senior Landscape Architect and Horticulturist
c. The Botanic Garden
d. Capitol Power Plant
e. Superintendent of Garages

The Architect budgets for the staff and activities of these units and manages their activities under policies set by the House Office Building Commission. This unit is made up of the Speaker and the majority and minority floor leaders. The gym is under the formal operational supervision of the Superintendent of House Office Buildings, but policies are established by an ad hoc committee of members. Parking is subject to the control of the Committee on House Administration, which not only makes general parking policies, but also actually assigns parking spaces.

*The Committee on House Administration.* The following operating units are under the formal control of the Committee on House Administration:

a. Restaurants
b. Barber Shops
c. Beauty Shop
d. House Information Systems
e. Office of Management Services

Sources of funding vary for these units and internal managers exist. But in each case subcommittees of House Administration supervise operations as well as set policy.

In addition, the committee is integrally involved in the daily operation of the House through the direction or control it exercises over a variety of services or activities. As previously noted, its chair must approve all expense vouchers drawing on the Contingent Fund; it controls and participates in the assignment of parking spaces; it reviews all consultant contracts; it approves all committee requests for special investigative money for staff and expenses; it has control over resolutions authorizing special printings of documents and materials; and, in addition to its wide-ranging authority over personnel practices in several major administrative units under the Employees Classification Act, it also has authority over the number of positions and salaries in the House contingents of the Capitol Police and Guide Service.

*Independent Support Offices.* The following units are under the partial or general policy or program control of various House committees, or joint House-Senate committees, but are responsible for their own operational management, personnel management, and budget estimates:

a. Congressional Research Service
b. General Accounting Office
c. Congressional Budget Office
d. Office of Technology Assessment
e. Government Printing Office

*Miscellaneous Units.* A variety of other officials and units exist that cannot be generally grouped or classified.

The Postmaster and Chaplain are elected by the House and perform their specialized functions independent of policy or operational control by other officers or committees. The Attending Physician is appointed by the Speaker of the House and the Senate majority leader. However, the Physician's employees are paid from funds budgeted to the Architect and from other titles of the Legislative Branch Appropriations Act. The majority and minority printers provide printing service to the party leadership offices and are appointed by the respective party leaders. Their salaries are paid from legislative appropriations. In addition, they provide printing services to members, committees, state societies, and various political groups on a fee basis. The Legislative Branch Appropriations Act also funds six minority employees who serve minority party leaders and members on the floor.

## THE DISTRIBUTION OF OPERATING RESPONSIBILITIES

Thus far this chapter has examined the distribution of authority in the House administrative system. Let us turn now to the complementary topic we identified earlier as the second focus of our analysis. That is, the distribution of functional or operational responsibilities that exists within the established patterns of authority; in short, the division of tasks or labor in the House administrative system.

The support services provided to the House fall into two broad categories—administrative and physical support, and legislative support. The first set of support functions are performed to provide House leaders, members, and committees, and their staffs, with the material resources and physical conditions they need to do their work. The second set of support functions have to do with facilitating the House's main function of legislating.

In both these areas, and especially with reference to administrative support services, the allocation of operating responsibilities has not developed in accordance with a carefully devised plan that focuses responsibility and accountability for whole functional areas on particular officials. Instead, responsibility within particular functional activities is fragmented among several units or officials. In some situations, the diffusion of responsibility either was a deliberate action to reduce the role of a particular official, or the result of an effort to build up the role of another. Some assignments have been the result of ad hoc arrangements designed to deal with a new or evolving need. Others developed out of compromises in connection with power struggles in the House or out of the force of particular personalities who had strong influence at a particular point in time.

### Administrative Support Processes

The diffusion of responsibility and accountability that characterizes the administrative system is best seen by examining how the various functional activities involved in the provision of support services are allocated among various House officials and units. Table 8.1 provides a summary chart of the division of tasks or operating responsibilities in the administrative support area.

Relying on table 8.1 as background, the major functional processes and the distribution of operating responsibilities in the provision of administrative support can be analyzed as follows.[3]

*Financial Administration.* The financial system of the House is composed of four separate processes: budget formulation and review,

**Table 8.1. *Administrative Support Units in the House by Functional Area***

| *Administrative Support Unit* | *Supervisor* |
|---|---|
| 1. *Finance* | |
| Finance Office | Clerk |
| House Bank | Sergeant at Arms |
| GAO (audits) | Independent |
| HIS (computer applications) | Committee on House Administration |
| House Administration Staff | Committee on House Administration |
| 2. *Procurement and Property Management* | |
| Office Supply Service | Clerk |
| Office Equipment Service | Clerk |
| Property Supply and Repair Service | Clerk |
| Architect (furniture design) | Architect |
| HIS (computer acquisition) | Committee on House Administration |
| 3. *Facilities and Services* | |
| Attending Physician | Speaker (and Senate Majority Leader) |
| Superintendent of House Office Buildings | Architect |
| Superintendent of Garages | Architect |
| Restaurants | Committee on House Administration |
| Barber Shops | Committee on House Administration<br>Doorkeeper |
| Beauty Shop | Committee on House Administration |
| Capitol Police | Capitol Police Board |
| Gym | Architect |
| Guide Service | Capitol Guide Service Board |
| HIS (computer applications) | Committee on House Administration |
| 4. *Communications* | |
| Telephone Exchange | Clerk |
| Recording Studio | Clerk |
| Majority and Minority Printers | Majority Leader<br>Minority Leader |
| Photographers | Speaker<br>Minority Leader |
| Publications Distribution Service | Doorkeeper |
| 5. *Personnel and Management* | |
| Office of Management Services | Committee on House Administration |
| HIS (computer applications) | Committee on House Administration |

expenditure and disbursement, financial accounting and reporting, and auditing. Performance of these functions is a responsibility performed, and in some cases closely shared, by several administrative units.

The House budget does not represent the results of a tightly managed effort designed to carry out centrally planned objectives. There rarely are such objectives, and no central office has responsibility to evolve them. Moreover, other than the need of the House and Senate to come into agreement with each other on overall congressional spending, these bodies are not subject to external review in determining their spending plans.

The main elements of annual spending, such as for members' salaries and expenses and staffing ratios, are fixed according to standing formulas, prescribed by statute or House rules. Accordingly, "budget" estimates tend to be routine calculations in line with these prior arrangements. Budget review consists largely of comparing requests with entitlements. The Committee on House Administration does exercise some budget control in cases where exceptions to given formulas are requested, where needs arise outside of such formulas, and where committees or subcommittees request special investigative money from the Contingent Fund to spend for staff or expenses that would not otherwise be authorized.

Since the House determines its own financial needs, it is not required to keep its expenditures within some centrally managed and planned total determined elsewhere. Also, unlike units of the federal executive branch, the House is not subject to requirements that it avoid or limit spending previously authorized. For these reasons, the House has not had to develop an elaborate central budget planning and expenditure control apparatus, such as is required by the president's Office of Management and Budget and departmental budget offices in their respective spheres. House expenditures control, such as it is, consists mostly of checks by the Clerk's office and the Committee on House Administration to determine if the spending units are using their funds for approved purposes and in the amounts authorized for those purposes.

The Clerk of the House gathers the budget estimates of the various House units, consolidates them, and files them with the president's Office of Management and Budget. In so doing, however, his role, with respect to other units, is essentially clerical and informational rather than controlling in nature. The Clerk either calculates what fixed statutory provisions require for generally defined salary and benefit items (e.g., clerk-hire), or provides information and assistance to units that they may use in developing estimates for particular items of salary and expense within their jurisdiction or control. Here too, quite often, these items are specified in some way or at least circumscribed by law or House rules (e.g., staff salary ranges or member office allowances).

The Office of Management and Budget does not have the authority to change House or Senate estimates, but merely includes them in the overall federal budget submitted by the president. As part of its annual consideration of this budget, the House reviews its own estimates. In doing so it relies primarily on the Legislative Branch Appropriations Subcommittee and the processes of passing the Legislative Branch Appropriations Act. Normally, however, the House and Senate accept each other's portions of this bill without change.

The task of paying for House goods and services is divided among several units and officials. The Sergeant at Arms provides the checks to pay members' salaries, certain mileage expenses of the members, and payments to the heirs of deceased members. The House restaurant pays its own supply and wages bills with the approval of the Committee on House Administration. The Clerk payrolls all other House employees and also carries the main load in expense disbursements. However, in all cases involving the Contingent Fund the processing of vouchers for payment is duplicative between the Clerk's office (Office of Finance) and the Committee on House Administration. The clerk's office determines whether the offices that submit purchase vouchers have the authority and funds for the requested expenditure, have complied with all requirements, and have the correct dollar figure. The Committee on House Administration then makes the final decision on payment, often after making its own review of the matters determined by the Clerk's office.

While the Clerk has the primary operating responsibility for keeping House accounts and preparing financial reports, the Sergeant at Arms keeps the accounts and makes reports on all funds he disburses. House committees make their own monthly reports to the Committee on House Administration for the uses of funds they draw from the Contingent Fund and must also certify their entire payrolls monthly to the chair of the House Administration Committee. The committee also makes and keeps accounts for various House units.

Audits are generally done by the General Accounting Office, either at the request of the Clerk or the Committee on House Administration, or pursuant to statutory requirements.

House Information Systems (HIS) provides computer and computer program design services in various areas of financial management and operations and the range of such services is continually increasing.

*Procurement and Property Management.* With the exception of procurement for house leadership offices, the leasing of equipment for members' district offices, and the buying of computer services, the Clerk of the House, under the rules of the House, has the authority to contract to buy the office supplies, office equipment, furniture, and furnishings used by House members, committees, and other units.

Under the Clerk, the Office Supply Service operates the Stationery Room, which sells stationery and other office supplies to all House offices and units. The Office Equipment Service, also under the Clerk, provides electrical and mechanical equipment to House offices and units, repairs small equipment, and contracts for the repair of major equipment. Another unit reporting to the Clerk, the Property Supply and Repair Service, supplies furniture and furnishings to House offices. These two units maintain stock control and inventory systems, with the help of computer programs and services supplied by House Information Services.

House Information Services, a unit that reports to the Committee on House Administration, has responsibility for buying computer equipment and supplies for House use. The procurement or leasing of furniture and equipment for the offices members maintain in their home districts is handled by the General Services Administration, with funds authorized by House resolution.

The Committee on House Administration is responsible for issuing the rules and regulations that establish procurement standards and procedures. Also, all procurement that uses money from the Contingent Fund must be approved by the committee. The types of equipment and the prices to be paid by the Clerk are specified in lists developed and maintained by the committee. Members, however, are free to use part of their clerk-hire allowance to acquire computer terminals of their choice for their own offices.

The Architect of the Capitol also is involved in furniture acquisition. His office is required by law to approve the designs and specifications for furniture to be acquired. He also has the responsibility to determine the need for new equipment, furniture, and furnishings for the House office buildings and Capitol.

*Facilities, Services, and Communications.* The Architect of the Capitol, operating under policy direction of the House Office Building Commission, has responsibility for nearly all aspects of physical plant development, repair, maintenance, and housekeeping in House facilities. He also is responsible for providing subway and elevator service and water, cooling, heating, and sewage systems. Exceptions to this concentration of responsibility are installation and operation of telephone service, which is the responsibility of the Clerk of the House, the provision of police and other security services, which is a responsibility of the Sergeant at Arms, and the assignment of parking places, which is a responsibility of the Committee on House Administration.

The Architect handles the administrative and other details involved in allocating space in House facilities. However, the responsibility for office moving is split between the Clerk and the Architect. The Clerk moves furniture and office equipment. The Architect moves material that is placed in files or boxes.

The remaining areas in this functional category also are characterized by fragmented operational responsibilities.

Printing: Generally, reports and other House documents are printed by the public printer. However, a majority and a minority printer each do a wide variety of other types of printed work for the members and leadership.

Recording: Radio and TV recordings for members are the operational responsibility of the Clerk, under policy control and supervision of a Special House Committee on the Recording Studio.

Photography: Photographic work is done by the Democratic and Republican photographers, who are appointed by the party leaders in the House.

Guide Service: Responsibility of the Sergeant at Arms of the House and Senate.

Barber Shops and Beauty Shop: These services get direction and supervision directly from the Committee on House Administration.

Bank: Operated directly by the Sergeant at Arms.

Folding and Packaging: Responsibility of the Doorkeeper, through the Publications Distribution Service.

Gym: The director of the gym is appointed by the Architect but is given policy direction by an Ad Hoc Committee on the House Gym.

Health and Medical: Responsibility of the Attending Physician who is appointed by the Speaker and the majority leader of the Senate.

Chaplain: Chaplain services are provided by a chaplain elected by the House.

Restaurants: Responsibility of an administrative officer, who operates the restaurants under direct supervision of the Committee on House Administration.

*Personnel and Management.* The Office of Management Services, under the policy control of the Committee on House Administration, has responsibility for providing advice on office management systems to House offices. However, various other units tend to be involved in this area also. Through the Clerk's office, equipment and furniture suppliers advise House members, committees, and other units on office management ideas, work process systems, and the capacities of various types of office equipment. The Architect of the Capitol is responsible for any changes in walls, doors, partitions, and built-in lighting fixtures that might be necessary in order to rearrange the work spaces of offices. Finally, House Information Systems, under control of the Committee on House Administration, provides advice to House offices on information use and retrieval systems involving computers.

The House does not operate its personnel system on the basis of civil service concepts, and it has exempted itself from nondiscrimination laws. Therefore, unlike the units of the executive branch, it has not had the need to develop a complex centrally monitored system to operate and police both merit and nondiscriminatory hiring, job classification, supervision, and termination procedures. For the most part, personnel arrangements are decentralized, with great latitude left to individual offices to decide such matters. Only with reference to several major administrative units do elements of overall control exist through the authority of the Committee on House Administration with reference to the number of positions, salaries, and job classifications.

The Office of Management Services provides help to House employees and others in seeking placement in House employment. Actual hiring, training, and termination of employees is handled by the employing offices. Administration of wage, salary, and fringe benefit systems is a mixed responsibility of employing offices, the Clerk of the House, the Sergeant at Arms, the Architect, and the Doorkeeper, in some cases under policies set by and subject to approval of the Committee on House Administration.

### Legislative Support Processes

The legislative support units can be grouped into two categories. The first includes the units that provide daily and basic forms of support in carrying on the legislative process. Most of these units are

**Table 8.2** ***Legislative Support Units in the House by Functional Area***

| *Legislative Support Unit* | *Supervisor* |
|---|---|
| 1. Daily Operations | |
| Parliamentarian | Speaker |
| Legislative Counsel | Speaker |
| Law Revision Counsel | Speaker |
| Reporters of Debates | Clerk |
| Reporters to Committees | Clerk |
| Enrolling-Digest Clerk | Clerk |
| Bill Clerk | Clerk |
| Journal Clerk | Clerk |
| Reading Clerk | Clerk |
| Tally Clerk | Clerk |
| House Library | Clerk |
| Pair Clerks | Sergeant at Arms |
| Minority Employees | Minority Leadership |
| Document Room | Doorkeeper |
| Cloakrooms | Doorkeeper |
| Pages | Doorkeeper |
| Doormen | Doorkeeper |
| Summary of Debate Clerks | Doorkeeper |
| House Information Systems | Committee on House Administration |
| 2. Research and Analysis | |
| Congressional Research Service | Independent (Library of Congress) |
| Congressional Budget Office | Independent |
| Office of Technology Assessment | Independent |
| General Accounting Office | Independent |
| House Information Systems | Committee on House Administration |

primarily concerned with activities on the floor, but some also provide important services to members and committees. The second category is made up of units that provide research and analysis services. Their primary function is to collect and interpret substantive information that will assist the House in its ability to make decisions that determine and control governmental policy.

Table 8.2 provides a summary chart of legislative support units organized in terms of these two basic functional areas or categories.

It may be noted that the Clerk's office has a major role in providing daily operational support on the floor as well as a major role in providing various forms of administrative support. Thus, the Clerk directs most of the support personnel on the floor who are directly and immediately involved in processing legislative materials.

However, other units and officials are also involved in a number of important ways. Parliamentary rulings and advice are the responsibility of the Parliamentarian. Advice to the leadership on legal matters and to committees and members on bill drafting is provided by the Legislative Counsel and his staff. These officials report to, and are supervised by, the Speaker.

Bill status reporting is a mixed responsibility, primarily involving efforts by the Clerk and House Information Systems. The latter unit also operates the electronic voting system and maintains data and records regarding it. The Doorkeeper has a role in helping members and their staffs make effective use of their time. The Doorkeeper's staff summarizes and distributes to members daily accounts of House proceedings, debates, and agenda, and operates the House document distribution activity.

The Doorkeeper also directs the work of the pages, operates the cloakroom, supervises the doormen, sees to housekeeping in the chamber and immediate siderooms, and provides limited food service in some of these areas. Lastly, the Doorkeeper operates the public galleries in conjunction with the Sergeant at Arms, who provides police and other security arrangements in and around these viewing areas.

The research and analysis units listed in table 8.2 are examined in depth in subsequent portions of this volume and need not be treated in any great detail here (see chaps. 9 and 11). A few broad characteristics that are relevant to the concerns of this chapter may, however, be noted. First, there is considerable overlapping or redundancy in the substantive services provided. Second, since these units respond or report to very different groups or officers, which are often noncongressional in character, there is little coordination or even consultation among them. Third, due both to their mandates and to time pressures, they generally serve committees far more than members and some committees far more than others. Nonetheless, it should also be noted that the primary load in terms of research and analysis is carried by staff personnel in member, committee, and party offices and thus that the provision for such assistance in support services external to those offices is and remains ancillary to the primary approach to providing them.

## GAPS, OVERLAPS, AND ANOMALIES IN RESPONSIBILITY AND ACCOUNTABILITY

In this section weaknesses in the House administrative system are identified on the basis of the preceding analysis of the existing distribution of authority and operating responsibilities. The House, to be sure, has particular characteristics as a public organization that make it different from executive branch organizations. Therefore, while some references are made to executive branch concepts, they are used only for purposes of perspective. Judgments as to weaknesses that are made here relate to problems that undermine or limit the effectiveness of the House administrative system in meeting the House's needs to discharge its steadily growing and increasingly complex mission as a legislative body.

### The Role of the Speaker

*The Speaker lacks clear policy and oversight authority in the House administrative system. Yet, when troubles develop, his own party members, the opposition party, the media, and the public hold the Speaker accountable.*

The Speaker's position in the House administrative system is an anomaly. Unlike the president in the executive branch, the Speaker is not positioned formally at the apex of the House administrative system. He is not even nominally in charge.

Though the Speaker tends to be held accountable when things go wrong, not uncommonly, he learns of operations problems or abuses and their details after the fact, through the media, grand jury proceedings, or from other sources. He does not have systematic operational reports coming to him, nor does he have a staff that can assist him in monitoring operations or alert him when facts, trends, and other indicators suggest trouble ahead.

The Speaker can be, and is, quite influential in the process of choosing the key administrative actors, such as the chair of the Committee on House Administration and the other elected House officers. However, once these people are on the job, he has to rely upon their judgment and performance to see to it that services are being handled satisfactorily. When breakdowns or abuses develop, and complaints from members or the media press in on him, the Speaker then finds himself pushed to quick ad hoc arrangements to deal with the immediate problem. When the Speaker finds that he has to act in the administrative area, he does so through his implied power as head of the majority party in the House and his skills of persuasion and bargaining, rather than on the basis of expressed authority in the Constitution, the law, or House rules.

**The Role of the Committee on House Administration**

*The oversight and review role of the Committee on House Administration is confused by its practice of also maintaining a direct day-by-day operations role in the conduct of a number of administrative support functions and in the approval of individual expense transactions.*

The Committee on House Administration, which has the oversight and review responsibility for many aspects of House administration, is involved in individual approval transactions for many items or services procured through use of Contingent Fund money. It approves the acquisition and uses of computers and the prices paid. It determines the types of furniture, office equipment, and furnishings bought, and the prices paid. It is involved in individual hiring approvals and the granting of parking places. It approves individual contracts.

Some might argue that the many-sided role of the committee gives it an excellent position from which to oversee most of the financial affairs of the House, and, thereby, to enable it to discover or avoid improprieties or waste. But the Wayne Hays scandal revealed some of the disadvantages of the committee's dual role as policy-maker and overseer on the one hand and as an operating unit on the other. Specifically, insofar as the committee functions at the transactional level of support operations, it has to accept direct responsibility for the quality of services provided for the money spent. Therefore, since the committee in many cases is reviewing its own acts, it is not in a good position to supply a fully objective or arms-length judgment of what is done or not done or how well it is done. No other unit is set up to supply this type of unbiased opinion. Also, the House does not have an objective source of review to develop judgments as to how the performance of the administrative support functions could be improved or as to what better policies could be adopted.

**The Role of the Architect of the Capitol**

*The Architect of the Capitol and the Clerk of the House have housekeeping, procurement, and other support functions that directly overlap or intertwine in ways that are confusing to House offices. In addition, the Architect of the Capitol gets policy direction and oversight from a number of congressional sources and is accountable to several policy-making bodies in the House.*

If a House office wants to improve office lighting by moving an installed light fixture, it must get the Architect's office to do this. But, if a table lamp is to be acquired, that acquisition must be made through the Clerk's office.

If an office wishes some files or boxes moved, the Architect must be called. If furniture or office equipment is to be moved, the Clerk does that.

These and a number of other overlaps confuse the members' staffs and cause delays and coordination problems in meeting office needs and timetables. These overlaps also blur accountability and frustrate members and their staffs.

The Architect reports to separate policy-making units of the House and Senate, respectively, for guidance on facilities planning, construction, and upkeep of the areas under jurisdiction of each body. However, he gets policy direction from several other sources in the House. For management of the House garages and assignment of parking places, he gets policy, and often operational guidance, from the Committee on House Administration. For management of the House gym, he gets guidance from the Ad Hoc Committee on the House Gym. For the rest of his functions relative to the House, he gets supervision and policy direction from the House Office Building Commission, which is made up of the Speaker and the majority and minority leaders of the House.

## Direction of Administrative Support Services

*The House lacks an official who has day-to-day responsibility for managing and coordinating its administrative support activities and for developing methods for upgrading the effectiveness of the services provided.*

As shown above, a number of House officials and units have responsibilities for providing administrative support services. Also, within particular service categories, responsibilities are fragmented. No one official, even in the staff of the Committee on House Administration, has the role of reviewing the effectiveness of the overall activity and seeing to the timely and effective coordination of its many parts. In the techniques of managing such areas as procurement, vouchering, and property accounting, the practices used in the House lag considerably behind the state of the art in other large public and private organizations. Yet, no one official has the responsibility or authority for devising, arguing for, and overseeing the initiation of basic improvements. No overall management assessment and improvement report is even prepared, let alone used, by the Speaker or the chair of the Committee on House Administration.

In view of the wide diffusion of authorities and responsibilities, the system lacks an official with adequate authority to get all the parties involved together to assess system-wide performance and consider general or specific improvements in an objective way. This is a critical gap at the operational level. Comparably, at the policy and oversight level, the Committee on House Administration has important gaps in its oversight authority. Moreover, it tends to blur its objectivity by performing operational roles in areas where it is supposed to provide the House with independent assessment and perspective on the effectiveness of how these same functions are performed.

**Direction of Legislative Support Services**

*The extensive responsibilities of the Clerk in the procurement and financial management areas and the fragmentation of responsibilities in the legislative support area leave no one official with the time, scope, and authority to oversee all aspects of legislative support to the House and to devise and implement broad improvements.*

The House's legislative load has grown massively in the past decade. Consequently, dealing with rapidly expanding information supply and demand problems that involve members, committee staffs, support units, government agencies, and the public has become a critical requirement and a frustrating challenge to all concerned. In many respects, however, the House's methods for gathering, using, and disseminating information in connection with the legislative process lag badly in terms of what might otherwise be possible within the capacities of evolving technology. House Information Systems, the Doorkeeper, the Committee on House Administration, the Clerk of the House, the Congressional Research Service, the Government Printer, the Speaker, and some of the other officials who advise the Speaker and the members about legislative procedures all have roles to play in devising improvements in the methods for handling the growing legislative load and for using and producing the expanding body of information needed before, while, and after the House acts on legislation.

**Financial Management**

*The House lacks an effective financial management system.*
The financial management system of the House is confusing,

too elaborate in some cases, and inadequate in others. Valuable staff time is lost in the duplicate processing of expenditure vouchers for approval through both the Clerk's office and the Committee on House Administration. The House lacks clear policies from the committee in many expenditure areas that could guide members and committees in determining what they can and cannot buy both with the Contingent Fund and other sources of money. Too many things are required to be approved by the committee, and too many individual vouchers have to be processed by all concerned. Neither the Clerk nor the committee keeps adequately structured expenditure classification reports that could be helpful in budget development and review from year to year. Also, contract management and performance data are not carefully developed and maintained to facilitate contract reviews. Generally, financial reports are inadequately conceived and maintained, and this gap provides no suitable basis for conducting a meaningful operational and financial audit program.

The House audit system is piecemeal, poorly articulated, and poorly supported because of inadequate and inconsistently kept operational and financial data. Consequently, the audits that are done often fail to provide timely warning to House leaders and the Committee on House Administration about abuses, gaps in policies and requirements, and failures to follow policies.

The failure of the House to have effective operational audits, plus the failure to have financial audits in some areas, leaves the House with inadequate means of assuring the public of the integrity of its administrative operations and expenditures.

**Personnel Management**

*The personnel system of the House is only partially formed, considering that the House is a public agency supported by taxes. It has none of the important ingredients and processes of a merit selection system. It has no watchdog or appeals system. Such abuses as discrimination on account of race, religion, or sex are usually uncovered by outside initiatives rather than by inside inspections and review processes, and rarely get systematic attention.*

House members usually defend vigorously their exemption from the merit processes and antidiscrimination laws that must be complied with by executive branch agencies. They argue that the members must have special and great latitude and flexibility in hiring and firing. In some respects, their arguments are valid. However, equally good arguments could be made about equivalent needs of many executive branch employers, who are accountable for carrying out highly critical public programs and objectives, and yet are sharply limited in their ability to hire and fire as necessary to get their jobs done. Moreover, in the discrimination area, the House increasingly is the subject of negative media comparisons and treatment.

The House personnel system is half-formed even in such relatively noncontroversial areas as job referrals, training, and employer/employee counseling. Surveys by the House Commission on Administrative Review in 1977 showed that member offices tend not to have a well-exercised service relationship with the House's Office of Placement. Also, most would-be House employees regularly bypass the Office and directly solicit individual member offices for jobs (Commission 1977*b*, vol. 2). Member office staffs often lack training on entering their jobs, and for the most part, learn as best they can, on the job. This situation not only leads to poor job entry conditions, and often ragged performance, but to an unnecessary and diverting drain on the time and energy of the other staff in both member and committee offices.

## CONCLUSIONS

The gaps, overlaps, and anomalies in the allocations of authority and responsibility for administrative and legislative support functions in the House impede effective management, both currently and prospectively.

Judgments relative to effective management go beyond drawing conclusions as to whether support activities are or are not performed adequately and cost-effectively. Concepts of "adequate" and "cost-effective" are relative terms. Both performance standards and costs take on shades of meaning as circumstances change. However, opinion surveys by the Commission on Administrative Review showed clearly that member and committee staffs in the House commonly are frustrated and puzzled in their efforts to get services from the various administrative support offices, and that these difficulties waste their time and often produce unsatisfactory outcomes that impede their work further (Commission 1977*b*, vol. 1). Indeed, many survey respondents noted that in the press of time in their busy offices, they function by "making do" with the administrative system, which means lowering their standards and expectations, or, as necessary, and where possible, circumventing known weak spots in the system.

Beyond considering day-to-day frustrations of users of the administrative system, judgments regarding its adequacy must be based upon the capacity of the system to meet future demands on the House.

The system, as presently constituted, is not adequately structured to meet today's demands, let alone those that are rapidly developing. As noted earlier, the House legislative load has grown considerably, and the House has experienced an explosion of subcommittees and staff. Consequently, expenditures and transactions for supplies, equipment, renovations, payrolls, fringe benefits, and information are steadily mounting, and those trends appear quite likely to continue. Labor/management issues are developing in House staff employment, and a number of scandals and abuses in spending and hiring practices have raised major public doubts about the integrity of House operations.

The deficiencies that exist pertain primarily to the administrative support area, though overlaps and anomalies also exist with reference to legislative support services. Indeed, it is the Clerk's dual position in both areas that is a major and pervasive source of weakness throughout the administrative system. With specific reference to administrative support services, however, it should be noted again that no one body in the House has a broad overview of the entire area since the Committee on House Administration has important gaps in its policy-making and oversight jurisdiction. Moreover, the objectivity of the committee in appraising performance of the administrative units it has responsibility for is blurred because it also uses the time of its staff and subcommittees actually to operate activities whose effectiveness it should be objectively evaluating.

Nor has the House provided itself with a highly competent manager who could provide day-to-day leadership in assuring adequate service results in all areas of administrative support and who would have the knowledge and perspective to see where and how basic service improvements and coordination could be instituted.

In the absence of a more comprehensive policy-making and oversight body in the administrative support area, the House will attempt to meet its growing workloads with no objective means for gaining a comprehension of how the several policy authorities and units are contributing to good or poor results overall. Comparably, without someone in a position to oversee and coordinate day-to-day operations throughout all aspects of administrative support, accountability for what is done or not done well will be difficult to pin down, and confusion and wasted motion will continue to result from member and staff frustration with the system.

Without the development of comprehensive and clearer policies, simpler procedures governing expenditure approvals, and more consistent, timely, and complete financial reports for members and committees, time will continue to be wasted, and useful audits will be hard to prepare. Without an adequate operational and financial audit program, financial abuses, policy lapses, and operational weaknesses can develop and continue without prompt detection and remedy.

In such circumstances, the House leaders and the members collectively will continue to be politically and personally vulnerable to bad publicity and charges of waste, mismanagement, and dishonesty because of the actions of a few that will have gone undetected by internal controls and unchecked by timely corrective action.

## NOTES

1. For a detailed compendium of House administrative units, including figures on salary expenditures and number of employees, see Commission 1977*a*, 5–28. In addition, see Commission 1977*b*, 1:96–166.
2. For a more detailed analysis of the Contingent Fund see Commission 1977*b*, 1: 170–174. Appropriations for such expenditures currently total about a third of the more than $300 million appropriated annually for the House. For detailed information on member expense allowances and their operation under the new consolidated allowance system see Congressional Quarterly 1980, 89–104.
3. For more detailed analysis of these functional processes see Commission 1977*b*, 1:167–602.

## REFERENCES

Commission on Administrative Review, U.S. Congress, House. 1977*a*. *Background Information on Administrative Units, Members' Offices and Committees and Leadership Offices*. 95th Cong., 1st sess. H. Doc. 95-178.

———. 1977*b*. *Final Report*. 2 vols. 95th Cong., 1st sess. H. Doc. 95-272.

Congressional Quarterly. 1980. *Congressional Ethics*. Washington: Congressional Quarterly Inc.

# Part III. Informing the Decision-Making Process

## *The Context of Information and Decision Making*

Thus far this volume has examined the contours of individual jobs or roles and the nature of primary work structures and processes. The character of the outputs the House seeks to produce for the political system is also a factor of substantial organizational significance. Systems of coordinated effort are not coordinated in a vacuum, but rather in terms of certain desired outputs. In the case of the House the desired outputs are decisions, but decisions of a very distinctive and demanding type. House decision-making needs in turn determine information needs and together these needs affect structure, behavior, and performance in highly significant ways. It is this facet or dimension of the House as an institution that we now wish to place in perspective.

### ROLES AND OUTPUTS

Desired outputs or products derive from and express in concrete form the character of an organization's functional role relative to its environment. Such roles are shaped or defined by basic aspects of value, linkage, and work that order relations and terms of exchange between an organization and its environment.

The values, linkages, and work that define or order the House's relationship to its environment make the manner in which it produces its outputs as important as their substantive content. In contrast to most organizations, its functional role thus has two facets of great and relatively equal importance.

Substantively viewed, the role of the House relates primarily to the policy and oversight responsibilities accorded it by the Constitution. Together with the Senate and president, the House is charged with serving as the basic definer of national or collective purpose through the formulation of law. In addition, the House, together with the Senate, is charged with overseeing executive performance to insure responsible, efficient, and nonarbitrary exercise of the authority vested in the president and bureaucracy by the laws and the Constitution.

Procedurally viewed, the role of the House encompasses considerations beyond those of the substantive content of action per se. Rather, it must perform its policy and oversight functions in such a way as to provide for consent as well as action, or to put the point another way, to base action on consent. The House, in short, both as a body and as a set of individual members, has representative functions as well as substantive functions. Indeed, the values, linkages, and work that specify its functional role establish and require a high degree of interdependence between the two. The House thus must satisfy its substantive functions largely through the performance of its procedural ones. In defining policy and/or exercising oversight it must reflect and accommodate citizen views and interest; it must act on behalf of society, but through democratic processes and procedures that are oriented to resolving political conflict or tension in the society.

In addition, the House has a number of derivative functions, functions that derive from its basic substantive and/or procedural roles. One is education, the familiarization of the electorate with issues, alternatives, and positions, to buttress the processes of electoral accountability and control. Another is constituent service. As part and parcel of their representative functions, members assume responsibility not only for looking after the general policy orientations and interests of their constituencies, but also for aiding their constituents as individuals or distinct sets of individuals in their dealings with the bureaucracy. Though such activities transform constituents into clients and members into lawyers or agents, they have long been recognized as legitimate and are supported by institutional resources.

In sum, then, the functional role of the House involves and takes the form of decisions. Yet, if the primary desired outputs of the House are decisions, they are decisions of a very special type. First, House outputs are not only abstract, as is true of all organizations whose primary products are decisions, but also highly value laden. They constitute key outputs in the authoritative decision-making processes of the state or political system and as such provide key determinations of the basic ends and means the society adopts when it acts as a collectivity. Second, House outputs have a highly individualistic component or base. The particular political system of which the House is a subsystem is a representative democracy. Hence, in contrast to many organizations, the House gives wide sway to individuals in producing its outputs. Certain output decisions are controlled by members as individuals so that the final institutional product is merely the sum of individual decisions. Moreover, in those important areas where decisions are collective products, outputs must still be based on the desires of all participants, must be reached collegially through voting. Interestingly enough, then, the House is both more and less a collective entity than the more bureaucratic organizations that typically exist in other sectors of societal life.

## INFORMATION NEEDS

As an organization whose primary desired outputs are decisions, the House is very dependent on its ability to gather and disseminate information effectively. Its decision-making needs, however, are not only highly distinctive, but also quite demanding. Its information needs, therefore, are also both highly distinctive and demanding.

To satisfy and maintain the primary and derivative aspects of its functional role, the House must make effective decisions, which, in fact, contribute to remedying or alleviating the problems or sources of distress to which they are addressed. Members and decision-making units thus need capacity to relate or adapt means to ends, to make rational decisions. They accordingly need the ability to mobilize and apply a variety of forms of information or knowledge: concrete or factual information about existing circumstances or conditions, empirical knowledge of the patterning of ends-means relationships, and familiarity with broad modes of analysis to frame or order the application of established knowledge to new facts or problems.

Nonetheless, the capacity for decision making at either individual or collective levels requires more than objective information. Political information regarding the subjective attitudes and preferences of electoral groups, other members, executive officials, etc., is also essential. In part this is true because objective information alone cannot provide a basis for choice. The decisions involved are, in general, highly value laden and must be made in a context in which there is usually value disagreement and fragility in existing knowledge regarding means-ends relationships. In part, however, it is also true because the primary decision-making processes and procedures themselves institutionalize concern for the maintenance and/or mobilization of support both externally with reference to electorates and internally with reference to majority construction. As noted earlier, it is both the genius and the faith of democracy to base the decisions vested in the House on "politics."

In short, then, decision making in the House at all levels involves highly overlapping mixes of objective and subjective factors or considerations. As a result, the need for information along both these dimensions is intense. Members and decision-making units need to know the facts, the range of alternatives, and the consequences of particular alternatives. But they also need to know the character, intensity, and distribution of attitudes and preferences among those actors whose support they need to stay in office, to use institutional structures and resources to advantage, or to build coalitions through bargaining and accommodation.

The sway accorded to the individual member in decision making also has critical impacts on the character of House information needs. On the one hand, demands for all types of information are extremely widespread or comprehensive. Division of labor in the House does not compartmentalize members in terms of functional tasks or processes. Rather, all members participate in all basic tasks or processes—lawmaking, oversight, constituent service, representation, etc. On the other hand, information needs are also extremely variable. In part this is due to the forms of division of labor that do exist in the House. Members represent distinct, geographical constituencies; vary in their committee assignments; and play different roles in partisan and ad hoc or informal groups. In part, however, it is due once again to the value-laden character of decision making and the limits of objective knowledge. To be useful or relevant, rather than merely interesting or enlightening, information has to be tailored or fine-tuned to individual requirements and particular situations. Objective analyses then remain largely academic unless related to member goals and interests and applied in the context of these factors and the level or stage of decision making concerned. Similarly, useful political information is also highly determined by context. All this is not to deny that facts and analysis discipline rational choice. But it is equally true that basic premises establish parameters that govern the relevance and significance of both factual and analytic knowledge, a point that assumes prime importance in a nonhierarchic organization that produces highly abstract and value-laden outputs.

Finally, the growth in the substantive and political burdens imposed by the workload and the accompanying expansion in the contours of the House as an organization have substantially magnified information needs. This is commonly recognized with reference to the forms of information needed to produce the outputs the House's functional role designates or requires. Thus, it is not only the factors discussed above that render House information needs demanding, but these factors in combination with the broad scope of governmental responsibility and the complexity of policy or interest alignments in late twentieth-century America.

Yet, the growth in workload burdens or pressures and in the scope of the House as an organization have also magnified information needs along another critical dimension. The House is now a large-scale organization and its needs for operational or management information have therefore greatly expanded. This is true both in the productive system and the support system. In the former regard the increase in the number of decision-making units and in staffs attached to these units, combined with workload pressures and the volatility of the legislative environment, has magnified and complicated the task of efficiently gathering and disseminating information regarding basic legislative operations such as bill status, committee and floor scheduling, and amendment tracking. In the latter regard the increase in staff and expense resources, combined with the decentralized and overlapping character of the productive and support systems, have magnified and complicated the task of efficiently gathering and disseminating information regarding the management of House resources and support units. Both discrete decision-making units and the House as an institution now require a variety of forms of management information to control the support functions that are supplied and to maximize their effectiveness.

## ISSUES AND CONSTRAINTS

We may conclude that information needs in the House are highly varied in content, extremely complex in their distribution patterns, and voluminous in nature. In truth, these needs cannot be met or fulfilled in their totality any more than the House can fully meet or fulfill the varied demands its functional role in the political system imposes. In both cases the goal must be to satisfice, not to optimize or maximize, the attainment of desired ends.

One mode of doing so, which has always been present but has grown more pronounced, is reliance on surrogates or expedients in decision making to replace or obviate the need for hard information. Some familiar examples are the use of special calendars or procedures, reliance on cues from trusted friends or groups, reliance on indicators of noncontroversiality, and simple benign neglect. Still, surrogates and expedients cannot be relied upon in the numerous instances in which the career, power, and/or policy interests of members are substantially engaged. In such instances the ability to mobilize and apply information becomes critical both substantively and politically. Yet one of the most frequent sources of complaint about the House concerns its ability to provide the information necessary for members to do their jobs and for the institution to perform at levels that will maintain its position and power in the political system.

The specific deficiencies perceived vary in nature. In general, they do not pertain to the sheer quantity of information that is supplied or accessible, but rather to its quality or utility both in terms of content and timeliness. Action to remedy or alleviate the situation thus involves three basic issues.

Perhaps the most important issue concerns the character of the priorities and strategies to be established and followed in seeking to improve the House's information capability. At present, normative disagreement over the mix of activities that best serve functional role demands, differences in perception or assessment of the various constraints posed by the internal and external environment of the House, and conflicts in the political and personal interests of members result in substantial amounts of disagreement and confusion in addressing information needs. Some examples easily come to mind. There is disagreement over whether Congress should seek to engage in policy analysis to any substantial degree or simply concentrate on the political tasks of accommodating interests and building majorities to pass policy proposals. There is dissatisfaction over the current scope and effectiveness of Congress's oversight role, but confusion over the incentives needed to augment it or the probable costs of doing so with reference to the performance of other important tasks. There is disagreement over the role, size, and quality of personal and committee staff and confusion over how to take greater advantage of units in the support system whose primary function is to provide factual and analytic information.

Disputes of this kind have been and remain difficult to resolve or even clarify. The underlying reality is that conflicts over congressional role demands are difficult to accommodate and the restrictive effects of constraints difficult to assess. For example, whereas the House as a body of lay politicians may be far better suited to political bargaining than objective analysis, it is also true that to cede a meaningful role in policy analysis is to render the body captive to the executive units or private groups that define and push new legislation. Quite understandably, then, the prevalent response to dissatisfaction has been ad hoc adjustment in areas where members' interests as individual political actors are unified rather than divided (e.g., staff expansion, the emergence of the DSG and other informal groups as prime information sources). Nonetheless, the point remains that hard choices are involved in substantially improving the quality of available information and that such choices require forging broad agreements over priorities and strategies in areas where disagreement and confusion now reign.

A second primary issue relates to the organization of the House's information capability, to the character of the institutional arrangements it should establish to serve its needs. Here, as well, inability to establish priorities among needs is a basic source of difficulty; but disagreement and confusion also derive from conflict and uncertainty over the form of these arrangements per se, over basic organizational questions or choices.

In the House, as in other organizations, flexibility or adaptability to information needs is constrained both by broad environmental factors and relationships and by the primary structures and processes employed to produce outputs. In the House these contextual constraints combine to render rational analysis of the efficiency and effectiveness of alternatives quite difficult, to render objective assessment of the costs and benefits of varying ways of distributing information tasks and resources quite tenuous. For example, information tasks and resources directly attached to units in the productive system typically involve advantages in terms of immediate relevance or utility, flexibility, and trustworthiness, but disadvantages in terms of professional expertise and regard for long-term factors. The converse is true of units in the support system. Yet all these qualities must be brought to bear in an integrated fashion to satisfy the House's information needs. Similarly, the high degree of functional overlap between units in the productive system and support units complicates choices in the distribution of information tasks and resources. We may remember that members and decision-making units are highly involved in managing staff and expense resources, while support units play key roles in providing legislative information with respect to both substance and operation. A final example concerns specialization, a primary form of organization response in any area. Given the broad and varied character of the work assigned to many decision-making units and support units and the decentralized and overlapping distributions of function and authority that prevail, it is often not easy to decide where or how to provide for specialization.

Nonetheless, difficulties relating to the assessment of benefits and costs in technical or objective terms are not the only or perhaps even the most important source of conflict and confusion over the manner in which the House should respond organizationally to its information needs. The House is a political institution and this context, when linked with the fact that control over information is itself a prime source of power, has a profound impact all its own. Organizational choices in the information area thus do not simply involve questions of the efficiency or effectiveness with which information is generated, distributed, and used; they also involve questions of the basic distribution of power in the House among various categories of members—among majority and minority members, among party leaders and the rest of the House, among committee leaders and committee members, among junior and senior members. This facet of the situation adds a whole new dimension to the problem which both further complicates the assessment of benefits and costs and narrows the alternatives that are truly open.

In organizing information processes, as elsewhere, the House has responded to the substantive and political difficulties it faces in a highly ad hoc fashion by relying on redundancy. Such an approach has definite advantages, given the character of both the needs and the constraints. Still, the duplication of tasks and resources across various locations is at best a partial solution. As present discontent over the quality of available information indicates, existing organizational forms or mechanisms are themselves flawed. Moreover, in a situation in which resources are strained, redundancy itself becomes as much an issue as a viable approach or strategy.

A third and final issue concerns the manner in which the House can best exploit the ongoing technological revolution in information handling. Thus far, computer applications in the House have expanded, but primarily in areas where the political benefits to members as individuals were high and/or where the political costs for members or groups of members relative to other types of benefits were low. Computer technology has accordingly largely been applied to legislative and administrative operations or management, to constituent service activities in member offices, and to the mobilization of budgetary information for a few key committees. Further and wider applications of the computer for legislative decision-making purposes pose a variety of problems and confront a number of constraints. How can computer technology be brought to bear so as to meet the need of members and decision-making units for facts and analyses that are relevant or useful in terms of their policy perspectives and political situations? Conversely, how can access to objective, political, and operational information be substantially enhanced through increases in computer services without doing damage to the already tenuous ability of party leaders to organize majorities and without control over such services becoming a significant factor in the distribution of internal power? Finally, how should the provision of expanded computer services be divided between productive and support units and how should costs be allocated and budgeted?

In sum, then, though extended and imaginative use of the computer offers one of the most promising avenues for improving the quality of the information available to members, the potential benefits should be kept in perspective. In the House, performance is not and cannot be determined by technology. Political factors and political skills are and will remain more basic. Thus, despite its dynamism and potential, increased computer usage must be accommodated to this underlying reality to be either functionally beneficial or politically feasible. Moreover, here as elsewhere, such accommodation must be accomplished in a context in which the precise contours of both the opportunities and the limits are veiled. Politics is not physics. Yet, this fact itself is a source of opportunity as well as limit.

# 9. Congressional Information Sources

*Louis Sandy Maisel*

## INTRODUCTION

Never is the pace of life for a member of Congress so frenetic as during the last hectic days before adjournment. Never are more demands made on members. Never do members need a greater command of the substance and consequences of such a diverse array of issues on which they are expected to be expert, on which they must make judgments which will affect public policy for years to come.

Consider the closing days of the 95th Congress (1978). During the final two weeks of that Congress, members of the House faced important votes on many of the major pieces of legislation which had formed the legislative agenda for the previous two years. They had to deal with the president's energy program, and with its complicated natural gas compromise. They were confronted with proposal after proposal as conferees struggled to draft a tax cut bill which the president would not veto. They were faced with yet another round of votes on the abortion language in the Defense Department and Labor-HEW appropriations bills. They had to vote on civil service reform; the airline deregulation bill; procedures for permissible wiretapping; a major ethics bill and individual charges brought against three of their colleagues by the Committee on Standards of Official Conduct; user fees for inland waterways and the construction of the controversial Dam 26 on the Mississippi, a proposal which has been before the Congress since Franklin Roosevelt's administration; the extension of CETA; a controversial foreign aid package; grazing fees on public lands; and the list goes on.

In addition, many less consequential pieces of legislation reached the floor during this period. And in committee rooms and conferences with the Senate, many members had to deal in intricate detail with variations on the main themes presented in broad legislative packages. They had to move from committee to committee, to conferences, to the floor, to meetings with White House lobbyists and others affected by pending proposals, and back and forth among these, switching gears as they switched issues. The amount of information required for the performance of their public duties is difficult to comprehend.

We must also remember that this frenzy of legislative activity was taking place in October of an election year. Most members were facing reelection the following month. Members not only had to deal with a mind-boggling array of substantive proposals coming before them, but they had to factor into their decisions an assessment of how these proposals would affect their individual districts. Thus, as an example, members were concerned not only with the effect that the airline deregulation bill would have on air service nationally and on the price of that service, but also with how it would affect the service offered to particular sections of their districts.

When members raced home to get in whatever campaigning was possible, they had to confront an entirely different set of concerns. In 1978, concern for inflation and means of reducing the tax burden were recurrent themes in elections throughout the country. However, in many districts members had to campaign on issues which were unique to their region and sometimes ones over which they had no control in Washington no matter how the election was resolved.

This chapter will deal with the information needs of members of Congress, with the internal and external information sources available to them, with the uses they make of these sources, and with the legislative implications which follow from the patterns of usage that will be identified.

This subject is filled with paradoxes. Members of Congress have access to an overwhelming amount of information; yet they often feel underinformed on the issues with which they are expected to be familiar. A wealth of information flows automatically into every member's office; yet it is often in a format which makes it all but unusable or it may arrive after the time when it was needed. Members set national policies; yet they often weigh the consequences of those policies from the parochial perspective of a particular district, state, or region. The information on which they base their conclusions most frequently deals with short-term political factors or public perceptions; yet their decisions have long-term policy consequences. These will be among the issues raised in this discussion.

## MEMBERS' INFORMATION NEEDS

A first priority is to determine the types of information which we must consider. Members have a need for at least four distinct types of information.

The first is *procedural or operational information.* They need to know what is happening on the floor, when bills are likely to come up, what is going on in their committees and subcommittees and in other committees and subcommittees, in the Senate as well as in the House, under what procedures certain pieces of legislation will be considered, when the House is likely to adjourn for the day, or for a week, and matters of that sort. These items are particularly important to members because they can only plan their schedules if they know when their presence will be needed on the floor or in committee. Obtaining this type of information was made somewhat easier by the scheduling reforms adopted at the beginning of the 95th Congress (Commission on Administrative Review 1977*d*). However, much of this information is still difficult to obtain and, at times of particularly heavy workload, such as near the end of a session, all but unobtainable.

As an example, the recorded messages through which each party's whip organization advises its membership of ongoing and pending floor action were unable to keep up with changes in schedules during the last weeks of the 95th Congress. As a result of late changes in floor schedules several members had to miss fundraising events planned for their reelection bids and at least one member had to make plans to participate in a debate with his election opponent by way of telephone connection set up in the Democratic cloakroom. Operational and procedural information is very important to members in terms of their own daily lives; lack of this type of information is a tremendously frustrating part of a member's job.

The second type of information which members need to receive might be referred to as *program information.* Members must be apprised of how much a proposal will cost, how many units will be purchased, what the cut-off level for eligibility will be for a certain program, where the program will be implemented, how the administration of a program will function, and like matters. Because there are so many issues with which they must be concerned, it is no mean feat for members to stay up-to-date with the relevant facts.

This category of information can be subdivided further. As specialization is the norm in the House, members are expected to have a much more detailed and sophisticated grasp of the information relating to some issues than to others. Thus, they need to know more about issues which come before their committees and subcommittees, or in which they have a special interest, than about other issues on which they are to vote but are not expected to assume a leading role. Still members are aware of their responsibility and want to have certain basic information on all matters on the legislative agenda. In addition, there is a whole array of subjects about which constituents expect members of Congress to be conversant, just because members are public people who are concerned with policy making. Most members feel it necessary to keep up with all issues before the public—whether legislation is pending or not—so that they can respond to the legitimate questions and concerns of their constituents. Finally, members need information which is specific to their district and to the unique concerns of their constituents. This type of information relates to the effects of pending legislation, to the impact of ongoing federal programs, and to many other factors as well. We will examine where members obtain these different types of information later in this chapter.

Factors other than those relating to details of a proposal enter into the judgments which members must make on pending proposals. The third type of information which members need might be described as *political "decision-making" information*. This is a most complex topic, one which has been the subject of a good deal of research by political scientists. Obviously members take many factors into account when determining how they are going to vote on certain issues, what positions they are going to take on pending pieces of legislation. The "facts" rarely speak for themselves. Members need to know how a particular proposal will affect their district, how it will affect other programs, who will be helped by it and who hurt, who is for it and who opposed to it, what compromises have been made, who have been the winners and who the losers, who is happy and who unhappy. All members of Congress claim that they seek the "best" public policy, but they would also admit that there is no objective answer to what is "best." They have to know how they should perceive a certain matter, given their ideological, geographic, political and personal considerations. They need a good deal of information beyond the factual substance of a matter in order to fill out their own decision-making paradigms.

The fourth category of information is *ongoing evaluative information*. In some ways this could be viewed as a subset of the third category. However, it is a more specialized type of information. Members need to know how programs are functioning and why they are functioning that way if they are to be able to review existing programs and plan new ones. Schick (1976), Jones (1976), Davidson (1976), and others have begun to explore Congress's ability to use policy analysis. In the final section of this chapter I will look at this problem as well.

## SOURCES OF INFORMATION

What then are the sources from which this variety of information is sought? Certainly the House is not without institutional sources to which the members can turn. In fact, with the expanding workload of the House and with the increased expectations of members' knowledge of public policy positions, the House has moved to increase the internal sources of information available to members (Commission on Administrative Review 1977*a*, 2[*Work Management*]:42–50). In addition, all members rely heavily on sources from outside of the House to provide the information needed to perform their tasks adequately.

### Internal Sources

The first and most important of the internal sources of information is the *congressional staff*, both personal staff and committee staff. In the 95th Congress, members were allotted a clerk-hire allowance of $255,144 annually for their personal staffs. Members could hire no more than eighteen staff employees and no more than one-twelfth of the total allowance could be expended in any one month. According to the payroll records of the Finance Office of the House, the average member of Congress employed 15.8 staff employees in April 1977. These employees were, of course, divided between the member's Washington office and those offices in the district. These employees are directly responsible to the members, serve at their pleasure, and are responsive to the needs which the members themselves define. Significant differences distinguish the ways in which various members allocate and employ their staffs, as befits an institution as decentralized and individualized as the House (see Fox and Hammond 1977).

In 1977 the twenty-two standing committees of the House employed 1,515 staff employees. Special, select, and ad hoc committees employed an additional 177 employees. These staff members served as a resource for the entire House. The degree to which they served individual members varied considerably according to specific employment relationships. In some cases, staff employees worked almost directly for one member, generally a subcommittee chair. This has become noticeably more true since the Democratic Caucus passed a rule allowing each subcommittee chair to hire one specific staff member to work for him or her on the subcommittee. In other cases the employee worked less for one member and more for the entire committee or subcommittee (or one party on that committee or subcommittee) as a collective.

The second internal source of information for members and for the House is the information *support agencies* of the legislative branch: the Congressional Research Service of the Library of Congress, the General Accounting Office, the Office of Technology Assessment, and the Congressional Budget Office. The Library and the GAO have long histories of serving congressional information needs. As the workload of the Congress has increased and the information needed by members has become more complex, these two agencies have expanded and diversified (see Jones 1976). The creation of the OTA in 1972 and the CBO in 1974 further added to the information resources available to the House.

Taken together, the four congressional support agencies, all of which the House shares with the Senate, have the capacity to provide the Congress with a great deal of important information. However, as with any such adjunct agencies, the impact which they have depends directly on the questions that they are asked, the way they respond, and the uses members make of those responses.

The third category of internal resources is comprised of the information services provided by the two *party organizations*. The whip organizations have traditionally provided members with information on upcoming issues and with statements concerning party positions on these matters. The capability of both whip organizations to provide these kinds of information has increased since 1970. For example the Democratic whip organization has been restructured, the deputy whip system is now more effective, and three new at-large whips have been added to assist with whip duties (U.S. Congress 1975). The Majority Whip Office provides members not only with schedules of bills to be debated and voted on, but also with short summaries of those bills (Whip Advisories) and with more detailed position papers on major pieces of legislation (Whip Issue Papers). The Republican party, through its whip office and the Republican Conference, provides its membership with similar information.[1]

In addition, the Democratic Policy and Steering Committee, the Republican Policy Committee, and the Republican Research Committee have taken on expanded roles in recent years. These groups have become more involved in setting party positions and in developing policy alternatives. As such they have provided members with information on legislation likely to come to the floor and on some of the political implications of that legislation. The Republican Research Committee maintains a number of task forces on specific problems which recur frequently and are unlikely to be "solved" through one piece of legislation. Both party organizations have become more involved with providing their members with material suitable for use in speeches back in the district. None of these groups, however, has sufficient staff to take on any significant amount of research itself. Rather, the "research" provided by these groups is frequently little more than rewriting and politicizing documents provided by committee staff. One function of this transmitting process seems to be to give more legitimacy to the positions taken by each party's members (and staff) at the committee level.

*"Nonofficial" groups* provide members of Congress with a different type of information. Approximately twenty nonofficial groups are currently active in the House.[2] Some of these are partisan groups (e.g., the Democratic Research Organization or the [Republican] Wednesday Group). Others are nonpartisan and form along lines of shared interest (e.g., the Congressional Black Caucus, the Congresswomen's Caucus, or the Blue Collar Caucus). While most of these organizations serve only the House, others serve the Senate as well (e.g., Members of Congress for Peace through Law or the Environmental Study Conference). Some have long histories and seem likely to persist (the Democratic Study Group); others have shorter histories and may well disappear, to be replaced by other ad hoc groups (e.g., the recently formed caucus of members from shipbuilding states).[3] These groups vary tremendously in the amount and quality of information that they provide to their members. Table 9.1 lists the "nonofficial" groups which were approved by the Committee on House Administration as legislative support agencies at the start of the 96th Congress (1979). These groups qualify for certain House benefits, such as telephones, but do not constitute all of the "nonofficial" groups currently active.

These organizations engage in a wide range of activities. Some provide information for their members on a specific set of issues; others provide digests of all pending legislation. Some view their role as lobbying for their principal concerns; others claim to serve a purely informational function. Collectively these nonofficial organizations are an important informational resource for most members of Congress.

The *computer capability* which the House has provided for its members also plays an important informational role for some mem-

**Table 9.1.** ***Nonofficial Groups of the House Approved by Committee on House Administration***

| |
|---|
| Bi-Partisan New York State Congressional Delegation |
| Congressional Black Caucus |
| Congressional Clearing House on the Future |
| Congressional Hispanic Caucus |
| Congressional Rural Caucus |
| Congressional Steel Caucus |
| Congressional Textile Caucus |
| Congresswomen's Caucus |
| Democratic Research Organization |
| Democratic Study Group |
| Environmental Study Conference |
| House Fair Employment Practices Committee |
| House Wednesday Group |
| Members of Congress for Peace through Law |
| New England Congressional Caucus |
| 94th Members Caucus |
| 95th Members Caucus |
| Northeast-Midwest Congressional Coalition |
| The Suburban Caucus |
| United Democrats of Congress |

bers. House Information Systems (HIS), established in 1971 under the auspices of the Committee on House Administration, is the central computer support facility in the House. HIS provides member and committee offices with data bases and software packages which are helpful to members and staff in fulfilling their need for information. In addition, members have a computer allowance which can be used to purchase information services from private vendors.

No discussion of internal sources of information for members of the House would be complete without mentioning an informal, but highly influential source, interaction with *colleagues*. In a very meaningful sense, members are always working. Even congressional small talk is about politics, about legislation, about the business of governing. Members spend a good deal of informal time with their colleagues—on the floor, in the cloakrooms, in the Members' Dining Room or in the gym, riding the subway to the Rayburn Building or walking the hallways between the Capitol and their offices, and elsewhere in Washington, a city dominated by talk of government. Whether in informal settings or in meetings called specifically to discuss legislation, members are constantly alert to gather new information from their colleagues. Others (e.g., Cherryholmes and Shapiro 1969; Clausen 1973; Fenno 1965, 1973; Kingdon 1973; Matthews and Stimson 1975) have demonstrated that patterns of interaction can be seen. Members tend to rely on the same colleagues as sources—like-minded members, others from their state, others who entered Congress with them, and other fairly natural groupings. Members often feel that only other members of Congress can view a problem from the same perspective they can; thus, they often give a good deal of credence to information imparted by their colleagues.

**External Sources**

Members gain political information from almost everyone they meet, but some sources from outside of the House can be isolated as more important than others. These sources, which in many ways have become institutionalized, can be divided into governmental and extra-governmental sources.

The *administration*, broadly defined, is an important source of information. Members and staff deal continuously with representatives of the White House and the various executive departments. There is also some interaction between federal agency officials in the field and the members who represent the districts they serve. Despite the fact that the House has begun to develop sources of information on federal programs independent of the executive branch, departmental officials still contribute heavily to what Congress knows of their programs. While members and staff are aware of the bias of this information, they still are forced to rely heavily on it.

Members of Congress also rely heavily on *state and local government officials* to provide them with information on the functioning of federal programs. It is often state and local officials who see most directly the impact of federal programs. They can also see how the administrative procedures for running a program are functioning.

Executive branch officials and state and local officials provide information to the Congress in much the same way as do nongovernmental *lobbyists*. In each case, the individual providing the information views a situation from a very particular perspective. Some members of Congress seek information from these sources because they share that perspective and need to bolster their arguments. In other cases members are seeking a range of views on a subject about which they have yet to form an opinion. Information from any of these sources can be imparted informally in conversation, through more formal requests for specific data, or in the very formal hearing process. Lobbyists are always interested in presenting their views to members of Congress. Members may or may not choose to hear the views of any particular lobbyist.

It should be remembered that all of these sources, like members of Congress, are absorbed with governmental decision making. They are constantly talking about these issues, building alliances, gaining and imparting information, working to improve their programs or the positions they represent. This is a very sophisticated interactive process. Each participant has a stake in the outcome of the legislative process. Each knows the stake and thus the bias of the others. Thus the information flow observed here is in reality a multiperson game in which the players interact, build coalitions, share information, and so on, while each is well aware of the rules of the game and the stakes, incentives, and biases of the others. They each know this is a continuing game as well, that today's allies may be tomorrow's adversaries and vice versa. This leads to the general acceptance of certain norms of behavior toward all who are part of the process.

Some would claim that the *media* are the neutral observers of this political game. In fact, they are participants as well. Much of the information which members rely on comes from the media. One has only to watch a newspaper delivery truck unload thousands of *New York Times* or *Washington Posts* around the Capitol daily to see how dependent members and staff are on the national media for basic information so that they can perform their daily tasks. When members are granting interviews, they are often gathering as much information as they are giving. They know that reporters speak with those on all sides of an issue.

Not only do members rely on the national media, but each individual member also follows the local media in his or her district. These are important sources through which members monitor the concerns prevalent in their districts. Through their choices of what news to cover, therefore, media representatives play an important role in determining what members perceive as important back home.

Any listing of external sources could be expanded almost indefinitely. Certainly members closely follow their mail from the district; they talk frequently with political allies in the district and with many ordinary constituents on their trips home. Some rely heavily on polling information; others draw on academic sources with whom they are familiar. All of these and many more help to fill members' information needs. Having outlined the sources of information potentially available to members, the next task is to analyze the uses members actually make of these sources.

## USAGE OF INFORMATION SOURCES

### Methodology

The data presented in this section are mostly drawn from the Obey Commission member and staff surveys (Commission on Administrative Review 1977*c*, 2:941–1120). The views expressed in those interviews have been supplemented by a series of interviews I conducted with a smaller group of members and staff in spring 1977 and again in late fall 1978. In all cases interviewees were assured anonymity. Consequently, quotations are cited without attribution.

The Obey Commission survey was commissioned in order to identify problems which members felt they had in obtaining necessary information. In achieving this goal, the survey identified not only problems and gaps in information, but it also revealed patterns of usage.

The data on information sources come from two different sets of questions. First, it should be noted that the commission questionnaire differentiated types of information members needed:

1. Things you need to know to handle your committee work.
2. Things you need to know to vote on legislation on the floor which *isn't* from a committee on which you sit.
3. Things you need to know about the wide range of public issues and government policies about which you are expected—as a public person—to have opinions and positions, even though these issues may never reach the floor.
4. Things you need to know about matters that relate specifically to your District, and/or the different needs and interests of your constituents.

(Commission on Administrative Review 1977*c*, vol. 2, Member Survey Wave II, Show Card "A")

These categories correspond roughly to the four subcategories of program information outlined above. For each of these categories members were asked questions about problems and solutions and then they were asked an open-ended question such as:

> Now thinking about all the different places you *could* go to get what you need to know to handle your committee work—your personal staff, committee staff, the Leadership, groups like the DSG or Republican Research Committee, various sources back in your District, groups here in Washington, and CRS, for ex-

ample—where *do* you turn to get what you need to know to handle your committee work—who do you *really rely on* for this kind of information? (PROBE: What *other sources* have you found to be particularly helpful in getting what you need to handle your committee work, either while the legislation is in committee, or when it reaches the floor?)

(Commission on Administrative Review 1977*c*, vol. 2, Member Survey Wave II, Question 3d. Questions 4d, 5d, and 6d were parallel for other types of information needs.)

The responses to these open-ended questions were coded and aggregated to provide the data relied upon to discuss members' actual use of the various potential sources of information available to them.

Legislative assistants were also asked a set of questions about information problems and sources. The importance of questioning these assistants can be emphasized if one notes the large extent to which members rely on staff for gathering information.

The questions asked the staff were similar to those asked members. However, legislative assistants were asked closed-ended questions on sources; they were also asked to evaluate the usefulness of these sources. The responses to these questions will be discussed below.

Before proceeding to the analysis of source usage, two additional factors should be noted. First, the categories of information distinguished by the commission do not precisely correspond to those used here. When one examines the problems cited by members, an extremely high percentage deal with the fact that they do not have enough time or do not get information on procedural matters soon enough. This emphasis relates to a growing frustration felt by members that they cannot do all they are expected to do in as thorough a way as they would like, that expectations of performance have exceeded pragmatic limits.

Second, while follow-up data were gathered on where personal staff (and to a lesser extent committee staff) gather information, it was not within the commission's charge to determine where other primary sources went for their information. Thus, as an example, if the party organizations rely heavily on committee staff or administration sources for information, that two-step process has not been revealed through the survey. It will be alluded to below, however.

**Usage Patterns**

Table 9.2 shows clearly that members rely most heavily on their own staffs in order to learn what they need to know to perform all

**Table 9.2.** ***Members' Use of Information Sources (in percentages)***

| Source | For Committee Work | | For Legislation Not from His/Her Committee(s) | | For Public Issues | | For District Matters | |
|---|---|---|---|---|---|---|---|---|
| Member's personal staff | 60 | | 57 | | 49 | | 51 | |
| Committee staff | 50 | | 29 | | 13 | | 18 | |
| Congressional support agencies | 27 | | 11 | | 30 | | 13 | |
| (CRS) | | (23) | | (11) | | (29) | | (13) |
| Nonofficial groups | 22 | | 37 | | 11 | | 7 | |
| (DSG) | | (18) | | (35) | | (9) | | (7) |
| Lobbyists | 23 | | 15 | | 16 | | 8 | |
| District sources | 20 | | 21 | | 16 | | 22 | |
| Personal reading and study | 14 | | 22 | | 55 | | 13 | |
| (Media) | | (14) | | (14) | | (36) | | (8) |
| Administration | 13 | | 6 | | 16 | | 46 | |
| Colleagues | 11 | | 38 | | 9 | | 7 | |
| Party organizations | 5 | | 27 | | 8 | | 3 | |
| (Whip's office) | | (3) | | (12) | | (4) | | (0) |
| (Research org.) | | (2) | | (15) | | (4) | | (3) |

NOTE: Percentages do not add up to 100; multiple responses were permitted. N = 149.

aspects of their jobs. It is apparent that members feel their staffs do become alter egos, that key staff employees learn to anticipate what their bosses need to know and how they will react once they have certain information. These remarks are typical of many:

> I myself don't have to go anywhere beyond my own staff. My LAs know how I think. I'm heavily reliant on them.
>
> On any issue I'll call in one or two staff people and we all kick it around to decide how I'll go.

For work in their own committees, members rely heavily on the staff employees of those committees as well. This is particularly true of those members who can appoint subcommittee staff; they feel the same loyalty holds as it does with their own office employees. It also seems to be more true for Republicans than for Democrats. Republicans tend to view minority staff as a collective resource while Democrats view committee staff mainly as responsive to the appointing member. The result is that junior Democrats are least likely to draw on committee staff to aid in their work. As one committee chairman saw the situation:

> Republicans on the committee have devised another approach [to staff serving subcommittee chairs]. All of their people, full and subcommittee staffs, are in a staff directorate managed by———, the chief GOP staff counsel. They've managed to reduce the balkanization of their staff through that method.

In a similar vein, the ranking Republican on another committee commented:

> I don't think the minority staff ought to work just for the ranking member. The people on our staff are not just attached to me. Even the people who work on specific subcommittees are not the property of the subcommittee's ranking member. We assign people to subject matters. If they cross over subcommittees, that's okay.

On the other hand, one junior Democrat noted:

> I pretty much have to use my LA for committee work. The staff is helpful, but they don't really feel they work for me.

Committee staff is much less frequently used by members for legislation not from their committees. Two other sources score much more highly, colleagues and nonofficial groups. Dependence on colleagues for this type of information corresponds to what one would expect. Members know that they are not expert on all matters. Consequently, they turn to like-minded colleagues who specialize in areas about which they know less:

> To me the way to use your colleagues is to analyze where their expertise is and to use it.

> My best sources are my colleagues on the responsible committees. The other Republicans let me know how I should go.

Similarly, the reference to nonofficial groups is not surprising. These data do reveal the importance of the Democratic Study

Group, however. Many observers have seen members scanning DSG reports on bills as they go to the floor. This is viewed as an invaluable source by many:

> I rely heavily on information from the DSG. If you can just digest all of that—which isn't easy sometimes—you are on your way to real understanding.

While few of the other nonofficial groups were specifically mentioned, Republican members tended to rely on the Republican Research Committee for similar types of information.

Yet another pattern emerges when members describe where they go for information they need to be kept generally up-to-date on public issues. Here personal staff is supplemented by personal reading and study—particularly reading of national newspapers and magazines[4]—and by use of the Congressional Research Service. Members have mixed feelings about the CRS. One comment seems to epitomize how many feel:

> It's like shooting craps. Sometimes you get good service and sometimes you don't. If you make contact with good people there, you'll get good services. But there are lots of "lemons." CRS seems to be spending a lot of time writing speeches and not enough on real research.

It should be noted that CRS is the only one of the support agencies which is mentioned more than occasionally as a source on which members rely for any kind of information.

Other than personal staff, the administration is the source most often used by members to get information on district matters. Many members interpreted this question to refer to casework. Thus, by "administration," they meant the relevant executive branch agency (19%), liaison office (7%), or regional office (3%). Others interpreted the question more broadly to mean, for example, how a program affected a certain district; they were then referring to departmental policy people, not to civil servants further down the line.

Because so many members rely primarily on their office staffs for information, in order to understand fully how members learn what they do, it is important to see how top legislative assistants (presumably those aides most involved in informing members about this aspect of their jobs) are informed. Table 9.3 addresses this subject.

**Table 9.3.** ***Legislative Assistants' Use of Information Sources (in percentages)***

| *Source* | *For Committee Work* (N = *142)* | *For Legislation Not from His/Her Committee(s)* (N = *144)* | *For Public Issues* (N = *145)* | *For District Matters* (N = *144)* |
|---|---|---|---|---|
| Other members' staffs | 64 | 57 | 50 | 51 |
| Committee staff | 95 | 78 | 71 | 27 |
| Party organization | 41 | 32 | 30 | |
| Committee documents | 73 | 74 | 59 | |
| CRS | 75 | 67 | 90 | 33 |
| GAO | 40 | 32 | 39 | |
| Nonofficial groups | 83 | 66 | 91 | |
| (DSG) | (47) | (66) | (48) | |
| Relevant chair of committee or subcommittee | 37 | 35 | | |
| Lobbyists | 77 | 75 | 71 | |
| State and local officials | 57 | 50 | 47 | 77 |
| Administration and executive branch | 54 | 40 | 56 | 42 D.C.<br>67 field |
| Media and reading | 47 | 56 | 76 | 58 |

NOTE: This table is derived from a series of questions on which legislative assistants were handed a card with a number of sources which other legislative assistants had suggested were helpful for gathering information in each category. The items listed on the cards varied with the type of information. The percentages recorded were those legislative assistants who found each source either "very helpful" or "fairly helpful" as opposed to "only somewhat" or "not at all helpful," under the assumption that those who chose one of the first two categories used the source more frequently. Some sources were listed only for one or two types of information, such as "Dear Colleague" letters. These have been eliminated from this table.

Table 9.3 lists percentages of legislative assistants who find each source of information either "very helpful" or "fairly helpful." It is thus only an approximate measure of what sources are used and should be interpreted with some care. However, some interesting patterns do emerge.

First, committee staff are heavily relied upon. Thus, the committee staff employees are imparting information to committee members through both steps in a two-step communications flow, directly to members and to members through their legislative assistants. Committee staff influence becomes even more evident when one notes that committee documents are also frequently mentioned as helpful. Committee staff prepare most of these documents so they have influence in this way as well.

Legislative assistants rely on lobbyists as well. Many interest groups in Washington routinely provide all congressional offices with statements of their positions on and evaluations of key issues. Staff employees seem to rely on these—as well as on other contacts with lobbyists—to be informed on a whole array of issues. As mentioned earlier, all of the players in this game know the incentives and biases of the others. Thus, it can be assumed that legislative assistants are selective in the advice they use.[5]

CRS and the DSG again stand out. The DSG percentages, of course, are much higher when only Democrats are tabulated. Many members get brief digests of what is to be voted on the floor from their staffs. Many of the legislative assistants are evidently using DSG digests as their prime source for preparing their summaries. Of all those polled, 51% (71% of the Democrats) found DSG materials to be "very helpful" for floor work not emanating from their member's committee. Only 4% of the Democratic legislative assistants found the DSG materials to be "not at all helpful"; undoubtedly most of these were staff employees of members who were not in the DSG.[6]

CRS is found "very helpful" especially for keeping abreast on public issues. In other areas, it tends to be "fairly helpful" more frequently. This leads to support for the quotation cited above on what CRS is in fact doing; more of its work involves short-term requests for specific information, material helpful in preparing speeches, for example, than longer term, more sophisticated research (see Commission on Information and Facilities [Brooks Commission] 1976, Part II).

What then can be concluded from this review of the sources of information on which members rely? Returning to the types of information outlined earlier in this chapter, it seems that most of the information sources relied on by members and legislative assistants are providing either procedural/operational information, program information, or "political decision-making" information. Members can find out what they are voting on, under what procedures (though they complain about the timeliness and format of this information). They can find out who is for a proposal and who is against it, and presumably why. Those are the kinds of information which the sources they currently turn to are adept at providing. However, they do not seem to place reliance on any sources of information which provide them with more objective, more sophisticated evaluative analysis of the needs of the country and the impact of legislative proposals. That is, members do not turn to sources which provide them with the policy analysis referred to earlier.

## IMPLICATIONS OF USAGE PATTERNS

Many years ago Richard Neustadt (1960) pointed out that presidents make decisions today that they cannot put off until tomorrow. They never have all of the information that they need; they obtain as much information as they can and then make the best decisions possible given that amount of information. Presidents are not necessarily happy with this way of reaching decisions, but it is inherent in the nature of the job.

Much the same can be said for members of Congress. They are called upon to make literally thousands of public policy decisions each year. While they might like all of the information possible to reach appropriate conclusions, their minimum requirements—and those on which they most frequently rely—are much less. One member responded almost derisively to the commission's questions on information:

> Information? What's information? Congressmen don't deal with "information." That's talk for political scientists. What I need to know is what people think. So I talk to———[his legislative assistant] and we decide what this is all about and we go with what we have. That might not fit your textbook description, but that's how we work around here.
>
> A common pattern is for members to get caught up in the hurly-burly of decision-making, the necessity of passing legislation, without having time to analyze and evaluate the long-term implications of their decisions.

However, members of Congress are not necessarily happy with the way in which they reach decisions. The Obey Commission survey asked members and legislative assistants about problems they have in obtaining information. In interesting ways, the problems related to the appropriateness of the sources upon which they relied for information.

For instance, few members expressed serious problems with finding out what they felt they needed to know about general public policy concerns. They may have been overwhelmed with the number of issues with which they were expected to be familiar, but they could cope. That was because they relied on media sources and talking with other people who were concerned about public policy. Those were the same sources that those who expected members to be conversant with these issues relied upon. The members were not expected to have detailed knowledge of these matters, rather they were expected to know as much as, or a little more than, those who asked about them, to have an informed opinion but not the last word. Because members of Congress are by their nature interested in public policy, and because discussions of public policy concerns dominate their lives, they do have the general familiarity expected of them. Government now pervades almost all aspects of our lives—and this pervasiveness may itself be a problem—but the sources of information used by members of Congress are precisely the appropriate ones for coping with others' expectations of what they will know about the issues of concern to their constituents.

On the other hand, members have serious problems in dealing with those matters on which they need enough information to make responsible decisions. Table 9.4 presents data on problems cited by members and by legislative assistants dealing with the information needed to cope with demands made by committee work and by required floor action on bills not emanating from a member's committee(s). References to procedural matters have been deleted because these concerns tend to deal with the timing, not the substance of the information available.

Table 9.4 shows that members and their assistants have few problems determining the positions of the various other actors in the political arena. That follows because they turn to those other actors to learn what they need to know to make decisions. That is, the administration, the House leadership, and the affected interest groups are among their prime sources of information.

However, they do express problems in getting other kinds of information normally thought to be necessary to arrive at rational decisions. The table shows clearly that members and staff have diffi-

**Table 9.4. *Difficulty in Obtaining Information, as Reported by Members and Legislative Assistants***

| | *For Committee Work* | | *For Legislation Not from Member's Committee(s)* | |
|---|---|---|---|---|
| *Subject* | *Members (%)* | *LAs (%)* | *Members (%)* | *LAs (%)* |
| Existing problems or needs addressed by legislation and what past efforts have produced | 40 | 32 | 39 | 41 |
| Other proposals currently being considered which relate to the problem being addressed | 40 | 45 | 34 | 55 |
| Likely impact of legislation on member's district | 34 | 40 | 40 | 58 |
| Likely impact of legislation nationally | 27 | 11 | 30 | 18 |
| Position of the administration on proposed legislation | 11 | 8 | 10 | 7 |
| Position of the House leadership on specific legislation | 9 | 9 | 6 | 5 |
| Position of affected interest groups on specific legislation | 5 | 8 | 7 | 4 |

NOTE: Percentages do not add up to 100; multiple responses permitted. N = 151.

culty getting information about the likely consequences of their actions and/or alternatives to their actions.[7] This conclusion follows logically from the earlier analysis of sources of information relied upon; that is, there is a dearth of evaluative material used and few sources are relied on which can supply them.

Are members having trouble getting information of this type because no appropriate sources exist, or because they do not choose to draw on those sources? Or is this lack of reliance on sophisticated policy analysis inherent in congressional—or governmental—or political—decision making?

These are critical, important questions. As the system currently functions, it could be argued that no incentive exists for members to seek out such information. Their job is to legislate, to vote on pending proposals, to avoid antagonizing constituents with controversial votes. If members felt they needed this kind of information, they would work harder to obtain it. The situation, however, appears to be fluid. Public opinion is moving toward demanding less government, more efficient government, lower taxes. Members of Congress will have to evaluate ongoing programs, to choose among them, to revise those which are not meeting expectations.

Early in the 96th Congress many members were complaining of the slow pace of the Congress. In part this was because members understood that their task in 1979 was different from what it had been earlier, but they were unequipped to deal with it. The institution needed different kinds of information to adopt to changing expectations, but individual members had yet to make this adaptation in the way in which they informed themselves, in the type of information they needed. It is unclear through what process—or if—this change will take place.

If members do perceive these new needs, do appropriate sources currently exist? Certain formal organizations currently in place could provide some such information, but their overall utility is limited. Few members or legislative assistants mentioned reliance on the OTA, the CBO, or the GAO. It seems likely that in part at least these agencies are too specialized to be useful for members in the context under discussion. The CRS has a slightly different limitation. Its mandate allows it to answer a wide range of questions; however, CRS researchers are indoctrinated with a norm of objectivity. Members do not want objective analysis; they require evaluations which take their own values into account. The internal information support agencies do not seem capable of fulfilling this need.

Outside of the Congress, there has been a tremendous emphasis in the academic community in recent years on policy analysis. Many of the major universities have developed public policy programs and have turned their attention away from theoretical discussions of political phenomena toward the most pragmatic kinds of analyses of the impact of public policies. However, the Congress has not made wide use of this resource either. University and academic sources of information were cited by relatively few members of Congress. The census of House personnel conducted by the commission did not reveal a large number of legislative assistants holding Masters of Public Policy or similar degrees. Rather the emphasis remains, as it traditionally has, on employing those with legal training.[8]

Why have members and staff not turned to these sources? Some might claim that it is too soon to detect a changing pattern, that the congressional support agencies are just gearing up to play a significant role in the decision-making process, that the academic community is just beginning to turn out qualified analysts, that the Congress will make increasing use of these resources. Certainly the evidence is not clear on this point. It is impossible to predict whether the Congress will move in these directions. Much may depend on the satisfaction of those members who do seek new and different sources.

Others (Jones 1976; Schick 1976) claim that the Congress is not an appropriate forum for policy analysis. They claim that members must make essentially political decisions and that objective policy analysis often does not take into account the factors that members of Congress view as most important. Though these observers did not have the benefit of the Obey Commission findings on problems members felt in obtaining information, it is unlikely that these findings would alter their opinions.

There are some important factors about the congressional environment which should be kept in mind. Perhaps the most important of these is the fact that it is an electric environment; something is always happening, and staffers like to be in on momentous events. Prestige among congressional staff is directly related to one's access to members and to key decisions. Often those decisions are defined as "key" in a very narrow context. That is, at any one time members may view a decision as critical which, viewed with a month's hindsight, looks mundane. However, what is important is that, at the time, the member thinks that decision is the most important thing in the world. The staff employee whom he consults on that decision basks in the glory of being in on an important matter. The member wants to consult with a staff employee whom she or he trusts completely, who knows how the member thinks in most cases and how that member's constituency will be affected, whose loyalty is unquestioned. Staff employees strive to reach a position in which they are so consulted. Staff employees do not want to miss the opportunity to be in on such important moments, to gain in prestige and (at least perceived) influence. Thus, one observes the phenomenon of many employees staying at their desks late into the evening—if their boss is still at work—so as not to be unavailable if called in for consultation on the next crisis. Staff employees do not like to think that their member—or the Congress—could proceed for even one evening or could make even one decision without their input. If a decision is reached without the benefit of consultation with a staff employee, the member might realize that the employee is not indispensable. That conclusion is one which a key employee wants his or her member to avoid at all costs.

This description of the relationship between a member and her or his key legislative assistants is directly relevant to the lack of policy analysis on the Hill. Those who are engaged in sophisticated, detailed policy analysis cannot always be concerned about the crisis of the moment. They are concerned with long-range forecasts, with details of costs and benefits from a program, with simulations of situations to predict likely consequences. They are concerned with demographic projections, with economic indicators. They do not need immediate access to a member in order to do their work effectively. They do not need to know what is happening every day. They do not need to know what is happening on the floor, what a particular interest group says, or what David Broder says the president is thinking. And therein lies the conflict. To date those engaged in this type of analysis have not been perceived as achieving positions as influential as the "fire-stopping" legislative assistant. Members have difficulty turning to people for some kinds of information who are not the same people they turn to in the day-to-day crises; thus the perception that these people do not have influence becomes something of a self-fulfilling prophecy.

In the House physical proximity to the chamber floor is a rough indication of in-House prestige. It is highly significant then that the Congressional Budget Office and the Office of Technology Assessment are both headquartered in the House annexes, separated not only from the floor but also from members' offices by wide avenues which stand as more of a psychological barrier than a physical one. Members do not perceive their need for these support agencies to do their daily jobs. Those who labor in OTA and the CBO are thus removed from the influence which accrues to those who have immediate access to members. It can be argued that legislative assistants who could spend time developing outside resources with that capability also see that this is not the way to influence and avoid that path.[9]

There is another aspect of the congressional decision-making environment which is equally relevant. Institutional resources in the Congress must serve two masters—the majority and the minority. They must attempt to give balanced presentations, objective analyses. In the executive branch, policy analysts serve only one master. They can, therefore, be explicit about their priorities and values. That kind of openness is necessary for policy evaluation to be relevant to governmental decision making. Certainly policy analysts exist in the Congress today. However, their evaluations are seldom the determining factor because members do not yet see how the information they provide is the relevant information for the decisions members must make. In order for this transition to be made, policy evaluation must be increased in terms of availability and quality and members must become aware of its "political" relevance.

This analysis assumes that the Congress must make a transition to additional reliance on policy analysis of the type discussed here if it is to maintain its place in our policy-making process. Without policy analysis the Congress will not be able to take the initiative in—or even to respond effectively to—the necessary changes in governmental programs, retrenching, increasing efficiency, and cutting back government, as the public clearly seems to be demanding. Without reliance on this kind of information, the Congress will be able only to respond to executive branch initiatives. Often the response will be to judge those initiatives on criteria which are not in fact relevant to the need of the times.

How then can the Congress make this transition? That is difficult to judge, and the appropriate mechanism remains to be found. It appears that it is necessary to remove the "ego-gratification" incentive from the employee while at the same time maintaining the closeness and trust necessary to have influence with the member. One mechanism which has been frequently mentioned but never tried is to provide the two parties' leaders with a corps of trusted staff employees, proven congressional veterans whose political instincts have been well tested and whose loyalty is beyond question, whose job it would be to serve as policy analysts for the leadership. Because of the partisan nature of the Congress, it would be essential to tie these employees to the party leaders. However, it would also be important to choose employees who had an institutional perspective, who could look beyond the crisis of the day to the years ahead. These employees could develop certain policy expertise; they could be temporarily assigned to certain committees; they could serve as liaison with and draw on experts from outside; in short, they could become an invaluable resource for the House as a whole, for the leadership, and for individual members. However, one should not underestimate the difficulties in instituting this type of staffing pattern. The barriers to the development of this type of resource are significant and may well be insurmountable.

Finally, what are the implications for the House as an institution—and for the government—if congressional decision making continues to be accomplished without the benefit of perhaps the most relevant kind of information, information about the consequences of past and future decisions? Two scenarios present themselves. The first is essentially more of the same. Decisions will be reached in the same ways. Members will feel that they are forced to decide without the information that they would like to have, but they will cope. Some will become frustrated and leave the House. Many more will find other aspects of congressional life attractive and continue on. The public will continue in its disenchantment with the Congress; the institution will continue to fall lower and lower in public esteem. But individual members, using the powers of the incumbent, will deflect this dissatisfaction away from themselves onto "that gang in Washington," from whom they are distinct, and they will continue to be reelected. And, we will continue to see the phenomenon that Richard Fenno has noted, that, despite the fact that Congress is the "broken branch," we continue to love our representatives (Fenno 1975). This is, of course, not a very pleasant scenario, because it will lead to increased dissatisfaction with the government generally and the overall loss of support for the system which Burnham has foreseen (1975).

The second scenario is more sanguine. It essentially projects that the public will make the link between the incumbent members of Congress and the dissatisfaction which they are expressing both with the Congress as an institution and with public policy. Or perhaps more realistically this scenario projects that members of Congress will foresee that the public will make the link. In any case,the result would be a move toward improving public policy, toward revamping the decision-making mechanisms of the Congress so that ineffective programs will be corrected or disposed of. Certainly the rhetoric of the 1978 congressional election implies that members of Congress see that they must move in this direction. However, there is little evidence from the results of that election that the taxpayer revolt is going to have immediate electoral consequences for incumbent members of Congress. Unless members of Congress foresee such consequences, it is unlikely that they will alter significantly the means through which they arrive at the kinds of decisions which have allowed them to persist in office.

## NOTES

The author would like to thank the Social Science Grants Committee of Colby College for its generous support of this research.

1. The two party organizations are funded differently and divide responsibilities slightly differently. For a detailed discussion see Commission on Administrative Review 1977*b*, 45–46.
2. It was difficult to arrive at a term to describe accurately the organizations included in this section. Frequently they are referred to as "infor-

mal" groups; however, many of them have very formal organizational structures which have persisted for some years. "Unofficial" does not seem quite accurate either; the House recognizes the legitimacy of these organizations by giving (at least some of them) office space and by not objecting to the fact that clerk-hire funds are used to pay employee salaries (again, for some of the groups and/or some employees of others). Some of these organizations can accurately be described as "ad hoc" groups, but this term seems inappropriate for organizations which have been in existence for two decades and which deal with all issues coming before the Congress. The term "nonofficial" was chosen in part at least because it is infrequently used and therefore has fewer set notions attached to it.

3. There is a tendency for groups, once formed, to persist at least at a minimal level, however. This is because the member most active in a group soon realizes that he or she has extra staff to deal with an issue of particular concern by using the group staff.
4. See Members' Survey Wave II, Codebook for Question 5d in Commission on Administrative Review 1977c, 2(*Survey Materials*):972.
5. It would be helpful to know how frequently committee staffs rely on lobbyists as well. Again a multi-step flow of information seems apparent. On the interrelationships among the actors in this legislative game see, for example, Cater 1964.
6. Again it would be helpful to have a systematic analysis of where the DSG gets its material. According to one former DSG staffer familiar with their research methods, "It is no secret. We go through the committee staff; we call committee staff people of our members on the committee; we read lots of committee prints." A more detailed study of DSG methods would be valuable.
7. It is interesting to note that legislative assistants feel that they have fewer problems in assessing the national impact of proposed legislation than do members themselves. One can only speculate on the reason for this finding. Perhaps it reflects the fact that staff employees are more likely to trust the assessment of the sources on which they rely than are members.
8. See chapter 7 of this book for a detailed discussion of congressional staff.
9. An interesting parallel can be drawn with the policy advisors to the president. At the beginning of the Nixon Administration, for instance, Daniel Patrick Moynihan and Henry Kissinger were assigned the task of taking the long view of domestic and foreign policy making respectively for the president. Within a short period of time, each saw that this was not the road to influence. Moynihan left the Urban Council and Kissinger began to involve himself with day-to-day foreign policy making, most noticeably with the Soviet Union and the People's Republic of China. Kissinger's influence was enhanced tremendously by taking on these new assignments. John Ehrlichman replaced Moynihan as the president's chief domestic advisor. His influence was substantial, most-

ly because the Domestic Council staff which he headed dealt largely with day-to-day decisions. See Cronin 1975; Maisel and Helmer 1976.

## REFERENCES


Burnham, Walter D. 1975. "American Politics in the 1970s: Beyond Party?" In *The Future of Political Parties*, ed. Louis Maisel and Paul M. Sacks, pp. 238–277. Beverly Hills: Sage.

Cater, Douglass. 1964. *Power in Washington*. New York: Random House.

Cherryholmes, Cleo H., and Shapiro, Michael J. 1969. *Representatives and Roll Calls*. Indianapolis: Bobbs-Merrill.

Clausen, Aage R. 1973. *How Congressmen Decide*. New York: St. Martin's.

Commission on Administrative Review, U.S. Congress, House. 1977*a*. *Administrative Reorganization and Legislative Management*. Communication from the chair. 2 vols. 95th Cong., 1st sess.

———. 1977*b*. *Background Information on Administrative Units, Members' Offices, and Committees and Leadership Offices*. 95th Cong., 1st sess. H. Doc. 95-178.

———. 1977*c*. *Final Report*. 2 vols. 95th Cong., 1st sess. H. Doc. 95-272.

———. 1977*d*. *Scheduling the Work of the House*. Communication from the chair. 95th Cong., 1st sess. H. Doc. 95-23.

Commission on Information and Facilities, U.S. Congress, House. 1976. *Inventory of Information Resources and Services Available to the U.S. House of Representatives*. Communication from the chair. 94th Cong., 2d sess.

Cronin, Thomas E. 1975. *The State of the Presidency*. Boston: Little, Brown.

Davidson, Roger H. 1976. "Congressional Committees: The Toughest Customers." *Policy Analysis* 2(Spring):299–325.

Fenno, Richard F., Jr. 1965. "The Internal Distribution of Influence: The House." In *The Congress and America's Future*, ed. David B. Truman, pp. 52–76. Englewood Cliffs, N.J.: Prentice-Hall.

———. 1973. *Congressmen in Committees*. Boston: Little, Brown.

———. 1975. "If, as Ralph Nader Says, Congress Is 'The Broken Branch,' How Come We Love Our Congressmen So Much?" In *Congress in Change: Evolution and Reform*, ed. Norman J. Ornstein, pp. 277–287. New York: Praeger.

Fox, Harrison W., Jr., and Hammond, Susan W. 1977. *Congressional Staffs: The Invisible Force in American Lawmaking*. New York: Free Press.

Jones, Charles O. 1976. "Why Congress Can't Do Policy Analysis (or words to that effect)." *Policy Analysis* 2(Spring):251–265.

Kingdon, John W. 1973. *Congressmen's Voting Decisions*. New York: Harper & Row.

Maisel, Louis, and Helmer, John. 1976. "High Level Domestic Advising: The Domestic Council in the Ford Administration." Paper presented at

1976 annual meeting of the Southern Political Science Association, Atlanta.

Matthews, Donald R., and Stimson, James A. 1975. *Yeas and Nays: Normal Decision-Making in the U.S. House of Representatives*. New York: Wiley.

Neustadt, Richard E. 1960. *Presidential Power*. New York: Wiley.

Schick, Allan. 1976. "The Supply and Demand for Analysis on Capitol Hill." *Policy Analysis* 2(Spring):215–235.

U.S. Congress, House. 1975. *History and Operation of the House Majority Whip Organization*. 94th Cong., 1st sess. H. Doc. 94-162.

# 10. Computer Usage in the House

*Jeffrey A. Goldberg*

At the foot of Jenkins Hill, well removed from the main congressional campus, stands a government building popularly known as the "Old FBI Building." This building was used for many years as a central repository for fingerprint records maintained by the FBI. It now houses, among other things, the primary computer facilities of the U.S. House of Representatives.

In order for the House to satisfy its need to support an ever-growing staff population, the Congress took over the old FBI building when the FBI moved its fingerprint records to the newly completed J. Edgar Hoover building. Because this newly acquired congressional office building was situated at some distance from the nexus of congressional activity, the building was used to house those congressional staff members who did not need to be in close proximity to the Capitol to provide assistance on short notice to members of Congress.

In most cases the availability of adequate telecommunications capabilities makes the physical location of a computer facility somewhat irrelevant. However, the fact that the primary computer hardware employed by the U.S. House of Representatives is situated on the periphery of the congressional community symbolizes the cautious approach the House has taken in adopting the use of information systems technology.

For the last twenty years computers have been heralded far and wide as invaluable tools for improving the efficiency of administrative operations, and for increasing human effectiveness in the decision-making processes. Indeed, the computational and records management capabilities of the computer have permitted private industry to reap substantial profits and savings in time and money. The academic and scientific communities have not been indifferent to the research benefits made possible through the use of the computer. And, of course, the administration of government, through the modern federal bureaucracy, would come to an abrupt halt if the plugs were pulled on all executive branch computers.

Thus, the computer has been successfully integrated into many different working environments. And, in most cases, a technology which was originally perceived as merely a useful tool has become an absolute necessity to the continued functioning of the work activities it was intended to facilitate.

But what place does information systems technology have within the legislative branch? How can the computer make its peace with an institution which does not evaluate the success or failure of its efforts in terms of time and motion efficiencies? Can the computer be effectively adapted to a decision-making process which rarely bases its operations on mathematical calculation?

While serious analysis of the use of information systems technology by the Congress has been limited, those who have studied the subject have generally arrived at the same conclusion, that is, that the multitude of complex national issues before the Congress have forced the institution to borrow from the experience of private industry and to "streamline" its customary practices and procedures so as to accelerate the traditionally lumbering legislative process. The Congress in general and the House in particular have been committed to an on-going process of identifying new methods and procedures for improving the overall efficiency and effectiveness of institutional operations. In recent years the computer has served as the centerpiece of many reform recommendations. In this regard, the terms "efficiency" and "effectiveness" are often described as the principal benefits to be derived from automation. The House, to its credit, has in most instances been careful not to confuse the two concepts when it has considered ways to improve its operations, recognizing that the benefits derived from improved "efficiency" may operate at cross purposes with institutional "effectiveness."

For example, use of information technology by individual members to acquire background information on pending legislation appears to offer a means for improving the member's knowledge for the purpose of legislative decision making. At the same time, however, this may reduce the ability of the leadership of the House to coordinate and direct the activities of the House in a deliberate fashion. If the computer offers to all members the opportunity to receive more relevant information, it also may contribute to the creation of a generally better informed member. As a result of the independent acquisition of information, the member is less likely to rely upon the leadership, and more likely to express independent points of view, thus thwarting the leadership's legislative goals. In these circumstances, the computer's contribution to improving the efficiency of the individual legislator in gathering information may stand as an obstacle to the effective processing of legislation by the House as an institution.

In considering the motivations of the House during the last decade in adopting the use of computer technology, it is important to avoid blanket assumptions. In each instance where a computer application has been implemented within the House, it is necessary to view the system first in terms of the original benefits for which it was designed and then to see if the intended benefits were realized in the actual implementation of the system. Finally, and perhaps most importantly, one should examine the unintended or unanticipated consequences of the implementation of a system, since these will be an important part of the impact that system has on the operation of the institution as a whole.

## EARLY DEVELOPMENTS

In the private sector the computer was first used as an administrative tool, and this was no less the case in the U.S. House of Representatives. In the late 1960s and early 1970s, the Clerk of the House employed the computer to assist with personnel/payroll processing and inventory control. During this period a few House committees used the computer to help with the production of their legislative calendars (an historical document containing a record of the legislative activity of the committee). Thus, the computer made its first inroads into the House by providing automated support for selected administrative activities of both the Clerk of the House and House committees.

As awareness of the potential benefits of automation began to grow within the House, there developed an interest in establishing a House unit which would have the principal responsibility for planning and implementing House computerization. In 1971 the House adopted a resolution providing for the establishment of the House Information Systems (HIS). Functioning under the jurisdiction of the Committee on House Administration, HIS had as its primary mission the planning and implementation of future computer applications within the House. In 1971, HIS began its work with a staff of one; in 1979 it maintained a staffing ceiling of 195 positions and an operating budget of over $9 million.

Upon its creation, HIS operated principally in support of the computer operations of the Clerk's financial management and inventory systems and the production of committee calendars. The major thrust of its early development efforts focused, however, on the design of an electronic voting system for the House chamber, and on the development of an automated bill status system for use by congressional staff in monitoring the current status of legislation.

With the adoption of the requirement for record teller votes as a result of the passage of the Legislative Reorganization Act of 1970, the House was virtually forced by time constraints to convert from its time consuming voice vote system to an electronic voting system. The implementation of the record teller vote meant, in effect, that recorded votes would be taken on most amendments which the House considered during debate in the Committee of the Whole. Prior to the enactment of this reform, recorded votes were usually taken on the floor only during the final passage of a piece of legislation.

Given the expectation of an increasing number of recorded votes, and the knowledge that the average voice vote took approximately thirty minutes to complete, the House moved to implement an automated voting system. But even as the House moved tentatively into the twentieth century with the installation of a computerized voting system, it retained its time-honored standards of decorum. For example, a mandatory design requirement was that the traditional decor of the House chamber not be violated as a result of installing monitors and voting stations on the House floor. Thus, all vote displays and vote recording equipment are inconspicuous except when there is a vote in progress.

The implementation of the electronic voting system provides a good example of how the intended benefits of computerization sometimes conceal unanticipated consequences. Allowing members to vote as they entered the House chamber at any of forty-four voting stations was intended to reduce by half the average time needed to take a roll call vote. However, roll call vote statistics gathered prior to and after the implementation of the electronic voting system demonstrate that, while the average time to record an individual roll call vote was indeed reduced by approximately 50 percent as a result of the use of the electronic voting system, the total time spent by the House in roll call voting increased in each succeeding session principally because more roll call votes were demanded.

To be sure, no simple or direct cause and effect relationship has been demonstrated between the implementation of the electronic voting system and the increase in the number of roll call votes taken within the House. In part, the increase in roll call votes can be attributed to a general increase in the volume of legislation. And surely some portion of the explanation lies in the introduction of record teller votes. But there is also strong reason to believe that the increase in the number of roll call votes is partially attributable to the implementation of the electronic voting system itself. On any individual roll call vote, the House is now inconvenienced for only half of the time required under the previous voice vote procedures. This has led some to argue that the relative ease with which it is now possible to undertake a vote using the electronic voting system has encouraged the initiation of an increased number of frivolous votes or quorum calls, as a dilatory tactic, causing a progressive increase in the total number of roll call votes. The savings in time which the voting system made possible for each individual roll call vote may thus have had the unintended consequence of encouraging members of Congress to demand many unnecessary or dilatory roll call votes, thereby increasing the overall time the House spends in voting.

Despite the uncertainty as to whether, on balance, the electronic voting system has increased or decreased the efficiency of the House, there can be no doubt that the use of the automated bill status system (LEGIS), introduced in 1973, has provided congressional staff with substantial time savings and efficiencies in the tracking of legislation. In its initial version, the LEGIS system functioned as a telephone inquiry service, allowing congressional staff to have a trained computer terminal operator retrieve the desired legislative information. Tracking all House and Senate bills and resolutions, the LEGIS data base could be accessed by bill number, sponsor or cosponsor, or by legislative subject. The LEGIS data base is updated nightly after all House and Senate committees are polled to determine changes in the status of legislation being considered in committee. In recent years, congressional staff have been able to access the LEGIS system directly through the use of computer terminals located within member or committee offices.

The LEGIS system is now most frequently used by congressional staff as a reference tool to respond to constituent inquiries regarding the status of a particular piece of legislation. Although it serves this useful reference function, the system has been criticized for failing to provide evaluative information, thus making it necessary for staff to communicate directly with committee and leadership personnel to determine the scheduling of a particular piece of legislation and the likelihood of its passage. This criticism does not point to any technical deficiencies in the system design of LEGIS (as the computer would be able to facilitate the transmission of any information entered into the system), rather it points to the continuing tension between the computer's capability to contribute to the "democratization" of information, on the one hand, and the realities of a political environment which dictates selective dissemination of information, on the other.

## LEGISLATIVE USES

In 1974, the Congressional Budget and Impoundment Control Act was passed by Congress. In addition to creating three new congressional organizations—the Congressional Budget Office and the House and Senate Budget Committees—the Budget Act created a new budget timetable and requirements for extensive budgetary information and analysis.

While the president continues to submit his annual budget request to the Congress and thereby establishes the limits and terms of congressional budgetary debate, clearly one of the fundamental objectives of the 1974 Budget Act was to create congressional institutions and procedures which would aid the Congress in asserting its independence from the executive branch in the annual formulation and assessment of the federal budget. To the extent that this objective has been realized, the computer has played an integral role. As a result of the passage of the Budget Act, both internal House computer resources and commercial resources were quickly brought to bear to assist the Congressional Budget Office and the House Appropriations and Budget Committees in fulfilling their responsibilities under the Budget Act.

At the beginning of each budget cycle, the Office of Management and Budget delivers to the Congress computer tapes containing the president's budget request for the coming fiscal year. These computer tapes are loaded onto House computer facilities and hundreds of specialized analyses are produced for the House Appropriations subcommittees and the House Budget Committee. In this way the computer is used to produce budget reports based on the unique analytical requirements of each House user. The manner in which these reports are produced to satisfy House analytical requirements often bears little resemblance to the computer format provided by OMB.

Use of automated support during the budget cycle has not been the exclusive privilege of the House Appropriations and Budget Committees or the Congressional Budget Office. In recent years the authorizing committees of the House have also experimented with the use of computers to assist in budget tracking and in the preparation of the annual compilation of "Views and Estimates" on reauthorization levels for continuing programs within their respective jurisdictions. Although the requirements for fiscal analysis were statutorially prescribed in the 1974 Budget Act, it has been computer technology which has allowed the statutory prescriptions to become a reality. Thus, in the case of congressional budget review, access to the computer has enhanced the Congress's ability to act independently of the executive in the formulation of the budget.

In certain respects the computational powers of the computer have also facilitated policy analysis and review by House committees. However, more than in any other area of computer utilization, committee use of automated resources in support of policy analysis and oversight responsibilities appears to be directly related to the academic or professional experience of each committee's staff. Committee personnel who have used computerized forecasting models and statistical packages prior to being employed by the House have encouraged committees to recognize the value of these analytical tools.

Econometric and economic forecasting models have been used to a limited extent by House committees. Computerized tax models have been available for use by the Joint Committee on Taxation as well as the Committee on Ways and Means. In addition, a computer package known as the Transfer Income Model (TRIM) has been used by the House Agriculture Committee to assist in the analysis of food stamp policy. Through the use of TRIM, the economic impact of changes in food stamp eligibility can be determined for recipient households. In 1979 the Committee on House Administration used a computer-generated statistical analysis of Federal Election Commission campaign contribution data in conjunction with its consideration of public financing legislation.

There has been moderate use of the computer in support of committee oversight responsibilities as well. In 1976, the Subcommittee on Oversight and Investigations of the Interstate and Foreign Commerce Committee published a report on Department of Commerce actions relating to the Arab boycott of businesses having financial dealings with the State of Israel. As background material for its investigation, the subcommittee established a boycott data file which was then used to analyze the Department of Commerce's activities. The House Committee on Science and Technology employed House computer facilities to conduct an oversight study of the distribution of research and development funds by the National

Science Foundation. And the House Appropriations Committee employed the House computer to process questionnaires used in a congressional survey of public attitudes toward federal regulations.

## ADMINISTRATIVE USES

In the past several years, automated support has also been expanded to facilitate administrative functions and document preparation by committees. The electronic capture of committee hearing transcripts has become a reality through the use of the computer. Not only has editorial and publication time been reduced through automation, but the overall cost of publishing committee hearings has been substantially reduced through the use by the Government Printing Office of electronic photocomposition equipment.

Not all automation projects involved with committee administrative needs have been unqualified successes. Indeed, the history of the Committee Meeting Information System (COMIS) provides an excellent example of an automated administrative system conflicting with fundamental institutional prerogatives.

As a part of the 1974 Committee Reform Amendments, the House adopted a rule which provided for voluntary participation by House committees in an automated committee scheduling system. If all House committees entered notices of scheduled meetings into the computer, the Committee Meeting Information System would permit any committee to determine which of its members was previously scheduled for other committee meetings. In this way, the computer was intended to help committee chairs minimize schedule conflicts, and in so doing, to improve member attendance at committee meetings. However, in the four years since COMIS became operational, only minimal use has been made of the system by House committees. This failure to successfully integrate COMIS into the committee scheduling process has revealed several important lessons regarding the application of advanced technology in a traditional legislative environment.

While one may attribute this low rate of participation to the voluntary nature of the House rule, it appears that the primary reason for the lack of participation is the basic conflict between the system's fundamental mission and the prerogatives of House committee chairs.

For the computer to serve as a useful tool for committee scheduling, all House committees would have to enter meeting information into a central data base which could be accessed by other committees. The presumption is that committee chairs would be willing to make meeting schedules available for review by others. Unfortunately this presumption assumes a level of collegiality among committee chairs which does not have any basis in fact. Moreover, there is no clear indication of a desire by committees to reduce member absenteeism at committee meetings through better scheduling. In fact, there may be occasions when a committee chair would want to encourage selective absenteeism among members whose presence might impede the actions of a committee. On such occasions the computer system, ostensibly designed to help reduce scheduling conflicts, could be used by the committee chair to promote selective absenteeism.

Thus, it is important to realize that in a legislative or any other environment, pure technology cannot be relied upon to manage itself. Not in this respect can one be assured that technology will be used for the salutary purpose for which it was designed.

At the beginning of the 96th Congress, the House established a new Select Committee on Committees to review the overall structure of the House committee system, including the issue of committee scheduling. There is a strong indication, at the time this is written, that the Select Committee's recommendations will include provisions for improving the committee scheduling process, including mandatory use of COMIS by all House committees. But even if the House adopts this recommendation, there is no assurance that the knowledge of potential scheduling conflicts will, in itself, reduce such conflicts for members of the House.

## MEMBER OFFICE USES

The introduction of sophisticated computer and word processing equipment into the member office environment has been another recent occurrence. The first year in which members were permitted to expend their official expense allowance on commercial computer equipment and services was 1975. While access to automated legislative information resources is centrally provided by the House, members must deal directly with commercial vendors to acquire computer terminals, word processing equipment, and external computer time-sharing services. Today over 300 members of the House use some form of direct computer support in managing office workloads and acquiring legislative information. In short, computer and word processing equipment is not automatically provided to all members of the House as standard office equipment. On the contrary, members are required to make individual budgetary choices regarding the acquisition of computer services. The fact that over 68% of the membership of the House has acquired some form of direct computer support is indicative of the widespread belief that the computer represents a cost-efficient tool which enhances the effectiveness of the member as both legislator and constituent ombudsman.

Within the member office there has been a natural tendency to apply computer and word processing technology to those areas where the workload is greatest. Thus automation was first used to assist member offices in responding to the large volume of incoming constituent correspondence. As a by-product of answering the mail, member offices have been able to use computer and word processing services to maintain constituent correspondence histories. By using the sophisticated selection and sorting capabilities of the computer, constituent correspondence histories can be retrieved to produce "follow-up" mailings on legislative subjects of interest to the constituents, and to produce numerical tabulations of incoming mail volume broken down by legislative issue. The computer also permits the member office to cross-reference incoming mail against relevant geographic indicators (e.g., zip code, town, county). A representative can thus determine the legislative concerns of his constituents as a function of their location within the district.

In this way, the computer has contributed to a partial redefinition of congressional representation. Automation within the member office facilitates communication not only with a broad constituency, but also with each individual constituent. From this perspective, increased computerization within the member office has not, as is commonly believed, encouraged greater "depersonalization" in congressional representation. Rather it has permitted members to "get in closer touch" with their constituencies.

Not everyone believes that this closer representational proximity is a good thing. Indeed the Founding Fathers, in establishing a representative democracy, were anxious to establish some distance between the government and the governed. In addition, some critics feel that in an age when the Congress has established strict limitations on the executive branch regarding the collection of data on individual citizens, it is inappropriate for the legislative branch to exclude itself from similar restrictions.

While computer and word processing support is generally applied first to the production of legislative correspondence, in a growing number of offices automation is being used to support other types of constituent services. Many offices use the computer to manage casework correspondence and to monitor the status of pending cases. By entering into the computer the anticipated response date of a federal agency, the computer can provide the member office with a list of all agencies which are delinquent in responding to a member's inquiry on behalf of a constituent. In addition, members are using their computer resources to assist with the tabulation and analysis of responses to constituent surveys.

Automated support is slowly beginning to be used in member offices to assist in administrative and record-keeping functions. The management of office finances and the maintenance of a member's schedule are just a few of the areas in which the computer has recently been tested. A small number of member offices have experimented with the use of the computer to assist in the evaluation of military academy applicants.

Among member offices using certain commercial computer services, an electronic mail service is available which provides a computer-assisted message transfer capability. In addition to permitting the transfer of messages between any two compatible offices, this electronic mail service allows an office to "broadcast" a message to multiple users. In this way, by entering one command, a "Dear Colleague" letter, for example, can be electronically transmitted to multiple member offices.

Members are also looking to advanced technology to provide better communication between their Washington and district office(s). As more members become interested in transferring office functions to the district in order to bring constituent service closer to the people and reduce overcrowding in the Washington office, computer technology is seen as a useful tool to facilitate this transition. Thus, a growing number of members are installing computer terminals and word processing equipment in their district office(s). In this way, the district office can communicate with its Washington counterpart for such coordinated activities as scheduling the member's time, transferring constituent requests, and management reporting (e.g., volume of cases processed, number of walk-in visitors, etc.). In addition, district offices are using their computer terminals for direct access to the legislative information resources stored in congressional computers located in Washington. With this direct access to information on the current legislative activities of the House, district staff have begun to feel more closely a part of legislative events occurring in Washington. This has tended to discourage the development of the "we/they" syndrome which often occurs between Washington and district staffs. And in fact, district staff, through direct access to legislative information resources, have been able to greatly assist Washington staff in responding to the legislative inquiries of constituents.

As indicated earlier, in addition to using the computer for correspondence management, administrative tasks, and communicating between Washington and the district, member offices which lease computer terminals have access to a number of legislative information resources. Known as the Member Information Network (MIN), the data bases available to member offices include:

LEGIS—the legislative status and tracking system

SOPAD—a system providing information on current House floor proceedings, including the current day's roll call vote results

FAPRS—a system used to research federal assistance programs

MBIS—a system providing current fiscal year and historical federal budget information

JURIS—a legal retrieval system used to research the U.S. Code and federal court cases

SCORPIO—a system operating on the Library of Congress computer, which provides access to such information resources as the Library of Congress card catalogue, a bibliographic citation file, abstracts of the *Congressional Record*, and an up-to-date computerized file of policy papers on over 200 major issues maintained by the Congressional Research Service

As reference resources, the data bases of the Member Information Network have been generally well received. However, as noted earlier in this chapter, there exists a significant gap between the factual and status information provided through the data bases and the kind of evaluative information that congressional staff require in order to fulfill their advisory responsibilities to the member for whom they work.

Because it is often necessary to go beyond the computer to acquire the necessary evaluative information, automated legislative information resources have been frequently criticized for not meeting the comprehensive information requirements of congressional decision makers. Indeed, those who have been trained to use the computer to retrieve legislative information directly frequently revert to old methods of acquiring needed information when the computer is unable to answer all their questions.

A relatively new automated service available to members, which is likely to have a substantial impact on future legislative decision making, is the House Geographic Data Base. This system is designed to provide representatives with timely, accurate, and concise data on the economic impact of federal assistance programs within their congressional districts. Thus, the staff of House Information Systems is working closely with federal agencies to acquire "machine readable" data on the distribution of funds under programs within a given agency's jurisdiction. In most cases the data provided by federal agencies does not use the congressional district as the primary geographical reference. It is surprising that the executive branch is not generally more attentive to congressional information requirements, inasmuch as the Congress must annually review program appropriations under each agency's jurisdiction. In any case, when program information is received from the various agencies, systems analysts "massage" the data in order to produce analysis reports broken down at the congressional district level. In rural congressional districts, where district lines are generally coterminous with county boundaries, it is relatively simple to separate federal funds distribution reports according to congressional district boundaries. Providing equivalent fiscal reports for congressional districts with greater population density is a more difficult task. To address this problem, systems analysts are attempting to develop federal funds distribution formulas which would be applicable to urban and suburban congressional districts.

## IMPLICATIONS

Computers are now an established fact of legislative life in the House of Representatives, an integral part of its operations. But, in many ways, computer utilization in the House is still in its infancy. The potential contributions of computers have really just begun to be explored. Hardly a month goes by without some member or committee finding a new way to employ computers to enhance workload management. Much of this story has yet to be written.

But the first decade of computer usage affords us experience enough to begin to assess their initial impact and to suggest some of their implications for the House and the legislative process. Some significant patterns and directions have begun to emerge, among which the following are most noteworthy.

*The use of computers has led to an increasing fiscalization of legislative analysis.* Inevitably computers focus attention on those substantive aspects of legislation that are quantifiable. Generally that means money. Automated data processing permits legislators and their staffs to examine the financial implications of new policies in much greater depth than was ever possible before the introduction of computers.

The benefits of this are significant. Econometric models can provide members with indications of the fiscal impacts and, in some cases, the personal financial impacts of new spending and taxing programs. Computers facilitate the effort to relate new programs to aggregate outlay and revenue calculations in the federal budget. Projections of program effects are "harder" and more systematic than previously. Computers thus have helped to eliminate some of the guesswork from the legislative process. Members can now evaluate new and old programs with a much clearer sense of their micro- and macroeconomic impacts.

But this is something of a mixed blessing. Because they are now so much easier to deal with, "the numbers" have taken on a much greater importance in legislative debates. The collective lay mentality, the institutionalized common mind on which the Founding Fathers placed such a high value, often seems to have given way now to an "auditor and accountant" perspective. In the contemporary idiom, the character of the "bottom line" is changing. Instead of concerning themselves with the physical, cultural, and sociological impacts of national programs, members' principal attention often focuses on how programs will affect tax rates, inflation, the value of the dollar, or the prospect for a balanced budget. Perhaps concentration on the financial impacts of new programs is inevitable in a time of economic distress; but, if so, this is a development that has been magnified significantly by the use of computers as tools of legislative analysis. In a substantial way, economic arguments have come to play a larger part in legislative debate because economics is more amenable to computer analysis than are sociology or philosophy.

*The fiscalization of legislative debate has also contributed to changes in the nature of coalition building in the House.* One of the things which computers now often permit is an instantaneous indication of the financial impact of policy changes on individual congressional districts. Before members determine their positions on a program or an amendment, they can avail themselves of information on how their districts stand to gain (or lose) economically from that policy change.

Because of this, the use of computers has had an increasingly prevalent impact on the character of majority building in the House. Bargaining, particularly on domestic spending programs, not often focuses on distribution formulas. Committee and party leaders have come to realize that members are unlikely to support a new policy proposal until the computer printouts show that their districts are treated fairly (and favorably) in the distribution of new spending authorized by the program.

Agreement was hammered out on the shape of the General Revenue Sharing Act of 1972, for instance, only after the members of the House Ways and Means Committee had tinkered frequently with the distribution formula. Each new formula was tested against an econometric model to determine how much money would be returned to each governmental jurisdiction in the country. Only when committee members were convinced of the appropriateness of allocations between poor and wealthy communities in their districts and between their districts and others of similar composition did they approve the program.

While computers may have helped members to understand program impacts on their districts, they have not eased the task of legislative coalition builders. They have enhanced the parochialism that is endemic in the House and, in so doing, they have given legislative debate a subtle but persistent thrust toward distributive policy making. Because the potential economic benefits of almost every program can now be individualized, the tendency has grown to treat every new policy proposal as a piece of pork barrel legislation. With this has come the propensity to build legislative coalitions based on little more than shared financial self-interest. Other common foundations of coalition development—party, philosophy, leadership authority, and committee deference—are consequently reduced in importance.

*Computers have also contributed indirectly to the weakening of party and committee leaders in the House.* Developments in the last decade have done much to fortify the independence of individual members of the House and to weaken the authority and influence of party and committee leaders. The introduction of computers is one of the several reasons for that.

Except for the two decades immediately surrounding the turn of this century, the power of House leaders has always rested primarily on informal techniques of influence. One of the most important of those was control over access to essential information, particularly information about scheduling, about the progress of bills within committees, and about the substantive impacts of legislation. With the expansion of staff resources, however, and with the advent of computerized data bases, there has been in the past decade a substantial democratization of information access.

Members who wish to know the schedule of floor debates or committee meetings, who are interested in the status of a bill in committee or in the other House, or who simply wish to inform themselves better about the substance of a policy proposal have less need to turn to party or committee leaders for that information. Much of it can now be had simply by punching a few keys on a computer terminal in a member's office or by a single phone call to a central information retrieval point. Inevitably, as members have become less dependent on their leaders for information, they have become less beholden to them as well. That has contributed, in no small measure, to their growing independence.

Finally, *computers have helped to even the balance of power between the legislative and executive branches of government.* So much has been done in the Congress in the past decade to enhance its independence from the executive branch that it is difficult to specify precisely the part that computers have played in that movement. It is clear, however, that the computer has accelerated the return of the Congress to co-equality.

Without a congressional capacity for accessing and analyzing government data bases, the Freedom of Information Act, the Budget and Impoundment Control Act, and the legislative veto would be little more than paper constraints on executive authority. Computers have helped to make them work. Major congressional investigations in the 1970s—the House impeachment inquiry, the Senate Watergate investigation, and the Senate's review of the domestic intelligence activities of the CIA, to name a few—all relied heavily on computers to organize and cross-check reams of information. In this and other ways, they have become an important aid in congressional oversight activities. Computers did not provide the incentive for a reinvigoration of the legislative role in legislative-executive relations, but once that goal had been set, they provided important support for its accomplishment.

Computers are no longer just a novelty on Capitol Hill. They have become—and will remain—an integral part of the legislative and administrative operations of the House of Representatives. The full impact of their use is not yet certain but, as the foregoing suggests, that impact is likely to extend well beyond a mere increase in efficiency. Computers will help to make the legislative workload more tolerable, to be sure; but it seems likely as well—in ways both intended and unintended—that they will also continue to affect internal authority structures, relationships between the branches of government, the shape of legislative coalitions, and the character of the representative process. The House has made a rapid and expanding commitment to computers. And, for that, it will never be the same again.

REFERENCES

Brademas, John. 1972. "Prognostications Regarding the Growth and Diversification of Computers in the Service of Society: The Congressional Role." In *Computers in the Service of Society*, ed. Robert L. Chartrand, pp. 147–158. New York: Pergamon Press.

Chartrand, Robert L. 1978. "Congressional Management and the Use of Information Technology." *Journal of Systems Management* 29(August): 10–15.

———; Janda, Kenneth; and Hugo, Michael, eds. 1968. *Information Support, Program Budgeting, and the Congress*. New York: Spartan Books.

Commission on Administrative Review, U.S. Congress, House. 1977. *Final Report*. 2 vols. 95th Cong., 1st sess. H. Doc. 95-272. 1:207–232.

Committee on House Administration, U.S. Congress, House. 1969. *First Progress Report of the Special Subcommittee on Electrical and Mechanical Office Equipment*. 91st Cong., 1st sess.

———. 1970. *Second Progress Report of the Special Subcommittee on Electrical and Mechanical Office Equipment*. 91st Cong., 2d sess.

Frantzich, Stephen E. 1978. "Congress by Computer." *Social Policy* 8(Jan./Feb.):42–45.

———. 1979. "Computerized Information Technology in the U.S. House of Representatives." *Legislative Studies Quarterly* 4(May):255–280.

Saloma, John S. 1969. *Congress and the New Politics*. Boston: Little, Brown.

Semling, Harold V., Jr. 1969. "Congress and the Computer." *Law and Computer Technology* 2(November):7–13.

# 11. The Evolving Role and Effectiveness of the Congressional Research Agencies

*James A. Thurber*

## INTRODUCTION

Information is a powerful resource in politics. Those calling for reform of Congress in the 1970s understood this axiom very clearly. The sweeping congressional reforms of the last decade brought new demands for independent and "democratized" information and analysis. In 1974, at the height of the push for more congressional control over information, former Senator Sam Ervin argued, "One of the main factors for the unfortunate mismatch in budget power between the legislative and executive branches has been the superior information resources of the President and executive agencies and the inability of Congress to obtain information which would enable it to take an independent position" (U.S. Congress 1974, S 3833).

Since 1974 Congress has provided itself with the most extensive and sophisticated information support system of any democratic legislative body in the world. Congress is now better able to challenge the president and the executive bureaucracy; it has made information more accessible to all, which has, in turn, contributed to a new decentralized power structure. Basic to this expansion of information resources has been the creation of the Congressional Budget Office (CBO) in 1975, the development of the Office of Technology Assessment (OTA) in 1972, and the growth of the traditional responsibilities of the General Accounting Office (GAO) and the Congressional Research Service (CRS).

The creation of the CBO and OTA and the major reforms in GAO and CRS have changed the information business on Capitol Hill significantly. This chapter seeks to examine these changes and has three central purposes: first, to describe the current structure of each agency and the kinds of information and analysis each provides; second, to assess the strengths and weaknesses of each

**Table 11.1.** ***Authorized Employees for the Congressional Support Agencies, 1970–1979***

| *Agency* | *Fiscal Year* 1970 | 1976 | 1979 | *Increase from 1970 to 1979* N | % |
|---|---|---|---|---|---|
| General Accounting Office | 4,471 | 5,126 | 5,264 | +793 | +17 |
| Congressional Research Service | 323 | 721 | 856 | +533 | +165 |
| Office of Technology Assessment (started 1972) | | 103 | 140 | +140 | |
| Congressional Budget Office (started 1974) | | 193 | 218 | +218 | |
| Total | 4,794 | 6,143 | 6,478 | +1,684 | +35 |

SOURCE: Committee on Appropriations, Subcommittee on Legislative Branch, U.S. Congress, House, January 1979. Personal communication.

agency; and third, to review the major issues facing the four agencies as an integrated information support system for Congress.

## THE SUPPORT AGENCIES

All four units have had significant staff expansions during the 1970–1979 reform years, as shown in table 11.1. A review of the structure and responsibilities of the CRS, GAO, OTA, and CBO also shows that growth in staff size has been accompanied by changes in the type and quantity of information available to Congress.

### Congressional Research Service

The Congressional Research Service (established in 1914, but until 1970 called the Legislative Reference Service) provides Congress with research, information, and reference assistance on public policy issues that Congress must consider. Prior to the Legislative Reorganization Act of 1970, CRS functioned primarily as a reference service. However, since the 1970 reorganization, the service has emphasized greater research and analytical support for committees and more freedom to provide assistance to committees and individual members on legislative matters. The primary goals of CRS are—

1. to provide analytical and research assistance to committees

**Table 11.2.** ***Requests for CRS Services, FY 1978***

| Source | Number | % |
|---|---|---|
| Members of House and Senate | 184,436 | 60 |
| Committees | 66,488 | 22 |
| Constituents | 55,555 | 18 |
| Total | 306,479 | 100 |

SOURCE: Unpublished memorandum, Office of the Director, Congressional Research Service, Library of Congress, Washington, D.C., May 1979.

**Table 11.3.** ***CRS Response Time to Requests, FY 1978***

| Response Time | Number of Requests Filled | % |
|---|---|---|
| Same day | 159,509 | 52 |
| 1 day | 33,028 | 11 |
| 2–5 days | 60,197 | 19 |
| 6–10 days | 20,766 | 7 |
| Over 10 days | 34,042 | 11 |
| Total | 306,479 | 100 |

SOURCE: Unpublished memorandum, Office of the Director, Congressional Research Service, Library of Congress, Washington, D.C., May 1979.

and members to support them in their legislative and oversight responsibilities;

2. to provide information and reference assistance to members and committees to support their lawmaking and oversight functions; and
3. to provide up-to-date information on the status and content of current legislative proposals (see Beckman 1975).

In 1979 CRS had more than 850 employees (a 165% increase since 1970), providing assistance of both general and specific nature, from routine factual questions to complex long term policy analyses. These requests for factual information and policy analysis came overwhelmingly from individual members of Congress (60%) and, next most frequently, from committees (22%). Constituent service is the lowest priority of CRS by law and the lowest number of requests (18%) came from constituents, as shown in table 11.2. Such requests, it should be noted, are referred through members.

CRS is equipped for speedy response to requests from members and committees, as shown in table 11.3. Its quick response capacity is shown by the 52% same-day response time for all requests. Only 11% of the requests could be called long-term analysis which took over ten days to prepare.

CRS documents and analyses are widely distributed to members and committees in Congress and their special seminars are widely attended. The service answered more than 306,000 inquiries for research and reference in fiscal year 1978. The output of in-depth analyses increased 13% over the previous year. To service these requests, CRS has had a history of steadily growing staff and appropriations—which totaled over $24 million for fiscal year 1979. The vast majority of congressional inquiries (88%) continue to be for factual information (see fig. 11.1). These reference inquiries come largely from member offices and take up about 41% of CRS time. Although most inquiries are for reference materials, more than half (54%) of the CRS staff hours are spent on analytical work.

## General Accounting Office

The GAO, established through the Budget and Accounting Act of 1921, performs wide-ranging services, including audits, reviews, evaluations, and analyses of the efficiency and effectiveness of fed-

Figure 11.1. *Types of CRS Inquiries Compared to Time Spent on Inquiries*

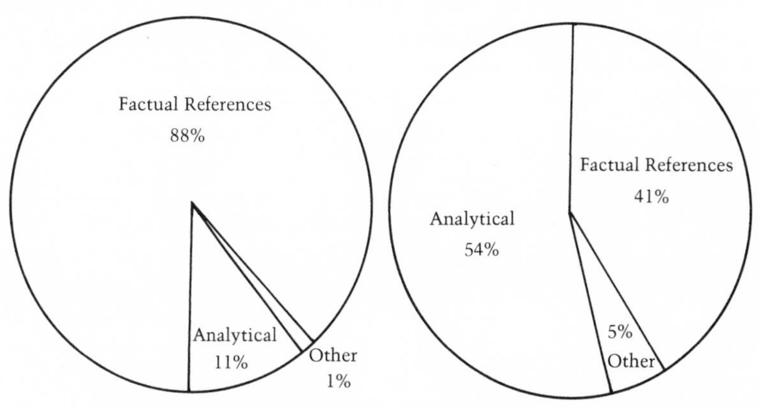


*Source*: Committee on Appropriations, U.S. Congress, House. 1977. *Hearings on Legislative Branch Appropriations for 1978*. 95th Cong., 1st sess.

eral programs, on behalf of Congress. Under the direction of the current Comptroller General of the United States, Elmer B. Staats, GAO has been transformed from primarily a voucher auditing agency to an agency with a sophisticated program evaluation component. It seeks to assess whether programs are achieving their original objectives and whether there are other ways of accomplishing program objectives at lower costs.

GAO services have been enlarged and improved in response to the size and complexity of the federal government. Several reform efforts in the 1970s have provided the authority and stimulus: the Legislative Reorganization Act of 1970 (31 U.S.C. 1151), the Congressional Budget and Impoundment Control Act of 1974 (88 Stat. 297), and the General Accounting Act of 1974 (88 Stat. 1959).

GAO's major functions are to—

1. assist the Congress in its legislative and oversight activities;
2. provide legal services;
3. audit and evaluate the programs, activities, and financial operations of federal departments and agencies;
4. help improve the financial management systems of federal agencies; and
5. settle claims and collect debts.

With a staff of 5,264 (70% of whom are professionals), GAO works on requests from committees and members about 43% of the time. A summary of the analyses and reports completed in fiscal year 1978 reveals the current distribution of GAO work (see table 11.4). Growing concern about fraud, abuse and error in government has increased pressure from Congress for the GAO to do even more. In response to this renewed concern, GAO has established a special Task Force on Fraud and Abuse for 1979 and 1980. During 1976 and 1977, savings attributable to GAO recommendations totaled $8.2 billion.

**Office of Technology Assessment**

The OTA, established by the Technology Assessment Act of 1972 (86 Stat. 979), assists Congress in planning for the consequences of the growth of technology. Its purpose is to provide Congress with information about the impacts, both beneficial and adverse, of technological applications, and to identify policy alternatives for technology-related issues. OTA's assessments cover the social, environmental, economic, and political impacts of technological applications. OTA has a bipartisan board, director, deputy director, and professional staff and consultants. OTA received funding in November 1973 and began operations in January 1974. It had 140 staff members

**Table 11.4.** ***Summary of GAO Reports for FY 1978***

| *Type of Reports* | *Number* | *%* |
|---|---|---|
| Reports to Congress generally | 349 | 31 |
| Reports to congressional committees | 323 | 28 |
| Reports to individual members | 167 | 15 |
| Reports to federal agency officials | 297 | 26 |
| Total | 1,136 | 100 |

SOURCE: General Accounting Office, U.S. Congress, 1979. *1978 Annual Report of the Comptroller General of the United States.* 96th Cong., 1st sess.

as of May 1979 and used 600 advisory panelists, 140 consultants, and numerous contractors in preparing its assessments.

The OTA board is made up of six senators, appointed by the President Pro Tempore of the Senate, and six representatives, appointed by the Speaker of the House, evenly divided by party. In 1978, Senator Edward Kennedy (D-Mass.) and Congressman Larry Winn, Jr. (R-Kans.) served as the chairman and vice chairman, respectively, of the board. The two posts alternate between the Senate and House each Congress. In FY 1978, OTA completed fifteen assessment reports covering a wide range of technological applications, including coal slurry pipelines, railroad safety, access across federal lands in Alaska, ocean thermal energy conversion, solar technology, urban transit, and many other important areas.

During 1977 and 1978, OTA went through a major internal reorganization after suffering from criticism for being too politicized and uneven in its reports. Before 1978, nearly all assessments undertaken by OTA were in response to requests from the chairs or ranking minority members of congressional committees. OTA board members were also major users of OTA staff. OTA was restructured from seven divisions with twenty-four members of the staff reporting directly to the director, to three major divisions (energy, materials, and global security; health and life sciences; and science, information, and transportation), each headed by an assistant director reporting to the director. It also developed a priority list of key issues considered of critical concern to the U.S. from more than 1,400 suggestions from public and private sources. From this list, OTA established an official priority list of thirty items on which to do in-depth analysis. All items on the list are complex emerging technological issues that OTA feels Congress is likely to face in the future.

After extensive oversight hearings on OTA in 1977 and 1978, the Subcommittee on Science, Research, and Technology of the House Committee on Science and Technology summarized its findings as follows:

> OTA has been set up to do a job for Congress which is: (a) essential, (b) not capable of being duplicated by other legislative entities, and (c) proving useful and is already relied upon. OTA should retain its basic operating method of depending to a large extent on out-of-house professional assistance in performing its assessments. Continued congressional support for OTA is warranted. [Committee on Science and Technology 1978]

## Congressional Budget Office

The CBO was created by the Congressional Budget and Impoundment Control Act of 1974 (88 Stat. 297) as the primary analytic and informational component of the reform effort. CBO's role is to provide the information that Congress needs to assume a more independent relationship with the president and executive branch in fashioning the budget. CBO has three primary responsibilities in assisting Congress with the budget process—

1. monitoring the economy and estimating its impact on government actions;
2. improving the flow and quality of budgetary information to members and committees; and
3. analyzing the costs and effects of alternative budgetary choices.

CBO meets these responsibilities first, by providing analysis and data to the Senate and House Budget Committees; second, by providing analytic assistance to the Appropriations, Ways and Means, and Finance Committees; and finally, by providing similar services to a very limited degree to other committees and members. Prior to the creation of CBO, Congress had no unit of its own, comparable to OMB, to provide budgetary analysis and information. CBO (through its director) is authorized to obtain data, estimates, statistical analyses, and other information from executive branch agencies, departments, and commissions, and allows Congress to be more independent of the president and the agencies in determining final budget figures.

CBO had a staff of 218 and a budget of $11.4 million for FY

**Table 11.5.** ***CBO Activities by Function for FY 1978***

| *Functional Activity* | *% of Time* |
|---|---|
| Scorekeeping | 13 |
| Bill costing | 20 |
| 5-year budget projections | 26 |
| Program analysis | 41 |

SOURCE: Interview with professional staff member in the Office of the Director, Congressional Budget Office, Washington, D.C., May 1979.

1979. The manner in which it allocates its time is shown in table 11.5.

"Scorekeeping," which takes 13% of CBO's time, consists of informing Congress periodically regarding the impact of recently enacted legislation on the spending limits in its most recent budget resolution. This function gives Congress increased budgetary control. CBO also helps committees determine the cost of programs proposed in pending bills (20% of its time) and projects the five-year impact of any bill reported by a House or Senate committee that provides new budget authority or tax expenditures (26% of its time). Most of its time (41%), however, is spent on program analysis for the two Budget Committees and other money committees of the Congress.

CBO is highly respected on Capitol Hill and has become an essential part of the complex new congressional budget system. It produces useful, timely, and highly professional economic and budget data for members and committees.

## ASSESSING THE SUPPORT AGENCIES

How well do the four agencies do their work? What do they do best? What do their primary clients—members and committees—think about their quality and usefulness? Analysis of the 1977 survey of House members and staff by the Commission on Administrative Review (Obey Commission) reveals specific answers to these questions. However, before the Obey Commission findings on member and staff evaluation of the agencies are discussed, it is essential to describe where members and their employees go to get information and analysis.

### Sources of Congressional Information

Do members and staff use the four support agencies extensively? Where do members get their data and analysis for committee work and floor votes? Where do they go for analysis of constituency problems? Several studies of congressional behavior suggest that legislators do not use information from the support agencies, but rely primarily on their colleagues, their constituents, and their staffs (see Kingdon 1973, Matthews and Stimson 1975, Kovenock 1973, and Entin 1973). In a 1976 survey of fifty House members, Zwier (1979) found that "specialists" (legislators who sit on the subcommittee initially considering a bill) ranked staff, the executive branch, interest groups, and constituents as the most important sources of information for their work. The "nonspecialist" respondents (legislators who do not sit on the subcommittee initially considering a bill) in Zwier's study relied almost entirely on traditional inside congressional sources: colleagues, constituents, the party whips, Democratic Study Group, and staff, in that order. No students of Congress have shown the four congressional support agencies to be important sources of information for members and legislative assistants. The Zwier study emphasizes the unimportance of the four agencies:

> The congressional research arms—the Congressional Research Service (CRS) and the General Accounting Office (GAO)—are not very important for either group of legislators, although more specialists (committee members) mentioned them. The time it takes for these organizations to produce more than superficial studies requires more precise planning than legislators may be willing or able to do. [Pp. 39–40]

Zwier also concluded in a footnote that CBO and OTA are of little consequence to House members: "It should be noted that the Congressional Budget Office and the Office of Technology Assessment were not mentioned by any of the respondents" (p. 42).

Yet, this may be a premature conclusion. Most studies on congressional decision making were completed before the reforms of the 1970s in the House of Representatives and the expansion of independent sources of analysis and information within Congress. As table 11.1 reveals, all four analytic support agencies grew significantly during the reforms of the 1970s. It is thus important to analyze postreform attitudes of members and their staffs about sources of congressional information. Conclusions about postreform sources of information can be drawn from the survey of House members and legislative assistants that was done by the Commission on Administrative Review (1977). The data gathered by the commission were based on responses from a quota sample of 149 members and 145 legislative assistants in the House of Representatives. The survey was administered in June and July of 1977, well after all reforms affecting the four analytic support agencies had been instituted.

How do members now perceive the agencies? Do they rely on them for information and analysis? Has expansion of staff and additional responsibilities meant that more members use their services? Table 11.6 shows that the four agencies were ranked very highly by members and legislative assistants. The agencies are second most important to legislative assistants working on both committee and floor responsibilities for their employers. Members rate the agencies very highly—third most important as sources of information for both committee work and analysis of general government policy. For information on district issues, members ranked CRS sixth, which is surprisingly high since district-oriented work is formally a low priority for CRS. Contrary to previous studies, members now seem to rely heavily upon the four support agencies for the most important aspects of their job: district service, committee work, floor responsibilities, and taking general policy stands. Legislative assistants follow their employers with a high regard and heavy use of the support agencies and rank all four services consistently high. There seems to be a two-step flow of communication from CRS to staff to member. The Obey Commission findings are in almost direct opposition to the 1976 survey of House members by Zwier (1979). Where Zwier found the four agencies of little or no importance, the members and staff responding to the Obey Commission survey found them to be significant sources of information and support. The differences between the Commission and Zwier studies may lie in the sample; the Obey Commission quota sample of 149 House members and 145 legislative assistants was much more extensive than the 50 members included in Zwier's study. Most likely the different sample sizes do not completely explain the different findings. Since the Obey survey was one year after Zwier's, an explanation of differences must also include recent growth in the agencies, turnover in membership, change in attitudes, wording of the questionnaires, and the focus by the Obey study on the role of staff in conjunction with members' views of the agencies.

**Table 11.6. *Ranking of Information Sources by House Members and Legislative Assistants***

| *Members' Information Sources for District Issues*[a] | *Members' Information Sources for General Government Policy*[a] | *Members' Information Sources for Committee Work*[a] | *Legislative Assistants' Ranking of Information Sources*[b] |
|---|---|---|---|
| 1. Administration (105) | 1. News media (119) | 1. Committee (134) | 1. Committee (63) |
| 2. Personal staff (93) | 2. Personal staff (98) | 2. Personal staff (121) | 2. Congressional support agencies—CRS/GAO (59) |
| 3. District (75) | 3. Congressional support agencies—All four (66) | 3. Congressional support agencies—All four (58) | 3. Partisan congressional organizations—DSG (31) |
| 4. Committee (44) | 4. District (33) | 4. Partisan congressional organizations (52) | 4. Interest groups (31) |
| 5. State and local government (15) | 5. Committee (28) | 5. Interest groups (45) | 5. Congressional reports (27) |
| 6. Congressional support agencies—CRS (13) | 6. Partisan congressional organizations (26) | 6. District (38) | 6. Personal staff in offices of committee members (25) |
| 7. Member's personal knowledge (8) | 7. Colleagues (19) | 7. Personal reading (30) | 7. Relevant subcommittee or committee chairs (18) |
| 8. Local news media (8) | 8. Member's personal knowledge (19) | 8. Administration (27) | 8. Specialized House caucuses (17) |
| 9. Interest groups (8) | 9. Administration (16) | 9. Colleagues (21) | 9. Party policy committees (15) |
| 10. Colleagues (7) | 10. Interest groups (13) | 10. House leadership (1) | 10. Administration (14) |

SOURCE: Commission on Administrative Review 1977, 2(*Survey Materials*):958–960, 972–973, 980–981, 1082–1084.

[a] Rankings in the first three columns were established by adding the number of times each source was mentioned by the respondents. This total is given in parentheses.

[b] Rankings reflect, and the figures in parentheses indicate, the number of legislative assistants who rated each information source "very helpful" with respect to legislation within the jurisdiction of committees on which their members serve.

**Variation in Usage**

The commission survey also shows that utilization of the four congressional support agencies varies significantly. Table 11.7 demonstrates widespread use of CRS, moderate use of GAO and CBO, and almost no general use of OTA by House legislative assistants. Combining the "very frequently" and "often" categories in table 11.7, CRS is by far the most utilized with 81% of the responses in these two levels. CBO is next with 29%, third is GAO with 26%, and OTA a distant fourth with only 4% in these two categories of use. CRS almost tripled its staff from 1970 to 1979 (see table 11.1), which seems to have been a good investment, considering the high utilization by legislative assistants in the House.

This varied pattern of use most likely stems from the varied legislative mandates of each agency, their newness in the cases of CBO and OTA, and lack of responsiveness to requests from the legislative assistant level. CBO, for example, is required to serve the Budget Committee first, the money committees next, and finally individual members. Because of this requirement CBO rarely gets to the individual member level of service.

**Evaluation of the Congressional Support Agencies**

Table 11.7 clearly shows that use of the four agencies varies tremendously. Does this varied utilization stem from unsatisfied congressional clients? Table 11.8 suggests a very high satisfaction with all four agencies. Combining the "very satisfied" and "fairly satis-

**Table 11.7.** ***Legislative Assistant Use of Congressional Support Agencies***

| *Frequency of Use* | *GAO (%)* | *CBO (%)* | *OTA (%)* | *CRS*[a] *(%)* |
|---|---|---|---|---|
| Very frequently | 5 | 8 | 1 | 32 |
| Often | 21 | 21 | 3 | 49 |
| Just some | 39 | 39 | 14 | 17 |
| Hardly ever | 29 | 26 | 29 | 2 |
| Not at all | 6 | 6 | 54 | 0 |
| Total % | 100 | 100 | 100 | 100 |

SOURCE: Commission on Administrative Review 1977, 2(*Survey Materials*):1102, 1107.

[a]Categories for CRS are: very often, regularly, only sometimes, hardly ever, and not sure.

**Table 11.8. *Legislative Assistant Satisfaction with Congressional Support Agencies***

| *Level of Satisfaction* | *GAO (%)* | *CBO (%)* | *OTA (%)* | *CRS District Work*[a] *(%)* | *CRS Non-assigned Committee Work*[a] *(%)* |
|---|---|---|---|---|---|
| Very satisfied | 38 | 33 | 22 | 14 | 42 |
| Fairly satisfied | 42 | 45 | 43 | 19 | 25 |
| Only some | 17 | 17 | 18 | 35 | 28 |
| Not at all | 4 | 5 | 18 | 32 | 5 |
| Total % | 100 | 100 | 100 | 100 | 100 |
| Total N | 134 | 133 | 60 | 144 | 144 |

SOURCE: Commission on Administrative Review 1977, 2(*Survey Materials*): 1089, 1101, 1108, 1109.
[a]Categories for CRS are: very helpful, fairly helpful, only somewhat helpful, and not helpful at all. The not at all category and the not sure category were combined for CRS committee work for purposes of comparison with the other responses. "Nonassigned" committee work refers to the work members do on issues and bills that are in or come from committees to which they are not assigned.

fied" categories, GAO fares best with an 80% rating by the legislative assistants. CBO is also highly respected with 78% of the respondents expressing high levels of satisfaction with their work. CRS is third with 67% and OTA last with 65% of the legislative assistants expressing high satisfaction. There is a big difference in satisfaction between CRS district work (33%) and CRS committee work (67%), which again presumably reflects the priorities set by CRS. Considering the selective use of each of these agencies as shown in table 11.7, legislative assistants have given the agencies impressive marks.

However, these are general or overall results. Let us use the commission data to look at the support agencies individually in greater depth.

CRS is used more extensively than the other three support agencies (table 11.7). A more detailed look at the frequency of use for several categories of basic service, shown in table 11.9, indicates that House legislative assistants use CRS primarily for basic information and reference materials (64% said they use CRS for this function "nearly all the time" or "most of the time"). The next most impor-

**Table 11.9. *Frequency of Use of CRS for Four Basic Services by Legislative Assistants*[a]**

| *Frequency of Use* | *Answering Constituent Questions (%)* | *Basic Information & Reference Materials (%)* | *Researching & Analyzing Public Policy Issues (%)* | *Writing Speeches, Reports, & Testimony (%)* |
|---|---|---|---|---|
| Nearly all the time | 4 | 20 | 10 | 7 |
| Most of the time | 8 | 44 | 34 | 19 |
| Some of the time | 66 | 34 | 48 | 43 |
| Hardly ever | 23 | 1 | 8 | 30 |
| Not at all | 0 | 1 | 0 | 1 |
| Total % | 100 | 100 | 100 | 100 |
| Total N | 145 | 145 | 145 | 145 |

SOURCE: Commission on Administrative Review 1977, 2(*Survey Materials*):1083, 1103, 1101, 1108, 1109.

[a] Question: "How often do you or other members of your legislative staff . . . rely on CRS, as opposed to someplace else, for (add each service category)? . . ."

tant category of service used by the legislative assistants is analysis and research (44% use CRS most or nearly all of the time). A quarter (26%) of the legislative assistants indicated they use CRS for writing reports and developing testimony. Finally, only 12% of the legislative assistants use CRS most or nearly all of the time to answer constituent questions. The pattern of utilization of these four services fits exactly the established priorities of CRS. Tables 11.8 and 11.9 demonstrate that legislative assistants do not use CRS for constituent work very often and they are most dissatisfied with CRS district work. Whether this dissatisfaction with CRS stems from unresponsiveness or poor quality work is unknown, but it may stem from the fact that congressional staffs know much more about constituent problems and district level issues than CRS and thus feel that no matter what CRS does for them, they can do a better job. In summary, CRS has a heavy demand for basic information and analysis of public policy issues, but little demand for more "personal" work such as constituent responsibilities and speech writing.

Of the four congressional support agencies, CRS and GAO's new policy analysis responsibilities resemble each other most closely. Some would also say that they are also natural competitors vying for more analytic work with their congressional clients. How do legislative assistants evaluate CRS and GAO services in these regards? On the service categories listed in table 11.10, CRS surpasses GAO in levels of client satisfaction. Despite the evidence presented earlier in table 11.8, this table discloses an impressive level of satisfaction with CRS with much lower scores for GAO. By combining the top two categories of satisfaction ("very helpful" and "fairly helpful") for these three basic services, more than two-thirds of the legislative assistants were satisfied with its support for committee work, its information and analysis for floor votes, and its information and analysis on general government policies and public issues. GAO, on the other hand, never surpasses the 40% level of satisfaction. Looking more closely at the figures for each of these three services, legislative assistants feel CRS is much better in assisting a member's assigned committee work (75% to 40%, combining the "very helpful" and "fairly helpful"). CRS also seems to assist members better for floor votes from committees on which they are not assigned than does GAO (67% to 32%). This may reflect the common belief that GAO perceives its primary clients as the committees and their chairs rather than the members generally. Release of GAO reports and access to analysis is often informally restricted by committees so that members cannot use these data for their floor vote preparation. In fairness to GAO, that agency's legislative mandate keeps its services a level away from most House legislative assistants, since most GAO employees are still doing government audits or policy analysis that has been initiated by committees. Only recently has GAO been allowed to branch into new and expanded analytic services for members (under the provisions of the Budget and Impoundment Control Act of 1974).

We may conclude, then, that despite the evidence presented in table 11.8, congressional users are much more satisfied with CRS than with GAO. GAO's higher score in table 11.8 is attributable to the far lower frequency of use (see table 11.7). Thus, different scores resulted (table 11.10) when the question was framed in terms of "helpfulness" rather than "satisfaction." In short, it would appear that, in part, the high levels of satisfaction with the GAO shown in table 11.8 were due to noninvolvement or low expectations.

How well is the Congressional Budget Office evaluated by its users? Key standing committee staff in the House of Representatives were asked to evaluate CBO on several of its responsibilities as set in the Budget and Impoundment Control Act. CBO received high marks for four of its key activities: budget scorekeeping, short-term budget projections, accuracy of authorization bill projections, and timeliness of authorization bill projections (see table 11.11). Well

**Table 11.10.** ***Evaluation of CRS and GAO Services by House Legislative Assistants***

| | *Specialist Committee and Floor Work* | | *Nonspecialist Committee and Floor Work* | | *Analysis of General Government Policies and Public Issues* | |
|---|---|---|---|---|---|---|
| *Level of Satisfaction* | *CRS (%)* | *GAO (%)* | *CRS (%)* | *GAO (%)* | *CRS (%)* | *GAO (%)* |
| Very helpful | 42 | 17 | 42 | 9 | 58 | 11 |
| Fairly helpful | 33 | 23 | 25 | 23 | 32 | 28 |
| Only somewhat helpful | 20 | 33 | 28 | 37 | 10 | 34 |
| Not at all helpful | 5 | 21 | 4 | 27 | 1 | 23 |
| Not sure | 0 | 6 | 1 | 4 | 0 | 4 |
| Total % | 100 | 100 | 100 | 100 | 100 | 100 |
| Total N | 142 | 142 | 144 | 144 | 144 | 144 |

SOURCE: Commission on Administrative Review 1977, 2(*Survey Materials*):1083, 1089, 1094, 1095, 1101.

over half of the committee staff responding regarded these key CBO services as being performed favorably. All other CBO services were at the 40% favorable level, which reflects the consistently high marks that CBO gets.

Considering its very short tenure, CBO seems to be doing very well in the eyes of its primary mandated users, the budget committees, the money panels, and other standing committees. Congressional committee staff seem to have accepted CBO as an important new source of timely and accurate analysis.

Finally, the low frequency of use with respect to OTA should be read in conjunction with its high satisfaction rating (see tables 11.7 and 11.8). The latter therefore cannot be accepted without question. In general, it may be said that OTA has as yet not attained the same levels of performance as the other support agencies.

## CONCLUSIONS AND ISSUES

It is clear that members and their staffs depend upon the four congressional support units to a much greater extent than previous studies of Congress have shown. Generally each agency received high evaluations from their clients. There seems to be an acceptance of the recent reforms that have allowed House members and staff an independent source of information and analysis, independent of the executive branch and interest groups. Although this new partnership between clients in the House (members, committees, and staff) and the four support agencies is working, there are several issues facing the support units that have not been directly addressed by the House nor by the units themselves. Three of the primary issues that must be faced by Congress and the support agencies are—

1. How can the quality and timeliness of analysis and information from the four support agencies be improved?
2. What is the appropriate mission and management structure for each of the four agencies? and
3. How can Congress improve its oversight of the four agencies?

The Commission on Administrative Review of the House understood these problems and established several specific objectives to improve the performance of the support units (1977, 1:8). Four of these objectives are directly relevant to the primary issues facing the support units, but each seems to have been ignored by the House and has had little or no impact on the information support systems in Congress:

**Table 11.11.** ***Evaluation of CBO Services or Products by Congressional Committee Staff***

| *Evaluation* | *Budget Scorekeeping (%)* | *Short-Term Budget Projections (%)* | *Five-Year Budget Projections (%)* | *Accuracy of Authorization Bill Projections (%)* | *Timeliness of Authorization Bill Projections (%)* | *Economic Analysis (%)* | *Response to Requests for Reports (%)* |
|---|---|---|---|---|---|---|---|
| Favorable | 73 | 58 | 42 | 74 | 84 | 47 | 42 |
| Neutral | 12 | 21 | 37 | 16 | 11 | 43 | 32 |
| Unfavorable | 15 | 21 | 21 | 10 | 5 | 10 | 26 |
| Total % | 100 | 100 | 100 | 100 | 100 | 100 | 100 |
| Total N | 26 | 19 | 24 | 19 | 19 | 21 | 19 |

SOURCE: Commission on Information and Facilities 1977*a*, 20.

NOTE: Respondents were staff members of House and Senate committees polled by the Commission on Information and Facilities. Responses were voluntary and the staffs of the House and Senate Appropriations, Senate Finance, and House Ways and Means committees are over-represented in this sample.

1. To create an administrative system with clear lines of authority and accountability;
2. To separate the responsibility for administrative policy direction and oversight from the responsibility for policy implementation;
3. To provide for a more effective and efficient distribution of functions without excessive consolidation or the disruption of services being well performed; and
4. To develop new and improved ways of utilizing legislative information from existing sources.

The Obey Commission can be faulted, however, for developing only one specific recommendation (out of forty-two) to pursue these objectives for the four analytic support agencies. The commission limited its recommendation to foresight and long-range analysis: "The legislative support agencies should be specifically directed to assist the Speaker and minority leader in assessing long-range issues" (1:678). There is little evidence that this recommendation has made any significant impact on the ability of the House leadership to do better long-term planning and foresight, although it is obviously an admirable goal. The Obey Commission made no recommendations for better administration and accountability, none on oversight, none on overlap, and none on new and improved utilization of agency information.

The Obey Commission has come and gone as have several other committees and commissions that have focused on the four support agencies, but the central problems remain: quality and timeliness of information and analysis, mission and management of the information system, and oversight of the agencies.

Although each of the agencies received above average report cards on their performance by members and staff, the central issue with regard to these providers of information continues to be the need for *better* information, not *more* information. This is supported by the Obey Commission in its comment on information:

> In past years, the problem of the Congress was one of having too little information; today, the issue is less a question of information quantity than it is one of information quality. Members and their staffs have very little time to wade through the multitude of documents, reports, tables, and analyses that are potentially available for their review. Today, the House places a high priority on having information that is accurate, relevant and concise. (1977, 1:188)

There is no doubt that much of the analysis on Capitol Hill is redundant, outdated, and highly subjective. That is partially a result of the nature of the congressional environment, but too often analysis is the continuation of politics by other means. Knowledge in Congress is not always power, but another person's ignorance certainly is. Without accurate and timely facts, it is extremely difficult to legislate. House Democratic Whip John Brademas of Indiana argued this point when describing the difficulties of the House in the 96th Congress, "It's very difficult to legislate when there is no consensus on fact and this is something we all understand" (Schram 1979).

There is a continual drive by members and staff to get more and more information, thinking that more is better. There is a similar drive that keeps a news reporter looking for the new "scoop." This is legitimate and understandable; however, it translates into a search for easy answers and quick analysis that drives out quality. Congress, the Obey Commission, and the four support agencies have not solved that problem yet, although significant progress has been made recently. Allan Schick argues that the problem of improving the quality of analysis might be an unresolvable issue under the present information support structure on Capitol Hill:

> One of the reasons for the persistent interest in creating an analytic institute for Congress is that none of the existing Congress-institutions devotes itself exclusively to research. With one exception, each must allocate a substantial portion of its resources to the everyday interests of Congress and to recurring functions assigned to it by law. As service agencies, these institutions are not free to develop their own work agendas, and each has experienced the chronic problem of routine activities, preempting analytic interests. (1976, 229)

Little has resulted from House or Senate commission studies of the four analytic support agencies. There still exists a decentralized system of authority and accountability over the units (see table 11.12). Each is responsible to a different set of committees and each has a different set of procedures for selecting directors who have varying lengths of appointment. Congressional policy direction, oversight, and policy implementation by the units have not been altered as a result of the numerous congressional studies. Policy direction and oversight are still done by the same committees and subcommittees that had authority over the agencies before the various evaluations of 1976–77. There is no sense that Congress is looking at the analysis and information services from the four units as a unified support system. Congress has not altered the overlap and frequently excessive competition among the four units; however, the new research does create an incentive to reduce overlap. Creative titles for projects sometimes undermine the Research Notification System (created in 1976) and cover up the amount of duplication that really exists. Duplication and overlap of activities may be a false issue in that members and committee chairs will often ask several agencies to do analysis knowing full well that each will take a different approach. Theoretically, those requesting the analysis will then have a more complete picture of a problem or policy. All four agencies were asked to evaluate President Carter's energy plan, for example. Each came up with a different view, presumably giving members a better mechanism for evaluating the president's proposal.

The problems facing the four analytic support units of Congress remain, but progress has been made. The internal management of the four support agencies has improved significantly during the 1970s, almost in spite of the findings and recommendations from the various study commissions and committees. OTA has made the most improvement through its reorganization, probably because it had so far to go. GAO has also made great strides forward under the leadership of Elmer Staats. Its image has changed from an agency of accountants with green eyeshades to one of tough policy analysts and program evaluators. Further evidence of this phenomenal success is the new Office of Program and Budget Analysis, a widely respected unit that produces high quality and timely analysis. CRS has also improved itself through expansion and management under the direction of Gilbert Gude. Its training sessions and seminars are widely attended and the usefulness and timeliness of its information and analysis has helped to give it high marks. Finally, CBO has an excellent national reputation for objective analysis, be it of a Democratic or Republican, congressional or presidential proposal. A measure of its success is the political criticism its director, Alice Rivlin, seems to receive from all sides at one time or another. These internal management improvements and enhanced reputations have occurred, but the nagging questions of management, control, overlap, quality, timeliness, and oversight of the four units as a *unified* information system for Congress still remain.

**Table 11.12.** ***Oversight and Management of CRS, CBO, OTA, and GAO***

| | *CRS* | *CBO* | *OTA* | *GAO* |
|---|---|---|---|---|
| Administrative Officer | Director | Director | Director | Comptroller General |
| Method of Appointment | Appointed by Librarian of Congress | Appointed by Speaker/President Pro Tem of the Senate (from recommendations of Chairs, House/Senate Budget Committees) | Appointed by OTA Board | Appointed by President (with advice and consent of the Senate) |
| Length of Appointment | Civil service | 4 years | 6 years | 15 years |
| Oversight Authority | | | | |
| House | Joint Committee on the Library<br>House Administration (Libraries & Memorials) | Budget | Science and Technology (Science, Research, & Technology) | Government Operations (Legislation & National Security) |
| Senate | Joint Committee on the Library | Budget | Rules | Governmental Affairs (Reports, Accounting, & Management) |
| Appropriations | | | | |
| House | Appropriations (Legislative) | Appropriations (Legislative) | Appropriations (Legislative) | Appropriations (Legislative) |
| Senate | Appropriations (Legislative) | Appropriations (Legislative) | Appropriations (Legislative) | Appropriations (Legislative) |

## REFERENCES

Beckman, Norman. 1975. "Use of a Staff Agency by the Congress: The Congressional Research Service." *The Bureaucrat* 3(January):401–415.

Capron, William. 1976. "The Congressional Budget Office." In *Congressional Support Agencies: A Compilation of Papers*, pp. 75–94. Commission on the Operation of the Senate. Washington, D.C.: U.S. Government Printing Office.

Carroll, James D. 1976. "Policy Analysis for Congress: A Review of the Congressional Research Service." In *Congressional Support Agencies: A Compilation of Papers*, pp. 4–30. Commission on the Operation of the Senate. Washington, D.C.: U.S. Government Printing Office.

Commission on Administrative Review, U.S. Congress, House. 1977. *Final Report*. 2 vols. 95th Cong., 1st sess. H. Doc. 95-272.

Commission on Information and Facilities, U.S. Congress, House. 1976. *The Office of Technology Assessment: A Study of Its Organizational Effectiveness*. 94th Cong., 2d sess. H. Doc. 94-538.

———. 1977*a*. *Congressional Budget Office: A Study of Its Organizational Effectiveness*. 95th Cong., 1st sess. H. Doc. 95-20.

———. 1977*b*. *Organizational Effectiveness of the Congressional Research Service*. 95th Cong., 1st sess. H. Doc. 95-19

Committee on Science and Technology, Subcommittee on Science, Research, and Technology, U.S. Congress, House. 1978. *Oversight Hearings on the Office of Technology Assessment*. 95th Cong., 2d sess.

Entin, Kenneth. 1973. "Information Exchange in Congress: The Case of the House Armed Services Committee." *Western Political Quarterly* 26 (September):427–439.

Griffith, Ernest. 1976. "Four Agency Comparative Study." In *Congressional Support Agencies: A Compilation of Papers*, pp. 95–148. Commission on the Operation of the Senate. Washington, D.C.: U.S. Government Printing Office.

Kingdon, John W. 1973. *Congressmen's Voting Decisions*. New York: Harper & Row.

Kovenock, David. 1973. "Influence in the U.S. House of Representatives: A Statistical Analysis of Communications." *American Politics Quarterly* 1(October):407–464.

Office of Technology Assessment. 1979. *Annual Report to the Congress for 1978*. Washington, D.C.: U.S. Government Printing Office.

Matthews, Donald R., and Stimson, James A. 1975. *Yeas and Nays: Normal Decision-Making in the U.S. House of Representatives*. New York: Wiley.

Pois, Joseph. 1976. "The General Accounting Office as a Congressional Resource." In *Congressional Support Agencies: A Compilation of Papers*, pp. 31–54. Commission on the Operation of the Senate. Washington, D.C.: U.S. Government Printing Office.

Schick, Allan. 1976. "The Supply and Demand for Analysis on Capitol Hill." *Policy Analysis* 2(Spring):215–235.

Schram, Martin. 1979. "Camp David: Civics at the Top with 11 House Democrats." *Washington Post*, June 4, 1979, p. A4.

Skolnikoff, Eugene B. 1976. "The Office of Technology Assessment." In *Congressional Support Agencies: A Compilation of Papers*, pp. 55–74. Commission on the Operation of the Senate. Washington, D.C.: U.S. Government Printing Office.

Thurber, James A. 1976. "Congressional Budget Reform and New Demands for Policy Analysis." *Policy Analysis* 2(Spring):197–214.

U.S. Congress, Senate. 1974. "Statement by Sen. Ervin." *Congressional Record*, 93rd Cong., 1st sess. March 19: S 3833.

Zwier, Robert. 1979. "The Search for Information: Specialists and Non-specialists in the U.S. House of Representatives." *Legislative Studies Quarterly* 4(February):31–42.

# Conclusion

# Organization and Innovation in the House of Representatives

*Joseph Cooper*

The preceding chapters of this book have dealt with a number of topics relevant to understanding how the House organizes and performs its work. The prologues to the various parts have sought to relate the topics examined in individual chapters and to identify important problems and issues. The purpose of this conclusion is even more synthetic. It is to define a framework in terms of which current House structures and processes can be described and analyzed in a systematic fashion and proposals for change evaluated both substantively and politically. This framework will rely on the detailed information contained in the preceding chapters and on a variety of concepts drawn from organization theory. Such concepts, it should be noted, underlay much of the analysis in the prologues, but they will be applied somewhat differently and more extensively in this chapter due to its broader scope.

## CURRENT ORGANIZATIONAL FEATURES

The House is no longer a small or part-time organization. This is amply demonstrated by the material presented in earlier chapters of this book, especially those written by Mackenzie, O'Donnell, Brady, Kieffer, and Hammond. As a result, the House shares many features with other large-scale organizations. It divides task responsibilities among a variety of distinct units. It employs large numbers of personnel. It relies heavily on formal rules and procedures. It distributes decision-making power differentially among participants. It constantly grapples with the problems of controlling conflict, motivating performance, and sustaining institutional loyalty. It strives to design and employ procedures and practices that will generate outputs that are adequate both quantitatively and qualitatively to the maintenance of environmental support.

Nonetheless, as the chapters in this book also suggest, the House differs from most large-scale organizations in substantial and significant ways. The following summary of salient organizational features is thus designed to pin down the major differences and similarities that exist in order to provide a basis for later analysis.

## Structure

Five salient structural characteristics of current House organization may be identified.[1]

A. *High Degree of Organizational Elaboration and Variation.* The organizational configuration of the House is both extremely elaborate and extremely varied. As the Hammond, Kieffer, Maisel, Brady, and Thurber chapters indicate, more than a thousand distinct units exist. These include member offices in Washington and the districts, committee and subcommittee units, party leadership, policy and research units, and a variety of ad hoc policy groups or caucuses. In addition, scores of administrative support units exist and provide a host of managerial, informational, logistical, and auxiliary services.[2]

B. *Limited but Complex Division of Task or Functional Responsibilities.* The numerous and varied units that exist render difficult any neat or succinct analysis of the bases of task division. Perhaps the best approach is to use the basic products or outputs of the House to define a framework for analysis. At this point in the chapter they may be seen in conventional terms: lawmaking, oversight, constituency service, representation, and education. Given these outputs plus the need for various types of administrative support, three primary systems of units may be identified.

1. Constituency Service System. This system is composed of member offices in Washington and the districts.

2. Policy System. This system is composed of member offices in Washington, committee and subcommittee units, party units and ad hoc groups, and the floor.

3. Administrative Support System. This system is composed of the independently established staff units that provide managerial, logistical, informational, and auxiliary support services to the host of member units that exist.

Having established this framework of analysis, the following aspects of limitation and complexity with respect to the functional division of labor may be noted.

In terms of limitation, the division of labor fails to structure or focus the activities of participants in as strict a fashion as is typical in most other organizations. This is particularly true of members. Their roles are not focused or specialized in relation to a single output system or even within output systems. To be sure, division of labor does take place. Members delegate tasks to staff, serve separate constituencies, and have different committee assignments. Nonetheless, member roles are comprehensive. They participate in critical ways in all output systems. Moreover, the character of their participation is largely left to their own determination and is therefore highly variable. As for staff, the degree to which tasks or activities are limited and focused varies greatly in relation to whether an independent staff unit or a member unit is involved, the precise character of the unit, and the level of position.

In terms of complexity, clear and distinct task or functional differentiation among and within the primary systems of units is far less marked than in most large-scale organizations. This is clearly indicated by many of the articles in this book, especially those written by Hammond, Kieffer, and Maisel. Thus, for example, member offices play a key role in both the constituency service system and the policy system; there is no specific organizational location for educational and representational outputs; and some units in the policy system, e.g., House Administration, have important discretionary functions and operational responsibilities in the administrative system. Similarly, within the three systems, highly overlapping divisions of task or function exist. This is particularly true in the policy system with reference to committee jurisdictions and in the administrative system generally. In sum, then, the organizational chart of the House resembles a maze rather than some neat network of units organized in either functional, product, or matrix terms.

C. *Limited Degree of Specialized Expertise.* A second aspect of division of labor, aside from division of task, relates to the degree to which organizational positions are defined in terms of, and occupied by persons who possess, credentials or qualifications in some recognized discipline or field of knowledge. Organizations vary greatly along this dimension. In the House, as the Hammond, Maisel, and Brady chapters indicate, the degree of professionalization is limited (see also Fox and Hammond 1977, 1–102).

The key participants, the members, are generalists, not specialists. To be sure, many have professional or specialized backgrounds. In addition, they can be termed "professionals" in the art of politics and they often acquire specialized forms of substantive knowledge through service. Nonetheless, they are not selected on the basis of professional qualifications; their positions are not defined in terms of professional specialties; and the exercise of their duties is not dependent on or circumscribed by the possession of particular forms of specialized expertise. The situation with respect to staff is somewhat different. Here too, however, the degree of professionalization is limited, even though the House now has more than ten thousand staff employees. This is particularly true of member office staff, which constitutes about two-thirds of the total. But it is also true of large components of committee, party, and administrative unit staff due both to political needs and to the large amounts of clerical or routine tasks that are involved in processing the workload.

D. *Extensive but Irregular Formalism.* Organizations vary in the degree of their formalism as well as in the character of their structural configurations and divisions of labor. That is to say, they vary in terms of the degree to which the rights and duties of particular positions are specified or codified and the degree to which processes are ordered or standardized by set procedures. As the Hammond, Kieffer, Brady, and O'Donnell chapters indicate, the House's situation is one of extensive but inconsistent formalization.

In the constituency service, policy, and administrative systems there is a high degree of specification with respect to staff numbers, salaries, and operating expenses. However, the overall degree of specification in these regards varies greatly both among and within the systems. Moreover, the heads of units in all systems have few formal limitations in the employment, assignment, direction, or treatment of staff. In the policy and administrative systems, procedures for processing the work are highly formalized. Thus, for example, there are few organizations, aside from military organizations, that have manuals of procedure as elaborate as the House manual of rules. In addition, individual member offices tend to develop set procedures in processing constituent business. However, except in some areas of administrative support and minor legislation, there is little formalization in terms of the application of standardized criteria or guidelines to govern the substance or content of decisions. In contrast to many other types of organizations, substantive aspects of decisions or actions are thus highly subject to shifting and variegated sets of considerations.

E. *Limited Centralization of Power.* A final organizational characteristic of great importance is the degree to which power over operations and outputs is concentrated or centralized. Both the chapters in this book and the general literature on the House testify to the fact that the current House is highly decentralized (see, for example, Patterson 1978; Dodd and Schott 1979, 58–155; and Keefe 1980, 61–101). This is true not only in relation to other types of organizations, but even in relation to its situation in other eras of its own history.

Aside from formal controls over staff members, salaries, and expense allowances, the constituency service system operates as if the House were composed of 435 separate and independent firms. In the policy system the Speaker and other leaders lack firm or decisive power over outcomes and even have limited control over scheduling and the terms of floor debate. In the administrative system power is decentralized and lines of authority unclear. However, as is possible and even necessary in a decentralized system, power within particular units can be quite concentrated. In the recent past this was true of committees and it remains true of member offices and many administrative units.

**Operations**

Structural characteristics are important, but they are not exhaustive. Even in summary form, any adequate description of the House in organizational terms must include salient operational or process characteristics as well.[3] Five such features may be identified.

A. *High Degree of Turbulence and Uncertainty.* As the Hammond, O'Donnell, and Maisel chapters indicate, internal operations in the House tend to be chaotic and ad hoc rather than orderly and predictable. The pace of the work varies greatly both for the House acting collectively on the floor and for particular House units and participants. Ability to foresee intense output demands or the kinds of problems that will arise in processing such demands is usually limited. Time constraints and conflicts are generally severe. Last, but not least, there is often great uncertainty with regard to the character and mix of the substantive and political factors that should govern decision making as well as the basic dimensions of the decision or output that will ultimately emerge. In sum, then, internal operations in the House tend to assume a crisis mode. The work is performed through confronting and responding to a series of distinct crises. This is particularly true of the policy system. However, turbulence and uncertainty in internal operations are also marked in the administrative system, due to its service relationship to the policy system, and they are present to a reduced, but substantial, degree in the constituency service system as well.

B. *High Degree of Dependence on External Sources of Information and Influence.* A prime characteristic of the twentieth century House has been its increased dependence on external groups, particularly presidential units and bureaucratic agencies. This is a feature of both the constituency service system and the policy system. In the former system members have become highly dependent on executive information and favors both to satisfy constituent requests and to advance their careers. In the latter system the House and its committee and party units have become highly dependent on executive policy formulation, substantive expertise, and political muscle. All this is amply demonstrated in the general literature on the current House and it is reinforced by the Cavanagh, Parker, Johannes, and Maisel chapters in this book.[4]

C. *Emphasis on Sufficiency Rather than Efficiency.* House operations are not oriented toward efficiency, toward minimizing units of cost per units of output. They are rather oriented to insuring that resources will be adequate or sufficient when needed, quite aside from strict considerations of cost. This is well documented in many of the chapters in this book. Note the extensive replications of staff and equipment in individual member offices and the resistance to central pools or facilities. Note the reliance on a contingency fund to handle the operating expenses of most House units and a large portion of committee staff costs. Note the additive rather than analytical character of the House budget process. Finally, note the redundancies in institutionalized sources of information for member units and the overlaps in managerial and logistical support services.[5]

D. *Pervasive Politicalization.* Substantive or technical rationality may be distinguished from political rationality. The former governs choice regarding the attainment of substantive ends by focusing on the direct or inherent relationship between such ends and means of attaining them. It assumes or requires value agreements and high levels of knowledge regarding actual, empirical relationships. The criteria for decision making thus pertain to the objective prerequisites of goal attainment, and disputes are resolved on the basis of shared values and technical knowledge. In contrast, political rationality governs choice regarding the attainment of substantive ends by focusing on the strategy and tactics of mobilizing opinion or support. It assumes or requires value conflict and/or limited knowledge of means-ends relationships. The criteria for decision making thus pertain to the subjective prerequisites of securing agreement, and disputes are resolved through the manipulation of inducements and the control of perception.[6]

In all organizational settings outputs require reliance on both substantive and political rationality. Nor are they applied in total isolation from one another or with purely contradictory effects. Rather, the character and impact of their interaction varies. The House, however, is an organization in which internal operations are highly politicized. This is true in the policy system in several respects. At the individual level the tendency of members to exploit positions and issues for career advantage has been ably analyzed by David Mayhew (1974). The Brady and Hammond chapters provide yet another indicator of its prevalence, that is, the high degree of control over staff given to members in order to insure feelings of trust and loyalty. At the group level it is common practice as well for parties and various other types of policy coalitions to exploit positions and issues for electoral advantage and/or to subordinate policy desires to the strategic and tactical necessities of building majority support. The Katz chapter provides an excellent illustration of both these tendencies and the Maisel chapter illustrates a related phenomenon, the reluctance to engage in policy analysis.

Similarly, the work of students of the Congress, such as Morris Fiorina, and Cavanagh, Parker, and Johannes in this volume, indicates that internal operations in the constituency service system are also highly politicized. This is true both in terms of basic motivation and the projection of an interested and helpful image to compensate for deficiencies in actual performance. Finally, strong elements of politicalization exist even in the administrative system, as shown by the existence of patronage employees, minority suspicions regarding the equity and objectivity that can be expected in the delivery of services, and the tendency of House Administration Committee members to use their powers in the administrative system to build personal credits with their colleagues.

E. *High Participation Costs and Rewards.* The contemporary House is an organization that involves many facets of its participants' lives and it does so in intense and demanding ways. Participation costs and rewards are therefore high. As the Cavanagh, Katz, and O'Donnell chapters suggest, this is particularly true of members. On the one hand, members suffer substantial impairments to privacy, heavy workload pressures, and fixed limits on salary and other sources of earned income. On the other hand, the House, far more than most other types of organizations, accommodates its structures and resources to member needs as individuals and allows members to use them to maintain or advance their careers. In addition, the House provides members with the opportunity to play important roles on a national stage and with generous fringe benefits of various kinds. It also nurtures a rich and intense group life which serves as a source of camaraderie, friendships, and mutual self-protection. As for staff, participation costs are also high in terms of time and personal loyalty, and so too are rewards, though more vicarious in nature and tied to the younger stage of life of most staff personnel.

## BASIC DETERMINANTS OF HOUSE ORGANIZATION

The structural and operational features listed above are not a result of chance. Rather, they are a product of the combined impact of certain fixed parameters, which are imposed by critical and enduring aspects of the House's environment, and the current states of certain situational variables, which are also components of that environment.

### Fixed Parameters

Organizations have roles relative to their environments and these roles may be conceptualized as environmental expectations regarding the functions an organization will perform for its environment and the modes of decision making it will employ in performing these functions.[7] Such roles, in turn, may be seen to be shaped or determined by the character of environmental values that bear on an organization and its outputs, by the forms of linkage through which transactions between an organization and its environment are conducted, and by the nature of the work assigned to or assumed by an organization.

To preserve their roles over time, organizations require levels of output capability adequate to satisfy environmental expectations. Output capability, in turn, rests on the degree to which organizational structures and processes can simultaneously provide for division of labor, integration, and motivation. The first is necessary to capitalize on the efforts and skills of individual participants; the second, to render the actions or decisions of the component parts of an organization supportive and cumulative; the last, to induce participants to fulfill the individual role demands that involvement in the organization entails. However, the same values, linkages, and work that shape or determine an organization's role also constrain its choices in satisfying these performance prerequisites or needs. Of necessity these factors have both functional and operational implications that limit the manner in which performance needs can be satisfied and accommodated. Organizations thus do not have free choice in designing internal structures and processes to generate output capability.[8]

This is not to say that all aspects of the values, linkages, or work that shape or determine role expectations are equally critical. Even among those that have important impacts, there is variation in the degree of abstraction and comprehensiveness. Those aspects that rank highest in these regards are necessarily the most determinative of role content and must be, and generally are, the most stable. They thus define fixed ranges of potential variation in structure and operations in response to variable environmental factors.

In the case of the House these fundamental and enduring aspects of value, linkage, and work can be summarized as follows. The values involved are basic conceptions of the normative requirements of a constitutional democratic state. In the American context this form of government is interpreted to mean representative democracy in a separation-of-powers framework. As a consequence, the legislative branch is enjoined to serve as the prime determiner of discretionary decisions on collective goals and as a prime overseer of the manner in which the executive branch exercises the authority vested in it by the constitution and laws. In addition, the legislative branch is enjoined to operate in a representative and democratic fashion as a precondition for the acceptance of the legitimacy of its concrete outputs. In this regard, however, there are some substantial elements of inconsistency. Both reasoned deliberation and majority rule on the basis of strict equality among individuals are valued. So too are strict adherence to constituent wishes and the exercise of independent judgment in the public interest.

The aspects of linkage that need to be noted reflect the influence of democratic and separation-of-powers values, but have stable and important impacts of their own on the organizational character of the House. Thus, plurality elections in distinct, geographically defined constituencies serve as the main form of linkage for mediating transactions with one primary component of the environment (the electorate), and formal constitutional arrangements and procedures for mediating transactions with the other (executive officials).

Finally, the relevant aspects of the type of work the House performs are closely tied to the values and linkages described above. As a democratic legislature in a separation-of-powers framework, the work of the House relates to the determination, implementation, and justification of collective goals. Its work is therefore value laden, abstract or non-material, variable and complex, and judged or assessed through electoral verdicts. Nonetheless, these features too have substantial and enduring effects of their own.

Given values, linkages, and work of this character, five parameters that limit the organizational flexibility of the House in a fixed or constant manner may be identified.

A. *Limited Institutional Control over the Character of the Workforce and the Distribution of Tasks.* The aspects of value and linkage outlined above bar any substantial degree of institutional control over the exit and entry of members. They also severely constrain the House's ability to add members or to divide functional tasks among them simply on the basis of workload needs. Rather, these needs must be weighed against and often subordinated to representative and deliberative ones. Last, but not least, they establish a sharp qualitative distinction among participants (i.e., members and staff), so that legitimacy considerations also become prime considerations in determining staff numbers and functions.

B. *Limited Institutional Control over the Dimensions and Mix of Output Goals.* The aspects of value and linkage outlined above significantly constrain institutional capacity to define the character of its output goals. Whereas many organizations have considerable flexibility in tailoring their outputs to maintain environmental support, the House typically encounters substantial difficulties in seeking to regulate, ward off, or choose among environmental demands. On the one hand, democratic and separation-of-powers values render the proper character and scope of House decisions or actions highly open to societal definition. Its role is to respond to national needs and grievances, not to avoid them because they pose problems that are complex, onerous, or difficult to resolve through processes of majority aggregation. On the other hand, electoral linkages through individual constituencies serve as ready channels for transmitting demands, provide strong incentives for responding to them, and give individual members great influence in determining the overall dimensions and mix of institutional output activities.

C. *Limited Institutional Tolerance for Hierarchy.* The values and linkages outlined above severely constrain the House's ability to concentrate decision-making power in its top leaders. Democratic values prohibit formal distributions of authority that vest leaders with the right to command desired behavior and also restrict formal distributions of influence that enable leaders to induce desired behavior through the control and manipulation of organizationally generated rewards and penalties. Limitations in this latter regard are also substantially reinforced by electoral linkages that place control over the entry and exit of members in the hands of external groups or forces.

The House thus has a low tolerance for hierarchy. In the constituency service system concepts of the formal equality of members render central direction and control difficult, except through limited and standardized rules and procedures. In the policy system representative and deliberative values require the House to resolve issues through voting on the basis of formal equality and structured opportunities for deliberation and accommodation. While parliamentary authority can be vested in top leaders, more stringent types of formal authority cannot. Similarly, while the organizational positions of top leaders inevitably place some rewards and penalties at their disposal, the range and strength of such inducements are restricted by the arrangements and procedures that collegial decision making involves, the direct ties between members and constituents, and the standardization in member pay, staff, and allowances that formal equality requires or promotes. In the administrative system the normal compatibility between bureaucracy and hierarchy is undermined by location within a democratic legislature. To concentrate power within this system without simultaneously concentrating control and responsibility in a House leader or unit threatens member control of an important segment of its staff. Yet, to concentrate power over the administrative system in a House leader or unit threatens to provide a fund of rewards and penalties that could be used to coerce or control members in substantive areas of decision making. The House accordingly faces far more problems concentrating power in its administrative system than most types of organizations.

D. *Limited Institutional Capacity to Rely on Objective Standards or Measures.* In democratic legislatures disagreements over the nature and priority of ends are pervasive and knowledge of the relationship between ends and means uncertain. The House's capacity to rely on objective decision-making criteria or performance measures is thus highly constrained by the character of its work. This is particularly true in the policy system. The House generally cannot resolve key policy issues in lawmaking or oversight disputes by bringing analytical techniques or criteria rooted in some established discipline to bear. Nor at subsequent points in time can the effectiveness of the outputs it has produced or the role individual members have played be assessed through measures that permit unambiguous and indisputable judgments. Rather, in important areas of policy, disputes over whether proposed outputs are proper and efficacious in terms of societal ends must be resolved through processes of majority aggregation based on accommodation. Similarly, institutional performance must be judged through interactive processes between members and constituents in which confusions over institutional and individual responsibility are endemic and in which symbolic acts and positive, personal evaluations function as important means of maintaining support.[9]

This is not to say that knowledge and analysis have no significant contribution to make in the policy process or that appearance totally dominates reality in assessments of performance. The greater the degree to which the House can bring valid knowledge of means and ends to bear, the greater the degree to which it can objectively circumscribe the task of accommodating divergent views and the greater the degree to which it can identify types of action that will in fact be efficacious. Similarly, despite the difficulties in pinning down and evaluating results, members must be able to justify their behavior in areas of policy salient to their constituents and they are affected politically by collective output failures, even if on an irregular basis. The point is simply that the work of the House is and must be far more open to subjective determination and assessment than is the case in many other types of organizations, such as hospitals and factories.

E. *Limited Institutional Capacity to Motivate Organizational Identification.* In all organizations individual interests conflict with institutional ones and present serious problems for organizational effectiveness. All organizations thus must and do strive both to merge individual and organizational interests and to maintain high levels of loyalty to the organization above and beyond narrow considerations of personal advantage. The House's ability to generate diffuse feelings of loyalty is strongly supported by democratic values and by the broad connection that exists between member power in the political system and the maintenance of congressional power. However, the House is severely limited in its ability to merge or identify individual and institutional interests in concrete and immediate terms and this element of weakness counters and often cancels out the impact of the institutional loyalties that exist.

Once again this effect is rooted in the values, linkages, and work outlined above. Democratic values limit the House's ability to distribute basic material rewards and penalties so as to identify individual and institutional interests. House linkages to the electorate and the executive provide inducements to pursue career goals at the expense of institutional needs for policy outputs as well as inducements to pursue policy goals by expanding executive power at the expense of institutional needs to maintain the specificity, scope, and autonomy of House decision making. The value-laden and abstract character of the work provide leeway to pursue career goals by manipulating appearance rather than contributing to institutional performance. Nor are the difficulties the House encounters in identifying individual and institutional interests limited to members. The same values and linkages that establish a qualitative distinction between members and staff combine with the character of the work to discourage formal bureaucratic arrangements regarding employment, pay, and job classification. Staff, especially in member units, are thus closely tied to members in terms of both material and nonmaterial rewards and, as a consequence, tend to have their loyalties absorbed by members, who function or act more as patrons than bureaucratic superiors.

**Situational Variables**

Despite their importance, the nature and dimensions of the House's salient organizational characteristics are never wholly or precisely determined by the fixed parameters established by its environment. Indeed, the history of the House is marked by substantial change in the degree of formalization, distribution of power, turbulence, organizational elaboration, etc. Rather than determining the basic or cardinal features of structure and operations at particular points in time, the fixed parameters provide only what their name implies—highly stable and circumscribed ranges of variation. Locations within these ranges are, in turn, highly influenced by a second type of environmental constraint—the states of certain key situational variables.

These situational variables also derive from the House's environment and consist of aspects of value, linkage, and work. These aspects, however, differ from those that define fixed parameters by their openness to change and their level of abstraction. They represent more fluid and more concrete facets of environmental values, linkage, and work. They thus define more variable and concrete dimensions of role expectations that are tied to and limited by the more determinative and fixed aspects of role previously outlined. Nonetheless, the states of these variables have a more definitive impact on the salient characteristics of House organization at particular points in time. By defining or expressing the concrete content of prevailing role expectations, they have more specific or precise functional and operational implications for the satisfaction of performance needs than more basic aspects of role. On the one hand, the states of these variables substantially determine the actual character of demands on output capability, that is, the levels of division of labor, integration, and motivation that must be provided if output capability is to be adequate to sustain the role expectations that exist. On the other hand, the states of these variables substantially shape or influence the actual manner in which internal arrangements can be established and ordered for the purpose of satisfying output demands, i.e., the primary ways in which capacity for division of labor, integration, and motivation can in fact be generated or provided.

Four key situational variables may be identified.

A. *The State of Environmental Demand.* We have noted certain fixed aspects of the work of the House (i.e., its value-laden, abstract or non-material, and variegated character). What is equally true, as the history of the House readily demonstrates, is that the volume of output demands, as well as the degree of their complexity, uniformity, and volatility, vary greatly over time. Change, however, has in general been undirectional with the result that the contemporary House operates in a very demanding and turbulent environment (Commission on Administrative Review 1977*b*, 1:14–40, 616–652). Increases in the quantity, complexity, and volatility of demands, especially in the last half century, have, in turn, had substantial impacts on House structures and operations. They have created pressures for more extensive and effective divisions of labor both in terms of divisions of tasks and specialized forms of expertise. In so doing they have also created pressures for enhanced integrative capacity through increases in formalization and/or centralization and pressures for additional capacity to motivate or reward members in the face of the expanding burdens of office.

B. *The State of Electoral Politics.* We have noted certain fixed aspects of the form of linkage that ties the House to its electoral environment—the selection of members by separate and distinct constituencies. What is equally true is that the more concrete facets of this form of linkage also vary greatly over time.

Among these facets are the following: the size and stability of constituencies, the sophistication of communication technology, the nature and complexity of citizen grievances and divisions, and the role of party in organizing and controlling election results. These factors, of course, are not unrelated, but the last is of special importance.

The impact of constituency linkages on House structures and operations differs markedly in relation to party strength both as an organization and as a policy coalition. In large part this is true because the House's capacity for integration is substantially affected by the character and success of aggregative processes at the electoral level. To the degree that party at this level can organize and express communalities of interest and view across constituencies and play an important role in the conduct of campaigns, party cohesion in the House will be high. Such cohesion, in turn, facilitates aggregation within the House by providing a stable base for organizing majorities across a range of issues and by permitting greater concentrations of rewards and penalties (drawn from both formal and party systems) in the hands of party leaders.

In this latter regard, what needs to be understood is that the House's low tolerance for hierarchy, as compared with a private corporation or government agency, does not mean that the degree to which power is concentrated cannot vary. As the Cannon House illustrates, distinctly higher concentrations of power in the form of influence (i.e., control over inducements) are possible in eras of great party strength than in eras of only moderate party strength or weakness. This, to be sure, requires substantial party influence over the linkage between constituencies and members and interpretations of democratic values that mitigate or negate highly individualistic or egalitarian conclusions. However, when fellow partisans in and out of the House share policy goals to a high and intense degree, party standing becomes a critical element in election and democratic values tend to be interpreted in a collectivist fashion. Majority rule is equated with party responsibility and the powers given to party leaders are legitimized in terms of their needs as agents of the party majority.

Nor is the significance of the role party performs in elections limited to its impact on the House's integrative capacity. When party displays substantial strength as an electoral force, the ability of the House to rely on policy rewards and party resources to temper individualistic pursuit of career goals at the expense of the institution is greatly augmented. However, in point of fact, party strength has varied greatly over time. Equally important, party has never wholly dominated the electoral process and has only intermittently exhibited great strength as a policy coalition. The House thus typically has serious difficulties providing adequate levels of integrative capacity or relying on forms of motivation that are closely adapted to institutional needs. The current House is no exception. On the contrary, the strength of party both as an organization and a policy coalition has declined substantially over the past half century (Brady, Cooper, and Hurley 1979; Clubb and Traugott 1977).

The other facets of linkage identified also have significant impacts. Their states both influence the overall level of party strength and the general texture of electoral politics, whatever the level of party strength. In short, they have both direct and indirect effects on the linkage between members and constituents. For both these reasons trends regarding them substantially affect both the character of performance needs and the manner in which they can be satisfied.

C. *State of Executive Roles and Resources.* We have noted certain fixed aspects of the linkage between the House and executive officials, i.e., that it is ordered by formal constitutional provisions. Here too, however, the more concrete facets of the linkage vary greatly over time. The role of the president in the legislative and administrative processes is thus far greater today than in the nineteenth century. So too, accordingly, are the organizational resources controlled by and the fund of rewards and penalties at the disposal of the president. Similarly, the role of executive agencies in shaping outcomes in the legislative process and exercising discretion in the administrative process is far greater today than in the nineteenth century. So too, accordingly, are the organizational resources controlled by and the fund of rewards and penalties at the disposal of the executive agencies.

Given its role as a democratic legislature operating in a separation of powers framework and the fixed parameters this role involves, the House throughout its history has never been able to avoid relying on executive advice, influence, and discretion. However, such reliance creates conflicting pressures for the organizational character of the House. On the one hand, expansions in executive roles and resources restrict the degree to which the House must provide its own sources of division of labor, integration, and motivation in order to produce outputs that will satisfy environmental demands for legislative actions that effectively remedy or alleviate societal problems and grievances. In so doing they relieve pressures on performance needs. On the other hand, expansions in executive roles and resources threaten the House's ability to maintain the degree of comprehensiveness in its substantive decisions and the degree of autonomy in making decisions that fixed and basic aspects of its role require. In so doing they increase pressures on performance needs.

The House therefore at any particular point in time must strive to order its structures and operations so as to maintain viable balances between direction and discretion and between dependence and autonomy in its relations with the executive. Its ability to do so, however, is not constant. When executive roles and resources are great, as is true today, their very dimensions limit congressional leeway (Cooper 1975; Dodd 1977). The state of such roles and resources thus affects both the character of performance needs and the manner in which they can be satisfied.

D. *State of Democratic Decision-Making Values.* We have noted certain stable, albeit highly abstract, aspects of democratic values that constrain House organizational characteristics in fixed and critical ways, i.e., the normative imperatives to base House decision making on collegiality, equality, and majority rule. However, interpretations of the more concrete or precise implications of these values vary greatly over time. This is true both in terms of conceptions of the content of particular values and in terms of resolutions of conflicts among them or between them and House needs for adequate levels of output capability. In the first regard, the manner in which the concept of majority rule is open to collectivist rather than individualistic interpretation has already been noted. Similarly, interpretations or the precise prerequisites of electoral accountability can also vary along other dimensions, such as the degree of openness required in internal processes or member affairs. In the second regard, the history of House rules and procedures is largely a story of varying patterns of accommodating conflicts between different democratic decision-making needs per se (e.g., strict majority rule versus ample opportunity for debate) and conflicts between democratic decision-making needs and performance needs (e.g., rule by the whole body based on the equality of members versus committee power based on specialization and deference).

This variation in interpretations of democratic values and of appropriate patterns of accommodation regarding them has a substantial impact on the character of House organization. The legitimacy needs that apply to House outputs are in general far more demanding than for most other types of organizational outputs. This is due to the fact that the operational implications of the fixed aspects of value present in the House's environment are quite stringent. They render the manner in which an output is produced far more influential in gaining environmental acceptance and the sheer functional effectiveness of the output per se far less controlling than in the case of a factory, hospital, or army. Nonetheless, the degree of limitation imposed on satisfying performance needs varies with the manner in which the implications of democratic values are interpreted and balanced. The more interpretations stress the equality and independence of members, and/or strict forms of accountability to constituencies on an individual basis, the greater the direct limits on output capability and the less room there is for accommodation. In the current House, as recent sunshine, ethics, and subcommittee reforms indicate, the state of democratic values imposes far harsher restrictions on integrative and motivational capacity than in all the preceding decades of this century (Dodd and Oppenheimer 1977; Keefe 1980, 148–157; Cooper 1970, 91–135).

## IMPACT ON HOUSE ORGANIZATION

As was suggested earlier, the salient organizational characteristics of the current House can be explained or accounted for in terms of the fixed parameters and situational variables we have identified. The former establish broad constraints on the manner in which performance needs for division of labor, integration, and motivation can be satisfied and accommodated. The states of the latter impose further constraints that operate within the limits set by fixed parameters. Their interaction determines the basic or cardinal structural and operational characteristics of the current House.[10]

### Structure

The first two structural characteristics concern the shape or configuration of House organization and the division of functional responsibilities it establishes. These features are the high degree of organizational elaboration and variation and the limited but complex division of tasks.

The current states of all the situational variables discussed above create intense pressures for organizational elaboration. The current state of environmental demand does so by generating voluminous, complex, variegated, and unpredictable demands for action; the current state of electoral politics does so by putting a premium on constituent service and spawning congeries of ad hoc and intense policy concerns; the current state of executive roles and resources does so by threatening Congress's ability to maintain the degree of specificity, scope, and autonomy in its decision making that its legislative role requires; and the current state of democratic values does so by prompting wider distributions of key organizational positions and resources. However, the House's ability to extend the character of its division of labor in an orderly, effective, and comprehensive fashion is highly restricted. The constraints derive both from limited institutional capacity to control the character of its work force and the distribution of tasks within it and from limited institutional tolerance for hierarchy, combined with weaknesses in the prime situational variable that determines capacity to centralize power—weaknesses in party strength.

Thus, although the pressures for organizational elaboration are intense and their impact reinforced by limited institutional capacity to regulate the workload, such elaboration takes place in an extremely rudimentary fashion. What occurs primarily is horizontal expansion or proliferation of units along existing product or staff support lines of differentiation. In short, units tend to be added along existing organizational dimensions in a piecemeal manner in response to particular and immediate needs without much vertical extension or integration of relationships or much redefinition or redistribution of tasks either within existing systems of units or among them. This, of course, is not surprising given limited integrative capacity, but it leads to high degrees of variation and overlapping. Moreover, despite substantial horizontal expansion, the overall dimensions and benefits of such expansion are restricted by limits on the House's ability to expand the size of the workforce, to confine members to specific tasks or units, and to control member work choices. As a consequence, expansion, even along horizontal dimensions, is limited in ways that differ significantly from the situation in a corporation or government agency. Equally important, to a large degree expansion simply increases pressure on members' time.

The third structural characteristic identified, limited degree of specialized expertise, concerns a complementary but distinct aspect of the division of labor. It is attributable primarily to limited institutional capacity to rely on objective standards and measures and limited institutional capacity to control the character of the workforce. This is not to say, however, that the states of the situational variables in recent decades have not had a moderating impact. They have generated pressures which have led since 1946 to substantial expansions in staff, including the addition of persons trained in some discipline or field of knowledge. Nonetheless, the number of "professionals" and the work locations where they can be usefully employed have continued to be circumscribed by the impact of the parameters just noted on the way in which the House's work is processed and on the selection of members and staff.

The fourth and fifth structural characteristics identified concern the degree of formalization and centralization and are highly interrelated. Integrative capacity can be supplied by formal rules and procedures as well as by hierarchical power in the form of authority and/or influence, i.e., by limiting discretion and standardizing action as well as by distributing discretion differentially. The House throughout its history has relied on formalization to compensate for deficiencies in its capacity both to generate and concentrate power. Quite understandably, it has found it far easier to provide certain basic levels and types of central control through establishing impersonal rules and procedures than through augmenting discretionary leadership control over outcomes. Hence, the degree of formalization has increased over time as the workload and number of units and participants have expanded. As indicated earlier, it is now quite extensive. Nonetheless, if extensive, it remains quite irregular in its areas of operation. This too is understandable. Given limited institutional capacity to rely on objective standards and measures, to control the character of the workforce, and to control output goals, the range and content of decision making about outputs cannot be highly regularized or standardized. Nor can basic aspects of staff selection and direction be as highly formalized as in bureaucratic organizations. In short, the House's basic nature as a political institution promotes formalization in some key regards, but also limits it in others. This was true in 1789 and it remains true today, as the current state of situational variables accentuates both tendencies.

The impact of fixed parameters and situational variables in limiting the degree of centralized power in the current House is more consistent. On the one hand, the House's ability to generate and concentrate power on the basis of conceptions of organizational authority and/or distributions of organizational inducements is limited by the fixed aspects of its environment that establish a low tolerance for hierarchy. On the other hand, its ability to generate and concentrate power within these boundaries is currently impaired by weaknesses in party strength, attachment to democratic norms that emphasize free and independent judgment, and existing patterns of dependence on executive initiative and influence. As a result, one key product system, constituency service, has been and remains extremely decentralized and the other, the policy system, has typically been and remains one in which leadership control is tenuous.

## Operations

The operational characteristics of current House organization also result from the interaction of fixed parameters and situational variables. However, the paths of influence vary. In some cases the impact of these factors is highly direct; in other cases there are both direct and indirect effects of substantial importance.

The high degree of turbulence and uncertainty in internal operations partly derives directly from the current state of environmental demand and the House's limited capacity to control the dimensions or mix of its output goals. However, it is also closely tied to some of the structural characteristics of the House: the high degree of organizational elaboration and variation; the low degree of centralization; and the irregularity or unevenness in formalization.

A second operational characteristic, the emphasis on sufficiency rather than efficiency, is also both a direct and an indirect effect. In part, this emphasis results from the high degree of turbulence and uncertainty that characterizes internal operations and thus only indirectly from the interaction of fixed parameters and situational variables. However, it also derives, in part, from the direct impact these factors have in limiting organizational capacities that are essential to distributing resources so as to minimize costs relative to organizational ends and priorities—the availability of objective standards and measures and the presence of concentrated leadership power.[11]

In contrast, the remaining three operational characteristics derive largely from the direct impacts of fixed parameters and situational variables.

Pervasive politicalization has been and remains a fundamental feature of House operations. This is true because virtually all the fixed parameters identified promote and support it. Limited institutional capacity to rely on objective standards and measures does so by restricting the role of established facts or accepted modes of analysis in resolving internal conflicts or election contests. Low institutional tolerance for hierarchy does so by requiring decision making to be highly collegial in nature and by restricting leadership authority and influence in such decision making. Limited institutional capacity to motivate organizational identification does so by forcing high degrees of accommodation to the reelection needs of members in the distribution and control of organizational positions and resources. And limited institutional capacity to control the character of the workforce or the distribution of tasks within it does so by freeing members to pursue career goals in manners of their own choosing. Moreover, in the current House, basic and enduring tendencies toward intense and extensive politicalization of operations and issues are further accentuated by the states of electoral politics and executive roles and resources. It is the combination of fixed parameters and the present states of these variables that gives color and tone to the recent portraits of member behavior drawn by such analysts as Mayhew (1974) and Fiorina (1977).

Similarly, the high degree of dependence on executive information and influence and the high levels of participation costs and rewards are also largely a direct result of the interaction of fixed parameters and situational variables. The high degree of executive dependence results from the fixed and variable factors that combine to strain output capability. These primarily include limited institutional control of the workforce and the distribution of tasks and limited institutional tolerance for hierarchy, on the one hand, and the current states of environmental demand, electoral politics, and democratic values on the other. High participation costs and rewards result from the combined impact of the fixed and variable factors that render service in the current House both intensely frustrating and rewarding. On the cost side limited institutional capacity to control the workload and the current states of environmental demand and electoral politics combine to make the burdens and pace of service in the House very demanding. In addition, low institutional tolerance for hierarchy and the current states of electoral politics and democratic values combine to limit opportunities to achieve broad policy goals. On the reward side the same factors that militate against the passage of broad policy programs preserve high levels of influence and dignity in the processes of government for members as individuals. In addition, the same factors that promote pervasive politicalization provide multiple opportunities to use organizational positions and resources to serve career goals.

## IMPACTS ON INNOVATION

The preceding explanation of salient organizational characteristics does not mean there is no room for innovation in the current House, no room for planned or deliberate changes in structure and/or operations that enhance organizational effectiveness. On the contrary, the same set of concepts we have used to explain the basic or cardinal structural and operational features of the current House can be applied both to explain why choice or flexibility exists in organizational design and to analyze the room or leeway that exists for innovation, for constructive or beneficial change.

In its full or complete sense, however, innovation involves two dimensions: the potential for beneficial change and the willingness of organization members to adopt such change.[12] These questions are related and even overlap, but they are subject to determination by different factors and criteria. Thus though fixed parameters and situational variables normally constrain both, they may do so to highly different degrees. Similarly, whereas the question of willingness is simply an empirical matter, the question of potential involves both empirical and normative considerations, given its relationship to role fulfillment.

In this section we shall focus on the problem of innovative potential, not on innovative capacity in any full or complete sense, though we shall also need to refer to constraints on willingness from time to time. In short, what we wish to analyze is the familiar problem of House reform, but we shall use the term innovation to signify "true" or "real" reform.

## General Considerations

Organizations by nature have a capacity for planned or deliberate action. They are therefore never mere prisoners of their environments. Though constrained by the character of the fixed parameters and situational variables in their environments, they nonetheless have the ability to react to discrepancies between performance and role expectations.[13] The character of such reaction, of course, varies in relation to whether the discrepancy involves an excess or deficiency of output capability relative to role expectations and whether the dependency relations that exist between the organization and the environment are favorable or unfavorable to the organization. Given the fact that the current situation of the House is clearly one in which there is a severe negative imbalance between output capability and role expectations as well as a high degree of dependency on the environment, we may confine ourselves to situations of this type, that is, to conditions of stress.

Typically, organizations, when confronted with stress, do not choose to die or disappear or to transform their roles in radical or fundamental ways. Such choices are rare and when they do occur they usually result from failures in an organization's ability to adapt to its environment over an extended period of time. Rather than dying or radically altering their roles, organizations under stress normally pursue two other strategies, either singly or in combination.

One such strategy is to seek to make structural and/or operational changes that increase output capability. To be sure, the ability of an organization to do so is limited by the nature of the fixed parameters and situational variables in its environment. As we have argued, these factors interact to shape and limit the manner in which performance needs can be satisfied and conflicts among them accommodated, and they manifest their influence through shaping and limiting salient structural and operational characteristics, such as basic or cardinal aspects of the distribution of power, use of formal rules and procedures, and politicalization of issues and operations. Nonetheless, the degree to which fixed parameters and situational variables control or direct such choices varies in terms of the severity of the constraints they impose. Hence, so too does their impact in shaping and limiting the detailed or specific features of structure and operations, the precise ways in which performance needs are satisfied and accommodated. In addition, there is a general tendency for the controlling or directive effect of these factors to diminish as more concrete and specific features of structure or operations become the focus of attention—how to procure typewriters or process vouchers as opposed to the general character of the distribution of administrative power or function.

Nor are these the only reasons why organizations can be seen to have choice or flexibility in seeking to satisfy and accommodate performance needs, albeit to varying degrees depending on their contexts and the level of output activity involved. The fact that organizations exist in dynamic rather than static environments is also of critical importance. At any specific point in time most of the particular and concrete features of structure and operations that exist reflect attempts to satisfy and balance performance needs, made in the context of the character of fixed parameters and situational variables at prior points in time. Moreover, some portion of these reflect attempts in which considerations other than sheer technical effectiveness played a determining role, attempts in which there were high degrees of tolerance for individual self-interest at the expense of institutional needs. However, insofar as situational variables alter so as to relieve or intensify stress, so too do the character and intensity of demands on performance needs. In the former case flexibility obviously increases. Yet, despite what might be initially presumed, opportunities for choice also increase in the latter case. The reasons are several.

First, though limited by the character of fixed parameters and situational variables, conditions of stress provide additional leeway to emphasize performance needs at the expense of legitimacy needs, to emphasize functional aspects of role at the expense of operational aspects. Second, though limited by the character of fixed parameters and situational variables, conditions of stress affect and alter the benefit-cost ratios of existing modes of satisfying and accommodating performance needs. Thus, though the range of options remains limited, forms of structure or operations that on balance served output capability may no longer do so. Similarly, forms of structure or operations that served individual self-interest at the expense of institutional needs may no longer be so tolerable. Third, reaction to dramatic changes in environmental values, linkages, or work typically results in mistakes. Forms of structure or operations are often adopted that enhance legitimacy or a particular performance need without due regard for the hidden costs or negative impacts on output capability generally.

Another primary strategy organizations may pursue, and usually do when attempts to enhance output capability fail to relieve stress, is to seek to alter their domains, their existing spheres of action both in terms of products and linkage. In so doing they seek to alter the more concrete aspects of role expectations without altering or disturbing basic or fundamental ones that are more abstract and more comprehensive. They may therefore change the concrete character and/or mix of their products without changing basic aspects of their functional roles as producers. Or they may change concrete aspects of their linkages to the environment while still maintaining a viable balance between autonomy and dependence. An example of the former is the transformation of the March of Dimes from an organization concerned exclusively with polio into one concerned with a variety of childhood diseases. An example of the latter is the addition of students or alumni to University Boards.[14] In either case the thrust of domain change is to maintain environmental support for basic aspects of role by bringing more particular and concrete role expectations into line with output capability rather than vice versa.

Here too, however, the ability of organizations to pursue this strategy is limited. But the primary source and character of the limits are quite different.

Fixed parameters and situational variables have far less restrictive impacts on innovation in domain than on innovation in output capability. Fixed parameters, we may recall, derive from stable and basic aspects of an organization's role and they constrain the manner in which it may seek to fulfill or satisfy them. As a consequence, the limits they impose pertain more to modes of operation than to the content of an organization's outputs and within modes of operation more to internal, decision-making arrangements than to external relations. Indeed, even insofar as the limits imposed by fixed parameters do pertain to aspects of output or linkage, the restrictive effects are exceedingly broad and do little to narrow potential choices regarding the character of outputs or linkages.

In short, then, fixed parameters speak more to the manner in which performance needs can be satisfied and accommodated than to the mix of outputs an organization should produce or the balances between autonomy and dependence it should establish. The fact that they severely constrain the willingness to innovate generally due to their impacts on the forms and bases of internal decision making thus does not mean that their impact on the potential for innovation is uniform. Rather, they have far less restrictive effect on beneficial change in domain than on expansions in output capability.

As for the states of the situational variables, they too, for roughly similar reasons, have less restrictive impacts on the potential for beneficial change in domain than on the potential for expanding output capability or the willingness to innovate generally. Note, for example, the differential impacts of the state of the election system or even the state of environmental demands in these regards on planned or deliberate change in the House, e.g., further extension of the role and power of House party leaders or units versus public financing of campaigns.

The primary limits on innovation in domain thus derive, as might well be expected given the nature of the strategy, from basic aspects of an organization's role per se, from stable and determinative aspects of the values, linkages, and work that relate an organization to its environment. They do not derive from fixed parameters. It is the basic aspects of an organization's role per se that primarily limit potential for innovation with respect to outputs or linkages, not the fixed impacts such aspects of role have in constraining an organization's ability to generate output capability or to regulate the character of demands on such capability. Nor do they derive from the states of situational variables. These factors embody or reflect more concrete and fluid aspects of environmental values, linkage, and work. They thus have a dual significance. They define the concrete character of existing output demands and external linkages and, in combination with fixed parameters, limit output capability. However, since the concrete implications of basic aspects of role in terms of both outputs or functions and external relations or linkages are open to varying interpretations, it is the degree of flexibility these aspects of role permit that primarily limits the potential for innovation in domain, not the states of the situational variables.

Innovation in domain thus hinges largely on the ability to alter less stable and concrete aspects of role expectations without altering or infringing more fundamental ones through deliberate changes in forms of activity and/or interaction. Leeway for such action thus necessarily varies in different organizational contexts in relation to the basic or inherent restrictiveness of stable and determinative aspects of environmental value, linkage, and work. For example, a prison or mental hospital has less leeway for domain change than a private business or university.

Before closing this discussion of general considerations, however, two additional points need to be noted. One relates to an important impact of fixed parameters and situational variables. Though the direct effects of these factors on innovation in domain are limited, they can have significant indirect effects through the limitations they impose on innovation in output capability. Thus, for example, it is difficult for a prison or mental hospital to combine both custodial and treatment goals, though role expectations often have altered to encompass both. The other relates to a serious danger that a strategy of domain change inevitably involves. Unless carefully guided and circumscribed, domain change can in time result in radical role change (e.g., the YMCA, WCTU, or House of Lords).[15]

### House Reform

Let us apply these considerations to the House. As is clear from our analysis of the fixed parameters and situational variables that exist in the House's environment and the manner in which they interact to shape salient features of House structure and operations, the contextual constraints that limit organizational flexibility in the current House are exceedingly severe. Hence, as long as the states of the situational variables do not alter in ways that substantially relax the severity of these limits, there is little room or leeway for major expansions in output capability.

Leeway for expanding capacity for division of labor has been largely consumed by staff and unit expansions that have occurred since 1946. Given the fixed parameters and situational variables that limit this capacity per se as well as those that limit integrative and motivational capacity, further major increases in staff and/or units would be counterproductive. Similarly, integrative capacity cannot be substantially increased through either centralization of power or formalization, given the high degree of formalization that already exists and the constraints that limit both these structural characteristics. The fact that sizable new concentrations of power (e.g., greater leadership control of committee appointments) or sizable additions to formalization (e.g., the introduction of a civil service system for staff) would not be acceptable, while true, is thus not the critical point insofar as the potential for innovation is concerned. What is critical is that legitimacy needs, imposed by basic aspects of the House's role as a democratic legislature, cannot accommodate substantial degrees of leadership power, given the states of electoral politics and democratic values, and that decision-making needs, imposed by the basic character of the House's work, render greater formalization of highly political relationships and processes undesirable. Finally, the House's ability to motivate members to fulfill their roles and identify their interests with those of the institution is also highly resistant to expansion. An organization that cannot hire or fire, differentially distribute material rewards in terms of position or performance, or consistently provide policy or normative satisfactions inevitably has serious problems in generating morale and loyalty, and this is especially so when the burdens and pace of work are taxing.

All this, however, is not to say that there is no room for innovation with respect to output capability. Opportunities to make beneficial changes exist for all the reasons cited above: the impact of stress in altering benefit-cost ratios; changes in situational variables that relax constraints to some degree; and the reduced restrictiveness of constraints at more particular and concrete levels of structure and operation. Conversely, the House can also avoid or correct changes that unnecessarily impair output capability. Thus, current conditions of stress make it possible to temper legitimacy needs in the service of output capability (e.g., by placing tighter restrictions on the ability of a limited number of members to secure recorded votes or by limiting dedication to openness in internal deliberations). Similarly, beneficial changes in satisfying and accommodating performance needs are possible. In terms of division of labor, the Obey Commission made a number of recommendations that involve net benefits for output capability. Among these are the following: redefinition of committee jurisdictions, functional consolidation in the administrative system, additional legislative staff for members, greater legislative use of the computer, and improvements in staff training and recruiting. In terms of integrative capacity, both conditions of stress and changes in the political character of the Democratic majority have produced incremental changes since 1970 that are of net benefit (e.g., Speaker nomination of Democratic members of the Rules Committee and sequential reference of bills with a time limit). Further possible gains include greater and perhaps more systematic use of ad hoc committees, clarifying lines of authority in the administrative system, and stricter limitation of subcommittee proliferation. Finally, even minor improvements in motivational capacity are possible, such as keeping member pay and benefits in line with inflation and restricting intrusions on privacy.[16]

Nonetheless, it remains true that increases in output capability can only be of marginal or incremental benefit. The House thus has no option but to adopt a strategy of domain change as well. The potential for innovation in domain is broader than may at first be perceived. Indeed, it is significantly broader than the potential for enhancing output capability.

In part this is true because, as has been suggested earlier, the interaction of fixed parameters and situational variables has far less restrictive effects on innovation in domain than on innovation in output capability. This, however, is not to deny that these factors have substantial restrictive effects. Yet, if we reiterate the distinction we have established between the potential for beneficial change and the willingness to adopt such change and recognize again that fixed parameters and situational variables may restrict organizational choice by limiting the potential and/or the willingness for beneficial change, our point remains valid. Most of the restrictive effects pertain to the latter rather than the former. Indeed, even the single fixed parameter that has direct implications for domain as well as performance or output capability, that is, limited institutional capacity to control output goals, derives much of its constraining force from its impact on willingness rather than its impact on potential. In other words, the fact that the House must respond to citizen demands and grievances is not as restrictive on domain change as the fact that the character and mix of output goals must ultimately be determined through summing the choices and desires of individual members.

In large part, however, the House's broader capability for innovation in domain derives from the flexibility provided by basic aspects of its role as a democratic legislature in a separation-of-powers framework. To be sure, the aspects of environmental values, linkages, and work that define this role also impose boundaries. In addition, the interaction of fixed parameters and situational variables does impose important indirect constraints by limiting output capability (e.g., by limiting increases in oversight without reductions in other outputs). Nonetheless, the House retains considerable leeway to adjust domain to basic aspects of role. There are many variants in the character and mix of outputs within its performance capabilities that can satisfy its need to function as the prime determiner of governmental policy and to serve as an effective channel for citizen demands and grievances. Similarly, there are many variants in forms of linkage to the executive and electorate that are compatible with both its performance capabilities and its need to balance elements of autonomy and dependency in its external relations. Moreover, choices regarding these variants are necessarily affected by current conditions. Thus, the impact of the states of situational variables on innovation in domain is not simply negative or restrictive. Rather, once again, stress produced by changes in these factors alters benefit-cost ratios and thereby augments flexibility in adjusting domain to role.

Given the relatively broad boundaries the House's role as a democratic legislature in a separation-of-powers framework involves, it is not surprising that the House throughout its history has engaged in substantial alterations in domain. In the nineteenth century such change was primarily expansive in nature and was supported by sizable increases in output capability. In this century as well there have been elements of expansion, supported by increases in output capability (e.g., growth in the scope of lawmaking, oversight, and constituent service). However, especially since the 1930s, these elements of expansion have been accompanied by substantial elements of contraction in response to severe conditions of stress. This is particularly true with respect to executive officials. As indicated by the great clamor and concern that presently exists with respect to bureaucratic power, the amount of policy discretion vested in executive officials has greatly increased while Congress's ability to guide or direct its exercise or to hold bureaucrats accountable for their actions has lagged far behind. Similarly, dependence on executive information and influence has also increased substantially.

The fact that the House in the past several decades has engaged in substantial alterations of domain therefore does not mean that such change has uniformly or even generally served to maintain critical aspects of its role in the political system. Rather, there have been dysfunctional effects of great consequence. On the one hand, though the degree of autonomy remains within tolerable limits, the amount of uncontrolled discretion delegated to executive officials has been so great as to impinge on the boundaries of the House's policy role, to threaten radical role change rather than merely adjustments in domain. On the other hand, the expansion in constituent service has compounded the problem. This is true not simply because of the amount of time and resources diverted from legislative work. Rather, the impact the current emphasis on constituency service has in transforming members into modern versions of old-time ward politicians is of equal, if not greater, importance since it undermines concern with policy questions per se and in so doing threatens the House's policy role from yet another direction.[17]

The root of these difficulties inheres in the manner in which fixed parameters and situational variables combine to induce such action. As we have suggested, though these factors do not narrowly restrict the potential for beneficial change in domain, they do seriously restrict the willingness of members to make changes that serve institutional needs. The domain change that has taken place has thus been largely determined by the desire of members to attain highly valued policy goals and/or to serve career interests, apart from and even at the expense of institutional needs. Domain change, as a result, has not served to relieve stress to any significant degree, or to relieve discrepancies between output capability and role expectations. Hence, a continuing sense of crisis has prevailed in recent decades, despite substantial changes in domain as well as important additions to output capability.

In short, the House has not capitalized on the potential for innovation in domain that exists. It accordingly needs to orchestrate domain change more closely with basic aspects of its role as a democratic legislature in a separation-of-powers framework. It needs to act to preserve its role as basic determiner of governmental policy goals and a prime guarantor of the fairness and efficiency of executive action implementing those goals, while still vesting considerable amounts of policy discretion and administrative flexibility in the hands of executive officials. Acts such as the War Powers Resolution of 1973 and the Budget and Impoundment Act of 1974 are thus steps in the right direction. So too are the earmarking of units, staff, and expense funds for review or oversight activities and increased use of the congressional veto in important areas of policy where it is difficult to write meaningful standards or guidelines into the enabling legislation.[18]

Similarly, to reinforce this effort the House needs to act to decrease the scope and importance of constituent service. Here, as in other areas of domain or output capability, conditions of stress have altered former benefit-cost ratios. The more emphasis placed on constituent service and the more staff and allowances provided to support this output, the more the ante is raised for everyone and the more every member is forced to assume the role of ward politician. This circle needs to be broken in the institution's interest, if not the individual member's. At the least, some aspects of constituent service might be centralized and/or subject to noncongressional appeals mechanisms. The former would do little, if anything, to impair levels of effectiveness that are presently low and the latter is the course the Congress has followed with respect to many areas of routine legislation it used to handle in the nineteenth century, such as claims. In terms of more drastic action, serious consideration should be given to altering traditional and fundamental aspects of the linkage between members and constituents, such as the length of the term, public financing of campaigns, and so on.

## CONCLUSION

In closing, some consideration of innovative capacity in its full or complete sense is in order. We have noted several times that fixed parameters and situational variables constrain this capacity by restricting the willingness to innovate as well as the potential for innovation. We have also argued with respect to changes in the House's domain that the former source of constraint is the more severe. This is also true with respect to expansions in the House's output capability and even a brief look at the fixed parameters and situational variables we have identified indicates why.

These factors have a number of highly restrictive effects on the willingness to innovate. First, they establish a wide gap between the institution's interests and those of individual members. Second, they place control over the adoption of innovative change in the hands of the whole body of members, rather than of a small group of leaders. Third, they define an institutional terrain which gives advantage to opponents of change. Fourth, they encourage attention to and emphasis on short-term policy and/or career goals rather than long-term institutional needs.

It is thus not surprising that major efforts at House reform usually fail. On the contrary, given the constraints that exist, it might well be expected that such efforts require the presence of special sets of catalysts to be successful. Among the most critical are a high degree of public concern and media support; a high, internal sense of crisis regarding the institution's standing or performance; leadership support; and the availability of "sweeteners," such as pay raises, to mobilize individual self-interest.[19]

Our analysis of the potential for beneficial change accordingly needs to be tempered by a sense of the hard realities that exist. Still, feelings of cynicism and despair also need to be kept in check. Prospects for piecemeal or ad hoc innovations, including some of importance, are less bleak than the prospects for comprehensive or large-scale ones. The gap between individual and institutional interests is periodically subject to contraction in particular and circumscribed contexts by increases in the intensity of feelings of crisis and public concern. Witness, for example, the current attempts to reclaim control over administrative rule making. In addition, changes in the states of the situational variables can have similar narrowing effects. Witness, for example, the caucus reforms noted above that have increased the Speaker's powers. Finally, in areas of structure or operations of less consequence where the gap is inherently limited, the sheer recognition of the need to improve performance can energize innovative activity. Witness, for example, the adoption of a number of the recommendations of the Obey Commission in the period since the defeat of its reform package.[20]

Moreover, the fact that conditions of stress are high, that substantial discrepancies exist between output capability and role expectations, should not be misinterpreted. High levels of stress derive to a significant degree from the demanding quality of current role expectations per se and should not be attributed simply to failures of performance. Thus, though the House has lost ground to the executive in the past half-century and has great difficulty defining programs that effectively respond to national needs, it remains a vital, energetic, and powerful actor in the political system.

In sum, then, though the maladies of the House as an institution are serious and chronic, they are far from terminal now. There is a clear and present danger that its power and position in the system will continue to erode. But the outcome is by no means clear. Nor will the House's openness to innovation determine the result. The challenges it now faces are rather only one critical aspect of a more general testing of the continuing viability of our democratic republic.

## NOTES

1. For conceptual analysis and empirical findings on salient structural characteristics in the general literature on organizations see the following: Hall 1977, 97–195; Harrison 1978, 204–285; Wieland and Ullrich 1976, 21–53; Melcher 1976; and Azumi and Hage 1972.
2. See the Commission on Administrative Review's *Background Information Report* (1977*a*) for lists of the various types of House units mentioned in the text.
3. For conceptual analysis and empirical findings on salient operational characteristics in the general literature on organizations see the following: Thompson 1967; Simon 1945; March and Simon 1958; Etzioni 1975, 3–103; Khandwalla 1977, 176–572; and Wieland and Ullrich 1976, 96–373.
4. See, for example, Fiorina 1977; Dodd and Schott 1979, 276–324; and Keefe 1980, 101–120. Increased dependence probably also characterizes relations with private groups due to increases in campaign costs, sub-

committee proliferation, and the use of single-issue lobbies (Dodd and Schott 1979, 181–184).

5. The emphasis on sufficiency appears to apply to political decision making as well. See the critique of minimal winning coalition theory in Lutz and Williams 1976.
6. For discussion of the character of political reason see Diesing 1962 and Lindbloom 1965. See also March and Simon 1958, 129–130.
7. For further elaboration of the analysis of environmental constraints, organizational roles, and impacts on the House, see Cooper and Brady 1973 and Cooper 1975, 1977. In addition, see Froman 1968.
8. For general material on environmental components, environmental impacts, and organizational roles, see Brinkerhoff and Kunz 1972; Hall 1977, 303–333; Khandwalla 1977, 326–355; Harrison 1978, 343–395; and Wieland and Ullrich 1976, 375–403.
9. For a pathbreaking analysis of the role of trust and empathy in relations between members and constituents, see Fenno 1978, 136–249.
10. For three classic studies in the general literature on organizations that explain or approach structure and process in terms of environmental constraints, see Lawrence and Lorsch 1967, Thompson 1967, and Galbraith 1977.
11. For a discussion of the role of power and values in attempts to base decision making on considerations of economic efficiency, see Wildavsky 1979, 127–221.
12. For general treatments of innovation in terms of both the normative or design dimension and the empirical or implementation dimension, see Kotter, Schlesinger, and Sathe 1979; Galbraith 1977; and Wieland and Ullrich 1976.
13. For analysis of the dynamics of interaction between organizations and their environments, including treatment of varying organizational situations and options, see Haas and Drabek 1973, Pfeffer and Salancik 1978, and Thompson 1967. For further elaboration of material in the text, see Cooper 1977.
14. For examples and analysis of domain change, see Thompson 1967, 25–50 and Haas and Drabek 1973, 215–300. Also see Pfeffer and Salancik 1978.
15. For examples and analysis of the problem, see Perrow 1978, 174–199.
16. For a review of reform proposals in the past decade, see Dodd and Oppenheimer 1977. In addition, see Congressional Quarterly reports on internal changes (1979) and ethics (1980).
17. For analysis of recent tendencies toward an increased emphasis on the role of the member as a dispenser of favors to constituents, see Fiorina 1977, Epstein and Frankovic 1980, and Payne 1979.
18. For analysis and examples of the growth of reliance on the legislative veto see Cohen 1977.
19. All these factors were present in the successful efforts to reorganize the committee system in 1946 and to change House rules on ethics in 1977. In contrast, they were weak or absent in the unsuccessful efforts to re-

organize the committee system in 1974 and to reorganize the administrative system in 1977. For a thoughtful and detailed analysis of the failure of the 1974 committee reforms, see Davidson 1979.

20. On current House efforts to regain control of administrative rule-making, see note 18 above and Cohen 1980, 1476. On caucus reforms see note 16 above. Some examples of actions taken by the House that are similar to proposals made by the Commission on Administrative Review in its reports on administrative reorganization and work management are the transfer of the committee reporters to the Clerk, the creation of a formal system for part-time employment, and the reorganization of the unit concerned with personnel recruitment and office management practices.

## REFERENCES


Azumi, Koya, and Hage, Jerald. 1972. *Organizational Systems*. Lexington, Mass.: D. C. Heath.

Brady, David; Cooper, Joseph; and Hurley, Patricia. 1979. "The Decline of Party in the House of Representatives, 1887–1968." *Legislative Studies Quarterly* 4(August):381–409.

Brinkerhoff, Merlin B., and Kunz, Phillip R., eds. 1972. *Complex Organizations and Their Environments*. Dubuque, Iowa: Wm. C. Brown.

Clubb, Jerome M., and Traugott, Sondra. 1977. "Partisan Cleavage and Cohesion in the House of Representatives, 1861–1974." *Journal of Interdisciplinary History* 7(Winter):375–403.

Cohen, Richard E. 1977. "Junior Members Seek Approval for Wider Use of the Legislative Veto." *National Journal* 9(August 6):1228–1232.

———. 1980. "Legislative Veto Battle Escalates—Should Congress Have the Last Word?" *National Journal* 12(September 6):1473–1477.

Commission on Administrative Review, U.S. Congress, House. 1977*a*. *Background Information on Administrative Units, Members' Offices, and Committees and Leadership Offices*. 95th Cong., 1st sess. H. Doc. 95-178.

———. 1977*b*. *Final Report*. Vol. 1 of 2. 95th Cong., 1st sess. H. Doc. 95-272.

Congressional Quarterly. 1979. *Inside Congress*. Washington: Congressional Quarterly.

———. 1980. *Congressional Ethics*. Washington: Congressional Quarterly.

Cooper, Joseph. 1970. *The Origins of the Standing Committees and the Development of the Modern House*. Houston: Rice University.

———. 1975. "Strengthening the Congress: An Organizational Analysis." *Harvard Journal on Legislation* 12(April):307–368.

———. 1977. "Congress in Organizational Perspective." In *Congress Reconsidered*, ed. Lawrence Dodd and Bruce Oppenheimer. New York: Praeger.

———, and Brady, David. 1973. "Organization Theory and Congressional Structure." Paper presented at 1973 annual meeting of American Political Science Association, New Orleans.

Davidson, Roger. 1979. "Paradigms of Innovation: House and Senate Committee Reorganizations." Paper presented at 1979 annual meeting of American Political Science Association.

———, and Oleszek, Walter. 1976. "Adaptation and Consolidation: Structural Innovation in the U.S. House of Representatives." *Legislative Studies Quarterly* 1(February):37–65.

Diesing, Paul. 1962. *Reason in Society*. Urbana: University of Illinois Press.

Dodd, Lawrence C. 1977. "Congress and the Quest for Power." In *Congress Reconsidered*, ed. Lawrence Dodd and Bruce Oppenheimer. New York: Praeger.

———, and Oppenheimer, Bruce. 1977. "The House in Transition." In *Congress Reconsidered*, ed. Lawrence Dodd and Bruce Oppenheimer. New York: Praeger.

———, and Schott, Richard L. 1979. *Congress and the Administrative State*. New York: Wiley.

Epstein, Laurily K., and Frankovic, Kathleen A. 1980. "The Representative as Ward Boss." Paper presented at Rice-Houston Conference on Congressional Elections, Houston, January 10–12.

Etzioni, Amitai. 1975. *A Comparative Analysis of Complex Organizations*. New York: Free Press.

Fenno, Richard F., Jr. 1978. *Home Style: House Members in Their Districts*. Boston: Little, Brown.

Fiorina, Morris P. 1977. *Congress: Keystone of the Washington Establishment*. New Haven: Yale University Press.

Fox, Harrison W., Jr., and Hammond, Susan W. 1977. *Congressional Staffs: The Invisible Force in American Lawmaking*. New York: Free Press.

Froman, Lewis A. 1968. "Organization Theory and the Explanation of Important Characteristics of Congress." *American Political Science Review* 62(June):518–527.

Galbraith, Jay. 1977. *Organizational Design*. Reading, Mass.: Addison-Wesley.

Haas, J. Eugene, and Drabek, Thomas E. 1973. *Complex Organizations: A Sociological Perspective*. New York: Macmillan.

Hall, Richard H. 1977. *Organizations: Structure and Process*. Englewood Cliffs, N.J.: Prentice-Hall.

Harrison, E. Frank. 1978. *Management and Organizations*. Boston: Houghton Mifflin.

Keefe, William J. 1980. *Congress and the American People*. Englewood Cliffs, N.J.: Prentice-Hall.

Khandwalla, Pradip N. 1977. *The Design of Organizations*. New York: Harcourt, Brace, Jovanovich.

Kotter, John P.; Schlesinger, Leonard A.; and Sathe, Vijay. 1979. *Organization: Text, Cases, and Readings on the Management of Organizational Design and Change*. Homewood, Ill.: Richard D. Irwin.

Lawrence, Paul, and Lorsch, Jay. 1967. *Organization and Environment*. Cambridge: Harvard University Press.

Lindbloom, Charles E. 1965. *The Intelligence of Democracy*. New York: Free Press.

Lutz, Donald S., and Williams, James R. 1976. *Minimum Coalitions in Legislatures: A Review of the Evidence*. Beverly Hills: Sage Publications.

March, James G., and Simon, Herbert A. 1958. *Organizations*. New York: Wiley.

Mayhew, David R. 1974. *Congress: The Electoral Connection*. New Haven: Yale University Press.

Melcher, Arlyn J. 1976. *Structure and Process of Organizations*. Englewood Cliffs, N.J.: Prentice-Hall.

Patterson, Samuel C. 1978. "The Semi-Sovereign Congress," in *The New American Political System*, ed. A. King. Washington: American Enterprise Institute.

Payne, James L. 1979. "The Personal Electoral Advantage of House Incumbents, 1936–1974." Paper presented at 1979 annual meeting of Southern Political Science Association.

Perrow, Charles. 1978. *Complex Organizations: A Critical Essay*. Glenview, Ill.: Scott, Foresman.

Pfeffer, Jeffrey, and Salancik, Gerald R. 1978. *The External Control of Organizations*. New York: Harper & Row.

Simon, Herbert A. 1945. *Administrative Behavior*. New York: Free Press.

Thompson, James D. 1967. *Organizations in Action*. New York: McGraw-Hill.

Wieland, George F., and Ullrich, Robert A. 1976. *Organizations: Behavior, Design, and Change*. Homewood, Ill.: Richard D. Irwin.

Wildavsky, Aaron. 1979. *The Politics of the Budgetary Process*. Boston: Little, Brown.

# Notes on Contributors

THE EDITORS

*Joseph Cooper* is the Dean of Social Sciences and Lena Gohlman Fox Professor of Political Science at Rice University. He served as staff director of the U.S. House Commission on Administrative Review. He is a past president of the Southwestern Political Science Association and a past secretary of the American Political Science Association. He is the author of the monograph *The Origins of the Standing Committees and the Development of the Modern House* and of numerous articles on the U.S. Congress. He is also co-editor of the *Sage Electoral Studies Yearbook*.

*G. Calvin Mackenzie* served as a senior staff member of the U.S. House Commission on Administrative Review and has also been a consultant to the Commission on the Operation of the U.S. Senate and the U.S. Senate Committee on Government Operations. He is an assistant professor of government at Colby College and author of *The Politics of Presidential Appointments*.

OTHER PARTICIPANTS

*David W. Brady* is a professor of political science at Rice University and serves as chairman of the National Science Foundation Committee on Congressional Elections. He is the author of *Congressional Voting in a Partisan Era* and the co-author of *Public Policy and Politics in America*. He is a member of the editorial board of *The Legislative Studies Quarterly* and served as a consultant to the U.S. House Commission on Administrative Review.

*Thomas E. Cavanagh* teaches in the government department at Wesleyan University. He is the author of several articles and papers on congressional behavior and elections. He served as assistant survey research director of the U.S. House Commission on Administrative Review.

*Jeffrey A. Goldberg* is currently special assistant to the director of the Office of Management Services administered by the Committee on House Administration. Previously, he has served as assistant manager for member services at House Information Systems and as a research analyst for the U.S. House Commission on Administrative Review.

*Susan Webb Hammond* is an associate professor in the School of Government and Public Administration at American University. She is the co-author of *Congressional Staffs: The Invisible Force in American Lawmaking* and has written a number of other articles on congressional staffing and operations. She served on the staffs of both the Commission on the Operation of the U.S. Senate and the U.S. House Commission on Administrative Review.

*John R. Johannes* is chairman of the political science department at Marquette University. He is the author of a number of articles on congressional processes, procedures, and decision making. He is currently engaged in an extensive analysis of congressional casework.

*Allan J. Katz* served as general counsel of the U.S. House Commission on Administrative Review. He is now deputy insurance commissioner for the State of Florida. He has also served as legislative director for Congressman David R. Obey, legislative counsel to former Congressman Bill Gunther, and counsel to the Select Committee on Ethics of the U.S. House of Representatives.

*Jarold A. Kieffer* served as director of the Task Force on Administrative Units of the U.S. House Commission on Administrative Review. In his distinguished career he has held a variety of top level and private posts. Among them are: Deputy Commissioner of Social Security; Assistant Administrator for Population and Humanitarian Assistance at AID; Director, President's Panel on Biomedical Research; Planning Board Member, National Security Council; Hoover Commission Staff; Professor of Public Policy and Administration and Head of Public Policy and Administration Division, School of Community Service and Public Affairs, University of Oregon; and Director of the National Committee on Careers for Older Americans. Currently, he is staff director of the 1981 White House Conference on the Aging.

*Louis Sandy Maisel* is an associate professor of government at Colby College. He served as director of the Task Force on Work Management of the U.S. House Commission on Administrative Review. He is co-editor of the *Sage Electoral Studies Yearbook* and the author of a number of articles on party politics, White House staffing, and congressional elections.

*Thomas J. O'Donnell* is an instructor of government at American University where he is completing his doctorate in political science. He has served on the staffs of the Committee on House Administration, U.S. House Commission on Administrative Review, and the Commission on the Operation of the U.S. Senate.

*Glenn R. Parker* is an associate professor of government at Florida State University. He is a former American Political Science Association (APSA) Congressional Fellow (1972–73) and is currently the recipient of a National Science Foundation grant to study committee decision making in the House of Representatives. He is the author of numerous articles on mass attitudes toward Congress, congressional elections, and committee decision making.

*James A. Thurber* now serves as director of the Battelle Memorial Institute's Human Affairs Research Centers, and is on leave from the School of Government and Public Administration at American University. He was an APSA Congressional Fellow in 1973–74 and has written extensively on various aspects of congressional behavior and reform. He has served on several congressional staffs, including the Temporary Select Committee to Study the Senate Committee System and the U.S. House Commission on Administrative Review.

# Index